T0293014

The Contest for Japan's Economic Future

The Contest for Japan's Economic Future

Entrepreneurs vs. Corporate Giants

RICHARD KATZ

OXFORD
UNIVERSITY PRESS

Oxford University Press is a department of the University of Oxford. It furthers
the University's objective of excellence in research, scholarship, and education
by publishing worldwide. Oxford is a registered trade mark of Oxford University
Press in the UK and certain other countries.

Published in the United States of America by Oxford University Press
198 Madison Avenue, New York, NY 10016, United States of America.

Library of Congress Control Number: 2023948937

ISBN 978-0-19-767510-6

DOI: 10.1093/oso/9780197675106.001.0001

Printed by Sheridan Books, Inc., United States of America

To all my teachers, including one who told a seventh-grade boy: someday, you'll write books.

Contents

Introduction: The Opportunity
of a Generation

Just like every genetic mutation, every new company is an experiment. Most fail. Only around half survive even four years. And like the rare beneficial mutations that have taken the biosphere from microbes to mammals, the few firms that flourish drive evolution in the economy. Between 1895 and 1930, a stunning 1,300 automobile companies were created in the United States—some propelled by gasoline, others by wood, by steam, and, ironically, even batteries. By the 1930s, only three companies of substantial size remained. In short, 99.8% of the experiments failed. And yet, the car itself not only survived; it remade our world. Again and again, we have witnessed this pattern, more recently in the rise of computers and the Internet.

It was this spirit of experimentation that drove what would become known as Japan's post–World War II economic miracle—when, in only 27 years (1946–1973), Japan transformed from a poor, mostly rural economy into an industrial powerhouse. It did so faster than any country before it and faster than all but China after it. This high-growth era was a wondrous age, a time when a 25-year-old son of a rural sake brewer, Akio Morita,[1] could start a tiny company and see it turn into SONY; an environment where the ill-educated son of a blacksmith named Soichiro Honda could create an enterprise that motorized bicycles and could build it into a giant automaker capable of challenging Toyota and Nissan. In fact, half of the 1,700 nonfinancial companies on Japan's stock market in 1989 were created after World War II (Whittaker 1997: 32).

As in all economic upsurges, countless failures vastly outnumbered the relatively few successes. Fortunately, the political economy of the times not only allowed the cream to rise, but also ensured that those who lost their livelihoods in the contest for success could find good new jobs, or even create another company. That everyone shared the benefits was made possible by

---

[1] Japanese names are written in Western style, with surname last.

The Contest for Japan's Economic Future. Richard Katz, Oxford University Press. © Richard Katz 2024.
DOI: 10.1093/oso/9780197675106.003.0001

the combination of high growth (9% per year during 1953–1973), full employment, equal distribution of income, and social mobility for those with
more talent than money. Economic progress and individual security reinforced each other, and that was essential to Japan's success. Since most new
ventures flop, unless a country makes it safe to fail, it will not generate enough
experiments. Too few failures mean too few triumphs.

If young firms act as a conveyor belt for new thinking and new
technologies, too many once-superb older companies lose their luster because they cannot toss aside the now-obsolescent systems responsible for
their original victories. A prime—and sad—example is SONY, which tried,
and failed, to produce a globally competitive personal computer (PC), smartphone, tablet, and e-reader. Even when the older firms do manage big course
corrections, it is often due to pressure from new arrivals. It was Tesla's rapid
rise that induced Ford, Volkswagen, and other giants to jump into electric vehicles (EVs). Unfortunately, most Japanese automakers, particularly
Toyota, are resisting the shift to EVs.

Just as new species supplant old species in nature, dynamic economies
need a regular turnover of leading firms. "Creative destruction" is what economist Joseph Schumpeter famously called it. If natural selection drives biological evolution, then "economic selection"—the advancement of the most
innovative—propels improvement in living standards. Such economic selection was the hallmark of Japan's high-growth era. The birth rate of new
companies—new companies relative to total existing companies—was a
high 12%, while the death rate was 5% (METI 2018a: 492).

If the public is to support creative destruction, modern capitalist
democracies must ensure that, while companies live and die, the turbulence
is not too destructive to individuals. Failure to heed this lesson lies behind
the current rise of populism in the United States and Europe (Broz et al. 2021;
Anelli et al. 2019).

Japan, unfortunately, provided a false answer to the real problem of
protecting those harmed by creative destruction. Its shift began in the late
1970s in response to the abrupt halving of economic growth following two
oil price shocks. The country's leaders slowed down creative destruction in
the name of social stability. The private-sector safety net that had made Japan
politically safe for economic selection was no longer sufficient. Yet, the perennial ruling party, the Liberal Democratic Party (LDP), refused to launch a
large overt government-funded safety net. Instead, they made a worker's current job at his current company the prime backup. That led to voter pressure

on politicians to prop up even the most moribund firms. The government even subsidized wages to maintain redundant workers, while making it harder for new challengers to replace even inferior incumbents. Among all rich countries, it is Japan where new companies find it hardest to get the external funding necessary for growth. Consequently, the birth and death rate of companies has plunged and is now one of the lowest among 27 rich countries (see Figure I.1).

In a typical rich country, up to half of all annual productivity growth—and thus per capita growth in gross domestic product (GDP)—comes not just from the birth of new, more efficient companies, but also from the exit of less productive ones. In Japan, however, firm turnover provides only about 10% of productivity growth (Acs et al. 2008; Decker et al. 2014: 12). No wonder overall GDP growth is so low.

What's often overlooked is that the birth rate is so low precisely because the death rate has been kept so low. New firms cannot get the labor, financing, and even the real estate they need, since they're being used by the older ones. That's why countries with the lowest company death rate also have the lowest birth rate (see again Figure I.1).

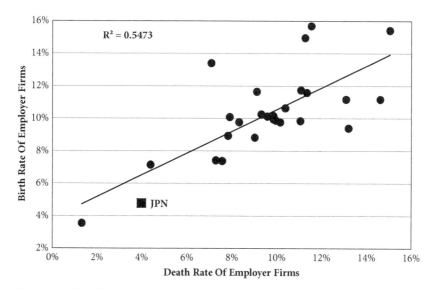

Figure I.1 Too few exits mean too few entrants.

Source: OECD (2019a).

Note: JPN = Japan. These figures refer only to firms that employ staff, not the self-employed, nor mom-and-pop shops with a couple of family employees.

The political enshrinement of stability—backed by the spurious claim that this was rooted in age-old Japanese values—provided the rationale for anti-competitive practices in the business world. The most successful companies of the high-growth era entrenched their dominance by erecting barriers against new upstarts, with the support of their allies in government. Consequently, only one of Japan's top 26 electronics hardware companies was born after 1959. By contrast, two-thirds of America's top 26 electronics manufacturers were founded after 1965, and a half were not yet in the Fortune 500 as late as 1991.

The problem for Japan is that its corporate giants, just like decades-old corporations in other economies, find it hard to change. Japan's leading firms were forged in the analog era when the vanguard of innovation was large, capital-intensive, vertically integrated companies that tried to do everything in-house. Today, we live in the digital era, and new technological regimes require new corporate institutions. Increasingly, the leading edge of innovation is found in smaller, more entrepreneurial companies. Moreover, many of those innovations yield viable commercial products via collaboration between the newcomers and the giants. The COVID vaccine bearing Pfizer's name was invented by a German-based startup, BioNTech, founded by immigrants from Turkey. It's a prime example of a digital-era business institution known as open innovation, a form of interfirm collaboration analyzed and promoted by Prof. Henry Chesbrough (Chesbrough et al. 2006a).

Japan, to be sure, throws a lot of money at digital technologies, but it ranks a dismal 63rd out of 63 economies in how much benefit the economy gets from that investment (IMD 2022: 103). Despite a 40% surge in global electronics sales from 2008 to 2021, every one of Japan's top 10 electronics hardware manufacturers saw its global sales slump, while total sales of Japanese electronics firms plunged about 30% (JEITA 2020: 2).

The abandonment of creative destruction is the reason Japan's growth remains anemic. An economy growing nearly 9% per year in the high-growth era, and then 4% as it matured in the mid-1970s–1980s, has slowed to just 0.7% over the past 30 years—despite promises by one prime minister after another to reach 2% growth (see Figure I.2). To bring back growth, the business world must once again become safe for new challengers. This does not require that Japan graft onto itself some foreign model, like neoliberalism; it simply needs to return to doing what it used to do so well.

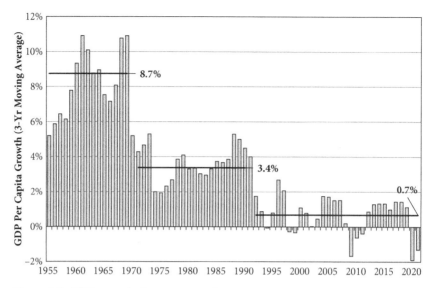

Figure I.2 GDP growth slows to a crawl.
Source: Penn World Tables 9.1 (2021); World Bank (2022).

The Good News

The good news is that, for the first time in a generation, Japan has the potential to rewrite its story. On the surface, the economy seems intractably stagnant and politics disappointingly unresponsive. Beneath the surface, reason for hope arises from six megatrends that add up to a tectonic shift in civil society. These include generational shifts in all sorts of attitudes, technological changes that alter the power balance between incumbents and newcomers, shifts in gender relations, the ramifications of the demographic crunch, the stimulative effects of globalization, and the political stresses induced by low economic growth.

"In my grandfather's generation, people had been so poor as children that a stable job at a big company was nirvana," explained Jun Tsusaka (Interview June 2018), the CEO of NSSK, a Tokyo-based private equity (PE) firm that buys and upgrades small and medium enterprises (SMEs).[2] "By the time of my father's generation, that salaryman job was boring and frustrating. But

---

[2] Small companies have less than 20 employees in manufacturing and 5 elsewhere; medium ones have 20–300 employees in manufacturing, 5–100 in wholesale trade and services, and 5–50 in retail.

they saw no alternative if they wanted a secure living. People today are more willing to leave a big, prestigious firm to take a new job at a new company so that they can have a more fulfilling life."

One of Japan's newest billionaires, Soichiro Minami, embodies three of the megatrends: generational change, a shift in technology, and globalization. Minami had been taught to look upon business as a vehicle to solve social problems by his mentor, Hiroshi Mikitani, the founder of the giant Rakuten Internet mall. Minami saw Japan's lifetime employment system as a hindrance to growth. Under that system, prominent companies do not hire people in mid-career. That makes it very risky for someone to leave a big company and either start, or work for, "the new kid on the block." If the latter fails, he would be unlikely to get a new job as lucrative as the one he had left. That is one of the primary reasons Japan has so few new innovative companies. Even so, a growing number of talented employees, especially those in their twenties and thirties, are willing to make a switch, and a growing number of companies are willing to make mid-career hires. The problem is putting them in touch with each other.

So, in 2009 at age 33, Minami set up a new Internet-based firm called Visional to act as a matchmaker. Job seekers earning at least ¥6 million[3] (about $46,000) per year post their résumés on Visional's BizReach website, and the 17,000 companies on the site contact them directly. In July 2021, the site attracted 1.4 million job seekers. Minami became a billionaire when he listed his company on the stock market in 2021. Like so many other entrepreneurs in Japan, Minami has a cosmopolitan background. His family lived in Canada for a few years during his childhood. He got his college degree at Tufts University in the United States and worked for Morgan Stanley in Tokyo (Lee et al. 2021).

Minami is not alone. Out of Japan's 55 billionaires in 2021, 11 had founded a company within the previous 25 years. This is the biggest infusion of new high-growth companies in decades. What makes these new billionaires different? They're young, cosmopolitan, and unconventional in their thinking. On average, they started their companies at age 30 and were billionaires by age 42. Many have lived abroad, studied at an overseas university, and/or worked for a foreign company. Most importantly, they had the independence of mind to see gaps in the market—and ways to fill them—to which executives at incumbent firms were blind. "You can't accomplish things

---

[3] Unless otherwise stated, all yen values are converted to dollars at ¥130/$.

without going against common knowledge," was how it was put by one of them, Taichiro Motoe, an American-born provider of online legal services (Glen Royal 2022). Rather than creating exotic inventions in areas like fintech or artificial intelligence (AI), most of these new billionaires simply use the latest technology to revolutionize existing prosaic businesses: from e-commerce that gives SMEs access to customers that they never had before, to online provision of medical information to doctors, or accounting services to SMEs. Most importantly, they're just the tip of the new company iceberg.

Certainly, these societal shifts are nowhere close to reaching the critical mass required for an economic revival. They're unlikely to do so without government action to nurture the positive trends. Nonetheless, for the first time in a generation, the opportunity is there.

How Startups Create Ripple Effects

As soon as I walked through the doors of Raksul, an 11-year-old startup, I felt the buzz of dozens of ambitious, bright people in their twenties and thirties. What a stark contrast to the sense of stiffness, even tedium, found among so many middle-aged managers at the giants. Just as striking was an abundance of female managers, a rare sight at traditional firms.

No one exemplifies this new generation more than Raksul's founder, Yasukane Matsumoto. In 2009, when Matsumoto was just 23 and one year out of the prestigious Keio University, an idea struck him that, a decade later, would lead *Forbes* magazine to name him Japan's top entrepreneur for 2018. By 2022, Raksul enjoyed sales of ¥30 billion ($231 million) and employed 440 people. Matsumoto hopes to reach $1.5 billion within another 5–10 years.

Like other brilliant ideas, Matsumoto's was elegant in its simplicity. Back in 2009, as an employee of A.T. Kearney, an American consulting firm, the young Matsumoto was advising some small printing companies. It dawned on him that printers could slash marketing costs by using the Internet as an auction platform. "I looked for a company that was already using that idea so I could go work for them," he explained. To his surprise, there was no such company. "So, I started one myself" (Interview, October 2019). He envisioned his new company as a kind of Uber for printing before Uber even existed.

In 2015, he extended the concept, creating an Uber for parcel delivery. While 90% of the delivery market is dominated by just three companies, another 30,000 scratch and claw for slices of the remaining 10%. With their trucks usually only 40% full, compared to 60% in Europe, making a living is tough. By helping drivers fill their trucks, Raksul became a serious force in parcel delivery without owning a single truck. There is nothing exotic about Raksul. It simply uses the power of the Internet to improve a very ordinary service.

Flower cutters or butchers post their delivery needs on Raksul's website, truckers say how much they will charge, and the lowest bid gets the job. The key is that a truck going from point A to point B within Tokyo adds very little cost, but lots of revenue, by going just a bit out of its way to pick up another package. Without the web, neither the butcher nor the trucker would know this opportunity existed. What's most exciting is the ripple effects. The florist and grocer get a good price, a saving that they can pass on to their customers. Drivers increase their income by up to 30% because they carry more packages for every mile they drive. Even the climate benefits since there are less carbon emissions per package. Finally, newcomers like Raksul push stodgy incumbents to up their game. Raksul's rapid expansion compelled the government-owned Japan Post to partner with it.

Getting more benefits with fewer hours of labor and with less equipment—improved productivity—is what raises living standards for both producers and consumers. At present, Raksul has enlisted 1,500 trucks, mostly in Tokyo. Imagine the benefits if more companies entered the field and this system covered all the cities and towns. Imagine the even greater benefits if enough comparable innovators revolutionized other traditional sectors.

When I spoke of Raksul to an American professor at a Japanese business school, she reacted, "It seems a bit sad that, in a country that has produced giants like Honda Soichiro [founder of Honda Motors], Matsushita Konosuke [founder of Panasonic], this generation is being symbolized by someone who has come up with an Uber for delivering flowers."

While this reaction is understandable, it misses the way in which a Japanese recovery will occur. At present, for every hour of work, Japanese laborers produce 37% less in goods and services than their American counterparts and 28% less than those in the Eurozone (OECD 2022a). Growth will be restored through a rather plebian process in which hundreds of thousands of now-lagging companies use the latest technology and management techniques to reach world benchmarks. Look at the American productivity revolution that began in the mid-1990s. Two-thirds of the acceleration of productivity growth came in the so-called old economy sectors, not the ones that produced the newest technologies, but the ones that utilized them (CEA 2001: 30). The same will be true of Japan. Transportation, for example, accounts for 7% of Japan's GDP. Suppose Japanese companies could transport goods at a 20% lower cost and 20% less carbon emissions per package. That alone would add 1.4% to the level of Japan's GDP, almost twice as much as Japan grows in a year.

In this process of making Japan more efficient, there will be some new giants, but there also need to be tens of thousands of smaller innovators like Raksul.

The professor added a more fundamental critique: "Stories like these have been around for a while. What is new?" She had a point. All too often in the past couple of decades, policymakers and journalists alike have sighted a couple of swallows and announced the spring. Such pronouncements warranted skepticism, and I've been one of the skeptics. Why, then, is today any different? It's the changing context: momentous changes in generational attitudes, gender relations, and technology, as well as the crying need for a solution to the stresses of aging and economic stagnation.

Gazelles versus Elephants

Say the word "entrepreneur" and people reflexively conjure up visions of geeky young men in Silicon Valley crowding into a garage strewn with empty pizza boxes and cans of Coke, all in the hopes of becoming a millionaire, maybe even a world-famous billionaire. In truth, such turbo-charged ventures are a very thin slice of American entrepreneurship. There are just 2,000 high-tech enterprises in Silicon Valley. By contrast, the United States is home to more than 50,000 high-growth enterprises, those with at least 10 employees which grow at least 20% per year for three years in a row. The comparable number in Korea is 16,000; it's 13,000 in the United Kingdom and 10,000 in France. We have no idea of the number in Japan because the government does not measure this (Bureau of the Census 2021; OECD 2021a).

Typically, a rapidly growing company starts at, say, 10 or 20 employees and grows to 60 or 200. Only a small fraction are in high-tech, 16% in Britain, for example (Brown et al. 2017: 13). Most simply find a way to create a new product, improve an existing one, or deliver a service more efficiently than existing companies. Consider Vision Dynamics Laboratory in Louisville, Kentucky. It's an independent lab that produces digital eyeglass lenses, glass lens surfaces, and related products. Its competitive edge is not just the nuts and bolts of low cost, high precision, and fast turnaround times, but also carving out a niche by producing low-volume varieties on behalf of bigger producers, enabling them to concentrate on more lucrative areas. Founded in 2007, it reached 75 employees and $11 million in sales in just 10 years (Karp 2017).

Rapidly growing companies are hardly the norm. The vast majority, like the corner grocer or haircutter, are quite content with staying tiny. While they're indispensable, they drive neither innovation nor growth. By contrast, the few that soar—typically just 4%–6% of all firms in rich countries—produce an outsized share of a nation's growth in jobs, innovation, and productivity. In 2009–2011, America's 100,000 fastest-growing companies amounted to just 2% of all employers but created 4.2 million new jobs, more than a third of the country's net job creation. Among the 14,000 fastest-growing companies during 2011–2017, the average one was just eight years old with 200 employees and $37 million in annual sales. Together, they employed almost 3 million people (Hathaway 2018; Clayton et al. 2013).

The youngest of these firms—those under five years old—have become so pivotal that they've earned their own nickname in official statistics. They are called "gazelles," after one of the fastest and most agile animals on earth. During the 1980s–1990s, American firms less than five years old supplied a stunning 60% of the growth in factory output per worker (Decker et al. 2014: 12).

In Japan, as elsewhere, gazelles are rare. Of all the newly entering enterprises in 2009–2013, just 4% of the entrants provided half of the entire productivity boost to Japan from the new entrants. After four years of existence, the average gazelle had 27 employees and sales of ¥58 million ($430,000) per employee. This compares to just 7 employees and sales of ¥14.5 ($111,000) per employee at the rest (METI 2017a: 58).

Unfortunately, unlike most rich countries, Japan does not regularly measure the number of high-growth firms. If governments measure what they consider important, it's telling that Japan has never done so.

If rapidly growing young firms are gazelles, older big companies are dubbed "elephants," while the tiny firms that stay tiny are "mice." The nicknames were coined by an American business consultant (Birch 1987). Like the elephant, companies such as Nippon Steel, Mitsukoshi (department stores), and Mitsubishi Heavy Industries are big and strong and certainly skillful along their existing paths, but, as they age, they lose the agility to change their path. IBM makes a lot of money, but it no longer calls the tune in computer technology. Toyota invented the hybrid car, but how well will it continue to fare if its CEO keeps denouncing fully electric vehicles as "overhyped" (Landers 2020)? After years of losses, SONY has regained profitability due to its presence in movies, music, and games. It also enjoys a 45% global market share in certain imaging sensors for smartphones, a $15 billion global market in 2021. But the latter is the exception. In how many other areas of electronics does the world still look to SONY for a continuous stream of revolutionary products? While a few of Japan's elephants—like Hitachi and Fujifilm—have reinvented themselves, successful reinventions are rare in any country.

Most of Japan's elephants are shrinking. During 2009–2014, Japanese companies established before 1984 shed 2.5 million workers, while those established after 2005 gained 2.5 million jobs (METI 2018a: 45).

To be sure, no economy can prosper on gazelles alone. Healthy elephants and mice are just as indispensable. It's getting the balance right that counts. Japan's leaders used to understand that, but today they favor elephants, even moribund ones, in ways that render gazelles a rare species. Only 8% of the government's financial aid to R&D goes to companies with fewer than 250 employees, the lowest share among rich countries (OECD 2014: 83). What Tokyo fails to grasp is that, as yesterday's cavorting gazelles become today's limping elephants, the economy needs new gazelles.

Consider the 1,800 companies that were on the First Section of the Tokyo Stock Exchange in both 2010 and 2020. The older the company, the lower its rate of growth. A typical company established way back in 1875–1894 is still big (annual sales of $1.2 billion), but its sales shrank during 2010–2020. Those founded during the century from 1895 to 1995 showed lackluster growth of just 2.7% per year. Only the 161 founded after 1995 grew rapidly: a median rate of 10% a year. Unfortunately, these gazelles are among the smallest on the list (a pitifully small $280 million in median sales per year), and their total revenue comprised a trivial 3% of the combined sales of the 1,800 top corporations (SPEEDA 2021).

Japan's problem is not that most of its elephants, like those elsewhere, lose their dynamism, but that it's so hard for upstarts to take their place. As of 2015, only 5% of Japan's 300 largest corporations had been founded in the 25 years since 1990. In the United States, by contrast, nearly half were founded after 1990 (OECD 2015a: 98).[4]

Japan's corporate giants are among the oldest in the world, with almost 600 companies more than a century old among the 1,800 largest on the stock

---

[4] Adjustments had to be made to the OECD's raw numbers, because, as the OECD pointed out, the 2000–2009 figures for Japan were inflated by a change in allowing holding companies, and the latter were listed on the stock market as new companies even when it was simply a change in legal status.

market (Morishita 2022). As of 2020, the Nikkei 225 index of the most elite companies had admitted only one company founded in this century. It's M3, a network of 6 million doctors around the world who share medical insights on the web. Firms that cannot get into this exclusive stock market club find it harder to raise enough capital for further expansion, and their founders won't get the big rewards that will encourage others to try. Going public made M3 founder Itaru Tanimura Japan's 40th richest person (M3 Inc. 2020).

Japan lacks not just enough new giants, but also the smaller gazelles. Japan gives birth to lots of new SMEs, but their growth rate is the lowest in the Organisation for Economic Co-operation and Development (OECD). A typical manufacturing or service startup in Japan starts off about the same size as elsewhere, with around 3–4 people for service firms and 5–10 for manufacturers. However, in other rich countries, a typical manufacturing startup more than triples its staff after 10 years; in Japan, it just doubles. Elsewhere, a typical service company doubles its staff in its first decade, in Japan, it grows only 30% (see Figure I.3). Japan performs even more poorly in highly digitized sectors (OECD 2019b: 151).

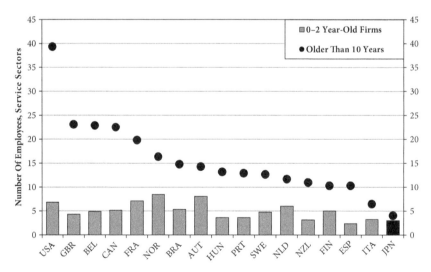

Figure I.3 Japanese startups show least growth in OECD. See country abbreviation code, pg. 12.

Source: Criscuolo et al. (2014: 30).

Note: AUS: Australia; AUT: Austria; BEL: Belgium; BRA: Brazil; CAN: Canada; CHE: Switzerland; CZE: Czechia; DEU: Germany; DNK: Denmark; ESP: Spain; FIN: Finland; FRA: France; GBR: United Kingdom; GER: Germany; GRC: Greece; HUN: Hungary; ISR: Israel; ITA: Italy; JPN: Japan; NLD: Netherlands; NOR: Norway; NZL: New Zealand; POL: Poland; PRT: Portugal; SVK: Slovak Republic; SWE: Sweden; UK: United Kingdom; USA: United States

Codes used in: Figure I.1, I.3, 2.1, 2.3, 12.1, 12.2, 16.2

Why We Care

Why should anyone care about gazelles and elephants? It's because living standards depend on it. People cannot consume more unless each worker produces more. And workers cannot produce more without a continuous cycle of economic selection.

Suppose each farmer had only the same equipment, fertilizer, and the like, as in 1910. The United States would need 71 million farmers. Suppose that calls were made with the same manual switchboards as a century ago. That would require 30 million operators. How about outlawing the PC so that 5 million secretaries could still earn a living by taking dictation, typing, and filing? Two-thirds of the entire workforce would have to be devoted to just these three jobs. Who then would make the tractors, phones, and computers, build the houses and office buildings, run the stores, provide healthcare, put out fires, or teach the children? For living standards to grow, some jobs need to be replaced by machines to make room for new jobs.

Most people realize that improved living standards require technological advancement. But it takes companies to convert new ideas into better products or to empower one worker to produce what used to take three. What makes new companies essential is that their imagination is not tethered to obsolescent products and outdated strategies. Few of the American companies that made radios could make the transition into TVs. Few producers of TVs remained in the era of PCs and cell phones.

There is a downside. While nations gain from creative destruction, not everyone within the nation reaps benefits. Some gain, while many others lose their jobs. Not every auto worker or farmer can become a computer programmer. Yes, progress creates more jobs than it destroys, and better-paying ones as well, but those caught in the transition can suffer. As will be shown in the discussion of flexicurity in Chapter 17, there are lots of ways to solve this problem.

However great the problems caused by growth, even greater are the problems generated by lack of growth.

Japanese companies facing low growth or declining sales are increasingly hiring low-paid non-regular workers. Most of the latter are part-time and temporary workers, whereas regular workers are full-time employees with job security and assorted fringe benefits. The non-regular share of the labor force has now reached nearly 40%, up from 15% in the 1980s. While regular workers, on average, earn ¥2,500 ($19) per hour, temporaries get just ¥1,660

($12), and part-timers only ¥1,050 ($8) (Japan Macro Advisors 2020a). Not surprisingly, 59% of Japanese men 30–34 with regular jobs are married or have been and by age 39, the share rises to 70%. Among non-regulars aged 30–34, it's just 22% (*Asahi* 2017: n.p.).

Equally heartbreaking are the straits of women over age 65 now living alone: 40% have fallen below the poverty line. A growing number endure the shame of having to shoplift in a country that prides itself on little crime. A third of all people now imprisoned for stealing are over age 60, up from 5% in 1960 (Fukada 2018). To make matters worse, old age benefits have been constricted because the Ministry of Finance (MOF) says low growth in tax revenue makes them unaffordable. By 2019, social security per senior was reduced by 20% from 1996, while healthcare spending per senior had been cut by 15% (Cabinet Office 2020).

Then there are the high-achieving high school students from disadvantaged families. Nearly a third have given up hope of being able to afford college. The government spends a smaller portion of GDP on education from primary grades through college than any other OECD country except one. Parents are forced to shell out thousands of dollars per year even for public schools (MEXT 2019).

These problems are not limited to small shares of the population. For those at the median income level, real (price-adjusted) per capita income fell 2% during 1995–2018 for those of working age, and 11% among seniors (OECD 2022j).[5]

Japan cannot resolve these problems without a productivity revolution. Let's see why. Suppose the number of workers grows 1% a year and each worker can produce 2% more output than the year before. Then, GDP will grow 3% per year (1% plus 2%). On the other hand, what if the number of workers starts falling 0.5% each year? To keep GDP growth at 3%, productivity growth would have to sharply accelerate to 3.5% (3.5% minus 0.5%). It's like running faster on the treadmill just to stay in place.

Japan's predicament is that, ever since 1990, aggregate work-hours, i.e., total work-hours of all workers combined, have fallen by 10%. That leaves increased GDP per hour as the only source of growth (see Figure I.4).

---

[5] Household incomes were adjusted for the number of people per household; the OECD's figures in current yen were adjusted by the Consumer Price Index by the author.

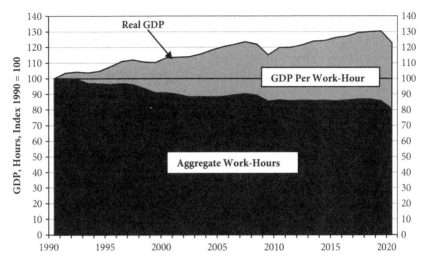

Figure I.4 Since 1990, productivity has been the only source of GDP growth.
Source: World Bank (2022); OECD (2022a).
Note: See text for definition of terms.

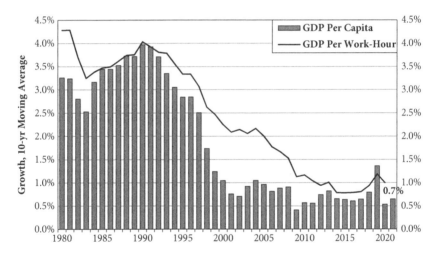

Figure I.5 Productivity slowdown leads to low growth in per capita GDP.
Source: OECD (2019g, 2022a). http://stats.oecd.org/Index.aspx?DataSetCode=PDB_GR.

Unfortunately, at the very time that productivity needs to accelerate, it has instead fallen off a cliff: from around 4% annual growth in the 1980s to just 0.8% per year in the past decade. As a result, per capita GDP growth has likewise plunged. In the last 10 years, it's averaged a meager 0.7% per year (see Figure I.5).

What a reversal of fortune. From 1950 to 1991, Japan's per capita GDP soared from just 21% of US levels to a peak of 83%. Then, what came to be called the "lost decades" pushed it back down to just 63% by 2020 (see Figure I.6). By contrast, the Eurozone kept pace, staying at 87% of the US level (OECD 2022a). In a rather shocking development, South Korea, Japan's former colony, surpassed it in real per capita GDP in 2018 (Katz 2021a).

It should be within Japan's power to achieve the required productivity revolution. It leads the world in new triadic patents, that is, those granted in the United States, Japan, and the European Union (OECD 2022c). Whatever technology it can't invent, it can buy from others. At 60%, it is second only to Korea in the share of 23–34-year-olds with a college degree (OECD 2022d). Germany and France match the United States in output per work-hour. Why not Japan? It's the failure of so many of its companies to keep pace with global benchmarks. This syndrome is particularly severe in industries not exposed to international competition.

Policymakers in Tokyo mistakenly believe that the magic solution is pouring more money into the latest machinery and software. It hasn't worked. Investments are necessary but hardly sufficient. As noted above, Japan's companies rank a depressing 63rd in the "bang for the buck" they get from their investments in digital technologies.

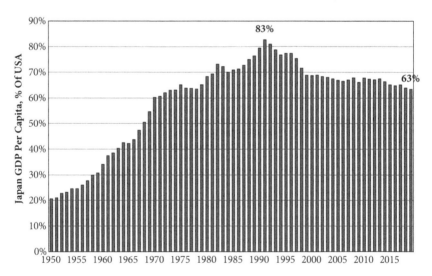

Figure I.6 Japan's catch-up in per capita GDP backpedals.
Source: Penn World Tables (2022).

Without igniting a productivity revolution, Japan will be hard-pressed to maintain living standards. And, without a host of new gazelles, Japan will be hard-pressed to ignite a productivity revolution. To do so, Tokyo needs to accept the necessity of creative destruction.

Don't Blame Japanese Culture

There are those who will tell you it cannot be done, that Japan's people are too conformist and risk-averse, that they all prefer the security of employment at one of the prestigious elephants. Not so. This is another one of those cultural myths that don't stand up to scrutiny—some of them deliberately propagated by Japanese elites to rationalize assorted power structures. If the myth were true, Japan would not have seen the effervescence of entrepreneurship that modernized it after the 1868 Meiji Restoration or its resurgence in the post–World War II economic miracle.

It's not that Japanese no longer wish to be entrepreneurs; it's that, beginning in the mid-1970s, changed conditions created more hurdles. During the high-growth era, of the half million Japanese who aspired to start a company, two-thirds actually did so. By 1997, Japan saw a doubling in the number of would-be entrepreneurs. However, only a third of them succeeded in starting a firm (METI 2002: 48). The upshot is that fewer Japanese start enterprises with non-family employees than in any other rich country (see Figure I.7).

The changed conditions were that assorted institutions, developed in the 20th century, that used to promote growth—from lifetime employment to the financial system—ossified into a rigid environment with high penalties for failure and low rewards for success.

What some misperceive as a culture of risk-aversion and conformity are behaviors that people adopted in response to the harsher environment. Change that environment and you change the behavior. This can already be seen in the labor market. A labor shortage induced by population decline has increased the bargaining power of workers with special expertise, like professionals in information and communications technologies (ICT). They are willing and able to shift jobs to better themselves.

Harry Hill, formerly the CEO of Oak Lawn Marketing (also known as direct marketer Shop Japan), recalled that, when Oak Lawn first tried to recruit university graduates in 2004, they got about six applications. "This year [2017]," he told me, "We got 3,000 applications." By 2017, Oak Lawn had

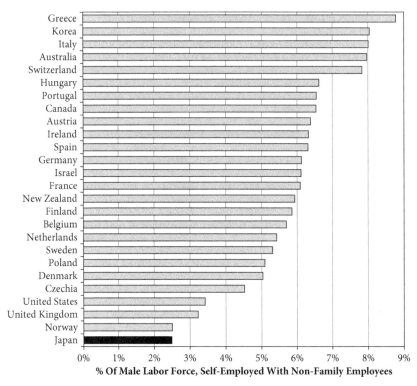

Figure I.7 Lowest rate of entrepreneurs with employees per male adults.

Source: OECD (2020c).

Note: The rate of among males was used because the gender gap in entrepreneurship is so much worse in Japan.

grown to sales of ¥68 billion ($523 million) and 450 employees. Besides the younger generation, a small but growing number of new staffers are veterans of big corporations in their late forties to early fifties. "They say to themselves: this is my last chance to do something interesting in my career before I retire"(Interview October 2017). Admittedly, this cohort is a small minority, but it's no longer trivial, and statistical evidence shows that it's growing. A sample based on three employment agencies found that the number of job-switchers over age 40 doubled between 2015 and 2020 (Suzuki 2022). Moreover, the shift from large companies to startups grew twice as fast as other types of switches (Suzuki and Nakai 2022).

Surprisingly, Japanese and American MBA (master of business administration) students are more like each other than either is to their French or Indian counterparts. Japanese scored highest or second-highest on agreement with statements like: "I love opposition; I feel driven to make a difference in my community and maybe the world," "Nothing is more exciting than seeing my ideas turn into reality," "No matter what the odds, if I believe in something, I will make it happen," and "I love to challenge the status quo" (Paul et al. 2017: 337).

These are the same attitudes once common among pioneering companies in the high-growth era (1950–1973). In the 1960s, Sharp developed a new kind of CMOS chip for handheld calculators even though it lacked experience in that field. Why even make such an attempt? Because, explained Hiroshi Inoue, the head of the team, "We were burning. Though we suffered setbacks, the young engineers who suffered them grew up to be the key people who supported Sharp's integrated circuit group" (Johnstone 1999: 78). Sharp's chip later helped Toshiba develop the world's first commercial laptop computer.

Today, young, ambitious, nonconformist visionaries are on the rise again. The trend is epitomized by Yoshihiro Maeda, the founder of the highly successful LINKERS company, and the winner of Nikkei Business Publications' Innovator of the Year award in 2015. In 2012, at age 34, Maeda realized that, in the digital age, it was counterproductive to cling to the "Not Invented Here Syndrome" among big companies: the refusal to source crucial components not invented within their corporate group. In this new world, they needed to collaborate with many others, including SMEs, as with Pfizer's COVID vaccine. LINKERS brings together larger firms and innovative SMEs, relying on both the Internet and a countrywide network of 1,700 local governments, chambers of commerce, banks, and individuals that it calls "coordinators."

One of LINKERS' famous early successes was its work for VIBE company, a part of the $7 billion Bandai Namco corporate group. VIBE was trying to develop a personal soundproof room that could be folded up and stored in a closet (e.g., for musicians practicing at home). Unable to design a sufficiently good one itself, VIBE spent a futile year searching for a partner. Finally, it contacted LINKERS. Within a week, LINKERS's network introduced it to a small firm called Kanda Sangyo. The resulting product, named Danbocchi, is available online and, by 2017, reached sales of ¥100 million ($770,000). That cash enabled Kanda Sangyo to expand its factory and hire more staff. As of 2019, when I met with Maeda, LINKERS had arranged nearly 900 such matches, and he expects LINKERS to hit $1 billion in revenue by 2030.

Maeda's aspirations go far beyond his own company and his personal wealth. He envisions a new legion of 1,000 innovators, each with annual sales in the range of hundreds of millions of dollars or even $1 billion. In Maeda's vision, these "Super Japan 1,000" companies will become hubs for tens of thousands of SMEs serving as suppliers, partners, and customers. He sees LINKERS midwifing the Super Japan 1,000 by sharing LINKERS' information on innovative SMEs with potential investors. Whether or not this vision works out, what's important is the willingness to experiment.

The Favorable Megatrends

Were this book being written a few decades ago, entrepreneurship revival on a sufficient scale would have seemed an impossible dream. The incumbent companies were too strong. Today, however, the megatrends have opened up new possibilities.

It's useful to start with technology because it can radically alter society's power structures. It's no coincidence that rock and roll and the transistor radio exploded simultaneously. Transistors eroded parental control over their children's listening habits because they cut the umbilical cord between the radio and the electric outlet. At the same time, Elvis Presley was the "killer app" that made the transistor a must-have item. This was a factor in the student protests a decade later. Similarly, the birth control pill unleashed an upheaval in gender relations (Halberstam 1993).

Today, e-commerce is shaking up the power balance between corporate giants and ambitious SMEs. Previously, SMEs had no alternative to the multi-tiered system of wholesalers that determined what products got onto store shelves, often acting on behalf of the big incumbents. E-commerce enables retailers and customers to bypass these gatekeepers.

Consider the ripple effects created by Rakuten, Japan's leading Internet mall. Founded in 1997 by the 32-year-old Hiroshi Mikitani, the company in 2022 empowered 56,000 ordinary SMEs to sell ¥5.6 trillion ($43 billion) worth of products to 110 million customers. One of them is Tansu No Gen, a furniture maker whose founder rejected e-commerce. When he died in 2002, his children joined Rakuten's network. Sales exploded from $1 million per year to $160 million in just 17 years. This also boosted the SME furniture makers.

Mikitani also exemplifies the globalization megatrend that has produced a surprisingly large share of Japan's successful entrepreneurs. His father taught at Yale for two years. Mikitani himself earned an MBA at Harvard and has made English the required language at company headquarters.

Askul is a great example of the change in generational attitudes, including gender relations. Having begun in 1993 as a four-person mail-order unit of a leading producer of office supplies, it exploded to almost ¥430 billion ($3.3 billion) in sales by 2022. Rather than have its own sales team, Askul partners with local independent retailers whom it refers to as "agents," even though these retailers are free to work with other suppliers. Noritomo Miyazawa, executive officer of Askul's Business to Business (B-to-B) segment, spoke of one retailer which, in 1994, had just two employees and ¥100 million ($770,000) in sales and was losing money. "Since becoming an agent for Askul, their sales have grown 60-fold and their staff to 33. It's one of our top 10 agents" (Interview October 2019). Its size empowers Askul to negotiate discounts as high as 30% from producers. That benefits the entire economy by reducing the inefficiencies of the traditional distribution system.

The success of these superstar gazelles helps the upcoming generation envision a better risk:reward ratio in either founding, or working for, a new company. Miyazawa came to Askul from Itochu, a giant trading company with $48 billion in revenue. "I thought that, if I joined a smaller company, I could become involved in a larger variety of assignments. Besides, senior managers at Askul listen to younger managers if they have a good idea." Saori Onsen, vice executive officer of Askul's B-to-B Strategy & Planning Unit, joined the firm in 2002 when she was in her late twenties. She shifted from a giant convenience store chain, saying, "I joined Askul because I thought I could have more challenges." Indeed. Her first responsibility was managing the website at a time when online sales were just getting off the ground.

Onsen exemplifies the shift in gender relations. So does Naho Kono, who joined Rakuten in 2003 and now runs the company's flagship Rakuten Ichiba marketplace. The unavailability of such opportunities at traditional firms has sent women flocking to the gazelles. Without the generational and gender shifts, even the best potential gazelles would have been hamstrung by what had been one of the greatest obstacles: an inability to hire talented mid-career staff.

This generational and gender shift saved Raksul, the Uber of parcel delivery. While founder Matsumoto is a visionary, he lacked experience in indispensable nuts and bolts management skills. This is not unusual; the same was true of Michael Dell, who had to hire a chief operations officer to avoid bankruptcy. Every year 40% of Raksul's staff quit, forcing Matsumoto to seek replacements. ICT pros in short supply see less risk in switching jobs to get a better situation. Without a remedy, Raksul could not survive. "So," he said, "I hired four high-class managers" (Interview October 2019). All had been working at foreign firms in Japan. Within a fairly short time, they reduced turnover to 5%–10% per year. Their solution was to keep impressing upon the staff that working for Raksul was not just about money, but also the company's mission. By working at Raksul, they were helping to create a better Japan.

"Were these veterans in their fifties?" I asked Matsumoto. "Oh no, people in their thirties," was the reply. He felt that managers who had spent most of their careers at older firms were too steeped in old ways and too insulated from overseas trends. That such managers were available to be hired illustrates the strength of the generational change.

"Startups like mine have a global experience and so my generation feels strange in Japanese culture," explained Matsumoto. "Most Japanese mainly get the information about Japan. But I spend a few months each year overseas. In our generation, things are freer and more liberal. We have lots of friends outside of Japan and, with the Internet, we can easily interact with them." "The whole of your generation feels that way? Or just the 5% or so that are doing things like you?" I asked. "Less than 5%," he replied. That may sound small, but if 5% of Japan's working adults created new firms with non-family employees, it would be a lot closer to the US level (see again Figure I.7).

The power of international exposure cannot be overstated. While a freshman at the prestigious Tokyo University, Mitsuru Izumo visited Bangladesh and saw that, despite having plenty of rice, Bangladeshis were malnourished. They couldn't afford nutrient-rich foods. He then heard about euglena, microalgae that would fill the gap if there were a practical way to turn it into food. As it happens, this globe-trotter spent his sophomore year at Stanford University where, not surprisingly, fellow students and teachers encouraged him to start his own company. His enterprise, called Euglena, produces a drink that can be found at Japan's Family Mart convenience store chain. As of 2022, it had reached annual revenues of ¥44 billion ($340 million). The revenue earned in Japan finances Euglena's donation of millions of euglena-based cookies to the children of Bangladesh. Would Euglena even exist if Izumo had spent all four years cocooned at Tokyo University?

The Politics of Reform in Japan

Japan's tragedy is that it would not take all that much change to catalyze economic revival, and yet the country's political leadership has been unable to make those changes.

Right now, given all the positive changes discussed above, the single biggest obstacle to generating a host of new companies is the dearth of external finance. Japan has few angel investors, those who provide seed money to startups. Meanwhile, banks are reluctant to lend growth capital, even to companies 10 years old or more. The problem is that companies that start too small for lack of funds end up staying small or failing altogether (Audretsch 2012). With would-be entrepreneurs forced to rely on themselves, family, and friends for funding, the talented but less affluent young are de facto excluded. This is a major reason why Japan has so few high-growth startups (see again Figure I.3).

There are about a half-dozen governmental measures regarding taxes and procurement that would make a huge difference. And for years, reformist officials have tried to get them implemented. Usually, they've been watered down to the point of ineffectiveness. Hopes were raised in 2021 when, for the first time, a Japanese prime minister declared the revival of entrepreneurship as a national goal essential to overall recovery. As part of his talk of creating "a new form of capitalism" in Japan, Fumio Kishida called for 100,000 new innovative, high-growth startups by 2027. Unfortunately, the one substantive measure Kishida offered, a tax incentive for investing in new companies, is poorly designed. And yet it would not take much of a tweak to make it as effective as such measures have been in countries like the United States, the United Kingdom, and France (see pp. 290–292).

But that is not the end of the story. As long as Japan's economy continues to stagnate, proposals like this will keep coming back to the fore. That's because the political impact of economic stagnation puts unending pressure on Tokyo to come up with a solution. Moreover, the depressed economy, as well as technological and generational shifts, are causing fissures among, and within, the assorted special interest groups upon which LDP power rests. Raising consumption taxes to support the growing ranks of the elderly creates discontent among middle-aged and younger families. In the business world, frustration at the immobility of the government and the main business federation, Keidanren, led a number of high-tech innovative companies in 2010 to start their own lobbying organization called the Japan Association of New Economy (JANE). By 2015, JANE already had more than 500 company members. It regularly meets with government officials and Diet members. The same changes are also causing new alliances among groups that previously felt no common ground. The more that similar fissures—and new alliances—emerge on other issues, the more likely is a shakeup of the socioeconomic coalition that has so far blocked serious structural reforms.

If the effort to revive entrepreneurship were simply a battle between reform and the status quo, the latter would have the advantage. The force of inertia is strong, particularly in a country where a single party has ruled for decades. However, the status quo is not on the menu of history. Without reform, Japan will be left with the harsh combination of poor productivity and an aging workforce, a recipe for declining living standards. Japan will either recover or suffer further decline; it will not stay the same. That condition is a recipe for political stress too intense for politicians to ignore. Over the past couple of decades, Japan's leaders have responded to the pressure by trying, and failing, to come up with a solution. This pressure will intensify.

This book will not only propose needed reforms, but also lay out the state of play between those trends driving reform and those resisting it. The hope is that showing the feasibility of real reform will make it more credible and increase the chances of success.

PART I

RISE AND FALL OF JAPANESE ENTREPRENEURSHIP

1

Entrepreneurship

From Effervescence to Rigidity

If Japan had never experienced an effervescence of entrepreneurship, then trying to implant it would be like grafting an alien practice onto inhospitable turf. In reality, modern Japan has experienced two extended bursts of entrepreneurship. It can do so again. Its current arrangements are not immutable artifacts of an age-old Japanese mindset; rather, they are products of history, institutions, and power, of decisions that mostly made sense when they were made, but whose time has passed.

Many of today's corporate elephants began as gazelles in the first entrepreneurial burst, from 1868 through 1926, named the Meiji and Taisho eras after the emperors then reigning. Prior to 1868, Japan had been an isolated feudal society. Back in 1635, in response to the emerging threat of European colonialism, its rulers had cut it off from virtually all foreign contact, all travel from or to Japan, a closure that lasted until the mid-1800s. China was the great power in the region. Japan was like something out of Europe's sixteenth century; 85% of the people lived in rural towns and villages. It had none of the modern machinery, steel mills, steam engines, telegraphs, railroads, postal system, or newspapers already pervading the United States and Europe. Nor modern-day business institutions like contemporary banking, the public corporation, or double-entry bookkeeping.

Then came the unimaginable. China, mighty China, was overpowered by Europeans, beginning with the Opium Wars. Fearing a similar fate, a group of young men overthrew the reigning military dynasty and took over Japan in the 1868 Meiji Restoration. Under the slogan "Rich Country, Strong Army," they fostered rapid industrialization through a combination of a dirigiste state and a host of new private companies. The takeoff was explosive. By the 1940s, only 75 years after its emergence from medievalism, Japan had an industrial base powerful enough to enable its military to seize almost all of Asia. Its planes and aircraft carriers were, for a while, almost able to fight the US Navy to a standstill. Although the state promoted industrialization,

The Contest for Japan's Economic Future. Richard Katz, Oxford University Press. © Richard Katz 2024.
DOI: 10.1093/oso/9780197675106.003.0002

it was a substantial cadre of private entrepreneurs, as well as family-based conglomerates, called *zaibatsu*, who founded the companies that made the ships, the steel, the machinery, the newspapers, universities, and all the rest. Many of these entrepreneurs were new entrants into the business world. Along with economic modernization came gradual political modernization, leading to elections, party-based governments, and, by 1925, universal suffrage for men.

Political modernization was interrupted during the militarist period of the 1930s–1940s when the state tightened its grip on the economy and new corporate conglomerates emerged in alliance with it, as did the auto companies as suppliers of trucks. In the transition after the war, the dominant corporate institutions, *zaibatsu* like Mitsui, Mitsubishi, and Sumitomo, were the subject of trust-busting by the US Occupation. In addition, nearly 2,000 executives from 187 leading companies were purged from having any leadership role in any company, even new ones, on the grounds of their cooperation with Japan's militarists. This opened the way for both new firms and new, younger business leaders, all eager to rebuild their country and catch up to the West. It also opened opportunities for older firms that had potential, but, for one reason or another, had faced limits to growth in the prewar period.

Postwar Hothouse

These entrepreneurial upstarts operated in a hothouse environment. When the war ended, Japan had lost a third of its factories and housing. Reconstruction and the drive to catch up drew in new companies. It took until 1953 to recover prewar levels of output. Then, during the 1953–1973 high-growth era, Japan raised itself from a poor agricultural country to a newly industrializing country (NIC). Per capita GDP increased fivefold from a level that, in 1953, was the same as a poor African country today (Penn World Tables 2021). Not unjustly did this receive the moniker "economic miracle."

By 1971, 40% of all industrial output consisted of products—from color TVs to petrochemicals to air conditioners—that had not existed in the Japanese market in 1951; 10% of output consisted of products that hadn't even been invented five years earlier. Japanese shipbuilders were the first to produce and market supertankers and, by the 1960s, had the most efficient shipbuilders in the world. Japanese manufacturers were often the first adapters of innovations like solid-state TV, and they learned how to make steel with less iron ore, less coking coal, and less energy than others needed (Katz 1998).

As Japan traversed its long march up the electronics value chain from transistor radios to computer memory chips, its American counterparts began to fear that the future would belong to Japan, a fear that led to the severe trade frictions of the 1980s–1990s. Repeatedly, Japanese firms invented and/or commercialized product after must-have product. Sometimes, this meant taking existing technologies that were not yet commercially feasible and inventing the necessary technical alterations. Japan's pioneering developments included: the microwave oven for consumers (invented by Sharp); the handheld battery-operated calculator (developed by Sharp in competition with America's Texas Instruments); various specialized electronic and computer chips that they turned into widely used industry standards, from CMOS to flash memories like NAND (Sharp and Toshiba); the consumer electronic watch (commercialized by Casio and Seiko); the transistor radio (invented by SONY); the video cassette recorder (VCR) for consumers (invented separately by SONY and Panasonic); SONY's Trinitron color TV; the single-lens reflex (SLR) camera and then the digital SLR camera (developed by Nikon and Canon); the compact disc (CD) (introduced by SONY); the Walkman (invented by SONY); the video camcorder and the CCD chip at its foundation (SONY); a laptop computer using the same DOS system powering PCs (invented by Toshiba); liquid crystal display (LCD) screens successively used in digital watches and calculators, laptops, and TVs (developed by Seiko and Sharp); the lithium-ion battery used in everything from cell phones to electric cars (commercialized by Sony and Asahi Kasei); the 1G cell phone network (NTT) and 3G cellphone (NTT Docomo); and flexible endoscopes (Olympus).

Many of these triumphs came in areas where US firms, or more established Japanese firms, could have led but chose not to do so, often because they simply could not see the commercial potential. Western Electric, the inventor of the transistor, could not imagine any commercial use for it—it was being used in US missiles—but SONY's founders did.

Back in the day, the Japanese were shortsightedly disparaged by many as good imitators because much of the technology they adapted came from American inventors. But this overlooks the supreme technical and commercial genius in taking one or more technologies seemingly ill-suited for commercial use and synthesizing the technical changes needed to make mass-market products. Sharp's work in CMOS chips and LCDs for calculators, and Toshiba's cooperation with Sharp on CMOS, eventually led to Toshiba's pioneering market leadership in laptop computers.

Of the 120 large electronics firms in 1979—those with at least 300 employees—nearly half had still been SMEs in 1955. In other words, from 1955 to 1979 it was still possible for an SME to become a large firm within just a couple of decades. Moderately large challengers like Seiko and Sharp could become giants. What we don't know is how many more electronics SMEs tried, and failed, and either closed down, got absorbed by their bigger brethren, or became one of the innumerable subcontractors to a big firm. What we do know is that, since no one can know in advance which approach will work, tolerating so many failures led to more triumphs. Entrepreneurial countries must be safe for failure (Kawai and Urata 2002: 41).

This happened throughout the economy. Among establishments[1] in all business sectors with at least 300 employees as of 1996, 40% were founded during 1954–1974. In 1962, nearly 16% of Japan's manufacturing firms were less than four years old. More than 60% of their founders established their firms when they were in their twenties or thirties, a pattern not too different from the global experience today (Kawai and Urata 2002: 45; Watanabe 1970: 539).

Not only were new firms being founded; many were exiting. Economic natural selection, if not perfect, was working to a large extent. This is what gave the high-growth era its high growth.

Burning to Succeed

Journalist Bob Johnstone (1999) put a human face on the rise of the Japanese electronics giants: ambitious and imaginative young and middle-aged technicians and businessmen, who were willing to bet their companies on revolutionary products in the hope of rising to the top of the heap.

Johnstone's story begins with the partnership of Tadashi Sasaki, a brilliant electrical engineer, and Tokuji Hayakawa, the founder of an obscure company called Hayakawa Electric Industry. Born into poverty, Hayakawa could not go beyond second grade; instead, he was apprenticed to earn money

---

[1] Each Toyota factory or sales outlet is an establishment. Establishments with at least 300 employees typically belong to firms with many thousands of employees.

for the family. In 1912, at the age of 29, he invented a belt buckle that didn't need to perforate the leather, earned a patent, and created his own firm. In 1951, at the age of 58, he took a chance on making TVs before any of the bigger players in Japan. His was the first company in Japan to come out with a working prototype; the following year it licensed patents from RCA.

Licensing patents was no mean feat in those early days. With foreign exchange so scarce, any firm wanting to import anything, including patents, had to apply to the predecessor of the current Ministry of Economy, Trade, and Industry (METI) then known as the Ministry of International Trade and Industry (MITI). Permission was not easy to get, particularly when the benefit was uncertain. Some years later, SONY had difficulty being allowed to spend $25,000 to buy the transistor license from Western Electric. Fortunately, Hayakawa garnered permission and, in 1953, came out with Japan's first commercial TV set. Its price was equivalent to 2.7 years of income for a government worker with a high school diploma. So, most were put in public places. As prices dropped, sales took off, and Hayakawa had a 60% market share. By 1955, other firms, after seeing Hayakawa's success, joined in, and its market share plunged to 25%. But with the market growing so rapidly, sales soared tenfold to $58 million, employees to 6,000, and exports accounted for 16% of revenue. That made the company bigger than SONY, and more profitable. Yet, as Hayakawa lamented, both SONY and the much larger Matsushita (Panasonic) were now growing faster. To prosper, or even just to survive, Hayakawa had to keep coming up with new, revolutionary, consumer products, and to do so ahead of the competition (Sharp 2020).

This is where Sasaki comes into the story. Upon returning from World War II, Sasaki went to work for a small company that produced the first transistor made in Japan, just ahead of SONY. Despite this technical accomplishment, the company was failing, and, in 1960, its banks insisted that it sell itself to Fujitsu. Sasaki had no desire to work for Fujitsu. What to do? Fate stepped in when Hayakawa requested a meeting. Sasaki came equipped with an idea just when Hayakawa had an urgent need for one. US military contractor Litton Industries had developed a magnetron that was suitable to run microwave ovens. Litton had never made a consumer model. Sasaki sold Hayakawa on the notion. In 1961, Hayakawa Electric came out with Japan's first microwave oven and in 1962 put it into mass production for restaurants. The company was risking a lot of capital, even though its balance sheet was so tenuous that it too was facing bank pressure to sell itself to a bigger firm. Nonetheless, Hayakawa once again bet the company and, once again, he won.

In thinking of still more revolutionary products to drive growth, Sasaki favored small, portable ones for consumers. His dream was an electronic calculator small enough to fit in the hand, which could run on batteries (which would require a new kind of semiconductor chip) and that everyone from a grocer to a housewife could use. It ended up in a race with another upstart company, Casio. Lots of companies that could have seized early market leadership backed off, including SONY and Texas Instruments (TI). The incident proved the wisdom of an observation by a president of Seiko Epson, which would invent the electronic digital watch and the serial dot matrix computer printer: "Technology has no intrinsic value. It takes on value only when manufacturers like us apply it to the products we make" (Johnstone 1999: 61).

Hayakawa came out with the first commercial transistor-based calculator in the world in 1964, in time for the New York World's Fair. But it weighed 55 pounds and cost almost $1,500. At both Hayakawa and Casio, the sales and technology people were skeptical that the product would ever be a commercial success. But Sasaki believed in what is now called the learning curve. The more units a firm produces over time, the more knowledge it gains in how to make it at a lower cost. That, in turn, makes it affordable, which increases sales, thereby sending the company further up the learning curve. TI would later claim to be the only non-Japanese firm to understand the learning curve.

A handheld, battery-operated calculator, Sasaki argued, was just an electronic abacus. The market would arise once the price was right. Getting it right required a new kind of chip, a variant of the CMOS. Hayakawa decided that, despite lacking any experience in this type of chip, the company had to produce its own, since none of the existing producers would make it in the volumes Hayakawa needed. But, as the leader of the CMOS team said, they were burning. In 1969, the company introduced a desktop calculator weighing four pounds and priced at $277. Within a year, it had sold its millionth calculator. Its success lured 60 companies into the field.

In 1970, upstart Hayakawa Electric—now with sales of more than $400 million, 14,000 employees, and 40% of its output being exported—changed its name to the one most people now know: Sharp. It continued to be a pioneer and market share leader in a host of new products, including LCD screens for TVs.

The story has a sad ending. Sharp eventually turned into not just an elephant, but a lame one, with sales falling after the 2007 peak of ¥9.56 trillion ($74 billion). Like other elephants, it rested on its laurels, such as stubbornly sticking to making LCD TVs even when the market shrank, and other countries could make them at a lower price. SONY and others did the same. Ultimately, Sharp had to be rescued in 2016 via a takeover by Taiwan's Foxconn.

Sharp was not alone, either in its triumph or its tragedy. The real mystery is why Japan stopped generating new companies like Sharp. The main answer is institutional obsolescence. When the circumstances change, so must institutions and practices. But institutions give birth to interest groups that benefit from their continuation, even when that damages society as a whole. Moreover, the mental paradigms attached to these institutions can ossify into ideological blinders. However, if even after a reasonable lag, a society is still unable to make the needed shift, then institutional obsolescence sets in.

Yesterday's strengths become today's weaknesses. That is Japan's tragedy. Precisely because its economic performance had been so miraculous, the institutions and practices that produced the miracle maintained their credibility long after they should have been transcended.

The System Succeeds

In the catch-up era through the mid-1970s, Japan was an NIC. It successfully applied an industrial policy appropriate to that stage of development. Even without that policy, Japan would have developed, but not at a 9% yearly clip for nearly a quarter century (1950–1973). The "miracle" was accelerating the natural process of economic catch-up into a very short period of time. (Katz 1998: 107–164).

At the outset of the miracle years, Japan was a poor country with more farmers than factory workers. Its chief exports were silk, toys, and textiles. But it was determined to catch up to the United States and Europe, and that meant—against the advice of the World Bank—promoting big, capital-intensive heavy-machinery sectors, like shipbuilding, steel, autos, electronics, and the like. Since it had little capital, labor productivity was low—compare the hourly output of a farmer with a tractor to one without it. In those days, the royal road to growth was promoting high rates of savings and investment, new technology (imported or home-grown), and companies large enough to afford the big investments. By 1970, a majority of Japan's manufacturing output and two-thirds of its exports came from just seven modern sectors, including synthetic textiles, chemicals, metals, and all sorts of machinery.

As Japan's industrial structure advanced, the leading businesses became a lot bigger. Traditionally, manufacturing had been dominated by companies with fewer than 300 employees. By 1970, 34% of all industrial output and 60% of all exports were being produced by just 200 companies, most of which were in those seven modern sectors (Rapp 1976).

In order to build up large firms in these modern sectors, the government regulated interest rates to lower the cost of capital.[2] Since, in the first couple of decades, there was more demand for investment capital than Japan's savings could supply, the government chose priority sectors, and the Bank of Japan (BOJ) worked with the leading banks to ration the scarce capital to those sectors and to favored firms within those sectors. By 1964, Japan stood fourth behind the United States, West Germany, and Britain in the percentage of exports based in modern industries benefiting from rapidly growing world demand.

A full quarter of Japan's growth came from economies of scale (i.e., a car company producing 1 million vehicles per year can produce each vehicle more cheaply than one making just 100,000). At the plant level, for big capital-intensive industries like steel and autos, factories need to reach a certain size to be efficient. At the industry level, a market that is big enough to support several leading firms creates a competitive pressure cooker that forces firms to keep improving their efficiency.

These policymakers, however, faced a catch-22. Companies could not get big until they were competitive enough to gain sales, but they could not become competitive until they were big enough to achieve economies of scale. How to square the circle? The government applied classic infant industry policies of subsidy and import protection to favored sectors. Japan's auto industry, for example, was almost wiped out by a flood of European imports during a brief interlude of free trade in 1953. In response to the European threat, MITI simply slammed on the brakes. Using its powers under the 1949 Foreign Exchange Law, MITI simply refused to allocate foreign exchange for the import of foreign cars beyond a minimal quota.[3] Not until 1965, when the industry had become competitive, did car imports begin to be liberalized. The industry also received enormous subsidies, helping it to engage in the necessary investment. These included not only huge tax breaks and below-market interest loans to the automakers themselves, but critical aid to key

---

[2] Interest rates began being gradually deregulated during the 1980s.
[3] While the law was not repealed until 1980, allocation of foreign exchange became superfluous once Japan began running regular trade surpluses in the mid-1960s.

supplier industries, from auto parts and machine tools to steel. For 15 years, from 1956 to 1972, 15% of all loans to the auto parts industry came from the government, and for some priority parts producers, the figure sometimes reached as high as 50%.

The plan worked so marvelously that it enshrined certain notions that had only temporary validity in the era of catch-up (e.g., the myth economies of scale would always be the key to competitiveness). In reality, being too big or too diversified is just as bad as being too small or too narrow. Merging two unhealthy giants does not create one healthy company. In a mature economy, the force of competition yields more productivity than economies of scale. Misreading the lessons of the miracle years is a big factor in Japan's underappreciation of the need for new entrepreneurs to fit the digital age.

The System Sours

High growth cannot continue forever. As economies mature, growth inevitably slows down. For Japan, the slowdown came abruptly, via the 1973 oil shock which sent the world into a severe recession. However, growth during 1975–1985 plunged much more than would have arisen from maturity alone: to a mere 2.7%. The reason is that, once an economy reaches maturity, industrial policy is not only superfluous but outright counterproductive (Katz 1998: 165–196).

Unfortunately, in response to low growth, the government not only maintained the tools of industrial policy but used them for a harmful purpose. Instead of promoting future winners, it turned to protecting losers. In the name of protecting firms and jobs—particularly among industry sectors and population segments supporting the ruling LDP—the government actively worked to slow creative destruction. In a host of industries, MITI created legal "recession cartels" to make sure there was no disruptive shakeout of weak firms in scores of what were called sunset industries like textiles, aluminum, petrochemicals, and even steel.[4]

Under the rubric of avoiding what the government labeled "excessive competition," Tokyo turned a blind eye to anti-competitive practices, including violations of the Anti-monopoly Law's restraint of trade provisions, such as when incumbents successfully pressured retailers not to let new

---

[4] Recession cartels became the source of US-Japan trade friction and are no longer used.

challengers gain shelf space, or pressured wholesale firms to limit their help to challengers, either foreign or domestic. Even when Japan Fair Trade Commission (JFTC) reports documented such practices, it failed to act (Katz 1998: 45, 176–177).

The number of sectors where incumbents retain this sort of power is dwindling. It was always weakest in sectors marked by fierce competition within Japan. Japanese retailers had no fear of offering their customers Compaq PCs in competition with NEC's during the "Compaq shock" of 1992, when Compaq launched a successful campaign to sell Windows-based PCs at much lower prices than NEC computers using a proprietary operating system. NEC suffered a huge loss in market share and lost its dominance. But anti-competitive practices remain remarkably persistent when Japanese buyers face a concentrated industry with a history of METI-authorized recession cartels. In 1997, an editor of one of Japan's biggest newspapers recalled asking his purchasing manager to import less expensive foreign newsprint. The manager replied that, if the company imported paper, its main supplier might not be as willing to assure supplies in a future time of shortage.

In 1973, the LDP passed the Large-Scale Retail Store Law so that tiny mom-and-pop retailers could veto the establishment of a store bigger than 5,400 square feet in their neighborhoods lest the more efficient giants wipe out the small fry. Not until these issues became a source of US-Japan economic friction would Japan reform the law in the early 1990s.

In short, creative destruction was replaced with destructive preservationism. The weakest firms were protected, driving out the merely mediocre. The average firm that shut down was actually more efficient than those which remained—the exact opposite of the normal pattern (Fukao and Kwon 2005).

The result of all this was the creation of a dual economy, a dysfunctional hybrid of super-strong companies in the export sectors, where they faced the crucible of fierce competition, and super-weak domestic sectors where the force of competition was much less. All economies have some amount of dualism, but, in Japan, the productivity gap between the international and domestic sectors was much bigger than elsewhere. In the 1990s, Japanese output per work-hour was 24% ahead of the United States in automaking, and 15% ahead in consumer electronics. But most Japanese worked in another Japan, the domestic-oriented goods and service sectors where productivity was 30%–40% less than in the United States.

The underlying weakness was hidden from the world, and from Japan itself, by the stellar performance of the internationalized industries. But this could not go on forever. Just as a bulb burns brightest just before it burns out, a bubble in stocks and property led to a crash in 1990, and the underlying corrosion of the economic foundation was revealed. The lost decades of the 1990s and 2000s were on (Katz 2022a).

Without Competition, There Is No Competitiveness

Some of the responses to the lost decades deepened the internal corrosion, including excessive reliance on near-zero interest rates, which had the side effect of shoring up zombie firms at the expense of healthier ones.

To make matters worse, when firms or products in important fields seemed threatened with failure, all too often, Japan's answer has been mergers, sometimes aided by government money. Whereas the government spoke of excess competition and the supposed magic of economies of scale, in reality, it is the Japanese industries with the fiercest internal competition that perform the best on the world stage (Sakakibara and Porter 2001). Those sectors where the same few leading companies have the same market ranking year after year after year—the sign of a cozy, even if tacit, cartel—tend to be laggards. As a South Korean minister in the reformist Kim Dae Jung government told conference attendees in 1999: "Without competition, there is no competitiveness."

Trapped in obsolete notions, METI even claimed that Samsung Electronics' rise was due to its domination of the domestic market. "South Korean corporations use the domestic market as a 'home base' for bold and rapid strategic investment in global markets" (METI 2010: 21). That, by the way, is the same argument that American trade hawks used against Japan in the 1980s–1990s. METI has applied the same logic to steel, autos, electric power, and oil refining. In reality, Samsung beat out SONY, Panasonic, and others due to better strategy and execution (Chang 2011).

In 2011, Japan passed a new law making it easier for mergers to pass antitrust screening. Instead of looking at the company's market share in Japan, the law mandated the JFTC to look at its share in the global market. This might make sense in industries where imports are large enough to impact prices and output, but METI has also used it to promote mergers in industries, with low levels of imports, like steel (imports were just 7% of sales in 2019). In

2012, with the aid of this law, METI promoted a merger of Japan's largest and third-largest steel firms, Nippon Steel and Sumitomo Metal, to create the world's second-largest steelmaker. While this gave the merged firm some more pricing power—at the expense of steel-consuming industries like autos that employ even more Japanese workers—it is doubtful that the merger raised efficiency. On the contrary, in 2020, Nippon Steel announced it would shut down a plant built only a decade earlier at a cost of nearly $500 million. In the case of the inefficient oil-refining sector, METI issued regulations in 2009 so that the Ministry, rather than the market, could dictate how much each oil refiner reduced capacity in order to rebalance supply and demand, and thereby raise prices. In a market situation, the least efficient plants would have borne the brunt.

Japan's government and firms tried the same approach in more dynamic sectors like electronics, often wasting both money and human capital. In 1999, NEC and Hitachi created a firm called Elpida via a merger of their memory chip (DRAM) divisions, later adding Mitsubishi's DRAM unit. It took just 13 years for Elpida's $5.6 billion bankruptcy to become the second largest in Japanese history up to that time. Eventually, the American firm Micron Technology bought it. The same year that Elpida failed, the government's Innovation Network Corporation of Japan (INCJ) spent $2 billion to engineer and finance the merger of the LCD screen divisions of Sony, Toshiba, and Hitachi into a new entity called Japan Display (JDI). To the usual claim of economies of scale, Tokyo added the techno-nationalist notion that LCD technology needed to be kept in Japanese hands. That seems a strange rationale since one of the reasons for JDI's red ink was that it kept emphasizing LCD products even as Korean competitors moved on to OLED (organic LED). In the ensuing eight years, Japan's banks and taxpayers have repeatedly been called upon to spend billions to keep this zombie firm walking, and INCJ has repeatedly quashed various efforts to bring in Chinese, Taiwanese, and foreign investors, as it had futilely tried with Sharp Corporation and Toshiba's memory chip unit. In the end, the financially strapped JDI sold off some of its facilities and then sold majority control to Ichigo Asset Management, an investment firm headed by an American, Scott Callon, who became JDI's chair (Fukase et al. 2016).

The rationale for preserving the elephants is that this protects jobs. But what it really does is protect full-time regular jobs at existing unhealthy firms, while depressing the creation of new jobs at either existing firms or new entrants. In a dynamic economy, lots of jobs disappear every year, but even more new jobs are created. In 2015, for example, 13.7 American jobs ended while 16.8 million new jobs were created, for a net gain of 3.1 million. In fact, there is evidence that the exit and entry of firms actually boosts overall job creation. That's because this process produces more successful growing firms that need more employees (Henrekson and Johannson 2010: 241).

Why have these counterproductive policies and practices remained dominant? It's the fact that the very flaws that fetter the economy are also the way Japan tries to avoid social dislocation. In the absence of a robust governmental social safety net, one's current job is the main social safety net. If the company fails, so will its workers. The result is immense political pressure to keep zombie companies alive. Were there a sufficiently robust government safety net, then firms might close, but their workers could be transitioned more easily to new firms. Chapter 17 will detail how flexicurity can overcome this dilemma.

2

Analog Mindset in a Digital World

Decades ago, economist Joseph Schumpeter, who coined the phrase "creative destruction," asked himself what kind of companies most promote innovation. Is it the nimble new entrants not beholden to past conventional wisdom who go on to supplant incumbents? Think of SONY developing the transistor radio, or Steve Jobs and Bill Gates toiling in their respective garages. Perhaps, instead, it's the giant companies with tens of thousands of employees, the cash to spend untold amounts on R&D, and the ability to exploit innovations via economies of scale in fabrication and marketing—in other words, giants like Toyota and Hitachi. In the US-Japan trade wars of the 1980s, American computer chip producers argued that their Japanese competitors could come out first with newer generations because they were part of huge industrial conglomerates (known as *keiretsu* in Japanese) that gave them access to abundant cheap money.[1]

Schumpeter named his first model (entrepreneur-led innovation) "creative destruction." The second model, corporate-led innovation, has been called "creative accumulation." Because Schumpeter emphasized the creative destruction side earlier in his career and creative accumulation later, some authors refer to these two models as Schumpeter Mark I and Schumpeter Mark II (Castellacci and Zheng 2010).

In practice, both models are seen in the business world. Which one best applies in any particular situation depends on the life cycle of a particular sector, that sector's characteristics, and the leading technologies of any era. When new industries or new technologies are taking off, a large number of new entrants give it a shot, and then the field narrows to a few successors, as in US autos beginning in 1895. It is after the field settles down that the divergence in long-standing sources of innovation emerges.

It's no longer 1895. To get off the ground, Tesla needed investors to pony up $19 billion in debt and equity during 2010–2018. Only because the incumbents were late to the electric vehicle (EV) game was it able to succeed.

---

[1] The prewar *zaibatsu* become reborn under the term *keiretsu*.

The Contest for Japan's Economic Future. Richard Katz, Oxford University Press. © Richard Katz 2024.
DOI: 10.1093/oso/9780197675106.003.0003

For a firm outside of the luxury niche to be profitable, it must sell at least 100,000 vehicles of any model. It cannot start small and grow organically.

Contrast that with Rakuten, which started its online marketplace with only six employees, one server, and 13 merchants selling on its network, or Raksul, which struggled for three years, with revenues of just $500,000 per year, and then got off the ground with just $2 million in venture capital (VC) financing. In industries with lower financial and scale barriers to entry, not only are markets more contestable, but there is a lot of turbulence. Consider how new e-retailers are compelling long-established brick-and-mortar retailers to downsize.

Many industries may start out with the entrepreneurial model only to shift with maturity to the corporate model. Sometimes there is a combination of the two models, as in the collaboration between pharmaceutical giants and the newer biotech companies discussed below.

In the postwar era when Japan rocketed itself to affluence, the majority of innovation leaders in rich countries were most often large, capital-intensive firms, with economies of scale and who tried to invent all of the parts they needed by themselves (a practice known as vertical integration). That was par for the course in the analog era. As Japan developed those industries, it too created giant, well-financed, vertically integrated globally competitive firms.

The features that made these Japanese giants so competitive in the analog era no longer serve them well in the digital era, a situation in which technology and products are changing so rapidly, where smaller companies can compete, and in which some products rely on so many technologies that no single company can master them all. In that situation, companies need to be part of collaborative networks to be competitive. With few exceptions, the giants who soared in the analog era have not been able to adjust to digitization. In fact, as will be detailed below, among 64 countries, Japan ranks dead last in the ability of its companies to use digital technology well. It's not easy for elephants to change their ways of thinking and operating anywhere. Japan exacerbates this problem by making it hard for them to be supplanted by new companies more adept at the new technological regime.

The 1940 System in the Postwar Era

While giant firms were appropriate to the analog era, neither their emergence in Japan, nor that of other economic institutions, was a purely organic development. On the contrary, it was the result of a series of decisions policymakers made in response to the needs of their time. Because many of these steps were taken around 1940 as part of wartime mobilization, economist Yukio Noguchi (1994) termed Japan's postwar setup the "1940 system." If these institutions and practices were created by leaders back then, they can be revised by current leaders to meet today's needs.

One aspect was the encouragement not just of giant firms, but of giant conglomerates. In the 1960s, the famous prewar *zaibatsu* (e.g., Mitsui, Mitsubishi, Sumitomo, etc.) recreated themselves with the support of the government, now calling themselves *keiretsu*. An individual *keiretsu*, with a bank as the hub, consisted of dozens of companies across a host of often-unrelated industries from insurance to machinery to beer. Hence, they were known as *horizontal keiretsu*. At their peak, they not only accounted for a sixth of all business sales, but by virtue of their dominance of banking and commerce and their buying/sales power, they were able to shape the opportunities available to non-*keiretsu* firms. In addition, with MITI acting as cheerleader, big firms and their allies, customers, suppliers, and banks held each other's shares (called cross-shareholding). This not only staved off unwanted purchases by foreign investors, but it also meant that firms could support each other in economic downturns or when they needed large infusions of capital. In some oligopolistic industries like urea, bearing steel, rails, and rubber, collusion was further cemented when leading firms bought stocks of their own *competitors*.

Subcontracting—whereby a host of small suppliers make items for one or two large customers—was also enhanced by the government under several war mobilization laws to form what would be called *vertical keiretsu* during the postwar era. For example, 40% of Toyota's subcontractors in the 1960s had become so during the wartime mobilization. In the postwar era, half of SMEs in manufacturing became subcontractors to the giants, and a lesser amount in other sectors. Toyota itself had ties to Mitsui's horizontal *keiretsu*.

Japan's current system of bank-centered finance—with only a small role for the bond and stock markets—was also a product of the 1940 system. Back in the 1920s, Japan's financial system was much like those in the West. A combination of banks, the stock market, and the bond market decided which firms got how much capital to produce which products. As late as 1931, the year that began Japan's attempted conquest of Asia with the seizure of Manchuria, 87% of new funds were supplied from the stock and bond markets, and bank lending played a minor role. Shareholders' influence on corporate decisions was strong and outside members of the boards of directors were common. In 1940, as part of the mobilization for war, Japan centralized finance under the Bank of Japan promoted large banks as the leading edge of capital allocation, and more or less got rid of the equity and debt markets. The Bank of Japan (BOJ) gained the authority to dictate lending priorities to private banks (Noguchi 1998).

Bank-centered finance continued after the war, with banks as the hub of the re-formed *keiretsu*. This meant that the financial system shoveled lots of cash toward the giants in the *keiretsu* or independent giants, like Nippon Steel or Panasonic. By contrast, those who would challenge the incumbents found getting loans much harder. It took a big political battle for the newer Kawasaki Steel to get funding (Katz 1998: 86–88).

A final feature of the 1940 system was lifetime employment, which had begun a few decades earlier, and was consolidated in the lead-up to war as part of the system that made sure the companies producing military supplies were assured of enough workers, while also preventing any labor tension from disrupting the war effort. It was consolidated even further after the war as a core element of Japan's political economy.

While the Japanese system used to be lionized as the rational, monolithic mobilizer of the strategic industries by a faction of Japanologists a few decades back (Katz 1998: 301–303), in reality, the state has been schizoid. Some practices boost dynamic industries, while another set makes them act to preserve their weaker brethren.

As Noguchi (cited in Katz 1998: 50) pointed out, many of the features of the system transfer income from the large efficient exporting industries to the less-efficient domestically oriented smaller firms. In addition, for many years the less-efficient sectors were protected from competition via import restrictions, limits on market entry, and price controls. Today, government credit guarantees and other financial measures achieve the same goal of keeping inefficient firms in business so as to avoid social dislocation.

Although proponents of the 1940 system claim that it is the product of long-standing Japanese culture and thus very resistant to change, Noguchi argues that these practices are not intrinsic to Japanese culture. Rather, having been artificially created by wartime policy, the system can be changed by policy. Alternatively, Noguchi presciently argued, it may be "destroyed" by the emergence of new technologies, as we are now seeing in the impact of digitalization. However, he warned, if the system persists, then "Japan's future is considerably endangered" (Noguchi 1994: 407).

Regime Change in Technology Requires Change in Institutions

Different technological regimes both give rise to, and require, different business institutions. However brilliantly big-company capitalism worked in the analog era, it is no longer sufficient in today's digital environment. In the digital regime, the leading edge of growth is research and software rather than heavy machinery, and knowledge-intensive industries more than capital-intensive ones. In fact, even the big capital-intensive industries, like autos, rely on software. Whereas a car is a car, no matter the changes in automotive technologies, a radio is not a cell phone or the cloud. In the digital regime, technology changes so fast that there is an even greater need for the turnover of firms and greater opportunities for gazelles. That, in turn, means an even greater need for flexible capital markets—including business angels, venture capital, private equity, and stock markets for newcomers (like NASDAQ in the US). The need to move away from bank-dominated finance has long been recognized in Japan, but angels, venture capital, and private equity are still at a very small scale (Whittaker and Cole 2006).

If Japan continues to lag in digital technologies, its growth potential will be very constrained because digital technologies have become key to growth everywhere. In the United States from 1998 through 2017, the digital economy—ranging from computer hardware and software, Internet and other digitized communications services, e-commerce, and so on—has grown four times as fast as the US economy as a whole; 90% of the digital economy is software and services, not hardware (Bureau of Economic Analysis 2019).

In the first several decades of the postwar era, investment in expensive physical capital was the name of the game. Today, intangible assets—for example, software, R&D, training of staff, marketing, and organizational improvements—are the linchpin. Spending a dollar on intangibles now boosts productivity and growth more than spending that same dollar on tangibles (see Figure 2.1).

Consequently, in countries like the United States, Holland, France, the United Kingdom, Austria, and Belgium, companies invest as much, or even more, in intangible capital than in buildings and equipment. Japan, however, devotes only 22% of its business investment to intangibles.

A very big part of intangible investment is software. However, for reasons having partly to do with its business practices (Cole and Nakata 2014),

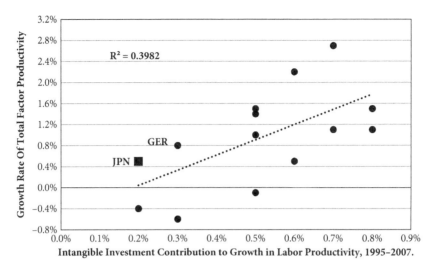

Figure 2.1 Low intangible investment rate slows Japan's productivity growth.
Source: Corrado et al. (2013: 280).

Japanese incumbents aren't that good in software. To top it off, Japan suffers a growing shortage of software programmers and systems integrators. This is becoming a big constraint on Japanese growth. For example, how will Toyota, Honda, and Nissan respond as software and related hardware grow to 30% of a car's value in 2030, up from 10% today (McKinsey 2018)?

Interestingly, Germany, whose big conglomerates and bank-centered finance resemble those of Japan, also has a low rate (30%) of intangible investment. This suggests that economic institutions, not national cultures, are the more important determinant of business strategies and competencies (Corrado et al. 2013).

Open Innovation

Open innovation—collaboration among unaffiliated companies, as seen in the invention of the Pfizer COVID vaccine—is one of the major institutional changes characterizing the digital era. While pharmaceuticals is the poster child, it applies in a host of industries, including mundane product areas like household cleaning goods.

Those changes not only have given greater prominence to entrepreneurial paths toward innovation, but also, in some sectors, have engendered a new partnership between entrepreneurs and corporate firms. Henry Chesbrough, who created the term "open innovation," is its primary promoter (Chesbrough 2006a). His work includes cooperation with Japanese giants working in Silicon Valley, discussed in Chapter 14.

Open innovation is the polar opposite of the innovation model that once prevailed throughout the rich countries and still prevails at Japanese giants: the so-called Not-Invented-Here syndrome. That's where companies themselves—or in cooperation with subordinate suppliers—produce all the components in their products, while rejecting those "not invented here." Supposedly, this keeps their products unique. Soichiro Honda, the founder of the Honda car company, famously declared in the 1960s, "We refuse to depend on anyone else." In a world where giant companies with deep pockets conducted most of the R&D and did not need so much software, such thinking made sense. It no longer does.

Honda learned this lesson the hard way. It tried to develop sensors in its vehicles that could avoid collisions. When it tested the sensors by using a dummy child, Honda's SUV mowed it down. It scored only 0.2 points out of 25, the worst of all tested vehicles. Even if Honda were eventually successful, the effort would have cost Honda lots of time, money, and sales. It finally gave in and bought off-the-shelf sensor technology from Germany's Bosch. The score soared to an almost perfect 24.4. While Honda's CEO has said the company is now more open to buying from others, its R&D veterans resist on the grounds that using only home-grown parts is "Honda's soul" (McLain 2018).

So far, the resistance forces are winning. A 2017 government survey found that more than 70% of all large-firm innovation was done completely in-house. When companies do collaborate, it's with other elephants; only 0.7% of large-company innovation involved collaboration with startups. Ulrike Schaede comments, "In most companies, employees were more concerned about protecting their careers than building something new" (Schaede 2020: 168).

One of the biggest drivers of institutional change in the digital era is a reduction in economies of scale in R&D. In the past, R&D was dominated by the largest firms, because it was so costly and because there were economies of scale and scope in doing it (e.g., expensive equipment whose cost could be spread among a large number of products).[2] However, with the advent of

---

[2] Economies of *scope* means that the more *related* products that a company produces, the lower its costs in each. By making cameras, photocopiers, and other office equipment based on optical technologies, Canon could make them at lower cost.

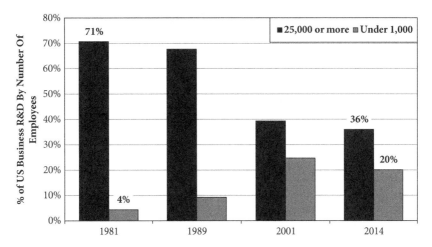

Figure 2.2 R&D spending shifts from giants to medium-sized firms.
Source: Chesbrough (2006a: 16); Wolfe (2016: 2).

cheap computer power, software, the Internet, and AI, bigger companies have a much smaller cost advantage in conducting R&D and thus in innovating new products and processes.

In 1981, 71% of the business R&D in the United States was conducted by giants with at least 25,000 employees; by 2014, the share had halved to 36%. Conversely, the share carried out by firms with less than 100 employees had risen to a stunning 8% (Chesbrough 2006a: 16). Similar changes have occurred in Europe, but less so in Japan. In 2015, only 7% of Japan's business R&D was conducted by firms with less than 500 employees, compared to 17% in the United States and 33% in France and the United Kingdom (see Figure 2.2).

In 2018, just 10 Japanese giants conducted almost half (43%) of all business R&D in the country (Oikawa 2019). Worse yet, Tokyo actually retards the R&D shift seen elsewhere; 92% of all Japanese government subsidies and tax breaks for R&D go to large firms, the highest share among OECD countries (see Figure 2.3). That's another reason so few gazelles live in Japan.

Cheap computer power is not the only reason for this shift in the size of companies able to conduct good R&D. Equally important is the difference in mindset between a big corporation and a gazelle. As will be detailed in Chapter 4, even when giant corporations try to transcend the mindset and practices that made them giants in the first place, they find it very hard to do so. The DNA of a gazelle, on the other hand, makes them rebel against

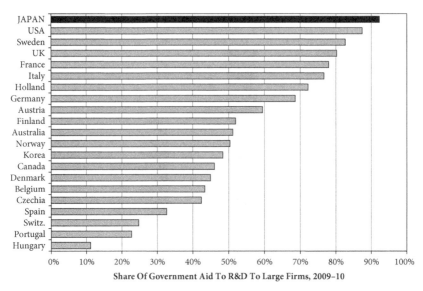

Figure 2.3 In Japan, 92% of government aid to R&D goes to large firms.
Source: OECD (2014: 83).
Note: see country code for abbreviations, pg. 12.

conventional wisdom and try something disruptive. After all, the only way for them to soar is by coming up with a new product or a better way of making an older one. Most of the time, the would-be gazelles are wrong. Incumbents know that and are understandably reluctant to embrace radical change. However, in the course of vetoing lots of bad ideas, they can't help missing the few good ones as well. Moreover, elephants often miss the potential of new products and technologies because they don't fit in with their conceptual and organizational paradigms. It often takes a new firm to see the potential in a radical but unproven idea—all the more reason an economy has to be safe for lots of failed experiments.

Chesbrough calls these missed opportunities "false negatives": thinking an idea is useless when it's actually terrific. For example, the microprocessors that turned Intel into a giant almost didn't happen. Intel developed its first microprocessor, the 4004, under a contract with a Japanese calculator company, Busicom, and in collaboration with the latter's engineers, one of whom was stationed at Intel. In the 1971 recession, Busicom wanted to renegotiate to get a lower price, and, in return, Intel's negotiators secured rights to sell the device to others. Most of Intel's own marketing people saw little commercial use for the product. The board of directors was divided—after all, its main product was memory chips, and it was still a struggling new firm with limited resources—but decided to take a chance. The rest is history.

Chesbrough notes that most companies consciously limit false *positives*, ideas that look good but turn out to be unviable. However, he says, few companies take steps to manage the risk of false negatives. He suggests that companies can track false negatives by licensing their patents that they think are useless and see what others do with them. At the same time, active collaboration via open innovation will help firms gain value from a patent that they are not equipped to exploit but that a partner might be able to (Chesbrough 2006b: 129).

Some elephants have learned that there are enough good ideas among some of the gazelles that they need to partner with them. In the United States, approximately half of all scientifically innovative new drugs are developed by modestly sized biotech firms, or by a partnership between universities and biotech firms. These biotech firms have the capacity to invent the drugs, but not the time and money needed to get regulatory approval or the capacity to manufacture, market, and distribute them. Big Pharma can do the latter much better. Consequently, pharmaceutical giants practicing open innovation perform better than those doing less of it (Rothaermel 2001). Similar partnerships are seen in Europe, albeit on a smaller scale. Although Tokyo has changed regulations to help biotech firms get off the ground, collaborative efforts in Japanese pharmaceuticals have not been as successful (Kneller 2010, 2013).

The trend is not limited to high-tech. In 2000, household supplies titan Procter & Gamble (P&G) faced the reality that its traditional, closed, in-house product-development system was running out of steam. Only 35% of its new products were achieving their financial targets. In response, P&G created a new strategy called "Connect and Develop" with a radical goal: that half of its new innovations would come out of collaboration between P&G and external partners. It achieved that goal in a mere five years. Within 10 years, P&G had engaged in more than 2,000 global partnerships and was getting more than 4,000 ideas per year that were good enough to merit further investigation. It then set a new goal: that $30 billion of its revenue (an amount equal to 40% of its total revenue in 2006) would stem from such collaboration (Huston and Sabab 2006).

Fear of falling behind is already beginning to break down some of the resistance in Japan. Toyota, Japan's biggest spender on R&D, now devotes

40% of its R&D budget to what it calls CASE technologies (i.e., connected, autonomous, shared, and electrified). Since these go beyond its in-house capabilities, it is forming alliances for joint development. "It is important to make partners," stated President Akio Toyoda (*Nikkei* 2018: n.p.).

KDDI—Japan's long-distance carrier in the days of the regulated, segmented telephone system—had to go into mobile phone service to stay alive. Since good apps are the key to competitiveness in cell phones, it set up a special group—called the Startup Relations Group—devoted to working with app startups. When I visited Tomohiro Ebata, director of KDDI's Global Business Development Department, and Eiji Toyokawa, group leader of the Startup Relations Group within that department, the first thing that struck me was their attire (khakis and open-collared shirts) and their way of talking about business. I might have been in Silicon Valley or at an incubator in Berlin. In fact, Ebata told me, the group was deliberately located away from corporate headquarters and put in the Shibuya neighborhood of Tokyo, the locus of many startups, in order to create and preserve its own collaborative culture, one different from that of the "suits." Recognizing that traditional corporate culture can crush the very qualities that it prizes in a startup, KDDI partners with the app developers rather than acquiring them.

Unfortunately, open innovation has progressed more slowly than elsewhere. Many firms think open innovation is little more than licensing someone else's technology, rather than real collaboration. The irony is that the vertical *keiretsu* have long practiced a kind of open innovation within the *keiretsu*, but many parent companies cannot comprehend how to do it outside the group. One reason is that, within the vertical *keiretsu*, a lord-and-servant relationship prevails. Not so in genuine open innovation.

Far too often, there is outright resistance from middle managers. Consider the case of Masatoshi Ueno, who is stationed in Silicon Valley by Asahi Glass to find American startups with which Asahi Glass can collaborate. One successful example is displays for cell phones in which a startup provides the thin glassine layer embedding the electronics, while Asahi Glass provides the glass substrate and does the fabrication and marketing. Ueno cannot get any project off the ground without support from some business unit back in headquarters. He constantly finds that, when he proposes a collaborative project, someone in the R&D department or a business unit will say: "Why are you going outside the company? We can do that job." They are afraid of no longer being indispensable and resist even when the CEO wants more open innovation. In each case, Ueno told me, "I have to find the right person to speak with inside of Asahi to get the authority to go ahead" (Interview March 2018). Japan is hardly alone in having corporate politics, but the degree of autonomy for someone like Ueno seems to be less than elsewhere.

METI is very interested in promoting open innovation. Consequently, as part of its goal of promoting more startups, the Kishida administration's Five-Year Plan spoke of providing some tax incentives for open innovation (Cabinet Office 2022c: 24–25). One incentive would provide tax breaks for companies that buy innovative startups, a big exit strategy for high-growth startups in the United States and Europe. A second would provide tax breaks for big companies that collaborate on R&D with startups. In the end, nothing along this line was included in the measures sent to the Diet in 2022. Reformers hope to find ways to get this implemented in the coming years.

Creative Destruction versus Creative Accumulation

There are plenty of industries in which innovation will continue to be led by the corporate giants—Schumpeter's creative accumulation model, Schumpeter Mark II. In some of these, like autos, Japan excels and has even increased its global market share. There will be others in which the entrepreneurial creative destruction model, Schumpeter Mark I, will have a comparative advantage.

Electronics firms in Japan have been flailing because, on the whole, more of the innovation in that industry has shifted to the Mark I model and/or an open innovation hybrid. Yes, Japanese firms still dominate certain subsectors in electronics and machinery, but those are exceptions. On the whole, the Japanese elephants are missing a pivotal trend: the shift in so many ICT/electronics sectors from domination by large vertically integrated firms with broad product lines to a web of smaller specialist firms in close collaboration, sometimes in partnership with one or two giants (Cole and Whittaker 2006: 8).

In fact, not only is ICT characterized by long-term collaboration among firms, but the firms collaborating range across a host of different industries or subindustries. In a sample of 149 different ICT technologies, the average number of patenting firms involved in the most frequently used technologies was a startling 219. Moreover, the share of innovations provided by the top three major innovators was low (Corrocher et al. 2003: 15).

At first blush, many are likely to see Amazon and Google as classic cases of companies that started off as entrepreneurs in the Mark I model and then became typical Mark II giants. In reality, both firms collaborate with a host of partners via open innovation. Consider Amazon's Alexa, a smart speaker that was used by 72 million customers as of early 2022. Outside developers created more than 30,000 "skills" (Amazon's term for apps that work with Alexa). These allow customers to control more than 4,000 smart home devices offered by 1,200 unique brands. Because of the sheer number of possible devices and possible skills, Amazon must rely on open innovation to ensure both widespread adoption of Alexa and continuous improvement (Thierry and Lescop 2009). At Google, both Android and Chrome are, in part, products of open innovation (Arcese et al. 2015).

Failure to understand open innovation played a pivotal role in the failed effort of SONY, NEC, Hitachi, Fujitsu, and Toshiba to re-enter the US market for desktop PCs in 1996 (Toshiba's earlier success had been in laptops). Darryl Brown of Dataquest was prescient in doubting their success, telling me, "The relationship of companies working together to make a PC is more like a cobweb than a pyramid. It requires partnering for product development with innumerable companies who are equals not subordinates" (Interview December 1996). When I asked Tim Errington, senior vice president for Sales and Marketing at Sony Information Technologies of America, he was confident that the PC venture would teach SONY all about "the business culture of third party partnering that we need to know for the next 50 years" (Interview December 1996). Unfortunately, that did not happen.

Failure to master the mindset of the digital era has wreaked havoc in Japan's machinery industry (whose subsectors range from machine tools to bulldozers, from dishwashers to computer chips). Such machinery accounted for half of all Japanese exports in the 1990s–early 2000s and was led by creative accumulation giants like Komatsu, Mitsubishi Heavy Industries, and Hitachi. Japan remains competitive in some niche areas. Fanuc, for example, in 2015 had a 65% market share in the controls for numerically controlled (CNC) machine tools. Olympus held roughly a 70% share of the global endoscope market in 2012, a market estimated to be worth approximately US$2.5 billion. Nidec has an 80% global market share in motors for hard disc drives and has the number one global share in a variety of motors for products like refrigerators, photocopies, and rice cookers.

Increasingly, however, all sorts of machines incorporate sophisticated software, including the Internet of Things (IoT), not an area of Japanese strength.

As that occurred and as other producers entered the market, Japan's share of global exports plummeted. In 1991, Japan had a bigger share than did the United States or Germany; by 2018, Japan was surpassed by both the United States and Germany. Japan's share would have fallen even more except for a 20% depreciation of the yen, which allowed Japanese firms to offer lower prices. Despite the price advantage, the volume of machines exported still fell by 6% at a time when global demand was growing. Since the sector is so export-dependent, domestic production fell as well (World Bank 2000 and assorted years).

Automobiles will be a very interesting test case. For almost a century, it has been a classic Mark II industry. As software's share of a car's cost rises, and as the market share of EVs grows, will that continue to be the case, or will autos become an open innovation hybrid as in pharmaceuticals or electronics? If so, how well will the Japanese automakers adapt?

Adapting to a Change in Regime

Here's the dilemma facing Japanese companies as entrepreneurial and open innovation trends rise in some of the industries that they have dominated in the past. No matter the country (at least among rich countries), the same group of industries tend to be in the same camp, that is, either Mark I, Mark II, or open innovation hybrids.

Firms where the giants dominate are ones in which there are large economies of scale and scope in both production and R&D and so the share of both output and patents by the top four or five firms is very high. The number of profitable players is relatively small, and it is hard for new firms to challenge the incumbents (Malerba and Orsenigo 1996).

Consequently, countries tend to specialize in the kind of industries in which their institutions enable them to excel. Because of Germany and Japan's orientation toward giant companies and bank-centered finance, they tend to have a comparative advantage in many Mark II (creative accumulation) industries. By contrast, Italy specializes in Mark I (creative destruction) fields. Countries like the United States and the United Kingdom are fortunate enough to do well in both types.

Importantly, as disruptive new technologies come into an existing industry, some Mark II industries become Mark I and vice versa. Electronics and pharmaceuticals come to mind.

If a country has the flexibility to generate both Mark I and Mark II companies, then, as the leadership in economy-wide innovation shifts, the country can shift with it. If, however, the country's institutions favor one model over the other, its role in world growth will shrink as global trends shift away from its forte. That is what happened to Japan. It rose in the global rankings of leading-edge industries when Mark II firms led the way. It fell back as digitalization and the Internet boosted Mark I sectors. Japan's difficulty in adjusting to regime change in technology markedly worsened a situation made difficult by its support for moribund companies in sunset sectors.

A shift in regime from corporate giant-led innovation to entrepreneurial-led innovation is usually triggered by some new disruptive technology that renders obsolete the dominant products or methods within a sector. The more disruptive that technological changes are to existing ways and the lower the incumbents' capabilities to adapt, then the greater the shake-up between incumbents and challengers, and the more likely a shift from creative accumulation to creative destruction (Landini et al. 2017).

The downfall of leading companies is more likely to occur when there is high lock-in behavior—also known as the incumbent trap—which is an inability to see the need to change or difficulty in executing a shift even if the need is perceived. The process seen in cell phones is a classic case. Motorola pioneered the product, having invented an analog-based cell phone. However, when the 1990s brought the digital mobile phone, Motorola stayed with analog for too long, and Nokia grabbed leadership by switching to digital. Neither company did well after the advent of the smartphone. Instead, leadership passed to Samsung and Apple, neither of which has previously been known as phone producers (Landini et al. 2017: 10).

Even though Japan's NTT invented the operating system for the world's first smartphone, its only market was, by law, Japan. Its Japanese hardware suppliers made the phone according to NTT's specifications, which did not meet global appetites. Hence, these electronics manufacturers lost their chance to become global suppliers.

One of the big reasons for lock-in behavior is sunk costs that the incumbent has put into both equipment and the training of staff in older methods. If the cost of switching is too high, and the benefits of the new methods too uncertain, the incumbent is prone to an unconscious underestimation of the need for change. It's not always unconscious. IBM was famous for buying up patents created by other firms just to prevent them from being used by anyone, lest they undercut IBM's existing technology.

New firms, on the other hand, having no sunk costs in now-obsolescent technologies, equipment, and ways of doing things, are more willing to take a chance on a promising technology even if the results are uncertain. That's another reason that new technologies are often associated with new firms (OECD 2001: 210).

Clayton Christensen, famous as the author of *The Innovator's Dilemma*, has documented how time and again, in fields as disparate as disc drives, tractors, and cameras, seemingly safe market leaders were replaced by newcomers due to some technology that the incumbents were predisposed to perceive as inferior. That predisposition stemmed from the fact that the innovation was incompatible with their current business model. Christensen coined the now-popular term "disruptive innovation" (Christensen 1997).

In industries characterized by frequent instances of radical technological change, a change in leadership from incumbents to challengers is common. But, when a dominant product or design has emerged, the product is more standardized, and disruptive technologies less frequent, then it is common for a few large leaders to emerge and for the sector to shift from Mark I to Mark II. On the other hand, the longer the period being looked at, the more likely it is that, even in sectors traditionally dominated by giants, some disruptive new technology will dethrone the incumbents. Some of the successful challengers will be gazelles, others will be giants in related sectors. It will be interesting to see whether the rise of EVs will produce a shakeup in the auto industry, including new competition from Chinese companies similar to the emergence of Japanese automakers in the 1970s. The Japanese companies got their chance when the sharp rise in oil prices gave rise to a demand for cars with better mileage.

In the postwar era, Japan engendered a host of entrepreneurs that grew into large companies that could prosper in the Mark II world of capital-intensive giants, but not as well in a Mark I world of knowledge-intensive entrepreneurs. When the world shifted, Japan had trouble shifting with it. Consequently, while Japan can maintain leadership, even dominance, in this or that particular product or sub-sector, the number of areas in which Japan sets the commercial trends keeps shrinking. Recognition of this problem is one of the drivers making elite groups more open to entrepreneurship than they have been in decades.

PART II
JAPAN'S RECOVERY REQUIRES MORE GAZELLES

3

The Need for a Productivity Revolution

Imagine the predicament facing a growing number of Japanese men in their thirties. Despite the years spent at extra cram schools and then graduation from good colleges, many can't find a full-time job at a good company. Since Japan's rigid labor laws make it extremely difficult to lay off permanent regular employees in downtimes, or when demand shifts away from a company's products, businesses now tend to fill open slots with part-time or temporary workers, who are called *non-regulars*. Worse yet, they typically pay temporaries a third less per hour and part-timers 60% less. Among men, 22% are non-regulars, up from just 7% in 1984, and 54% of women, up from 32% (Statistics Bureau 2022b). These are stunning figures for a society that a few decades ago proudly proclaimed, "We're all middle class."

What counts as a personal tragedy for each worker translates into economic corrosion for Japan as a whole. The growing resort to non-regular workers eats away at Japan's main resource: its human capital. These are the skills that enable workers to get the most out of up-to-date technology, to suggest improvements to the work routine and machinery, and to be able to fix equipment breakdowns.

Unfortunately, firms are reluctant to spend money training workers who may be working elsewhere in a few years. Among 1,066 companies, 92% provided training for regular workers, but just 42% did so for non-regulars. These firms are being penny-wise, pound-foolish. As the International Monetary Fund (IMF) pointed out, Japanese workers who receive less training are less productive (Aoyagi and Ganelli 2016: 6–7). Meanwhile, company spending on off-the-job training for all workers, regular or non-regular, has dropped 40% since 1991 (JPC 2020). In the past, Japan's companies used to provide more training than those elsewhere, and that was a major factor in its competitive edge. Today, it is losing that edge. Out of 22 OECD countries, Japan comes in 19th in the share of business value-added invested in on- and off-the-job training, and 18th in the share of the workforce receiving some form of training (OECD 2015e: 110).

The Contest for Japan's Economic Future. Richard Katz, Oxford University Press. © Richard Katz 2024.
DOI: 10.1093/oso/9780197675106.003.0004

In 2014, Nippon Steel & Sumitomo Metal, the main supplier to Toyota and other automakers, had to stop operations at its Nagoya steel plant for more than a day because of a power failure. Weeks later, the plant was still operating at 10%–20% below capacity. The trouble happened while employees were doing work they had not done before. The required maintenance expertise had not been passed on to the current workforce. At chemical plants, accidents caused by insufficient training have resulted in serious injuries, even deaths (Nakamura et al. 2014).

Short-sighted managers, brought up on the idea that training and lifetime employment go together, may think they'll save money by not training non-regulars. In the long run, they'll lose money, because the non-regulars they hire in the future will not have been trained by their previous employer and thus will bring even lower skill levels to the job. In Denmark, where job-switching is common, I asked a CEO about the risk of spending money to train workers who leave. His reply was: "What if we don't train the worker and he stays?" Not to mention that the new workers will come to his firm trained by their previous employer.

The trend also puts downward pressure on real wages, not just for non-regulars, but for all. After soaring during most of the postwar era, real compensation per worker (wages and benefits) has been stagnant since the 1990s. Even though output per work-hour rose 30% from 1997 through 2019, real compensation per hour rose a negligible 1% (see Figure 3.1).

The gap between productivity and wages is never mentioned by companies boasting of increased rates of return on equity (ROE). It's true that profits per worker soared 66% at the 5,000 biggest firms between 1996 and 2021, even though sales per staffer fell 2%. The reason is that wages per worker were cut by 4% (MOF 2022a). ROE produced that way is not genuine efficiency. Nor is it a sustainable pattern; after all, who will buy their products?

Finally, the low marriage rate among non-regular workers accelerates Japan's demographic decline, thereby shrinking the number of workers able to support the growing ranks of retirees. That induces the government to raise the consumption tax, which further weakens already feeble domestic demand.

The elderly are particularly afflicted by the consequences of low growth. Imagine that you've saved for decades, hoping that the interest income would help pay for the groceries. Instead, you've suffered a quarter century of near-zero interest rates. As of early 2020, the average interest rate on time deposits was just 0.055%. So, if you are like the average elderly household, you've got

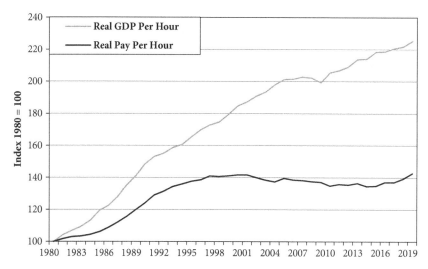

Figure 3.1 Real compensation stops growing, though output per worker up.
Source: OECD (2022a, 2022b).

¥14.9 million ($114,000) in bank deposits (Statistics Bureau 2020b), but those savings bring you a meaningless ¥8,211 ($63)! per year.

You can run down your savings, but how will you manage if, like the typical 65-year-old, you can expect to live another 20 years if you're a man and 25 years if you're a woman? You may have to go back to work as a non-regular, as half of those aged 65–69 do. While some may go back because they are still vigorous, all too many cannot afford to retire.

These low interest rates are not just the result of the Bank of Japan's monetary stimulus. They also result from the low productivity of capital (how much GDP increases for every additional dollar of capital stock in buildings, machinery, software, and R&D). Among 21 rich countries, Japan ranks fourth from the bottom (see Figure 3.2). If the productivity of capital is low, then the financial returns that banks, pension funds, or life insurance annuities can give to beneficiaries will also be low.

If not for government money, 65% of Japan's elderly would be in poverty. It is public pensions and other benefits that have reduced their poverty rate to 17% among those aged 65–74 and 23% for those 75 and older (OECD 2019f). Unfortunately, making up for the shortfall has become increasingly difficult, as the number of seniors rose from 12% of the population in 1990 to 29% in 2020 and will hit 35% by 2040.

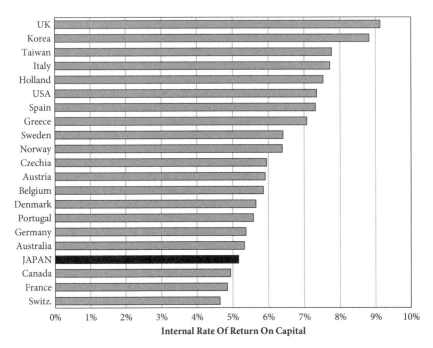

Figure 3.2 Low productivity of capital In Japan.

Source: Penn World Tables 9.1 (2021).

Note: PW 9.1's measure of this productivity of capital is called the Internal Rate of Return (IRR).

With fewer and fewer working-age people available to support more and more retirees, keeping up seniors' income cannot occur unless each working person produces an awful lot more (see Figure 3.3). Yes, Tokyo can raise tax rates, but the growth of the tax base depends on per capita GDP growth. Without an acceleration of productivity growth, Japan is forced to choose between two bad alternatives: cutting benefits for the elderly, or raising tax rates on the working generation. Tokyo has chosen both. It doubled the consumption tax from 5% in 2014 to 10% in 2019. At the same time, the government cut social security per senior by a fifth from its 1996 peak of ¥1.92 million ($14,800) to just ¥1.49 million ($11,400) in 2019. Healthcare spending was slashed by 15% from ¥520,000 ($4,000) in 1999 to ¥440,000 ($3,400) in 2019 (Cabinet Office 2020).

Better economic growth would not make all these problems go away, but it would make them much more manageable. Given Japan's demographics, that requires a productivity revolution (see again Figure I.4 in the Introduction).

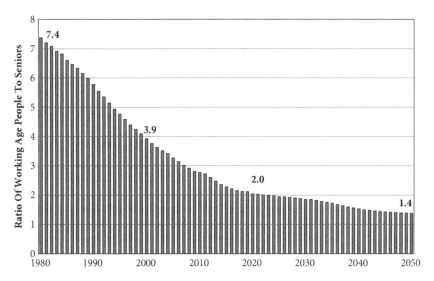

Figure 3.3 Fewer workers to support each senior.
Source: Japan Macro Advisors (2020b).

Those Who Say Japan Is Doing Fine

There are economists who would insist that this book offers a solution in search of a problem. Japan, they claim, is doing no worse than other rich countries. It's ironic that the most prominent proponent of this view is Paul Krugman since for years he doled out jeremiads that Japan was doomed unless the country created sustainable 2% inflation, something the Bank of Japan acknowledges it has still failed to do. He does not appear to have said how he resolves that contradiction. It's important to understand why this contention is wrong since it would seem to justify a failure to reform.

Krugman argues that aging is virtually the only reason why Japan looks bad in international comparisons. Instead of per capita GDP, he says we should look at GDP per working-age adult (age 15–64). By that measure, Japan during 1993–2013 performed almost as well as the United States and a bit better than Europe (Krugman 2014).

If Krugman were right, there would be no productivity problem in Japan. But he's not. Use different years and one gets very different results, depending on short-term events. If a country's unemployment rate goes up by 5 percentage points—as did Europe during 2007–2013, because of its austerity-ridden response to the 2008–2009 financial meltdown—then Krugman's measure sinks sharply. Then, when Europe revived and unemployment fell by 4%, Krugman's measure bounced back. Such yo-yo effects have nothing to do with genuine efficiency and productivity. The same temporary statistical illusion arises if, as in Japan, there is a sudden influx of women and the elderly into the workforce. The more distant we get from the Euro crisis, the more Japan falls in Krugman's measure.

Lagging Productivity

Instead of a productivity revolution, Japan has suffered a devolution. A severe decline in productivity growth has put into reverse decades of postwar catch-up to American living standards (see again Figure I.6 in the Introduction).

Worse yet, Japan is now lagging behind the United States and Germany in some areas where it once led the world. In advanced manufacturing—electrical and optical equipment, industrial machinery, and transport equipment—McKinsey Global Institute (Desvaux et. al 2015: 9) reports: "Japan's advanced manufacturers once raised the bar for the rest of the world in efficiency and quality, but today their labor productivity is 29% below that of the US sector and 32% below Germany's." For example, productivity in retail—which employs 9% of the workforce—is 35% below the US level. There has been some improvement since 1991 when reform of the Large-Scale Retail Store Law loosened restrictions on the spread of more efficient large stores. Nonetheless, productivity growth in retail is just half the pace of the US retail sector.

In 1997, Japan ranked 10th in real per capita GDP among 29 OECD countries; by 2019 (pre-COVID) it had fallen to 16th. In 1997, Japan's per capita GDP was just 7% below the average in the Group of Seven (G7: US, Japan, UK, France, Germany, Italy, Canada); by 2019, it was 17% below them (OECD 2022a).

The Advantage of Backwardness

There is a big silver lining in this dark cloud. Japan is so far behind global benchmarks in so many sectors that it could have a burst of growth just by taking 20 years to catch up to the other six other members of the G7. Assuming for the sake of easy arithmetic that the output per hour in the other six countries grows 1% per year, then, in 20 years, it would reach $75 per hour. To reach the same $75, Japan's productivity growth would have to be 2.5% per year for 20 years. At this pace, parents would see their children live twice as well as they do. The tax base would be rising fast enough to support the aging population without onerous tax hikes.

Can Japan plausibly do this? Yes. In fact, it would return Japan to just a bit above its 2.2% performance in the 1990s. There is no fundamental economic reason why Japan, with such an educated and talented population, abundant savings to fund investments, and access to the world's technology, cannot reach the same levels of output as other rich countries.

The primary obstacle is the structural flaws in its private businesses, which is the main argument of this book. Some of these flaws stem from a regulatory system aimed at protecting the inefficient. Japanese consumers got a taste of this in Christmas 2015 when they couldn't find enough butter on the shelves to make their traditional Christmas cakes.[1]

How is it possible for a rich nation to run short of something as basic as butter? The Ministry of Agriculture (MAFF) claimed Japan's cows were so exhausted by that summer's heat wave that they couldn't produce enough milk. Peel back another layer of the onion, and you find the stranglehold of Japan's giant farm collective called Japan Agriculture (JA). It has traditionally been a major support base for the ruling LDP, which is why it remains exempt from Japan's Anti-Monopoly Law. In order to protect the inefficient dairy farmers with tiny farms on Japan's densely populated main island of Honshu—where 80% of the people live—it has prevented imports of dairy products from Japan's sparsely settled northern island of Hokkaido. Large farms there make its dairy farmers far more efficient. The LDP stood by as JA played the role of the Christmas grinch. No wonder Japanese households spend more on food than people elsewhere (see Figure 3.4). Imagine what a little creative destruction would do to make food production more efficient, bring down prices for consumers, and liberate purchasing power for other items.

Knowledge-Based Capital

Japanese policymakers make two big strategic mistakes when they think about generating growth. For one, as noted earlier, they are seduced by the

---

[1] Christmas is a secular holiday in Japan.

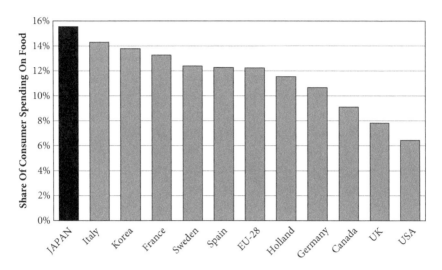

Figure 3.4 Japanese consumers pay high food prices for protection of farmers.
Source: OECD (2020d).
Note: This counts only food eaten at home.

glamour of artificial intelligence, nanotechnology, and the like. Instead, as in the American productivity revolution, it is Japan's currently lagging sectors that will either continue to sink the economy or save it.

Tokyo also presumes that the royal road to more productivity is more capital investment. But Japanese companies already invest a lot: 16% of GDP these days, compared to 13.5% for American companies. Eventually, such investment eventually runs into the law of diminishing returns.[2] Back in the mid-1960s, Japan could increase its GDP by almost 13 cents for every dollar of new investment, compared to 10 cents for the other six G7 countries. As these countries got richer and ran into diminishing returns, the benefit for each dollar of new investment inevitably diminished. But it diminished far more in Japan, and it now has one of the lowest returns on investment among 21 rich countries (see again Figure 3.2).

As discussed above, the majority of new investment these days is in intangible resources, including knowledge-based capital (KBC). KBC includes not just better technology, but also an increase in the ability of firms and their workers to get the most out of it. It includes three main elements: R&D;

---

[2] The first tractor that a village of farmers gets raises their output by a lot. The second tractor also raises output, but not by as much. With each additional tractor per farmer, the gains get smaller, eventually becoming negative.

computer software; and economic competencies, which includes training of workers, improving management skills, and developing better corporate strategies.

Once again, the problem is not investing too little, but getting too little bang for the buck. Out of 21 OECD countries, Japan invests 8.1% of its GDP on KBC, compared to an OECD average of 6.7%. On R&D, Japan invests 2.4% of GDP, much higher than the 1.5% average. Where Japan falls short is in investments in economic competencies. Japan comes in last at just 1.8% of GDP, much lower than the average of 3.2%. This matters because economic competencies are what convert good technical ideas, as well as physical and human resources, into superior commercial activities. Economic competencies range from worker training to managerial strategy, to corporate organization, and other commercial skills. What matters is not how much a country invests, but how much it benefits from that investment. On that front, Japan comes in last in the OECD in terms of the boost to labor productivity for each dollar invested in KBC. KBC contributed 0.5 percentage points to labor productivity growth per year during 1995–2007, but in Japan, it contributed just 0.3 points (OECD 2015a: 65).

Consider, for example, how convenience stores in Finland used ICT to increase sales and profits. Every time a customer bought something, the optical scanner registered it, and this drawdown of stock on store shelves was counted and replacements ordered automatically over the Internet. At first, that simply reduced the costs of a task they had been doing all along: inventory control. Beyond that, it also achieved something the store previously could not have achieved at any cost, using so-called big data. It told convenience store owners in Finland that they could increase sales by putting beer and baby diapers right next to each other! "The thing is to mine the data," explained Jouni Laitinen, a Finn who got his PhD at the Tokyo Institute of Technology. "You look at your sales on a Friday evening, and you see a big pop in sales of both diapers and beer. What's going on is that young couples who don't go out because of their baby, decide to watch a movie at home. They go to the store intending to buy diapers. But, if they see the beer nearby, they say, 'Oh, the weekend is here; I'm going to get some beer.' Now, I used to work in a supermarket, and we'd never put beer near the diapers. Alcohol is harmful for kids; it's a bad association. But when you use the new software to analyze the data, you can pick up that kind of pattern, figure out what it means, and you can sell" (Interview October 2019). Customers who purchase one sort of product can be sent marketing information on related products.

United Parcel Service (UPS) in the United States used big data by putting sensors into every delivery truck to monitor conditions that typically precede a part breaking down, like temperature or metallurgical stress. This avoids expensive breakdowns of a truck filled with parcels. Nissan has put similar sensors into its Leaf cars.

Japanese firms tend to use KBC like they use software, mostly for cutting costs of existing activities, rather than for creating strategic value. In a 2013 survey, nearly half of Japanese said their top use of information technology was for operational improvements like cost-cutting; just 22% talked of developing better products and services. The reverse was true of American managers: 41% said the top use was developing better products and services and 30% spoke of improving their business models (Cole and Nakata 2014).

Smarter tools need smarter workers. Consider what today's auto mechanic needs to know to work on the software-filled car of today compared to a couple decades back. Fortunately for Japan, it has an advantage. The World Bank measures human capital not only by years of education—in which Japan excels—but also by how much a student has learned, as shown by international tests on reading, math, and science. Here, too, Japan excels. On an index from 0 to 1, Japan's score is 0.84, higher than any other G7 country. The US score is the lowest among the G7, at 0.76, mainly because of the huge inequalities in educational attainment and learning among students according to their socioeconomic status (World Bank 2022). The American problem on this front may be much harder to solve than the Japanese one.

The World Bank index does not include the impact of schooling on GDP growth. When this facet of human capital is included, Japan is not taking best advantage of the skills of its people. It came in 13th among rich countries (Penn World Tables 2021).

Poor Total Factor Productivity

The best predictor of a country's long-term growth is a measure called total factor productivity (TFP). It combines the productivity of labor with the productivity of capital. An example of labor productivity is how much steel a worker can produce in an hour. Capital productivity measures how much output someone can produce with the latest PC compared to an old PC with a slow processor and inability to connect to the Internet.

If a country increases its total inputs of both work hours and its stock of capital by 2% per year, and its GDP grows by 3%, that 1 percentage point difference in output reflects a 1% rise in TFP. At the most basic level, TFP is improved by better technology in the narrow sense of adding the Internet to a PC. More broadly, TFP can be improved by anything that lets a firm produce more output with the same level of inputs, for example, how well it uses KBC.

While a country can increase labor productivity by giving each worker more tools, eventually this process runs into diminishing returns and growth will eventually slow. That's what happened to Japan. The only way to maintain growth over the long haul is with continual improvements in TFP. During 1985–2017, in a typical rich country, only half (55%) of the improvement in labor productivity came from raising the ratio of capital to labor. The other half (45%) came from improvement in TFP (OECD 2022e).

In Japan, by contrast, TFP contributes much less to growth. It was not always so. During the high-growth era, Japan's TFP grew by leaps and bounds, for a total increase of 75%, compared to 44% on average among the United States, the United Kingdom, Canada, France, and Germany. In part, that's because Japan was catching technologically up to these richer countries. By contrast, during 1990–2017, Japan's TFP increased by a total of just 3%, a figure dwarfed by these other five countries' increase of 16% (see Figure 3.5).

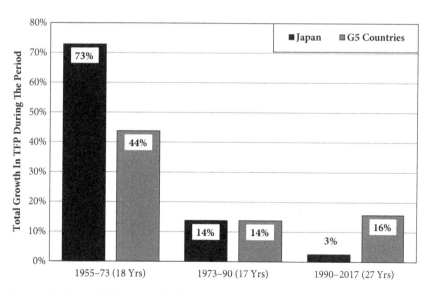

Figure 3.5 Japan's TFP: From leader to laggard.
Source: Penn World Tables 9.1 (2021).

By 1992, for example, despite using 22% more capital and 40% more labor per capita than the United States, Japan's output per capita was 23% *less* (MGI 1996). More inputs getting less output is the very definition of poor TFP.

Some put the blame for poor TFP on Japan's shift to a services economy. They note that while TFP in manufacturing nearly tripled from 1970 to 2010, it grew only 20% in services. In fact, during the lost decades, service sector TFP actually fell back a bit from its 1990 peak (see Figure 3.6).

However, other countries going through a similar shift have not suffered as large a TFP deceleration as Japan. Rather than deindustrialization, Japan's key problem is the lack of TFP growth in non-manufacturing sectors. In part, this reflects the low level of R&D in the service sector, which accounted for only 9% of business R&D in 2011, well below the OECD average of 38%. Other factors include low corporate profitability and corporations hoarding cash rather than investing in modernization.

There is a myth that services are inherently less productive than manufacturing, that they provide only low-skilled jobs, and that they cannot be exported. That's true of some personal services, like haircuts or taxis. However, a third of the 46 million new service jobs created in mature economies during 1996–2006 were in the highest-skilled and highest-paid

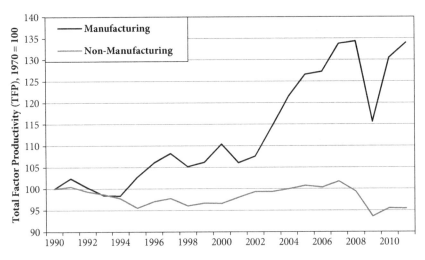

Figure 3.6 TFP in manufacturing vs. services.
Source: OECD (2015a: 63).

categories—professional, technical, managerial, and administrative occupations. German service exports today nearly match manufactured exports, when one considers the service sector inputs into manufacturing (e.g., ICT services). MGI projects that service exports will amount to a third of all rich country exports by 2030.

Think of productivity growth in musical performance. Two centuries ago, if you wanted to hear Beethoven's Eroica Symphony, you had to be one of the few dozen VIPs invited to Prince Lobkowitz's home or be among the fortunate few to attend a rare public concert. Today, you can download it. Musicians still need 60 seconds to perform the minute waltz, but today they can reach hundreds of millions at a trivial cost per listener.

Company Managers Produce Productivity

In the end, it is companies that produce productivity. Much of this involves decisions by executives about strategy and product development, what products to give up, how much to invest in what areas, human resource management, and all the other unglamorous nuts and bolts of management.

The poster child for the dramatic impact of improved management was a joint venture to produce Toyota Corollas established in 1984 between Toyota and General Motors called NUMMI (New United Motor Manufacturing, Inc.) NUMMI took over a GM plant in California so notorious for bad labor relations that GM shut it down. Absenteeism was high, and so was drunkenness, and even sabotage. When NUMMI, largely run by Toyota managers, came in, it rehired the same union workers, redesigned the assembly line, improved lighting, and, most of all, worked with the labor union and individual workers. Absenteeism, sabotage, and defect rates plunged. They produced twice as many cars with the same number of workers. It had the best quality of any GM plant. GM managers who worked at NUMMI were said to have become "missionaries for the NUMMI way," but had little luck converting others at GM. GM pulled out of the venture in 2009. Today, that same plant now produces Teslas.

Managers, however, do not make their decisions in a vacuum. They do so in the context of the business ecosystem, and these differ in the robustness of competition, the flexibility of labor markets, and the quality of financial markets. Raise the same individuals in a different business ecosystem and they will act differently. Changing the ecosystem, however, may not change mindsets at existing firms, because firms have their own culture—a group mindset that is often hard to change. This is what some in Japan call the "big company disease," the subject of the next chapter.

4

Big Company Disease

They Can't See the Gorilla

It's one of the most spectacular experiments in psychology, one only fully appreciated by those who've participated. Hundreds of people in an auditorium are shown a film. Two teams, one in black and the other in white, pass several basketballs to their teammates. The assignment is to count the number of times the white team passes a ball. No one is to speak a word. Only a few titters here and there break the silence. At the end, most people offered the correct answer. When the professor then asked who saw the gorilla, just half of the hands go up; everyone else sits in bewilderment. When the film is reshown, guffaws fill the hall. No one can believe they failed to see the man in the gorilla suit who entered the game, pounded his chest, and then walked away (Simons 2010). Yet, on less startling levels, this sort of thing happens in daily life all the time.

The experiment's originator, Daniel Simons, says that, when told about it, 90% of people are sure they'd see a gorilla, but, in experiments, only half do. People find it surprisingly hard to see something that contradicts their expectations. Similarly, people who've come to think the world works one way find it hard to accept conflicting evidence, a tendency called confirmation bias.

Corporate Blind Spots

Big organizations are systematically afflicted by confirmation bias and legacy thinking. In fact, the malady is often worse in organizations than in individuals. This stems from groupthink, difficulty in giving up long-held views—especially successful ones—and the tendency of organizations to hire those most likely to assimilate their mindset, rather than challenge it. The most insidious result is not that people fear speaking up, but that they cannot perceive problems in the first place. Worse yet, unlike in the gorilla

The Contest for Japan's Economic Future. Richard Katz, Oxford University Press. © Richard Katz 2024.
DOI: 10.1093/oso/9780197675106.003.0005

experiment, an organization's inability to recognize a glitch can persist even when outsiders point it out.

More often than not, failure to see the gorilla afflicts even the most well-intentioned leaders of old established companies. That's a problem for Japan because, when Tokyo talks about business reform, the focus has largely been on corporate governance measures for the few thousand publicly listed corporations. But, due to these perceptual blinders, improved governance rules do not necessarily lead to better strategy and execution. Besides, however necessary corporate reform may be, only 10% of the labor force works for big companies. Recovery requires addressing problems at the companies employing the other 90%.

It's often the most successful firms that are blindest to new needs and opportunities. Robert Cole and Hugh Whittaker stress that the more successful a firm is, the more it reinforces the path that brought it to success in terms of the markets on which it focuses, the way it trains its workers, and its relationships with suppliers. As it does so, it inherently ignores, and thus lets atrophy, capabilities that might have enabled it to comprehend new situations and execute other options. Consequently, when the firm is hit with an unfamiliar competitive threat, it may not even realize it's a threat. Even if it does, it tends to rely on familiar solutions that fail to work in the new context (Cole and Whittaker 2006: 13).

All too often, bureaucracies cannot see solutions right in front of their noses, even when they are looking for them. Consider the Silicon Valley outposts that some Japanese corporate giants created to learn about the latest trends. Kenji Kushida reports, "If the information the Silicon Valley employee sent to headquarters was too cutting-edge—so far so that the strategy and management departments did not get a good sense of what the potential was—the Silicon Valley reports were not acted upon." As a result, staffers began sending back to headquarters slightly older information that was already common knowledge. The latter was better received better by the Japanese headquarters because it seemed more familiar to them. This, of course, defeated the purpose of the outpost (Kushida 2015: 49).

Worse yet, executives often act like losing gamblers who won't leave the table until they have made up their losses, explains Daniel Kahneman, a psychologist who won the Nobel Prize in Economics. They keep spending money on fallen stars, convincing themselves that the product in question is just going through a bad patch, and thereby leaving insufficient human resources and capital for new opportunities (Kahneman 2011: 345–346).

Think of the billions of dollars in losses for SONY, Panasonic, and others before these companies finally downsized TV production, or abandoned it altogether. SONY's TV unit reportedly lost money eight years in a row during 2005–2012.

Sometimes an emotional stake adds to the blind spot. Perhaps the superior who helped a manager move up the ladder was among those who created the market for that product. So, ditching the product can feel like a betrayal of one's mentor. Conceptual rigidity is reinforced when executives tied to a certain way of thinking promote those who think the same way. This problem is particularly severe in Japan due to the lifetime employment system. As late as 2001, 82% of managers in Japan's larger firms, including the top executives, had worked at that company for their entire career. This compares to 18% in the United States. The situation has changed somewhat in recent years since some Japanese companies are hiring some managers in mid-career. Even so, it remains the dominant practice (Takenoshita 2008).

In the early 1980s, Omron CEO Kazuma Tateishi nicknamed these syndromes the "big company disease" in an article that made a big splash (Hoefle (2017). His recognition of these problems has helped Omron reduce them. Founded in 1933, the company remained an innovator despite becoming huge ($8.3 billion in sales in 2019). Among other innovations, it developed the world's first electronic ticket gate, which was named an IEEE Milestone in 2007.[1] It was also one of the first manufacturers of automated teller machines with magnetic stripe card readers. In 2013, Thomson Reuters listed it as one of the Top 100 Global Innovators.

Case Study: The Fight at Fujitsu

Attachment to a lucrative customer base is another source of corporate blinders. Such was the case at Fujitsu, where two divisions within the company clashed over the best technology for Internet network routers. The relationships each division had built up with their respective customer bases biased each division's perception about which direction the technology would ultimately take (Cole 2005; Cole 2006).

In the mid- and late 1990s, Fujitsu had two groups working on Internet-related technologies. One was the Communications Systems Group (CSG),

---

[1] IEEE is the Institute of Electrical and Electronics Engineers.

which had always focused on sales to the telecom sector, particularly Nippon Telephone and Telegraph (NTT), a state-owned monopoly in local telephone service undergoing partial privatization. Fujitsu was one of four big suppliers to NTT and was used to making equipment according to NTT specifications. Since NTT was prohibited by law from operating abroad until 1999, global markets did not shape thinking at either NTT or the CSG group at Fujitsu. By contrast, Fujitsu's Computer and Information Processing Group (CIPG) focused on sales of computer equipment to all sorts of operating companies in finance, manufacturing, and so on.

The two divisions' different perspectives came into conflict when advances in technology, particularly the Internet, created a fusion of telecommunications and the computer. One reason was that NTT, not its suppliers, was charting the technological path in the equipment they provided to it and therefore had inordinate influence over Fujitsu's CSG. When it came to networking equipment, the physical backbone of the Internet, and the question of the best software for broadband transmission, NTT placed all of its bets on the combination of Asynchronous Transfer Mode (ATM) and the Integrated Services Digital Network (ISDN), respectively. Critics joked that ISDN stood for "I Still Don't Need It." In 1991, Fujitsu became the first company worldwide to offer an ATM switching system that enabled high speed, two-way transmission and routing of voice, video, and data simultaneously.

There was a competing technology, the one that eventually conquered the world: Transmission Control Protocol (TCP) and the Internet Protocol (IP). NTT disparaged it because, in some ways, it seemed inferior. For example, as late as the early 2000s, 3% of all Internet packets of data were dropped en route and the system had to re-transmit them for successful communication. NTT, with its 99.999% standard of reliability, disdained this approach. This scenario is classic with disruptive technologies, Clayton Christensen points out. Initially, they have kinks that induce incumbents to dismiss them, but they have features that attract customers. Over time, the kinks are worked out and eventually they displace the previous technology.

The real attraction to NTT was that ATM/ISDN augmented NTT's existing technology, and, being hardware-centric, fit in with the skill set of NTT and its suppliers. By contrast, TCP/IP is software-centric and rendered NTT's existing technology worthless.

The issue here is not a matter of technological competence, but of conceptual blind spots. In fact, a team at NTT's Research Laboratories was working on TCP/IP development without the knowledge of senior management. One member of the group, Ken Murakami, developed a high-speed protocol for IP and demonstrated its effectiveness by building a system between Kyoto and Tokyo. The higher-ups at NTT dismissed it because it "was not ATM." So, Murakami made it available to Cisco, and the latter implemented a version of it on its own routers.

Given the importance of NTT purchases to Fujitsu, the latter's top executives put its money into routers for the telecom carriers, not for the enterprises wanting to use the Internet. When TCP/IP ended up beating out ATM/ISDN, Fujitsu was reduced in 2004 to distributing networking equipment made by Cisco and a competing firm called Juniper. Fujitsu's total revenue topped out in 2007 at ¥5.3 trillion ($41 billion) and by 2019 had fallen by one-third to just ¥3.8 ($29 billion). The company is still big and profitable, of course, but a company that formerly had the ability to challenge IBM in mainframe computers is now an also-ran.

Whenever a new technology comes into view, only trial and error will tell which one prevails. That's precisely why progress requires an environment where many companies can try different approaches. The problem is not that corporate leaders at NTT and its suppliers made a miscalculation; it's that they were unable to see the possibilities and risks objectively.

NTT is hardly the only giant encumbered by the big company disease. Bell Labs had difficulty developing competitive products vis-à-vis Cisco. AT&T was slow to recognize the significance of the Internet. It mattered more in Japan because NTT and its family of suppliers were the only game in town. In the United States, there was room for entirely new players, like Cisco, to grow and become dominant quite rapidly. Cisco had been founded in 1984 by two students at Stanford. By 2019, revenue had exploded to $52 billion. NTT's strategic blunder would not have mattered as much if new Japanese companies could have entered the field as Cisco did in the United States, or if the Japanese telecom market had been more open to foreign players early on (Cole 2005: 15).

According to the cliché, American companies are good at radical change, while Japanese companies are better at incremental change. That misses the point. Japanese giants, like those elsewhere, are quite open to radical technological changes, as long as they don't disrupt the business model that has brought them success. Toyota was the first automaker in the world to come out with a hybrid car, but has been resistant to electric vehicles. It was a Japanese company that came out with the world's first supertanker for oil. Japanese electronics firms were first with a consumer-oriented VCR, the

Walkman, and many other products. All were radical in their time; none disrupted their business model. The real distinction between incumbents and challengers in any country, argues Christensen, is not between radical and incremental change, but between changes that sustain a firm's business model and those that undermine it. Cole stresses that "a better business model beats a better technology" (Cole 2004: 8).

The Fujitsu story casts further doubt on the now-popular notion that improvement in Japanese corporate governance is the road to better corporate performance. It is hard to see how setting an 8% goal for return on equity or adding a few outside members to NTT's board of directors would have changed any of this. It's not as if NTT was trying to end up writing off billions of dollars by choosing the wrong technology. Its leaders genuinely believed they were heading toward commercial supremacy. Could a few outside directors have had both the technical expertise and clout to overrule NTT's own technologists? Competition is the more powerful force in effecting better corporate performance, and some of that competition needs to come from new companies.

Competition: The Road to Better Corporate Management

In a 1993 report, the McKinsey Global Institute compared labor productivity levels in Japan, the United States, and Germany in nine manufacturing sectors ranging from autos to beer. In steel, Japan's productivity was 50% higher than in the United States; in food processing, its productivity was 40% lower. Still, Japan employed more people in food processing than in autos, auto parts, steel, and metalworking put together (MGI 1993).

The productivity gaps were not primarily determined by tangible factors such as the educational level of the workers, the age of machinery, or capital:labor ratios, but by the vision and effectiveness of the executives. And the latter is heavily influenced by the degree of competition. A study by McKinsey Global Institute shows that managers do not come up with better solutions because they are smarter, work harder, or go to better business schools. Instead, they perform better when innovation and efficiency are the price of survival. "Global competitiveness is a bit like tennis—you improve by playing against people who are better than you" (Lewis et al. 1993).

All countries have a certain amount of dualism, a combination of leading sectors and laggard ones. But in neither the United States nor Germany is the gap in productivity, or in international exposure among various sectors, any-where near as severe as in Japan.

Nor is poor productivity in Japan limited to low-tech industries, like textiles or food processing. It afflicted even telecommunications, particularly in the old days when, due to NTT's monopoly in local phone service, it em-ployed 95% of all workers in telecom. Japan's TFP in telecom was 23% below the level of its American counterparts (MGI 1992: 192).

One of the best studies of how this applies to Japan is an article by Mariko Sakakibara, a former METI official, and Michael E. Porter, the famed ex-pert on business strategy (Sakakibara and Porter 2001). They measure the intensity of market competition by the size of shifts in market share within an industry. Continual big shifts in market share—and in market ranking—signify fierce competition. Excessive stability in market share indicates out-right collusion, or else a tacit non-aggression pact. The extreme case is Japan's flat glass industry, where three companies had an unchanging 50:30:20 split of the market for three decades.

Looking at 77 products between 1973 and 1990, the scholars measured how well companies did in the export market where they were pitted against the world's best. Instability in the *domestic* market share did a better job in predicting these companies' share of the global export market than did economies of scale, spending on R&D, or any other factor. Executives in low-competition sectors received little penalty when they underperformed. By contrast, when firms facing intense competition at home lost a big slice of their market share, or profits plunged, CEOs were replaced, often at the in-sistence of their banks, who had much more power than shareholders.

Do Japan's Banks and Capital Markets Impose Discipline on Corporations?

The famed economist John Hicks wrote: "The best of all monopoly profits is a quiet life [for executives]" (Hicks 1935: 8). All around the world, executives in firms with less competitive pressure reduce stress by failing to strive as much. They even have a higher life expectancy. Executives and managers at firms insulated from intense market competition and/or discipline from financial markets are more risk-averse, as well as less imaginative. Many executives and managers just five to ten years from retirement ask them-selves: Why shake things up when I'll get blamed for any failure, while the fruits of success may not show up until after I've left? Even when CEOs try to shake up their firm, they often face passive-aggressive resistance from the big gray cloud of subordinate managers.

Research confirms that Hicks's thesis applies in Japan, where shareholder power is weak. Executives who need not fear being ousted by a shareholder revolt are more conservative in their investments, less likely to withdraw from a product line when it goes sour, and less likely to undertake corporate restructuring. By contrast, when managers are closely monitored by institutional investors and independent directors, they are more likely to be decisive. The measure used in the study was the degree of cross-shareholding and stable shareholding. The first refers to company A and B holding shares of each other; the second refers to shareholders who keep their holdings indefinitely—regardless of performance—as part of an alliance. It would include a firm's banks, *keiretsu* allies, suppliers, customers, and sometimes even competitors. The greater the degree of cross-shareholding and stable shareholding, the more cautious are the executives (Ikeda et al. 2017: 1).

Shareholder power has always been weak because, when firms needed outside money, they looked to their banks, not the equity markets. So, in the past, banks could substitute for shareholders in imposing discipline. Not any longer. Banks have lost much of their power to oust poorly performing executives and/or send some of their own personnel to help run the troubled firm. That's because, on average, the electronic vaults of non-financial companies are stuffed with cash. At Japan's biggest 5,000 firms, cash flow is greater than their investments in new plant and equipment and R&D to the tune of 3% of GDP; at all corporations, the excess cash flow equals more than 5%–6% of GDP (see Figure 4.1). With no need to raise outside cash, executives can be either empire-builders or "quiet lifers," as they choose, without too much interference or discipline from the financial markets.

There are those who say shareholder power has increased because the ratio of *cross*-shareholding has dropped dramatically from 35% in 1990 to just 10% in 2018. In reality, however, 60% of listed companies still report that they have *stable* shareholders accounting for 40%–60% of their shareholder base, who can be counted on to side with management (Usami et al. 2019).

The influx of foreign investors—who collectively own 30% of all shares by value, up from almost nothing two decades ago—has so far had much less impact on behavior than many, including me, had expected. The foreign shareholder-led revolt at Toshiba in 2021–2022 made global headlines

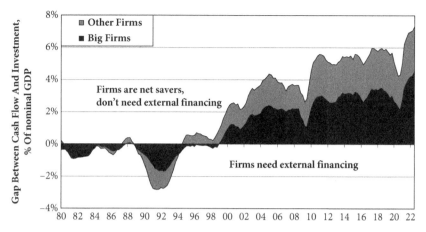

Figure 4.1 Business is net saver to the tune of 5%–6% of GDP.
Source: MOF (2023a).

in part because it was such a rare exception, and even there, as of February 2023, has so far frustrated efforts at reorganization of the company.

If you want to measure shareholder power, check out the dividend payout ratio: dividends as a share of net profits. Companies that cannot profitably reinvest their profits should return a big chunk of it to shareholders. Hence, for years, activists and foreign investors have asked corporations to raise dividends. Yet, on average, the payout ratio is not substantially higher today than it was in the 1980s–1990s. It's still about 20%–30%, compared to around 50% in the United States (Japan Exchange Group 2021a). If and when it starts to rise in a big way across many companies, that would signal an impactful leap in shareholder power.[2]

What about institutional investors? Nikko Research tracked the votes of 17 leading Japanese institutional investors at the 2017 annual meetings. These 17 had signed the "Principles for Responsible Investment" promoted by the much-lauded new Stewardship Code issued by the Financial Services Agency (FSA) in 2014. At only seven of the few thousand annual meetings that year, did any shareholders even present a proposal for a dividend increase. Twelve of the 17 institutional investors sided with management

---

[2] Instead, companies keep increasing stock buybacks, which do not commit the company to a certain dividend in the future, and which raise stock prices. It's beyond the scope of this book, but in the case of Japan, reliable dividends are better for the economy than ad hoc stock buybacks.

against the dividend hike all seven times. One sided with petitioners five times, and two did so only once (Okasen 2017).

On the other hand, some experts see signs of a less confrontational form of nudging. At the June 2019 annual meetings, a record 54 companies faced shareholder proposals, of which 12 came from institutional investors. None was approved. But the real action may have taken place before the meeting, when management made some concessions to head off an embarrassing vote. Declining levels of reliable support for management may be leading to the increasing frequency with which issues are settled before they become public via a vote at the annual meeting (Usami et al. 2019).

A Competing Story

While gazelles are the heroes of this book, there's another version of the Japan story, one in which elephants are the heroes. It is a tale told by Ulrike Schaede in her award-winning book, *The Business Reinvention of Japan* (Schaede 2020). In her view, the lost decades, rather than lost, were a time of transition, a period when Japan's corporate giants re-engineered themselves, focused on core competencies, and adopted what she calls an aggregate niche strategy.

It doesn't matter that we no longer see retail store shelves dominated by SONYs and Panasonics, she argues. What matters today is the indispensable Japanese-made parts inside. It's not just the well-known case of Japanese-made chips inside cell phones. She cites the cases of Japanese companies dominating the global market share in small electric motors in cars, such as for seats, windows, and wipers (estimated at 80%), vehicle power steering (40%), carbon fiber (66%), and advanced sensors (between 40% and 70%, depending on the type). For certain areas of medical and office automation equipment, Japan's combined global share exceeds 70%. Referring to a list of products in which Japan shines put together by a Japanese government agency called NEDO,[3] Schaede reports that, among 931 products across a wide range of industries in 2017, Japanese companies had over 50% of global market share in 309 products, including more than 75% in 112 products, and 100% in 57 products. While the sales volume of each niche may look small, when you add them all together, she contends, the aggregate volume is quite large (Schaede 2020: 78).

---

[3] New Energy and Industrial Technology Development Organization.

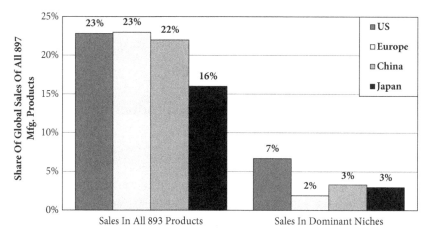

Figure 4.2 Niches too small for "aggregate niche strategy."
Source: NEDO (2018).

Unfortunately, the numbers don't appear to back up her conclusion.[4] Yes, there are a lot of niche products dominated by Japanese companies, just as there are niche products dominated by American or European producers. However, the aggregate does not add up to very much. With duplicates removed, there were 893 products with a total global sales volume of a considerable $10.8 trillion (NEDO 2018). However, Japan's market share among all 893 was just 16%, significantly behind the 23% share each for the United States and Europe and 22% for China (see Figure 4.2).

In the products where Japanese companies enjoyed a majority share, the median sales volume was a tiny $206 million. In fact, Japan is most dominant in niches where the sales are the smallest. As a result, Japan's total global sales in those products added up to a measly 3% of the total global sales of all 893 products.

What's remarkable is that, in a list designed to show off Japanese strengths, the typical American-dominated product enjoyed bigger global sales. Consequently, the sales of American companies in their dominant products added up to 6.7% of global sales of all 893 products, more than double Japan's share (see again Figure 4.2).

---

[4] Although Schaede and I disagree, she was kind enough to send me an Excel file she had prepared based on the NEDO data so that I could do my own analysis.

5

Gazelles

A Keystone Species for Productivity

A keystone species is one whose removal can cause an entire ecosystem to decay. Take the wolves of Yellowstone National Park (Farquhar 2019). When they were banned from the park in 1925, the deer and elk population exploded and then ate so many leaves that the trees withered. Without their strong roots binding the soil, riverbanks eroded. The entire ecosystem decayed. When the wolves were finally returned in 1995, their restoration of balance between prey and predator not only helped bring back lush trees, bald eagles, and the beaver—another keystone species—but, through a spectacular chain reaction, helped reverse soil erosion and fortify the riverbanks.

Gazelles are keystone companies. Without their new ideas, new products, and better ways of producing old products—not to mention how they push moribund firms to the exits—progress in productivity would be as tenuous as the riverbanks of Yellowstone without the wolves.

Only in part is this because gazelles have higher productivity than the firms they replace. As noted in the Introduction, during the 1980s–1990s American firms less than five years old supplied a stunning 60% of the growth in factory output per worker. At least as important is how gazelles improve the productivity of their customers, suppliers, and, very importantly, some of the elephants that they challenge. Recall how Raksul's Uber-like system for parcel delivery lifted trucking productivity and earnings while lowering carbon emissions, as well as how its rise compelled Japan Post to partner with it.

Very often, gazelles come into existence because they spot a gap in the marketplace that no incumbent even noticed, and they invent imaginative ways to fill it. The more that these gazelles succeed, the more that other entrepreneurs will be inclined to jump into that market, either to partner with them or else to try to beat them at their own game. Just by succeeding, gazelles catalyze their own partners, spinoffs, and competitors. Those

The Contest for Japan's Economic Future. Richard Katz, Oxford University Press. © Richard Katz 2024.
DOI: 10.1093/oso/9780197675106.003.0006

that become superstars, like Google, spawn an untold number of satellite companies using Google for this or that purpose. Elephants, too, will be induced to move into a market they had previously overlooked. as in the response of the auto giants to the rise of Tesla. This type of thing happens every day, albeit less spectacularly. So far, this book has emphasized the role of gazelles in supplanting elephants. What's also very important is that gazelles can also change technology regimes because at least some incumbent firms will feel compelled to emulate them, or even partner with them.

As the OECD points out, industries with a high rate of new entries have higher average levels of productivity. The reason is that, by increasing competitive pressures on the incumbents, new entries indirectly stimulate technological progress, even when the growth in efficiency appears to take place within incumbent firms (Baily 2003: 128, 138–139).

While the size of this spillover effect is hard to measure, we do have one estimate for the United States, and the same logic would apply to Japan. The US birth rate of new firms has declined sharply since 1980, as detailed below. As a result, labor productivity in 2015 was calculated as 3.1% lower, and real median household income was $1,600 lower, than they would have been had the 1980 company birth rate continued. The cumulative lost income over 35 years was several times higher (Alon et al. 2017: 1, 13).

Gazelles' Main Impact: Job Transfers, Not Job Creation

Let's look more deeply at the mechanism by which new high-growth firms raise labor productivity. While they create a disproportionate share of *net* new jobs, what really adds to productivity is the kind of jobs they create. Labor productivity in the gazelles is much higher than in either the inferior firms forced out of the market, or in most of the continuing firms. So, the real contribution of the gazelles is not job creation but job transfer, that is, transferring workers from low-productivity firms and jobs to high-productivity firms and jobs.

In the United States, only about 8%–10% of the workforce is shifted each year through the birth and death of firms. And yet, a variety of studies show that the entry and exit of firms account for 30%–40% of TFP growth in the United States and Europe (Bureau of the Census 2016; Foster et al. 2005: 45; Katz 2002: 226). In Japan, by contrast, firm turnover provided only 16% of TFP growth during 1980–2005, and almost none during 2000–2005 (Fukao

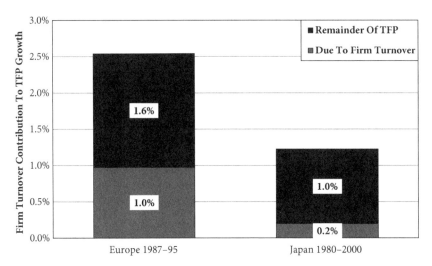

Figure 5.1 Low firm turnover produces low TFP growth.
Source: Fukao (2019).

2019). This is a major reason why overall TFP growth is so slow in Japan compared to North America and Europe (see Figure 5.1).

To understand how this happens, we must first distinguish between *gross* and *net* job creation. Across the OECD, 25%–45% of the labor force leave their jobs every year (voluntarily or involuntarily) and find new jobs. Net job creation is thus a very thin slice of gross creation. An amazingly thin slice of firms accounts for a surprisingly large proportion of net job creation. Among firms of all ages in the United States, the 1% fastest-growing created 40% of *net* new jobs during the first decade of the twenty-first century. Among younger firms aged 3–5 years, there were 42,000 gazelles. They amounted to 0.8% of all firms but created 10% of net new jobs. Most of these 42,000 younger firms were SMEs. Nearly 80% ranged from 20 to 99 employees, while another 16% had 100–250 staffers. However, they already added up to a few million employees in dynamic companies. Studies of Canada and Europe have found similar results (see Figure 5.2) (Stangler 2010: 5–7; Henrekson and Johansson 2010: 230; Bureau of Labor Statistics 2020; OECD 2009: 119).

In most of the OECD—but not Japan—the greatest downsizing of payrolls happens at the least efficient firms, only some of which go out of business. The upshot is that fluidity in the labor market and ease of entry and exit aid productivity growth. Equally important, the firms investing in up-to-date equipment have the highest rate of job growth, because their modernization

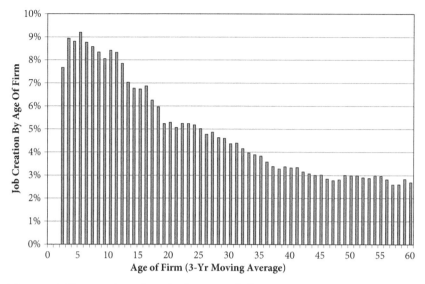

Figure 5.2 Younger firms have higher rate of job creation.
Source: OECD (2009: 142–144).

accelerates their growth in sales. So, while technology destroys some jobs, it creates even more new jobs (OECD 2009: 120, 142–144; Fukao and Kwon 2005).

Even when stodgy elephants remain in business, it is normal for newer, more efficient leaders to take market share. At Amazon, for example, the annual revenue per worker in 2015 was $491,000, compared to just $155,000 at Barnes & Noble bookstores. Costco's revenue per worker, at $210,000, was much better than the $140,000 at Sears. The redistribution of workers from less efficient to more efficient firms provides another addition to labor productivity. In a better world, this improvement in productivity would automatically translate into higher wages, as it did for most of period since the 1800s. As detailed below, that linkage has been broken in almost all rich countries since the 1980s.[1]

Japan lags in taking advantage of this source of productivity growth. Not only is the rate of entry and exit low, but it suffers from adverse selection. On average, the firms forced out have a *higher* level of TFP than the average firm

---

[1] However, public outrage has forced some of these American giants to grant higher wages, e.g., a minimum wage of $15 per hour.

that stays. The exit process perversely lowers TFP, instead of raising it as in other countries (METI 2017a: 45–47). In fact, during 1995–2005, this negative exit effect was so large that it more than offset the positive entry effect from the rise of newer, more innovative firms.

How could this adverse selection have occurred? As noted above, the thin government social safety net makes a worker's job at his current company his prime safety net. That puts inordinate pressure on the government to protect inferior firms and outright zombies. That often leads to an excess of firms in a product area and downward pressure on prices that can turn profits into losses for some firms. On top of that, the zombies get more direct and indirect support than do the merely mediocre. For example, the low-productivity zombies were able to get more bank loans than the average profitable firm, even if was troubled. The upshot is that the zombies can remain in the market while the merely mediocre are forced out. Scholars have documented that this problem has been going on for at least four decades (Fukao and Kwon 2005: 12–16).[2]

It's Broader than High-Tech and Venture Capital

The popular image of gazelles relies on the romance of Silicon Valley but, as noted earlier, high-tech accounts for only a fraction of gazelles.

Netflix is a spectacular example of a new firm displacing an existing giant by using a technology now almost 250 years old: the US Postal Service. Not so long ago, people went to the local video store to rent a video cassette, and later a DVD. Then came Netflix in 1998. It started off with $2.5 million, much of which came from the mother of one of the co-founders. The idea came to one of the founders when he was forced to pay $40 in overdue fines after returning *Apollo 13* well past its due date. Initially, the big difference between Netflix and Blockbuster (then America's biggest video rental chain) was that Netflix delivered DVDs by mail, rather than having brick-and-mortar stores. Netflix's advantages were a larger selection as well as lower cost. Customers paid a monthly fee, rented one film at a time, and kept it as they wanted without late return penalties. Once online streaming arrived in 2007, Blockbuster was driven out of business within a few years. The irony is that, in 2000, when Netflix was desperate for cash, its executives visited

---

[2] The authors graciously provided updated data based on their paper.

Blockbuster three times, offering to sell them a 49% stake in Netflix for just $49 million, and suggesting that Blockbuster make Netflix its streaming arm down the road. Blockbuster turned them down flat. Twenty years later, a 49% share in Netflix was worth $92 billion.

Tokushimaru food delivery is as low-tech as it gets. Its founder, a 42-year-old community organizer named Tatsuya Sumitomo, saw a need created by the megatrend of Japan's demographic crunch. The latter has given rise to many companies aimed at meeting various needs among the growing ranks of the aged—needs often ignored by the incumbents. In this case, the need was for mobile food delivery in communities tagged as food deserts. Almost 4 million seniors live in depopulating towns now too small to support a grocery store. By 2025, the food desert population will hit 6 million (*Yomiuri* 2014).

In 2012, he created Tokushimaru to send trucks to these towns, each packed with 1,500 items. Tokushimaru operates via a partnership with local grocery stores. He designed the trucks and trains the drivers, who become sales agents for the local stores. The drivers buy the products from the stores, with the proviso that they can return any unsold items, and the store sells the perishable ones at a discount. One feature displays a classic Japanese trait: since the agents come to know their aging customers, they alert local authorities of a possible problem if a regular customer living alone fails to show up.

As of early 2020, Tokushimaru had allied with 120 supermarket companies with a total of 1,700 stores. It had 500 trucks all over Japan and hoped to double that by 2022. In 2017, Tokushimaru was bought up by Oisix ra Daichi, an online vegetable delivery service created in 2012, with revenue of ¥115 billion ($884 million) in 2022. Tokushimaru now has a partnership with Ito-Yakado's 7-Eleven, Japan's largest convenience store chain.

Once a startup like Tokushimaru does something like this, it seems so obvious one wonders why bigger firms didn't think of it themselves. The fact is that such myopia is common. It underscores not just why new firms are necessary, but also how their arrival provokes older firms to move with the times.

When people think of innovation, the first thing that comes to mind is a new product like the automobile or the Internet. However, many of the most impactful innovations focus on producing better processes, rather than new products. Among the most famous are Henry Ford's development of the assembly line and Toyota's just-in-time production system. One of the most interesting among recent SME process innovators is a Swedish company that was named Ergonomidesign when I visited in 2007. In 2016, it was bought out by McKinsey and is now called McKinsey Design. At the time of McKinsey's buyout, it had around 90 employees and branches in several other countries.

In 1988, Scandinavian Airlines (SAS) turned to Ergonomidesign for help. The simple coffee pot was giving SAS a big, costly headache. Its flight attendants were regularly getting wrist injuries from pouring coffee from a traditionally designed pot. Some even needed surgery. Most airlines would have had Ergonomidesign work with their engineers. Ergonomidesign's innovation was to work instead with the flight attendants. Three of its ergonomic engineers watched the attendants pour over and over again. They noticed that the traditional design forced the attendants to bend their wrists every time they poured. Maria Benkzton, a co-founder of the company and a co-designer of the pot, proudly explained, "We moved the handle to the center of gravity, and we made it so that you could pour it with a straight wrist just by rotating the arm." Injuries quickly fell, as did healthcare costs and absenteeism. Moreover, attendants could safely pour more coffee in less time. The Museum of Modern Art in New York made this humble pot a part of its permanent collection. In the past three decades, over 30 airlines have adopted the pot and have deployed 500,000 of them. When I told this story to a flight attendant on a major US airline, she said the "suits" at her employer would never involve its attendants in such an issue.

While venture capital (VC) is part and parcel of Silicon Valley's glamor, the overwhelming majority of US startups do not rely upon VC money or even professional angel investors, the earliest investors who provide seed money to get off the ground. The Kauffman Foundation Firm Survey, the longest and largest longitudinal study of entrepreneurs to date, shows that among 5,000 startups, just 4.4% of startup funding came from VCs and just 5.8% from angels (Morelix 2013). Most of the money comes from entrepreneurs using their personal savings, maxing out their credit cards, and borrowing from family and friends. Even among the high-growth firms within these 5,000, only 6.5% raised VC money and just 7.7% of them raised money from angels. VC-backed firms are the exception. Venture capitalists are focused on firms that either want to go on the stock market or else get bought up by a bigger firm—cases where the founders are more concerned with their financial return than with retaining control; 37% of the firms that went public on the US stock market between 1980 and 2015 were funded by VCs (McSparron-Edwards 2016). For the ordinary gazelle that will never go on the stock market, explained Jeffrey Char, "Using VC money is like putting rocket fuel in your Corolla" (Interview April 2016).

Gazelles: A Rare Species in Japan

Some argue that Japan does not need any reform to promote gazelles, that there are plenty. The problem is that they always point to the same 10 or 20 names: the few, the famous, the VC-financed superstars. These are names such as Mercari, Japan's counterpart to eBay; DeNA, a host for mobile and e-commerce sites; game developers like Mixi and Gree; Line, a digital wallet producer; Zozo, a huge online fashion retailer; Smart News, a news aggregator; Preferred Networks, a developer of AI systems; and Liquid Group, which operates an exchange for cryptocurrencies. They are among Japan's very few unicorns or former unicorns, ventures that had been valued by private investors at $1 billion or more before they were listed on the stock market or acquired by a larger company.

The fact that these companies have prospered is a good sign. However, their numbers pale in comparison to those elsewhere. Out of more than 1,000 unicorns around the world in April 2022, just five were located in Japan. This compares to 562 in the United States, 173 in China, 65 in India, 43 in the United Kingdom, 26 in Germany, 12 in South Korea, 7 in Israel, and 114 more in the 11 other countries ahead of Japan (CB Insights 2022).

Where, however, are the many, the unknown, the ones relying on the savings of founders, family, and friends? In other countries, thousands of new gazelles are founded every year. Japan, by contrast, has never submitted a number to the OECD, and, in 2019, officials at METI told me that there was no current plan to track it. In reading years of METI's annual White Papers on Small and Medium Enterprises, I cannot recall ever coming across the term "gazelle." The available evidence, however, makes it clear that the number is small. Rather than focus on the need for gazelles, Tokyo once again chased the shiny object, announcing in 2018 a goal of 20 unicorns by 2023, but no strategy to achieve the goal.

The problem in Japan is not in creating a new company, but in making it grow. Sure, most SMEs are mice and wish to remain so, but many would like to become gazelles and cannot. There are more than 4 million enterprises in Japan, of which 86% have fewer than 10 staffers and employ a fifth of all company employees. At the other pole, just 14% of employees work for

567 companies with a staff of at least 5,000 (Economic Census for Business Frame 2014).

The OECD tracked micro SMEs, those that started with fewer than 10 employees, and charted their fate. Those that survived and grew to the "small category" (10–49 staffers) provided 40% of net job growth in the typical OECD country during their first three years; in Japan, it was just 23%, the lowest among the group (Criscuolo et al. 2014: 32).

Unquestionably, Japan has become a less dangerous place for gazelles than it used to be. However, it is not yet as safe as it needs to be. In 2012, when Shinzo Abe became prime minister, he promised to launch a program of structural reforms that would greatly improve the situation. Unfortunately, as we'll see in the next chapter, he didn't even really try.

6

Abenomics

A Tale of Lost Opportunities

All Shinzo Abe had to do was to carry out his famous three arrows of Abenomics: monetary stimulus, fiscal stimulus, and structural reform. Had he done so, Japan would have been well on the way to recovery. That he did not is a tale of lost opportunities.

None of the three arrows can work without the other two. Yet Abe took only one of his arrows seriously: monetary stimulus. His salesmanship of the three arrows helped keep him in power longer than any previous prime minister. He was a salesman who did not believe in his own product (Katz 2014).

Abe can be judged by his own goal: returning Japan to annual real growth of 2%. In reality, growth averaged just 0.8% per year during his tenure, and much of that was due to recovery from the five years of average negative growth following the 2008–09 global financial cataclysm (see Figure 6.1).

The First Arrow: A Confidence Game

Ultimately, Abenomics was a confidence game, in the literal sense: the false theory that lack of confidence was the root cause of Japan's long malaise. If only prices started rising again, his advisors told him, Japanese would have more faith in the future. Consumers would spend more. Companies would invest more, hire more, and raise wages.

This belief led Abe to place all his bets on the 2013 promise by Bank of Japan Governor Haruhiko Kuroda that he could achieve 2% inflation within just two years. He did not even come close (see Figure 6.2).

In denial of the obvious failure, Abe kept relying almost entirely on the monetary arrow while neglecting the other two. When it came to fiscal

The Contest for Japan's Economic Future. Richard Katz, Oxford University Press. © Richard Katz 2024.
DOI: 10.1093/oso/9780197675106.003.0007

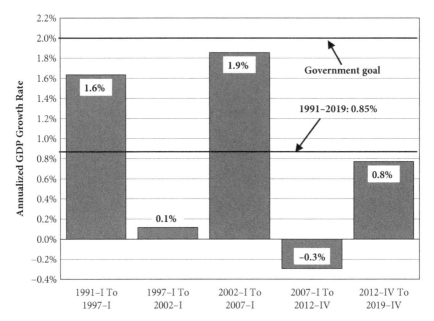

Figure 6.1   Stop-go growth.
Source: Cabinet Office (2022a).
Note: Ends before COVID.

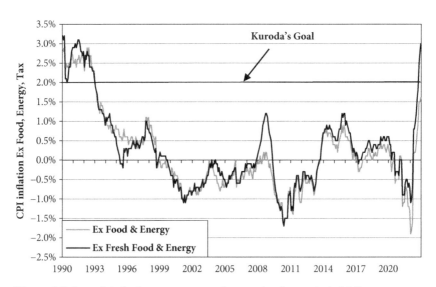

Figure 6.2   Japan's inflation never came close to the domestic-led 2%.
Source: Statistics Bureau (2022a).
Note: CPI excluding food, energy, and the consumption tax; see text regarding 2021–2022 surge.

stimulus, Abe had one foot on the gas pedal and the other, a heavier foot, on the brake. As for structural reform, Abe was long on lofty goals but short on any strategy to achieve them. On the contrary, time and again he sided with the vested interests to block reform.

Kuroda's promise of 2% inflation within two years was based on the illusory premise of a self-fulfilling prophecy, formally known as rational expectations. He was urged on this course by not only advisors in Japan but also some from abroad, most notably Nobel Prize–winner Paul Krugman. The theory held that, if the BOJ promised to achieve 2% inflation, and vowed to create lots of money to do so, then the public would believe 2% inflation was around the corner. Consumers would rush to buy more before prices went up and companies would rush to invest and hire before prices and interest rates rose. These actions would, via the law of supply and demand, push those prices up. In short: if they believe it, it will happen. In 2015 Kuroda explained his strategy with a Peter Pan theory: "the moment you doubt whether you can fly, you cease forever to be able to do it." Alas, outside of Neverland, happy thoughts lift neither lost boys nor lost decades.

There was an initial spurt of inflation for a couple of years, but then it fizzled out. From April 2015 through the end of 2019, inflation averaged a barely visible 0.3% per year. More than 90% of the entire rise in the consumer price index (excluding hikes in the consumption tax) was driven by import-heavy items. That's a transfer of income from Japanese households to foreign producers. This no more helps Japan than it does when OPEC raises oil prices. The same syndrome of imported inflation was true in the 2021–2023 surge of prices. This was not the healthy domestic demand-led 2% inflation that Kuroda had promised.

Deflation was never the cause of Japan's troubles; rather, it was a symptom of poor demand. The best predictor of the ups and downs of inflation/deflation has been the gap between full-capacity GDP and actual GDP 6–9 months earlier When GDP was at, or slightly above, full capacity—as measured by the so-called output gap—the rate of inflation rose. When actual GDP was below its full potential, inflation rates fell back (see Figure 6.3). Trying to cure Japan's anemic growth by raising prices is like trying to cure a fever by putting ice on the thermometer.

The benefits of monetary stimulus may have outweighed the cost, but overreliance on monetary policy alone had bigger costs than the available

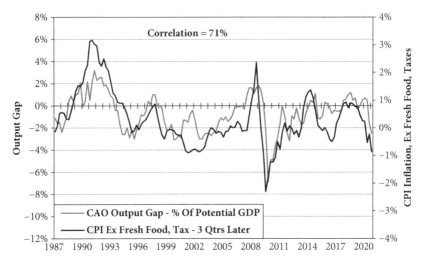

Figure 6.3 Output gap, not BOJ money, shapes ups and downs of inflation/deflation.

Source: Cabinet Office (2022b); Statistics Bureau (2022a).

Note: Stops before COVID and invasion of Ukraine, which distorted output and prices due to global supply problems.

alternatives. For almost a quarter century, interest rates had been kept close to zero, hurting the elderly who depended on interest income. The BOJ policy created a gargantuan transfer of income from tens of millions of household savers to company borrowers, thereby hurting consumer purchasing power. At the same time, a host of zombie firms are being propped up by near-zero interest rates. Monetary stimulus should have been used to finance stronger fiscal stimulus and to ease the downside effects of structural reforms, such as ones allowing the exit of zombie firms and helping their workers transition to new jobs. It should have been just one arrow in the package of three.

As with the rest of the world, Japan experienced a bout of inflation in the wake of COVID and the Russian invasion of Ukraine. Headline inflation hit a peak a bit above 4% and then, as of the summer of 2023, had fallen back to a bit above 3% However, this was not the healthy inflation the Bank of Japan was seeking. On the contrary, 90% of the rise in prices in 2022–23 came in the import-sensitive food and energy sector. This was imported inflation, caused by the rise in global commodity prices and the depreciation of the yen, which makes imports even more expensive. This kind of inflation weakens the economy even more (Katz 2023a, n.p.)

Second Arrow: Fiscal Stimulus Turned on Its Head

The original concept of the second arrow was fiscal stimulus until Japan recovered, followed by gradual tightening to bring down Japan's chronic budget deficit. In reality, Abe implemented fiscal tightening almost immediately in line with Finance Ministry diktats. What Abe gave the economy via monetary policy, he took away via fiscal tightening.

The measure of the fiscal stimulus is the primary structural deficit, what the deficit would be if the economy were operating at its full potential. When Abe returned to power, the structural deficit was 6.6% of potential GDP. Abe lowered it to 2.8%. This was done via some spending cuts, but mostly via a doubling of the consumption tax from 5% to 10%. The average yearly fiscal tightening took away 0.6% of GDP in an economy growing only 0.9% (OECD 2021b).

For almost 50 years since the late 1970s, the Ministry of Finance frightened prime ministers into pushing fiscal austerity by warning that Japan's high national debt risked a fiscal implosion. In 2010, they pointed to the Euro debt crisis as Japan's potential future. It was a fable. The only European countries that suffered a meltdown in 2010 were those that had not only big government deficits at home, but also lots of borrowing from foreign countries. There was no crisis in any country that, like Japan, could finance its own debt without borrowing overseas (Katz 2022b).

Even if Japan had been vulnerable, the BOJ's massive purchase of Japan Government Bonds (JGBs) slashed this vulnerability. The net government debt held by *private* investors—which is what matters for the risk of a crash—shrank from a peak of 148% of GDP just before Abe's ascension to 98% by late 2022, while the BOJ owns a tiny bit more (see Figure 6.4). In borrowing from the BOJ, the government is, in essence, borrowing from itself. As of 2022, despite some rise in interest rates on government bonds, the government's interest payments to private investors had fallen to a trivial 0.5% of GDP and were projected in late 2022 to be just 0.4% in 2024 (OECD 2023a).

In Japan's situation, monetary and fiscal policies are each impotent without the other. When firms cannot sell as much as they produce, they are not going to invest in new equipment just because the BOJ promises inflation or lowers the interest rate to the floor. What will cause them to invest is more demand for their products. That's what fiscal stimulus, more government spending or tax cuts, provides. On the other side of the coin, as fiscal

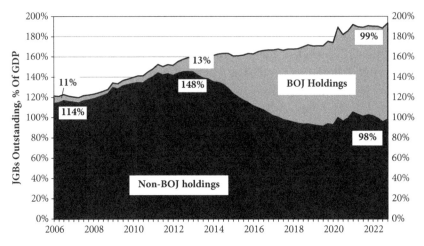

Figure 6.4 BOJ purchase of JGBs reduces net government debt.
Source: MOF (2023b); BOJ (2023a).

stimulus makes the economy grow larger and companies decide to invest in more equipment, there needs to be a proportionate increase in the money supply. Otherwise, interest rates will rise and that, in turn, will offset some of the desired stimulative effects of fiscal measures. Consequently, for fiscal stimulus to work well, it needs to be accompanied by sufficient monetary accommodation.

Admittedly, too much of past stimulus was used for boondoggles, like the notorious "bridges to nowhere" that provided construction jobs for part-time farmers, an important voter base. There is, however, no reason money could not be spent more productively, for example, on truly free public education (see Chapter 18).

Fiscal-Monetary Stimulus: Anesthesia or Narcotic?

If macroeconomic stimulus alone—that is, fiscal plus monetary stimulus—were enough to cure Japan of its economic lethargy, it would long since have done so. Japan has been running near-zero interest rates for more than a quarter century and chronic budget deficits even longer.

How did Japan become such a stimulus addict? The root cause is a chronic shortfall of private domestic demand. For decades, textbooks have taught that, for a market economy to be stable over the long term, wages have to grow around the same pace as output. If people cannot afford to buy what producers put on the store shelves, then producers will stop making them, companies will stop expanding capacity, and the economy will fall into recession. Consequently, ever since the mid-1800s, wages throughout the industrial world have, over the long haul, grown in tandem with GDP. Across the rich world, something changed beginning in the 1980s, and wages started growing only half as fast as GDP during 1997–2019 (Katz 2021c). Japan had the worst gap, with almost no growth in real compensation during that period (see again Figure 3.1 in Chapter 3).

If neither consumers nor companies are spending enough to buy what Japan could produce at full employment, someone else has to be the "buyer of last resort." For the past several decades, that has either been the government via chronic deficits or foreigners via Japan's chronic trade surplus. As with deflation, Japan's chronic budget deficit is a symptom of its problems, not the cause.

To correct the problem of structurally deficient private demand, Japan has to get employers to pay higher wages, as the IMF recommended (Aoyagi et al. 2016). Abe did that to a limited degree. For example, he pushed regular 3% hikes in the minimum wage and wanted to do so even faster until they reached ¥1,000 ($7.70) per hour. By 2019, they had reached ¥961 ($7.40). The fact is that an increase in the minimum wage would raise wages not only for workers beneath the minimum, but also for low-paid workers 10%–15% above the minimum. In 2016, the IMF calculated that, among full-timer workers, about 10% of men and 29% of women were paid less than ¥1,000 per hour. Among part-timers, the share was about 54% for men and 66% for women (Aoyagi et al. 2016: 7).

Abe and Kuroda and later Kishida did hector big corporations to hike wages by 2% per year, but companies do not raise wages just because of speeches by a prime minister. While Abe and Kishida asked for measures they had no power to extract, they refrained from doing what was in their power: enforcing the law against wage discrimination vis-à-vis women and non-regular workers.

In a transfer of income from households to corporations, and thus a further depression of demand, Tokyo raised the consumption tax on people, while cutting the income tax on corporations, from 39.5% in 2010 to 30.6% by 2020. The government claimed this would boost demand by prompting companies to invest more. This claim is belied by the fact that companies were unable to invest even the huge cash flow they were already taking in; the shortfall equaled 5%–6% of GDP in recent years (see again Figure 4.1 in Chapter 4). Nor did they send the cash out to shareholders via dividends or substantially hike wages. The tax cut just added to the fallow mountain of money in their electronic vaults.

In 2021, Kishida promised to reverse this transfer when he campaigned for the LDP presidency and thus the prime ministership. Correctly pointing out that "[i]f the fruits of growth are not redistributed [to households], consumption and demand will not increase," he contended that this syndrome was a major reason Japanese growth was so low. Using the hyperbole beloved by Japanese prime ministers, he said he was calling for "a new form of capitalism" in which there was a "virtuous cycle" between growth and distribution, including wage hikes (Katz 2022d). In reality, this was not any sort of new capitalism, but a return to what had been standard in capitalism since the mid-1800s: wages and GDP growing in tandem. In fact, economic textbooks since the 1960s have demonstrated that if wages do not keep up with GDP, then the macroeconomy will become unstable and growth will be hurt (Katz 2021c).

While it's terrific that a Japanese prime minister finally pointed out this fundamental flaw afflicting the economy, in the end, Kishida ended up doing very little of substance to remedy the problem. Asking companies to raise wages, or repeating past ineffective tax incentives, is not the same as taking the steps needed to impel them to raise wages. The latter would include measures like enforcing laws regarding equal pay for equal work and accelerating hikes in the minimum wage. Finally, in 2023, the government decided to raise the minimum wage to ¥1,000 as of 2024—13 years after first setting that goal.

In Japan, macroeconomic stimulus and structural reform need each other. Stimulus has been tried and, in the absence of reform, the economy needs larger and larger doses. At the same time, the initial depressive effects of structural reform, stopping the support for zombies, are so severe that it cannot be implemented without a macroeconomic safety net. As METI official Tatsuya Terazawa wrote, macroeconomic stimulus can be either as "anesthesia to ease the pain" of structural reform, or else as "morphine" to cover up the pain and avoid reform (Terazawa 2001). Abe, like his predecessors, chose the latter.

Third Arrow Has No Feathers

If any prime minister had the clout to push through the politically difficult third of his arrows—structural reforms aimed at raising Japan's growth
rate—it was Shinzo Abe. He had been given an unprecedented mandate by
the voters: more than two-thirds of the seats in the powerful Lower House of
the Diet for three elections in a row. He faced no viable opposition party, nor
any serious dissent within his own LDP. He increased the power of the prime
minister over the senior bureaucrats by effectively making the appointment
of 600 top officials subject to prime ministerial approval; previously the
Ministries themselves decided on all of their promotions (Mulgan 2018: 43–
48). Hence, when he pledged to be a "drill bit" breaking up the bedrock of
special interests, when he vowed "no sacred cows," people believed him.

All of this makes it a puzzle why, time and time again, he conceded to the
special interests. Consider the examples:

In 2013, Rakuten chieftain Mikitani recommended to a blue-ribbon advisory council to Abe that Tokyo permit online sales of prescription drugs to
lower prices, as in some other rich countries. Back in 2009, Rakuten had won
a Supreme Court decision against the government, enabling online sales of
nonprescription drugs. When the Abe administration rejected the recom-
mendation, due to urging from the 100,000-member pharmaceutical lobby,
Mikitani quit the panel, telling a news conference, "Abe's growth strategy was
about bringing down regulatory barriers and cultivating new businesses and
services. It's disheartening to see that now going in the opposite direction. . . .
I'm fed up" (Layne 2013). Rakuten again sued but lost. The ban remains as of
early 2022.

One of the biggest hits to household budgets is the high cost of food (see
again Figure 3.4 in Chapter 3). That results not only from tariffs and quotas
against less expensive imports, but also from the monopoly of JA (Japan
Agriculture), the gargantuan farm cooperative. JA is an octopus with dozens
of tentacles. It has 250,000 employees. It runs a trading company that sells
farmers supplies at high prices and buys their output, often at low prices.
JA's bank is the second largest in Japan. Its insurance and trading arms are
among the largest. Yet, because it has been key to LDP dominance in Japan's
rural areas, it has long been exempted from the Anti-Monopoly Law. Abe's
own regulatory reform council recommended breaking up JA, spinning off
its wholesale and marketing arms into purely private companies, restricting

co-op membership by part-time farmers, and more. Instead, Abe instead worked out a deal that Abe claimed cut JA's power, but that most observers felt watered down the advisory group's recommendations. When JA President Akira Banzai spoke at the Foreign Correspondents Club, the moderator asked him, "So, you agreed [to the deal with Abe] because there won't be much, if any, change. Is that accurate?" Banzai replied: "It's premature to lead to any conclusion about whether there will be any change or not" (FCCJ 2015: n.p.).

Academics working on another advisory council recommended that Japan achieve more flexibility in the labor market by making it easier for firms to lay off regular workers as long as they provided a big severance package. They reasoned that this would provide companies with more flexibility while preserving some security for workers. Representatives from big companies said that they wanted greater rights to lay off regular workers without being forced to give severance pay. Union representatives wanted no change in the strict protections that Japanese law and court decisions have given workers against involuntary layoffs. Abe did not intervene to break the stand-off, and little happened. On the contrary, he tried, and failed, to change the law so that employers could lay off regular workers with no mandated severance package.

Abe's supporters claim that job growth of more than 3 million into the workforce was a big victory, but it is hard to see how it's progress to put women and seniors into dead-end, low-wage non-regular work. Regarding his promise that 30% of managers would be women by 2020, the arrow couldn't fly. Nor did Abe take any steps to enforce equal pay laws for women and non-regulars.

Abe's supporters also laud assorted measures aimed at improving corporate governance at the big publicly listed corporations. First, as noted above, these big corporations employ only a small sliver of the labor force. Moreover, better corporate governance does not necessarily lead to better corporate strategy and performance in the absence of strong competition.

In the end, with a few exceptions, the third arrow amounted to little more than worthy wishes. While many of the reforms discussed would have indirectly helped entrepreneurship, one of the items would have given a big direct boost to entrepreneurship: doubling the entry and exit rate of companies to 10%. However, nothing was done to help this happen. Another goal that would have promoted entrepreneurship would have greatly increased inward foreign direct investment (FDI), the buying of domestic firms by foreign corporations, or the setting up of brand new facilities by them. FDI helps entrepreneurship because foreign firms are far more likely to partner with, and buy from, startups than are traditional domestic giants. While FDI did increase somewhat during Abe's tenure, the trend growth of FDI did not accelerate during Abe's tenure. What needs to be done to overcome the big obstacles to inward FDI will be detailed below.

Abe's coddling of special interests was no worse than his predecessors; his shortcomings stand out only because they are in such contrast to his repeated pledges. Why Abe acted as he did is a bit of a mystery. Some suggested that he wanted to spend his limited political capital on security issues. The fact is that he had the clout to do both. There is little question that Abe wanted the economy to revive but, for some reason, he would not do what it would take to get results. Cynics say all his talk about the third arrow was just rhetoric to appeal to voters and foreign stock market investors whom he repeatedly exhorted to "buy my Abenomics." Abe's political advisers believed higher stock prices would boost Abe's approval ratings. One of his advisors told him that, if he wanted a comeback, he had to convince voters that he had a dramatic plan for economic revival and that this, not security issues as in 2006, was his top priority. He may have believed the line peddled by some of his advisors that monetary stimulus was all that was needed for recovery. If so, then why spend his political capital on steps that would alienate powerful special interests?

Abe's pulse quickened when talking about security issues, but he was bored by the details of economic policy. Some bureaucrats who had initially been so enthusiastic told me of their gradual disenchantment, of seeing his eyes glaze over when they briefed him on this or that reform. Indeed, six years earlier, when Abe succeeded Koizumi for a one-year stint, he immediately readmitted to the LDP all of the Diet members that Koizumi had expelled for voting against Koizumi's postal reform.

Abe often claimed that his efforts were Japan's last chance for revival. The muse of history is kind in giving nations plenty of last chances. The failure of Abenomics does not mean Japan is doomed, merely that Abe blew his opening.

PART III

WHO BECOMES
AN ENTREPRENEUR?

7

Risk-Averse Culture or Risk versus Reward?

"Is it a chicken-and-egg problem?" I asked Mikihide Katsumata, president of the government's Innovation Network Corporation of Japan (INCJ), an organization tasked with, among other things, investing like a VC firm in promising startups (Interview October 2017). I wondered whether too many potential Japanese entrepreneurs didn't even try because they felt they could not get VC funding, and VCs couldn't attract enough investor money because they saw too few entrepreneurial opportunities. His answer came as a surprise. "It's not a chicken and egg issue; it's an egg issue. There are not enough entrepreneurs. Up until five or six years ago, not many people in Japan dared to start a growing business. They tended to go to bigger companies."

It was surprising to hear that from the head of an organization charged with funding such opportunities, but it's not an unusual one. On the contrary, the Japanese have been told so many times that they are too risk-averse and conformist to start a business on their own that many have come to believe it.

To the extent that this view holds any water, it provides no more than a fraction of the story. The anti-entrepreneurial cliché is no truer than when Japanese were told a couple of decades ago that, for cultural reasons, Japanese liked to save, and Americans liked to spend. Then, changing economic conditions lowered Japan's household savings from double-digit rates to a level even lower than their American counterparts. For decades it was said that Japanese were inherently non-litigious. Then the fees for filing cases were dropped and lawsuits jumped. As detailed below, the memes of "corporation as family" and "employee loyalty to the company" stem not from age-old culture but from a propaganda campaign by employers beginning early

The Contest for Japan's Economic Future. Richard Katz, Oxford University Press. © Richard Katz 2024.
DOI: 10.1093/oso/9780197675106.003.0008

in the 20th century. In fact, many of the alleged age-old cultural traditions are modern reifications—very new wine bottled to look like vintage (Vlastos 1998).

I have repeatedly asked 20-something urban career women in Tokyo: in terms of your hopes, dreams, frustrations, and sense of self, are you more like your grandmother or your counterpart in New York? Almost invariably, the reply is their counterpart in New York. In the initial post–World War II years, when Japan was still a very traditional agricultural society, most marriages were still arranged. Now that the country is highly urban and more women receive higher education, arranged marriages have virtually disappeared. This transformation is typical of modernization in all countries.

Cultural explanations of economic behavior have proved highly problematic. In the 1950s, scholars pointed to Confucianism as the cause of Japan's economic backwardness, not realizing that the miracle was already taking off. Then, success in Japan, followed by Korea, Taiwan, China, and so many others, led to a 180-degree reversal. Confucianism, it was now argued, drove that success. A prime example was Ronald Dore's influential 1977 book, *Taking Japan Seriously: A Confucian Perspective on Leading Economic Issues*. Next came the 1997–1998 financial cataclysm in Asia, and yet another reversal. Now, Confucianism was to blame because it led to crony capitalism. It is hard to see how a theory that claims to explain everything, and its opposite, actually explains much at all (Whyte 1994).

No one denies that cultural differences among countries have some impact, but is it 80% of the story, or just 20%? While culture changes slowly, how that manifests itself in behavior changes far more rapidly in response to changing conditions. Is Korean culture that of South Korea, or the North? Is Chinese culture that of Mao's China, Deng Xiaoping's China, or of Taiwan or Singapore? It is changing conditions, not culture, which explains why American rates of entrepreneurship have fallen over the last four decades, as detailed below. Delving into those changing conditions, whether in Japan or the United States, not only provides a better explanation; more importantly, it gives policymakers levers to change outcomes by changing the socioeconomic context.

Adverse Risk-Reward Ratio

Japanese thinking of starting a potential gazelle face a far more adverse risk-reward ratio than do Americans or Europeans.

Consider the lifetime employment practices that stem—not from the era of Prince Shotoku in the 7th century[1]—but from top-down changes introduced after World War I and World War II. Someone leaving a good regular job at a big firm to start a new firm, or work for one, has little chance of ever being hired as a regular at another top firm if the startup goes belly-up. Firms that invest in training workers do not want them to take that knowledge elsewhere, and so they've created an informal no-poaching pact among themselves. Not surprisingly, then, when surveyed about their biggest fear in starting a business, Japanese respondents came in first in answering "losing a secure job with a guaranteed annual income" (OECD 2013b: 86).

Beyond this, much more than elsewhere, banks in Japan are very loath to lend to an SME without collateral and/or a personal guarantee. If the firm fails, the borrower will have to use one's house, savings accounts, and so forth (details below).

If an SME fails, the owner and co-guarantor can seek personal bankruptcy, but Japan's personal bankruptcy laws are very harsh. Research has shown that the more draconian the bankruptcy laws, the lower the rate of entrepreneurship (Solomon 2014; Eberhart et al. 2017).

In a survey of 24 rich countries (OECD 2013b: 83), Japan came in last in the number of respondents who said that the school system helped to develop a sense of initiative and an entrepreneurial attitude (18% vs. an OECD average of 50%) and last in saying school gave them the skills and know-how to run a business (20%).

The proverbial Japanese mother reluctant to have her daughter marry an entrepreneur has a realistic sense of the stumbling blocks. It's no different than the comedically frantic mother in a Jane Austen novel feverishly seeking a good marriage for her daughter; the Austen mother knew that, absent a good marriage, the young woman risked penury in an age that offered daughters of the gentry little right to inherit and few ways to earn a living.

We heard a classic in-law anecdote from Jeffrey Char, an American serial entrepreneur who married a Japanese woman. Char likes to create new companies, bring them to a certain size, and then sell them, only to start anew on another firm. When he was running the firm, they were happy he

---

[1] Prince Shotoku (574–622 CE) is revered for bringing Buddhism and Confucianism to Japan, unifying warring clans into a unified state, creating a constitution, and instilling various cultural attitudes, such as *wa* (harmony).

had a lucrative job. When he sold one—at a profit—they worried he was jobless again.

On the other hand, consider my cousin, who was working at Hewlett-Packard during the dot.com boom of the 1990s. His boss—who had developed a server that had four times the capacity with no more heat—wanted to start a new firm and take my cousin with him. If they succeeded, they'd be millionaires. What if they failed? HP offered to buy around 10%–15% of the new firm and promised that they could get their old jobs back. Needless to say, his mother-in-law was delighted.[2]

Put my cousin in the Japanese situation and bring Japanese citizens to Silicon Valley and each of their behaviors would be very different.

Assessing the Evidence for the Risk-Averse, Conformist Explanation

There are widely cited studies that are interpreted as showing that Japanese are more risk-averse and conformist and thus lack the entrepreneurial impulse. The Global Entrepreneurship Monitor, for example, repeatedly shows Japan coming in at or near the bottom in all sorts of entrepreneurial attitudes, including perceived opportunities (49th out of 49); perceived capabilities in entrepreneurial skills (49th of 49); fear of failure (9th highest out of 49); and seeing entrepreneurship as a good career choice (46th out of 49th) (GEM 2018–2019: 88).

A closer look at the data suggests, not that Japanese are inherently more fearful, but that there is more to fear. In a survey, about 37% of Japanese men reported that they would rather take a risk and start a new business than work for someone else, which is about 80% as high as the median country. But just 20% think it's feasible, only half the typical rate (OECD 2020f). So, the biggest difference is not the desire to become an entrepreneur, but the perception of its prudence, given conditions in Japan. While fixing deep-seated cultural proclivities is hard, remedying adverse risk-reward ratios in a country's environment is far less difficult.

The most widely cited scholarly source on this topic is Geert Hofstede. In 1965, Hofstede founded the personnel research department of IBM

---

[2] As it turned out, the venture became a victim of bad timing: the arrival of the dot.com bust; but my cousin easily found a new position.

Europe. Between 1967 and 1973, he ran a large survey regarding differences in values of 117,000 IBM employees across different countries. He is cited so often, partly because he collected the most comprehensive cross-country data. His data and commentary appeared to show Japanese as both risk-averse and collectivist, both attitudes that Hofstede says militate against entrepreneurship. He showed similar handicaps in other Asian countries. Then came the Asian economic miracle; lo and behold, Hofstede came out with his own "Confucianism is good" commentary. In his version, not all Confucian attitudes help growth, only the attitudes that he favors (Hofstede and Bond 1988).

Few scholars citing Hofstede have bothered to note that IBM has its own culture, and that the company selects those within each country most amenable to its culture. It turns out that other Japanese display very different attitudes from IBM employees. In one example, noted above, Japanese and American MBA students shared a wide variety of attitudes such as "I love being a champion for my ideas, even against others," and "I love to challenge the status quo." This all sounds much like the burning technological adventurers we saw at Sharp in the 1960s.

A common symbol of the alleged Japanese urge to conform are the oft-published photos of new college grads, both male and female, showing up on recruitment day at a prestigious firm, all wearing identical black suits with white shirts or blouses. People infer that this is how it has always been. Yet, Professor Tadashi Takiguchi, who teaches entrepreneurship at Waseda University, showed me a newspaper article demonstrating that this is a fairly recent development. *Nikkei* (2010) ran an article with two contrasting photos: both on recruitment day at Japan Airlines, one from 1986 and one from 2010. In the former, the women, while conservatively attired, were as different from each other as one would see in other countries; in the latter, they were wearing the "uniform" (*Nikkei* 2010).

Nikkei saw the change as the product of cutbacks in hiring. It seems that, during what was called the "ice age for jobs" in the lost decades, college grads, desperate to get good jobs, started reading advice books, and the latter all tended to advocate the black suit/white top uniform. This is one of the many ways in which, since 1990, so many Japanese young adults have become more cautious, while a smaller share have become more adventurous.

Often, behavior interpreted as conformity is something else altogether, as was demonstrated by Toshio Yamagishi, a retired professor of psychology, in a remarkable variation on the famous "red pen" experiment (Yamagishi et al. 2008). In a 1999 experiment, when members of a group were given a box with four blue pens and one red, 70% of Americans, but only 53% of Japanese, selected the red pen. Note that even among the Japanese, a slight majority chose the unique pen. Yamagishi believed that the motivation of the Japanese was not conformity, but rather sociability and concern for reputation. He then ran the experiment with new participants, telling them that they were the last to choose. With concern about the desires of others no longer a factor, the number of Japanese choosing the unique pen rose to the same level as the Americans. When asked about going to a store with just one red and four blue pens on the shelf—where offending someone else was not an issue—slightly more Japanese than Americans said that they would "definitely" choose the unique pen.

Changed Promotion System Trained Employees to Avoid Risk

One can easily find some risk-averse attitudes among employees on the managerial track. Much of this reflects new criteria for promotion that began in the big banks in the 1970s and then spread throughout much of the corporate world. Called *genten shugi* (loosely translated as "demerit system"), here's how it works. Under a positive assessment system (*katen shugi*), staffers aiming for promotion get positive evaluations for achievements that meet or exceed the performance goal. Under the *genten shugi* system, the employees get negative evaluations for mistakes or failures. But it's asymmetric: no extra credit is given for outstanding success; that is regarded as just doing one's job. The result is predictable. People focus on avoiding mistakes; they stay away from ideas outside the box. A potential home-run hitter will limit himself to singles to avoid striking out. People do innovate, but in conformity with current business models. This is not a cultural proclivity; it's a learned behavior rooted in one type of incentive system, a relatively recent one at that. Under a different system, it would be unlearned. However, those who have climbed the ladder via the *genten shugi* system tend to recruit and promote those comfortable with that approach. While many companies like SONY and Nomura Securities have abandoned *genten shugi*, many others still adhere to it.

A survey found that *genten shugi* hurt bank performance in dealing with troubled customers. The survey asked 1,000 early and mid-career bank employees whether the personnel evaluation systems in their workplaces were primarily demerit-based or merit-based, the former being one in which "bank officers get *irreversible* negative marks if they fail [emphasis added]." Nearly half the respondents said their bank relied strongly on *genten shugi*. The survey then asked whether one of their bank's strengths is "to provide support to a company [borrower] until the very end." This would include the more challenging task of helping the firm improve its strategy and management, a practice that used to be a mainstay of Japanese banking. Even in banks using a merit-based system, only 55% still provided SMEs with that kind of advice and support. It was even worse, just 45%, in the demerit-based banks, and a truly dismal 20% in banks that were intensifying their reliance on *genten shugi* (Yamori and Yoneda 2019).

It is not impossible for decades-old corporate giants to change practices ingrained by counterproductive promotion criteria, but it often takes a big shock. Two of the most famous cases of reform occurred when companies hit rock bottom and were taken over by foreign enterprises: Nissan and Sharp. Notably, both cases involved the intervention of foreign firms.

Before the alliance with Renault in 1999, Nissan had suffered net losses in seven years out of eight. Renault, having bought 37% of Nissan, installed Carlos Ghosn as CEO and he brought it to record profitability within just a couple of years. "A friend of mine joined Nissan forty years ago," Professor Higashide recalled when we met in June 2018. A creative man when he was young, the friend eventually rose to administrative manager in global marketing and later quality management. "But by the time he was in his mid-forties, he had become so bureaucratic. He didn't want to try anything new, and just did what he was asked." When Renault came in, said Higashide, his friend's mindset dramatically changed in just two years because he was asked to come up with solutions. "So, people's mindset has been shifted from 'I don't want to make any mistakes,' to 'We need to try something.'" Sharp went through similar changes after being purchased by Foxconn of Taiwan.

Entrepreneurs Have Their Own Culture

Suppose for the sake of argument that the typical Japanese citizen was, by nature, more risk-averse than those in other countries; the fact is that ambitious entrepreneurs are a small minority in all countries, and they have a distinct personality type. When cross-country studies focused only on entrepreneurs, the results for Japan were similar to those elsewhere. One study found that "desire for self-actualization and creativity, which are individualist motives, tended to drive founders of Japanese high-technology startups." Another found that, in 13 countries, founders of new companies had different attitudes from non-founders. In fact, successful Japanese founders of entrepreneurial firms had more in common with successful American entrepreneurs than with other Japanese executives (Tiessen 1997: 372; McGrath and McMillan 1992; Deshpande et al. 2013: 231, 244).

A young, iconoclastic Bill Gates or Steve Jobs working out of a garage is the common image of a successful entrepreneur. That, however, is the exception, not the rule. The more common experience was captured in a survey by Ernst and Young, creators of the World Entrepreneur of the Year Program. More than half of the founders previously spent time in traditional employment before setting out on their own. Moreover, they reported that the knowledge and experience gained at a university and then in a traditional corporate environment were vital to their future success (Ernst and Young 2011: 5).

At the same time, not everyone can become an entrepreneur. Research has shown that they bear some common personality traits. Among the most important is a sense of self-efficacy, the belief that one's own actions can create desired results. This is complemented by a mindset that sees opportunities where others see disruption, along with an acceptance of calculated risk and a tolerance of failure (Ernst and Young 2011: 5).

Entrepreneurs across the world also tend to share a personality type and set of attitudes called entrepreneurial orientation, which includes such desires as: achieving a higher position for myself in society, adding challenge to my life, improving my own abilities, improving the quality of life for my family and myself, and having high personal earnings. A study of this found that, to a degree that surprised them, American and Japanese entrepreneurs shared this personality type (Deshpande et al. 2013: 240).

Some observers would offer the rejoinder that, even if Japanese entrepreneurs share the same personality type as entrepreneurs elsewhere, Japan engenders fewer people with entrepreneurial personalities than other countries. There may be some truth to this. If most entrepreneurs have a corporate background and attitudes like *genten shugi* are far too common, or companies give managers little autonomy, that would undoubtedly have an impact. In any case, as the next few chapters will argue, the primary obstacle in Japan lies in a harsh institutional environment that provides fewer of the ingredients that lead people to try entrepreneurialism, plus smaller rewards for success as well as harsher penalties for failure than elsewhere.

Even in countries widely considered to be entrepreneurial, like the United States, it's only a thin slice of the population that starts companies with non-family employees: just 3.9% of men in the typical OECD country versus 1.4% in Japan (OECD 2022f).[3] So, Japan's shortfall from the rest of the OECD is just 2.5 percentage points. It would not take more than an additional couple percent of Japan's adults to become entrepreneurs—and a larger group willing to work for them—to alter the country's dynamic. If Japan could ameliorate some of the factors inhibiting people from even trying, and impeding the success of those who dare, reducing the entrepreneurship gap seems a very attainable goal. Policies and politics, not culture, will be the primary determinants of whether or not Japan takes the right road. We can see below the same forces in action by looking at the decline in entrepreneurship in the United States.

What Does Declining Entrepreneurship in the United States Tell Us about Japan?

Few Americans, caught up in the romance of Silicon Valley, are even aware that the United States is no longer anywhere near as entrepreneurial as it used to be. Four decades ago, the number of new companies born every year added up to 14% of existing companies; these days, the birth rate is just 8%. In 1988, 30% of all employees worked for companies under 10 years old. By 2018, this had almost halved to just 18%. This, economists say, is one of the major factors in the disappointing growth of American GDP and living standards.

What explains this decline? Those preferring cultural explanations point out that Japan comes in 9th among 49 countries in the prevalence of fear of failure (GEM 2019: 88). But, consider this: the share of 25–34-year-old Americans saying fear of failure deterred them from starting their own business jumped from 24% in 2001 to 41% in 2015. Surveys of young adults show that desire to become an entrepreneur is as strong as ever. However,

---

[3] The rates for men are chosen because female entrepreneurship in Japan is extraordinarily low.

Americans aged 18–34 report that they are deterred by a lack of access to credit and risks in the economy (Kauffman Foundation 2011).

Imagine you've just graduated from college, and, like so many of your cohorts, you've had to borrow $32,000 to pay for it. If you're a typical grad, your payments will add up to about $4,800 per year while your salary during your first five years will be about $48,000. So, your payments will take a hefty 10% of your earnings. If you lose your job, you'll still owe $400 every month. If you've gone on to get a graduate degree—as is the case with a quarter of entrepreneurs—you've added another $66,000 in debt. You could end up still paying off that debt in your forties, just like Barack and Michelle Obama— that's if you get a good job. If you don't get that good job, or you lose the one you had, you may default on your loans, as one out of every five graduates does. It will become hard for you to borrow even to buy a car, let alone buy a home or start a business.

Given all this, how willing would you be to risk leaving a high-paying se- cure job to take the risk of taking that exciting job at a new company, let alone starting one, when you know that it's more likely to go out of business than succeed?

In 2015, economists at the Federal Reserve found that over the years 2000– 2009 just a few percentage points increase in student debt as a share of all consumer debt caused a 12% decrease in the number of new firms with 5–9 employees and a 6% decline in startups with at least 20 employees (Ambrose et al. 2015: 5, 16). The Kaufmann Foundation summed it up: "Saddled with student loan debt," now in the stratosphere at $1.7 trillion for 44 mil- lion Americans, "millennials can't afford to be entrepreneurs" (Simon and Barr 2015).

Then there is the obstacle of America's employer-based healthcare insur- ance system. Health insurance is so expensive that many employees are loath to leave a job with good health insurance to create, or work for, a startup that cannot afford to provide it. Obamacare has helped, but not enough to make a difference in business formation.

The slowdown in US productivity growth in recent years has not been caused by any deceleration in the rate of technological innovation. Rather, it's the decline in the business conveyer belt: the growth of companies able to turn that innovation into desirable products. Not only are there fewer startups, but the businesses most important in spurring recent innovations are having difficulty expanding, and thus, their innovations are failing to make as much impact on the economy as a whole (Bureau of Labor Statistics 2021: n.p.).

Whether we look at the United States or Japan, the evidence seems overwhelming: economic and political conditions, not national cultures, best explain changes in the rate of entrepreneurship.

8

Who Doesn't Get to Become
an Entrepreneur?

One of the reasons Japan has so few entrepreneurs is that certain sections of society are de facto excluded. Older people start fewer new growth-oriented businesses, and Japan is aging. Women face even higher obstacles to entrepreneurship than men, from a lack of managerial experience at traditional companies to greater difficulty in getting credit from banks. And, in a country where early-stage finance is scarce, people who aren't affluent won't have the access to the funds needed for a successful startup.

The aging of Japan is a double-edged sword. On the one hand, it intensifies the need for a productivity revolution. On the other hand, it reduces the capability to pull off such a revolution. Not only do aging societies produce fewer entrepreneurs, but SMEs run by older executives perform less well.

In Japan, as elsewhere, most entrepreneurs start their companies between the ages of 27 and 43 and have had experience at a bigger firm before starting their own. Most people under 27 have too little experience in seeing how a business works and in managing others. Fewer people over 43 are as open to fresh ideas (Liang et al. 2014).

Unfortunately, as a population ages, more and more of the managerial posts are filled with the middle-aged, leaving fewer slots for the young to fill. Consequently, employees don't get their first management post until they are far older than in the past. Back in the high-growth era, Japan was a young country, with a median age of just 24 in 1955, gradually reaching 37 in 1990. By 2019, however, the median had risen to 47 (see Figure 8.1).

As Japan aged, it took longer for young employees to become managers. Back in 1976, among all those reaching the first managerial rung—subsection chief (*kakaricho*)—32% did so no later than age 35. By 2016, that share was down to 14%. Worse yet, 68% had to wait until they were over age 40. In 1976, 25% of those becoming department chiefs (*bucho*), the highest management rank below director, did so before age 40; by 2016, only 10% did so.

The Contest for Japan's Economic Future. Richard Katz, Oxford University Press. © Richard Katz 2024.
DOI: 10.1093/oso/9780197675106.003.0009

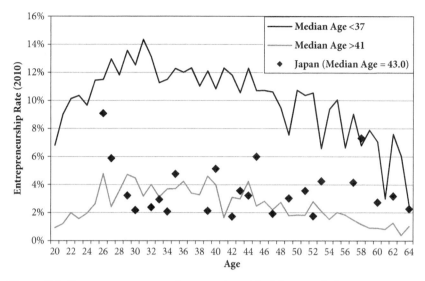

Figure 8.1 Fewer entrepreneurs in countries with older populations.

Source: Liang et al. (2014).

Note: The share of entrepreneurs per age cohort in Japan is lower than the "over 41" gray line until age 40 or so, and then increasingly higher than the gray line from age 50 onward.

Those without at least some managerial experience may start an SME, but they don't do as well unless they're able to hire skilled managers. No matter how great the founder's vision, lack of managerial experience does not bode well for company growth, or even survival (see Figure 8.2).

A younger population is just one of the reasons for the fact that half of America's top 10 high-tech companies in 2014 were founded in the previous 20 years, and their founder's age averaged a mere 28. In countries where the median age is under 37, around 10% of people from age 20 to 64 are entrepreneurs with non-family employees; by contrast, the figure is just 2.5% in countries where the median age is over 41 (Liang et al. 2014: 8).

The consequence of aging is not just fewer startups, but that more of Japan's founders are older. Back in 1979, a quarter of founders were under 30; by 2012, this was down to 12%, and a third of new SMEs were created by people over age 60 (METI 2014: 184). One reason for the latter figure is that, at medium and large firms, Japanese lifetime employees are forced to retire from their high-paying jobs at around age 60 (it used to be 55, and the government wants firms to raise it to 65). If they need to work, many can get a second career, sometimes at the firm from which they just retired, but at a

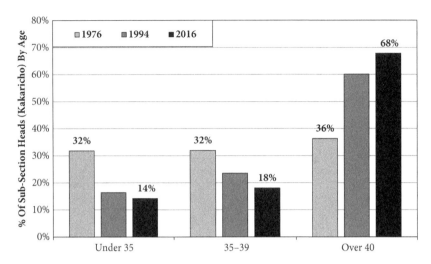

Figure 8.2 As Japan aged, employees had to wait longer to become managers.
Source: Dore (1996: 9); 2016 data: MHLW (2016).
Note: 1976 and 1994 data cover firms with at least 1,000 employees.

lower salary. Alternatively, they can start a tiny company with perhaps a few non-family employees. These older founders aim at being mice, not gazelles.

There is a silver lining in the gray cloud here. Many of these retirees would be a valuable resource if only there were a system to link with them younger, smaller startups. They know enough about management to be consultants to would-be founders of gazelles who have vision but insufficient experience, as we saw at Raksul.

All this has led to two adverse trends. First, the age of owners/CEOs is rising, and the age of the SME itself is rising, with Japanese SMEs being the oldest among 18 countries in the OECD (see Figure 8.3). Thirty years ago, the average age of retirement of a CEO at an SME was around 62; now it's around 70 and rising (METI 2018a: 357).

SMEs led by those over age 60 or 65 simply don't perform as well as those with young leaders. Elderly owners tend to put priority on making sure that their company can survive, not taking the sometimes-risky steps needed to make it thrive. This was brought home to me when I heard the story of a metallurgical firm bought out by NSSK, a low-and-mid-cap private equity firm in Tokyo. Founded in 2014, its business strategy is to buy firms that are already good and have the potential to be even better—often firms with an aging owner having no clear successor. NSSK CEO Jun Tsusaka, a veteran of

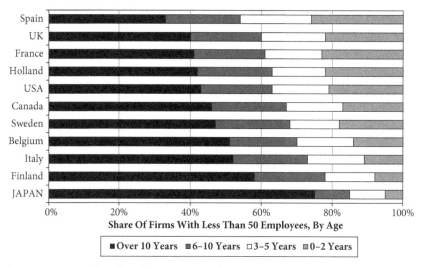

Figure 8.3 Japan has the oldest SMEs in the OECD.

Source: Criscuolo et al. (2014: 28).

Note: To avoid clutter, only 11 of the 18 countries are shown in the chart.

US private equity giant TPG, told me that the metallurgical firm was profitable and doing well enough but hardly setting the world on fire. Its CEO, who was in his sixties, wanted to retire and turn the top job over to the plant manager, a non-relative who was age 43. But there was a snag that afflicts most such firms. In order to get loans from the banks, the new CEO would also have to provide his own personal guarantee for the bank loans the retiring CEO had obtained. That is, if the firm failed, he would be personally liable for the firm's debt. The plant manager could not afford it.

Consequently, the CEO sold the firm 100% to NSSK. All the banks that had been hesitant to lend were now falling all over themselves to do so. They figured NSSK had done the due diligence. NSSK made the same plant manager the new CEO.

Revenues tripled and profits quadrupled within just a few years. How was this possible? "We invested a lot in the most modern machinery and increased capacity," Tsusaka explained (Interview June 2018). If that's all it took, then, why, I wondered, didn't the old CEO do it? Was this a case, I asked Tsusaka, of an older CEO just wanting to sustain the status quo and not take a risk by borrowing and investing, whereas the younger man was focused on the future? "It was," he replied. The older CEO was thinking how risky it would be to borrow to invest; the younger man about how risky it would be *not* to invest, how vulnerable his company would be if his competitors modernized and expanded, but he did not. Younger executives and entrepreneurs are not necessarily more tolerant of risk; sometimes, they just have a different perception of where the risk lies.

This story is hardly unique. Firms headed by young managers are more likely to accept innovations that differ quite radically from their predecessors (Acemoglu et al. 2014). METI data show that SMEs headed by older executives regularly perform less well than those headed by younger leaders. Among medium-sized enterprises run by executives age 70 years and older, only 16% reported that profits were rising, compared to 28% for firms run by someone under 40. Looking toward the future, only 32% of elderly executives wanted to expand the company versus 56% of executives under 40 (METI 2013: 126). While achieving high growth is hard at all firms, older CEOs succeed less often than their younger counterparts (see Figure 8.4), often because their views are stuck in strategies that no longer work. The rate of profit is consistently and measurably higher at firms that have replaced their aging CEO manager with one between the ages of 55 and 64 (METI 2016a: 463).

Katsuyuki Kamei, a professor who teaches entrepreneurship at Kansai University, told me of his own experiences with the generation gap. Often, older CEOs of SMEs will send their son or daughter—whom they expect to

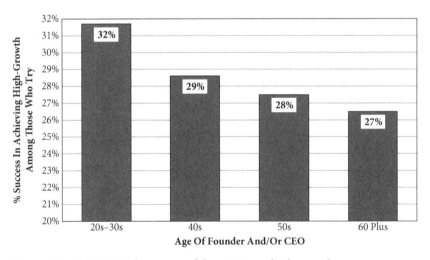

Figure 8.4 Older CEOs less successful in attaining high growth.

Source: METI (2017a: 211).

Note: Figures show the percentage of SMEs achieving high growth only among those seeking that as a goal, as opposed to seeking stable growth, or mere survival.

succeed them—to a business school to pick up basic management skills that many SME executives lack due to their on-the-job training approach. "But then," recounts Kamei, "They don't listen when the child says, 'I learned such and such about the management of finance.' Understanding finance is a very basic thing, but many SME managers don't actually know very much about it. So, these older SME leaders are happy to see their children gain some skills, but they don't welcome any ideas different from their own" (Interview October 2019).

If You Start Too Small, You'll Never Get Bigger

New enterprises that start off too small stay small—if they survive at all. Those who start off with sufficient equipment and staff are more likely not only to survive, but thrive (Audretsch 2012; Agarwal et al. 2001). That takes money. One study showed that, for every additional $100,000 that an entrepreneur was able to plow into his new company, revenue was 35% higher and hiring was 24% higher (Frid and Wyman 2016: 26).

Since access to credit does not come easy in any country, founders have to fall back on their own funds or that of friends and family. In Japan, the problem is even more severe. In a survey of 1,000 Japanese startups, a third of the companies relied entirely on the founder's own assets; 57% of the money for all 1,000 came from the founders' own assets. Only half the firms obtained any credit at all from lending institutions, private or governmental (Higuchi et al. 2007; Kutsuna and Yasuda 2005).

A study in Germany found that, among firms that invested less than 20,000 Deutsche marks (DM), only 45% survived five years. By contrast, for firms starting off with 50,000 DM or more, the five-year survival rate was 84% (Brüderl et al. 1992: 235). In a study of 5,000 American startups three years after their founding date, the firms that got business loans from banks from the start achieved double the revenue of firms with no loans (Cole and Sokolyk 2018: 24). Most importantly, when would-be entrepreneurs have trouble getting outside funding, the overall growth of the economy is lower (Kambayashi 2017: 79).

Unfortunately, would-be founders in their twenties and thirties—those most likely to create gazelles—have little financial assets of their own. Three of out every five founders in that age group reported that their financial assets were too small to suit the needs of the new company (METI 2002: 54).

Where wealth plays the role of gatekeeper, who can't get through the door? Not the wealthy with talent, nor the poor with neither talent nor ambition. Rather, it's the less affluent with both talent and drive. In the United States, insufficient funding kept 1.3% of the population from trying entrepreneurship (Evans and Jovanovic 1989). While 1.3% may sound small, it's a big number relative to current entrepreneurship rates: just 1.4% of men in Japan versus 3.9% in the typical OECD country (OECD 2020f).

In 2010, Takehiko Yasuda pioneered investigations of this issue in Japan. Looking at more than 600 firms with up to 20 employees, he examined which factors most determined whether a firm was profitable at age 10. He included the age of the firm as well as its owner, its size, the owner's education, income level, wealth, parental occupations, experience in business, gender, and size of a previous employer. Wealth, or lack of it, was by far the most important factor. Comparing founders with personal assets of more than ¥30 million ($230,000 versus those with less than ¥5 million ($38,000), he found that 82% more of the firms with richer founders were profitable compared to the baseline (Yasuda 2010).

In the absence of sufficient credit, it is no small thing in Japan to put together the necessary funding. In 2001, the average cost of starting a new enterprise was ¥15.4 million ($118,000) (METI 2002: 56). That's 4.6 times the annual compensation of a 30–34-year-old male regular employee with a college degree at that time (MHLW 2002). For a small, but nontrivial fraction, the initial required investment was ¥40–80 million ($310,000–620,000) or more.

Given that wages in Japan are determined more by seniority than by occupation, the predicament is particularly hard for younger employees. In 2000, only 25% of male employees had incomes above ¥5 million ($38,000), but that was the income of 75% of all founders of new SMEs aged 3–8 years. Only 1% of male employees had incomes above ¥10 million ($77,000), but a third of the owners of young SMEs had incomes that high (see Figure 8.5).

If new SMEs had greater access to credit, then the founders' wealth would not matter. Because such access is deficient, 72% of Japan's new SMEs are created by more affluent people and by those over 40 years old (Yasuda 2006: 14, 16). When people under age 40 do create SMEs, their financial constraints cause the firms to start off smaller, with fewer workers, less investment in equipment, and less R&D. SMEs younger than 10 years who are able to get a loan are also able to expand their capital stock far more. How

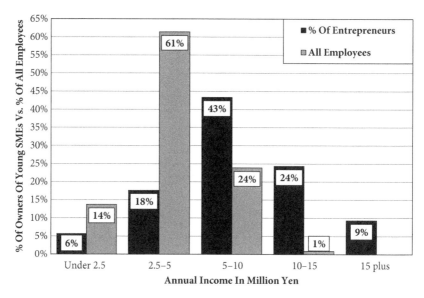

Figure 8.5 Entrepreneurs in Japan need high incomes.
Source: Yasuda (2006: 16); MHLW (2017c).
Note: Employee income for males only (who earn more than women).

many potential gazelles failed to fulfill that potential merely for lack of funds (see Figure 8.6)?

The Hit to R&D and Innovation

Surprisingly, R&D is often an even stronger contributor to a firm's growth than its investment in tangible assets, and this appears to be even truer for newcomers. For a would-be gazelle, it is innovation in either products or processes that leads customers to their door. METI found that, while innovating companies of all ages and sizes grow faster, the growth gap between the innovators and non-innovators is even stronger for younger, smaller companies (METI 2002: 87).

The downside is that R&D and innovation are not without risk. Smaller firms that spend a lot of money on trying to develop patents are more likely to fail than those who don't try. But, if they do survive, then they grow much faster (Motohashi 2011: 12). The outcome is not always in the entrepreneur's control. A promising entrepreneur can spend a lot of time and money on

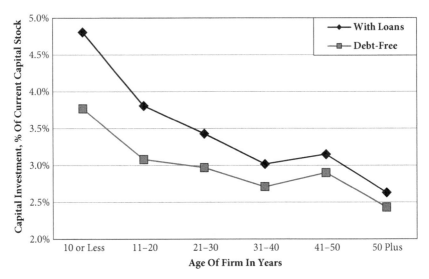

Figure 8.6 Young SMEs without loans cannot invest as much.
Source: METI (2016a: 340).

Note: If a firm has ¥100 million worth of plant, equipment, and software, and adds another ¥5 million in a given year, the investment ratio is 5%.

developing new products or processes, only to see them fail. This was brought home to me when I met with Masahiro Ito, who as a young man created his own company to develop a smartphone operating system that he believed could compete with NTT Docomo's then-dominant iMode system. He wasn't the only one; Android beat him to the punch and Ito's company was finished. Fortunately for him, he was hired by Start Today, a highly successful startup, and became its CEO for engineering. He is happy at Start Today, but a part of him still wishes he had his own company. Credit can tide a company over during rough patches that are not as fatal as Android was for Ito. Consequently, the problems of scarce bank financing for SMEs, in general, apply even more strongly to would-be innovators among the SMEs, due to their higher level of risk (Okamuro 2006). In the absence of fallback options like Start Today, how many young entrepreneurs would even try?

Rather than take that chance, too many potential innovators choose to optimize their chances of survival by limiting their investment in R&D. In Japan, the share of patents held by medium-sized enterprises (20–250 employees) compared to all firms is the lowest in the OECD: just 27% compared to 60% in a typical country (OECD 2013a: 195).

Up or Out

A firm has to reach a certain minimum efficient scale (MES) in order to be competitive. This scale, of course, differs from sector to sector. An agribusiness cultivating cucumbers can be a lot smaller than a company assembling autos. However, there's a catch-22: it cannot reach the MES until it's either competitive enough to seize market share or has access to credit to keep it going until it reaches the required size (Harada 2003).

Insufficient credit not only leads many promising firms to fail because they cannot reach MES quickly enough, but also affects what strategy they choose. For example, more initial capital permits a retail store to carry a broader mix of merchandise, or a firm to undertake more ambitious projects. Six of eight prior studies showed more initial capital was associated with better long-term performance (Cooper et al. 1997: 19).

This produces a very strong up-or-out trend among potential gazelles. Firms that can reach MES within a few years not only survive but go on to thrive. As they grow, they become more productive, via learning curve effects, economies of scale, and the like. At the same time, the more productive they become, the more they increase their competitiveness and see their profits soar, enabling them to finance even more investment and R&D. Some are funded internally and some because they can now attract more credit. This virtuous cycle turns good growth into high growth, and, in a few cases, explosive growth. These firms become the gazelles. On the other hand, if they fail to get on a trajectory to reach the MES quickly, then the money runs out and they die. Half of new entrants are gone in just four years (Motohashi 2011: 8).

The dearth of credit for newcomers in Japan causes all too many entrepreneurs to avoid productive sectors where the MES is too high. It also denies innovative SMEs the breathing space needed to endure the initial experimental phase when the path forward is not clear-cut (Cooper et al. 1997: 14–15). If a firm has access to credit, it can withstand rough times. If it knows it will have no such access, it is more likely to limit its investments lest it run into trouble. Sometimes, there is a trade-off between steps needed for a firm to thrive and the caution needed to ensure that it survives. Japan's death of capital tips the balance too much toward surviving rather than thriving.

Think of the consequences for Japan when initial wealth, more than talent or education, divides those who dare from those with too little money to dare.

Career Women—Hidden Treasure for Gazelles

Walk into a newer firm in Japan and you'll see a sight rare at many traditional ones: lots of career women and even female managers. That difference tells us a lot about why entrepreneurs are harder to find in Japan. Countries where women play a smaller role in the labor force have fewer entrepreneurs. Founders of new firms with non-family employees are only a small percentage of the labor force in the typical OECD country, just 6% of men and 2% of women. If half the population is forced to play a smaller role in the economy, then the pool of potential entrepreneurs is that much smaller.

As detailed earlier, the typical founder of an employer company is someone age 27–43 with at least some managerial experience. Unfortunately, few women get these managerial experiences, and those who do, get them much later in life. The result is that Japan has the lowest rate of female entrepreneurship in the OECD; just 0.6% of employed women are employers with non-family staff, compared to 2.2% in the median OECD country. Every country shows a gender gap, but Japan's gap is the worst in the OECD. There are just 2 women entrepreneurs for every 10 men; elsewhere it's double that ratio (OECD 2022f, 2020g).

Several handicaps limit women's chances at entrepreneurship. For one, they are paid less even when other factors, like occupation and education, are equal. Men and women with university degrees start off at around the same pay at age 20–24. By the time the male reaches 50–54, his pay has almost tripled, but a woman's has only doubled (MHLW 2014). According to the World Economic Forum (2020: 201–202), among 153 countries in 2020, Japan ranked 67th for gender wage equality, 110th for the number of professional and technical workers, and 131st for leadership roles in government and managerial roles in companies.

Having lower salaries means that women accumulate less money to pour into a firm, so a female-founded firm is likely to be smaller and hence less successful; 77% of women had to rely on their own funds plus help from family members, compared to 53% of men. Beyond that, banks are even more reluctant to lend to women. Only 12% of female-owned startups got bank loans versus 26% for men (Higuchi et al. 2007: 180).

At the same time, as detailed below, women face discrimination in getting on the management ladder, and those who do get posts get them later in life. Hence, fewer of them have the experience required for a successful, growing firm.

All this discrimination is at odds with Japan's Labor Standards Act, whose words seem quite clear: "An employer shall not engage in discriminatory treatment of a woman as compared with a man with respect to wages by reason of the worker being a woman." In addition, the Equal Employment Opportunity Law (EEOL) forbids discriminating against women on matters of promotion, or even using criteria that appear to be gender-neutral but result in discrimination. These laws are routinely ignored and there is no government agency mandated to enforce them. The victim must spend her time and money to seek redress in court. Worse yet, class-action lawsuits are not available in labor cases.

A lawyer who always represents companies in such suits told me that his clients routinely get around the "equal pay for equal work" principle by tweaking the job description to argue that it is not equal work. The courts almost always back the employer in such cases. Even when, in response to complaints, a government agency finds that a firm has violated the law, it is just given an administrative order to rectify its practice but is not penalized.

Partly in reaction to the anti-discrimination clauses of the 1986 EEOL, firms created two separate tracks: *ippan shoku* (clerical or general track) dominated by women and nicknamed "the mommy track," and the *sogo shoku* (managerial track) dominated by men. As late as 1992, 40% of firms had no problem justifying the track system by saying that they put women into jobs "for which the female sensitivity can best be used" (Gelb 2000: 391). At age 45, a person on the management track will earn nearly 2.5 times as much as his counterpart on the general track (Futagami 2010: 10). As of 2011, about half of firms with at least 1,000 employees still acknowledged using this two-track system.

Those familiar with talk of "womenomics" have heard that the Japanese prime minister pledged to raise the share of female managers from less than 10% to 30% in just seven years. What they may not know is that the prime minister who first announced this 30% goal was not Shinzo Abe in 2013, but Junichiro Koizumi 10 years earlier. Abe merely reiterated the same goal with the same target date of 2020. Just two years later, Abe admitted it was not going to happen and cut back the goal to 15%.

Those women who do get promoted to managerial roles acquire them much later in life. Consequently, there are far fewer women in the pivotal 27–43 age cohort with managerial experience. Within five years of joining the management track at a sizable firm, 14% of the men have been promoted to the post of *kacho* (section leader), but just 1% of the women. By the 20th year (age 42 for a college grad), a third of the men have attained the level of *kacho* or higher, but just 8% of the women (see Figure 8.7).

Many firms seeking to show good numbers give women a managerial title, but not the authority and the experience that normally come with that. In one study, a 38-year-old male deputy general manager in a bank's investment banking section reported that he does not see many female managers in the workplace who possess real organizational power. "Many of them have been given the job title but no subordinates to manage" (Nemoto 2016: 133–134).

Another unenforced law forbids "maternity harassment," whereby women getting pregnant are pressured to leave their job or accept a demotion. They're forced to choose between career and family. As result, in 2014, in companies with at least 300 employees, just 30% of female *kachos* are married with children, compared to 78% of male *kachos*. The comparable figures at the higher, *bucho* level are 33% and 81% (JILPT 2014).

To be sure, there's been progress over the last 30 years, but at a snail's pace. Thirty years ago, women held less than 5% of *kakaricho* posts, the first rung on the ladder, and one attained by almost all men; by 2020, the female share was up to 21%. The female share of *kachos* has risen from 2% to 11%. Among *buchos*, it has risen from 1.3% to 8.5% (Nemoto 2016: 4; Olcott and Oliver 2014: 5; Gender Equality Bureau 2022: 4).

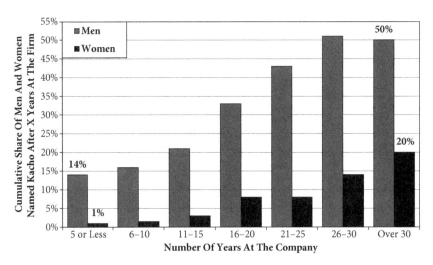

Figure 8.7 Fewer women get to climb the managerial ladder.
Source: Yamaguchi (2016: 9).

One driver of progress is a generational shift in attitudes about a woman's role in society, sparked in part by the 1986 EEOL. Until that law, more than half of women who continued education beyond high school were shunted off to junior (two-year) colleges that taught women to be ladies, meaning attractive in the marriage market. At the time, nearly 30% of marriages were still arranged and 95% of young single women had jobs, but at unsatisfying low-paid positions. Believing that the law would ensure genuine career opportunities—which meant not only money but independence—women flocked to full four-year colleges. Even though the law did not lead to fully equal opportunity, women still enjoyed large salary gains for every year spent at a four-year college. Not surprisingly, then, the number of women graduating from four-year colleges exploded from just a third of male graduates to almost 80% today.

Career Women Flock to Gazelles

A situation terrible for women turns out to be beneficial for gazelles: a flock of talented women seeking to work for them. As noted earlier, lifetime employment makes recruiting staff, including managers, one of the most difficult hurdles for new SMEs. Consequently, many new companies have been eager to hire these women, and they, in turn, have joined them. Askul, the online retailer of office supplies, is just one of many examples. It grew from just 130 staffers in 2002 to 3,500 as of early 2020. One of the reasons is that women comprise 37% of the 800 employees at Askul Corp. (not the entire Askul group), as well as an impressive 20% of its managers at the level of *bucho* or higher. The company has set a goal of 30% female managers. One of these women (discussed earlier) is Saori Onsen, vice executive officer of the B-to-B Strategy & Planning Unit.

The giant Recruit Holdings—which, among other things, helps link up companies and talented people—found it hard to recruit men when it began way back in 1960. So, it recruited women, and, as of early 2022, women still comprise half of the company's 16,500 employees in Japan and 28% of its managers. It appointed its first female president in 1997. As of 2021, its chief operating officer was not only one of the few women in such a high post, but also the youngest female board director among Nikkei 225 companies. By 2030, the company aims to reach gender parity in all positions, including board membership.

At Shop Japan, Harry Hill said that when he became CEO in 2006, 30% of the managers were women, but by 2017, this had risen to 55%. At the level of upper management, the female ratio was just 15%. Still, he added, "It's pretty clear that 10 or 15 years from now, this company is probably going to be run by women. I think last year, five out of six of our recruits were women. And it wasn't that we were just looking for women. They were the best, and the most aggressive."

This suggests mutual reinforcement between two trends. On the one hand, would-be gazelles' need for staffing encourages them to hire more women, including as managers. On the other hand, the availability of talented women will help more potential gazelles get off the ground.

Perhaps the most encouraging news is that companies with more female managers achieve higher productivity and higher profitability (Yamaguchi 2011, 2012). Moreover, those with active programs for work-life balance (WLB)—which reduces the family versus career dilemma for women— also achieve better financial results. If these companies can seize market share from the laggards, that might force the laggards to up their game. So far, however, as is typically the case, managerial perceptions of these financial realities lag far behind facts on the ground, particularly when company managers "can't see the gorilla." Yamaguchi reports that, among companies with at least 300 employees, just 14% are promoters of comprehensive WLB policies and child and family care programs, whereas roughly half either do nothing at all along this line, or do nearly nothing. There are surely many trends in the right direction, but the pace remains glacial.

9

Corporate *Intra*preneurship
Breeds Entrepreneurs

Medium and large firms are breeding grounds for entrepreneurs. In fact, there is a whole school of thought about this called "knowledge-spillover theory." According to Zoltan Acs, a leading analyst of entrepreneurship, and his coauthors, a majority of entrepreneurs are employees perceiving opportunities that their employer either cannot see, or else cannot find any way to exploit within its existing business model (Acs et al. 2009). The most notorious case is Steve Wozniak, an employee of Hewlett-Packard (HP) who co-invented the first Apple computer with Steve Jobs. Wozniak was contractually obligated to give HP the right of first refusal, but the "suits" at HP dismissed it as a hobbyist's toy, and the rest is history. Remarkably, during 1899 to 1988, the number of new American *firms* in any given year hinged on the number of new *patents* the previous year. The implication is that, when incumbent firms fail to exploit these patents, employees leave the firm to start their own (Acs and Varga 2005: 325). We saw above how Yasukane Matsumoto left A. T. Kearney and created Raksul because no other firm was implementing an idea like his.

A surprisingly large number of spillover entrepreneurs had previously operated in their employers as *intra*preneurs, a term not well known by the general public. Whereas *entre*preneurs set up new firms, *intra*preneurs create their own innovations inside established firms by working independently on projects they devise.

In the typical country, including Japan, 60% of intrapreneurs go on to become entrepreneurs. Not surprisingly then, except for the Nordic countries and Belgium, countries that have more intrapreneurs tend to generate more entrepreneurs. Here's the problem: in Japan, just 2% of all corporate employees are permitted to lead intrapreneurial projects, compared to 5.4% in the United States and a 4.3% median among 23 rich OECD countries; Japan is fourth from the bottom (Stam and Stenkula 2017: 16; GEM 2013: 25).

The Contest for Japan's Economic Future. Richard Katz, Oxford University Press. © Richard Katz 2024.
DOI: 10.1093/oso/9780197675106.003.0010

Intrapreneurship began a century ago when America's 3M, now a $36 billion firm, encouraged its researchers to spend 15% of their time on projects of their own choosing. When a project failed, it was discussed in in-house seminars. Some of 3M's biggest successes have come out of these failures, the most famous being the post-it note. In that case, an adhesive did not work for the intended purpose, but someone else thought of another use. Other famous products of intrapreneurship are Google's Gmail, the JAVA programming language, and the best-selling Elixir acoustical guitar strings.

The most dramatic story of intrapreneurship in Japan—a case that highlights the difficulties in Japanese elephants—is Ken Kutaragi, the father of SONY's PlayStation. In fiscal 2021, the games unit provided 27% of SONY's total revenue and 29% of its profits. Yet, it took a fight with most of SONY's senior management to get it off the ground. Having loved as a child to take toys apart to see how they worked, Kutaragi joined SONY as an electrical engineer in 1975. In the early 1980s, he noticed that the sound quality on his daughter's Nintendo was poor. Since SONY was not in the game business, his bosses allowed him to develop a specialized sound chip as a consultant to Nintendo. When his chip sent Nintendo's sales skyward, some of the executives wanted to fire him. Fortunately, CEO Norio Ohga backed Kutaragi. Perhaps Ohga saw himself in Kutaragi since both in their younger days had dreamed of singing opera. When Kutaragi developed the PlayStation, most of SONY's leaders dismissed it as a toy and, once again, some wanted to dismiss him and his toy. Once again, Ohga backed Kutaragi.

Trust and Challenge Your Employees

One would think Japan would have more intrapreneurship since it shares many of the usual ingredients that promote it. Among rich countries, Japan comes in second only to Korea in the share of 25–64-year-olds with a college degree, at 30%. Japan is a leader in the number of triadic patents (i.e., those granted in the US, Japan, and EU), including in cutting-edge fields. It has the fifth-highest ratio of R&D to GDP in the world. Moreover, studies have shown that firms with more intrapreneurship have higher sales, profit margins, and market share (Pearce and Carland 1996). By some calculations, in-house innovation is a better route to growth and profitability than the giants' acquisition binge.

The key missing ingredient at traditional Japanese companies is how the executives see the employees. If employees are seen as trustworthy by their bosses, then companies are more willing to give employees some freedom to pursue their own ambitions regarding innovation. Gifford Pinchot, an American inventor and entrepreneur who coined the term *intrapreneurship* in 1978, argued that if a firm employs technical people with a high desire for achievement, it need only create the appropriate environment and intrapreneurs will emerge. In-group trust, such as within companies and between a company and its suppliers, is often quite high in Japan.

What, then, is holding Japan back? Management mindsets. It's one thing for Toyota to trust its assembly-line workers to follow detailed instructions about halting the line when a defect is seen, or to come up with suggestions about how to improve a task they're performing. It's quite another to allow employees to develop their own projects instead of following the hierarchy of the R&D department.

Employee autonomy was one of the most important factors in promoting intrapreneurship. In one study, employees were asked whether they have autonomy in shaping how they do their job and opportunities to learn new skills on the job. Among the 21 countries surveyed, the responses ranged from 7% in Greece to 48% in Denmark. There was an extremely high 87% correlation between the degree of autonomy and the extent of intrapreneurship (Stam and Stenkula 2017). Unfortunately, Japan was not included in the survey. However, centralized R&D departments there seem more resistant than those elsewhere to giving up control, as we saw earlier in the case of Masatoshi Ueno of Asahi Glass.

Then there is the danger to an intrapreneur's status if his project fails, due to the *genten shugi* attitude regarding promotion. If baseball can laud batters who get out two-thirds of the time, why can't companies? Gen Isayama, whose World Innovation Lab in Silicon Valley helps big Japanese corporations collaborate with innovative US startups, told me, "I had to go to the Human Resource (HR) departments and say: 'Can you please make sure that the people who take a risk by contributing to this business have their efforts reflected in their promotion speed or bonus—whether the project is successful or not?' Otherwise, we're not going to get the best people to work with us" (Interview March 2018). Isayama only works with companies that are willing to comply. The majority of Japanese companies, he said, are still not willing.

In four rich countries, 25% of intrapreneurs said that they took a personal risk—mostly a potential loss of status in the firm—by becoming intrapreneurs (Bosma et al. 2010). In most big Japanese firms, the risk is much higher. "The culture of traditional corporations is organized to avoid this idea of autonomy," explained Tadashi Takiguchi, who teaches entrepreneurship at Waseda University while being one of the leaders of a VC spinoff called WERU Investment. Even at the university, he noted, engineers and scientists don't accept failure as the price of success. At some companies, the situation became even more rigid after 1990 in reaction to the growth of technological uncertainty in the digital age. "*Genten shugi*, the mindset to avoid failure, cannot work in the age of uncertainty. If a company is facing uncertainty, we have to manage the system to accept failures. But increasingly, Japanese corporations have been trying to manage for certainty, rather than figure out how to work with uncertainty" (Interview March 2020).

Takiguchi insists that, while the Japanese companies that have made this shift are rare, they show the possibilities. One is Sharp, which almost went bankrupt in the early 2010s, despite having superb technology. For example, in 2013 it created the world's most efficient solar cell to date, converting a record 44% of sunlight into electricity (Mathias 2013). Yet, like SONY and Panasonic, it kept on betting the company on TVs despite repeated losses. Beginning in 2012, Taiwan's Foxconn bought increasing stakes in Sharp and, in 2016, a controlling interest. The government-backed INCJ put in a rival bid, on techno-nationalist grounds, but Sharp chose Foxconn anyway. And now the company is doing well.

Takiguchi's colleague at Waseda and WERU Investments, Hironori Higashide, pointed to Sharp as a remarkable example of how companies can change when new management trusts and challenges the employees. When Foxconn came in, they replaced the *genten shugi* mindset with something more symmetrical, including rewards for success. Most importantly, failure at trying something exceptional became more acceptable. In addition, people were allowed to work for part of the time on their own projects if they were intended to benefit the company. Not everyone could adapt, and many of the older employees left Sharp. But now Sharp is profitable again and producing good new products.

One of the most splendid exceptions of an older Japanese company promoting intrapreneurship is Recruit Holdings, a global leader in HR technology. In fiscal 2022, Recruit boasted revenues of ¥2.87 trillion ($22 billion). Almost half came from overseas, up from less than 4% in 2011. When, in

2017, Takiguchi took a look at several new companies on the stock market created by Waseda graduates, it turned out that half the founders had previously been Recruit employees.

Recruit was founded in 1960 by Hiromasa Ezoe, then a student of educational psychology at the University of Tokyo. The purpose was to connect university graduates seeking jobs to corporations seeking new recruits. It has since then moved into matchmaking for job seekers at any stage in their careers, and in recent years has expanded into other industries.

Ezoe developed a corporate culture with the core value known as "bet on passion" (*ko no soncho*), explained Recruit spokesperson Kana Ueda. "We believe that, if employees concentrate on what they love, it will bring out their best" (Interview April 2022). In 1982, Recruit created the RING program to promote intrapreneurship. It takes the form of a contest among different business proposals, of which there are about 1,000 each year (some sponsored by a team). Senior staffers advise applicants. Less than 1% are accepted for implementation. The winners get funding and they run the new business.

Some of Recruit's hottest services have emerged from that process, including Zexy, which provides a magazine and online platform for wedding planning, and Study Sapuri, which offers online learning. Naturally, not all succeed, but Recruit does not penalize those who take a chance and fail. "We learn through all these experiences—learning what doesn't work is as important as learning what does—this approach is fundamental to our growth as individuals and as a business," added Ueda. She pointed to the example of Mio Kashiwamura, who, in her late twenties, proposed that Recruit bring Zexy to China. While the idea did not work out in the long term, that experience was part of the process that led to her role today as an executive corporate officer. "In other companies, people might consider it a failure, but we consider that type of experience vital. If people feel afraid of trying new ideas, we lose. We constantly encourage people to explore new ways of doing things."

Recruit itself is an example of coming back from failure. It was almost felled by a 1989 political bribery scandal for which Ezoe was later convicted and was soon hurt even further by the popping of the property bubble in 1990. Ezoe resigned. And yet, the company's resurrection is now a *Harvard Business Review* case study (Sucher and Gupta 2018).

Recruit hopes its employees will want to start their new businesses within Recruit, but, if someone is determined to strike out on their own, then

Recruit encourages them. Some who have tried and failed have come back to Recruit. Ueda herself is an example of the type of person Recruit attracts. Having graduated from the prestigious Keio University, she went to work for a major bank where, she soon realized, being a woman limited her advancement. So, in less than a year, she switched to Recruit.

While Recruit is 60 years old, Takiguchi commented that "the new companies being listed in the stock market today—at least when the founder has an entrepreneurial mindset—can become some of the best incubators for future entrepreneurs by providing intrapreneurial experience." He pointed to CyberAgent. Founded in 1998, CyberAgent provides a variety of Internet-based services and in 2021 enjoyed revenue of ¥666 billion ($5.1 billion). It, too, runs internal competitions for new business proposals. Those that are selected are turned into subsidiaries with an unusual degree of autonomy from headquarters, including hiring their own personnel and independence on day-to-day operations. Many of the subsidiary CEOs are in their twenties. Interestingly, the program was begun as an effort to counter the high turnover of skilled employees, and it worked brilliantly on that front. Part of the firm's "code of conduct" is "Give a second chance to those who challenged." During 2010–2017, 111 new subsidiaries were created, 23 of which failed and were shut down, but their leaders found that CyberAgent did indeed give them a "second chance" (Delbridge et al. 2019).

Recruit and CyberAgent act as if they are trying to fight the "knowledge-spillover" pattern: to create opportunities within the firm so that imaginative people won't feel the need to leave in order to turn their idea into a viable business.

Easier Said than Done

Fostering intrapreneurship is easier said than done, particularly in older, more traditional companies. Consider the case of Panasonic. In 2016, the Appliance Company (AC)—Panasonic's division for consumer electronics and home appliances—created a tiny unit (just 12 people as of 2019) devoted to nurturing intrapreneurs. The unit is called Game Changer Catapult. Its founder, Masa Fukata, a senior manager previously in charge of developing new products, hopes that, by 2025, Catapult will have launched between 20 and 100 new firms, some of them with annual sales as high as ¥100–¥300 million ($770,000–2.3 million). The impetus for Catapult came when Fukata noticed that "[w]e stopped the TV business and other businesses, but we weren't really creating new businesses" (Interview October 2019).

Still, it remains an uphill climb to convince managers at Panasonic to accept ideas not coming out of the R&D hierarchy. Consider one early proposal: a machine for softening food. It is aimed at elderly people who have difficulty swallowing regular food and dislike having to be restricted to paste and the like. This product was the vision of two female quality assurance officers, Tokie Mizuno and Megumi Ogawa, who had worked for Panasonic for decades. They got the idea from seeing the eating difficulties of their grandfather and father, respectively. When Catapult proposed that AC adopt this product, it rebuffed them, contending that the market was too small. In reality, about two million people each in Japan, the United States, and Europe suffer from such problems, and the market for specialty food for the elderly is predicted to reach ¥154 billion ($1.2 billion) by 2025. So, when the notion made a big splash at the South by Southwest (SXSW) entrepreneurial fair in Texas in 2017, AC leaders changed their minds and tried to develop it, but eventually gave up.

Fortunately, Catapult had prepared a fallback option. Along with Scrum Ventures—a US VC fund created and headed by a Japanese national—it formed a joint venture called BeeEdge. When Panasonic managers abandoned the idea, BeeEdge invested in a new firm, called Gifmo, to develop the product. Sales of Delisofter, which looks like a rice cooker, began in 2020 with a price tag of ¥47,300 ($363). Gifmo expects to sell tens of thousands in the coming few years.

One of the first new companies to arise from Catapult is called Mitsubachi (Honeybee) Products. Developed by Hatsumi Ura, a female manager in her forties, Mitsubachi's first new product is a machine for making high-class hot chocolate at home, called Infini Mix. The company is also developing its own chocolates for the machine. Once again, Panasonic managers rejected the notion, so BeeEdge funded it. Ura became president of the new firm. She invested some of her own money and sales have begun.

Staffers submitted about 120 proposals during 2016–2018, a tiny number in a division with 11,000 employees. Each year, seven are chosen for presentation at big fairs like Slush Tokyo (Slush originated in Finland) and SXSW in Austin, Texas. The ones that receive the best reception there are funded by Catapult.

When Panasonic's Masa Fukata talks about his ambitions for Game Changer Catapult, he radiates the energy of a middle manager younger than himself. There are probably lots of senior managers like Fukata hidden in giant corporations. Unfortunately, most seem to have been drained of their enthusiasm by the time they reach Fukata's status. And, so, part of Fukata's skill set is learning how to master corporate politics. Back in 2016, Fukata gained the enthusiastic support of Tetsuro Homma. Homma has since moved on to a new position, and it remains to be seen how supportive his successors will be in the coming years.

Nor can intrapreneurship succeed if staffers are afraid to offer a new idea that might fail, as most do. Catapult was designed to overcome this hindrance. If a staffer's proposal is accepted for prototype and proof-of-concept (POC) development, the intrapreneur is transferred from his regular division to Catapult and, in most cases, to a new independent firm. If that new firm succeeds, the intrapreneur will get rich. But if it fails, he can get his job back at Panasonic, a most unusual practice. But will his failure affect future promotion? "Probably," admitted Fukata. His own view is that someone who tried and failed "would have value to come back to Panasonic by providing ideas and experience."

The biggest obstacle may be the "not invented by us" mindset still prevailing at most of Japan's corporate giants. Panasonic's internal sections almost invariably come up with some reason to refuse to develop products coming out of Catapult. The unsaid reason, says Fukuda, is that "the idea came from someone not officially assigned to develop products."

There is a ray of hope. The HR department recognizes that talented young people are more attracted to a firm offering such opportunities. "HR loves our activities," explained Fukata, "because those passionate young people will make us successful. If they go elsewhere, we'll decline."

The Need to Attract Young Passionate Workers

Panasonic is not alone. In a number of ways, big traditional firms have had to change their ways to accommodate the generational changes in attitudes, such as the growth of mid-career hiring discussed above. One of those new ways is captured by a new term that has come to Japan: *inter*preneurship. Unlike intrapreneurship, which is acting like an entrepreneur within one's company, *inter*preneurship means trying an independent venture outside the company, while still maintaining one's job. People can experiment without the risk of giving up their regular pay.

Traditionally, Japanese corporations would not let their employees engage in side jobs. Today, however, explained Fukata, "Some have started to accept it due to high pressure from younger employees who are entrepreneurial and want to learn faster through these outside activities." It's not just about individual fulfillment. With faith in a lifetime job falling, said Fukata, interpreneurship enables workers to "get accustomed to a challenging environment in which they may eventually need to swim, given this uncertain working environment."

Fukata himself reflects the changing attitudes to which traditional companies need to respond. He retired from Panasonic in late 2021, five years ahead of the usual age, in order to help promote and coach interpreneurs within a company called Sundred. He left Game Changer Catapult in the hands of someone 15 years younger.

10

Universities as Entrepreneurial Communities

It was at a May 2016 New York conference bringing together venture capitalists and would-be entrepreneurs from Japan and the United States that I first met Jasper Cheng, a young man in his early twenties who had worked for an Internet of Things (IoT) startup and then a larger firm. The chance meeting attuned me to the pivotal role of entrepreneurial communities: "People think that entrepreneurs are loners," he said, "It's just the opposite. Entrepreneurship is a social activity." As a bright student growing up in New York City, he figured he'd go to a university known as a feeder institution for Wall Street and work there. As it turned out, he attended Berkeley. "No one I met there was thinking about Wall Street. My peers at Berkeley saw themselves pushing for the future. Like me, they threw themselves at entrepreneurship in order to create value and change, or they chose to accept an offer from a producer based on how they would have a hand in changing the world. Many of my peers who started at Google and the like often quit after a year or two to pursue their own ideas or join a fledgling startup." Cheng himself, as a senior at Berkeley, co-founded a startup with a fellow student. Though the attempt failed, and he's since worked for bigger companies to gain experience, he says that someday he may again be involved with a startup.

The lesson was reinforced when I went to Berlin to look at the startup experience there, and learned about an area of town, straddling the location of the torn-down Berlin Wall, where entrepreneurs could rent cheap office space and socialize when the day was done. It was there that I learned about "FuckUp Nights." Every month, young hopefuls get together at a big restaurant, where, fueled by food, alcohol, and camaraderie, they tell how they "fucked up" this or that attempt, to peals of laughter and applause. Greeting failure with laughter—and thereby learning from that failure—is the goal. Shame is turned away at the door. The Silicon Valley mantra has gone global: "If you haven't failed at least twice, you've got no guts." The official

The Contest for Japan's Economic Future. Richard Katz, Oxford University Press. © Richard Katz 2024.
DOI: 10.1093/oso/9780197675106.003.0011

website of "FuckUp Nights" claims events in 90 countries with 15,000 stories of failure and a million attendees (Fuckup 2022).

Tokyo, too, has "FuckUp Nights," not to mention an entrepreneurial base in the Shibuya section of Tokyo nicknamed "Bit Valley." It is run by ImpactHub, the host of a work-sharing space. There are more than 1,200 members in Tokyo, and a typical event has 60–100 in attendance (FuckUp Nights Tokyo 2022).

Admittedly, FuckUp nights is a special artifact of venture enterprises, those seeking VC money in hopes of taking off like a rocket ship. Ordinary gazelles do not share this culture. But Japan's participation shows that people are embedded in all sorts of cultures, not just their national psychology. Venture firms have their own globalized culture in the way they dress, where they live and work, how they talk—and Japanese hopefuls are full participants (see KDDI story above).

Give Them a Chance to Know an Entrepreneur

Given the social nature of entrepreneurship, it's not surprising that those who personally know entrepreneurs are far more likely to become one themselves. It could be a family member, a friend, a professor, or a co-worker. When METI asked young people what sparked their initial interest in starting a business, the top answer, "to make money" (32%), was followed very closely by "influence from entrepreneurs that I know" (30%); 65%–75% of Japanese running a company, or hoping to do so, know a current entrepreneur, often a friend or relative. Among those with no desire to start their own firm, just 34% know an entrepreneur (METI 2014: 193, 222). So, few entrepreneurs today means fewer tomorrow, and more today means even more down the road.

Universities Are Pivotal

Universities play a vital role, whether by creating a community of friends and mentors or providing direct input from an entrepreneur or a professor with business experience.

In Japan, as elsewhere, chums from high school and university often join together to create a startup. One famous case, Uzabase, was created by three young men in 2008, two of whom attended high school together. The founders had worked for several years at foreign-owned securities firms and believed they could offer a better method of gathering and disseminating business information. They formed Uzabase as a B-to-B service. By 2022, just 14 years after its founding, Uzabase employees reached almost 800 and revenues hit ¥18 billion ($138 million). Its board includes Professor Masahiro Kotosaka, a veteran entrepreneur who has taught business-creation courses at Keio since 2017. He's also on the board of Raksul, as well as Appirits, a company founded by three Keio students that is now on the stock market.

As a student at Keio in 1999–2004, Kotosaka and a half-dozen schoolmates created three different startups. Then he worked for McKinsey and earned a doctorate in management studies at Oxford. Practicing what he would go on to preach, he spent four years running three profitable IT/retail businesses. "Twenty years ago," Kotosaka mused, "student entrepreneurs were so rare at Keio that a TV station came to interview me and spent 15 minutes on this story." Around 2010 or so, "it became much, much easier to start a growing business." One reason was that digital technology drove down the cost of a new business. "Back then, if you wanted to have people pay by credit card, you needed to pay for a security system and that was very expensive. Now you can just go to Amazon or someone like that." The other big factor was the creation of an ecosystem of people like himself, experienced entrepreneurs who are able to mentor younger aspirants. "Many of them are running VC or PE firms that provide both money and advice" (Interview October 2017).

How many of the 120 students in his undergraduate course on business creation intended to start their own firm, I wondered. "Half," he answered to my great surprise. "To be honest, it's a unique situation because this particular campus, Keio SFC, is famous for incubating startups and this was a business creation course."

There was an additional factor. Kotosaka had invited a famous "angel" investor to speak to the class. It was Naoko Aoyagi, the CEO of GREE International. GREE's parent had been founded in 2004 by Yoshikazu Tanaka, a former employee of Rakuten. Today, GREE is one of Japan's two leading online gaming and social network companies. In 2022, it enjoyed annual revenues of ¥75 billion ($577 million) and 1,500 employees. Aoyagi asked Kotosaka's students to prepare a business plan for a startup and promised to fund the best project to the tune of ¥3 million ($23,000). As it turned out, he found three projects worth funding and promised to fund all three.

Ten years ago, would half the class have desired to start their own companies? "No," came Kotosaka's swift reply.

Unfortunately, there's little systematic data on the career choices of those who have taken these entrepreneurship courses. Not even the universities seem to track this. However, Kotosaka found some valuable information. In 1997, the Tokyo Stock Exchange created a new section called MOTHERS to be a launching pad for innovative startups, akin to NASDAQ. Examining the profiles of nearly 4,000 executives and directors at 500 companies that had gone public via initial public offerings (IPOs) on MOTHERS between 1997 and 2017, Kotosaka found a remarkable change. "Initially, there were almost no university graduates," he explained. "A tiny fragment came from big traditional firms like SONY or NTT. But now the companies doing IPOs are led by people with real professional experience. They are university graduates who have worked at some of the big innovative firms founded in the past few decades, or they've worked for foreign-affiliated companies, like consultants or securities firms."

Tokyo University versus MIT and Stanford

If, in 2006, the still-active companies created by living alumni of the Massachusetts Institute of Technology (MIT) were a nation, their global revenues of nearly $2 trillion would have been equal to the GDP of the world's 11th-largest economy. Their employees totaled 3.3 million, mostly at companies now employing at least 10,000. Half of their combined global revenues exist in companies that use technology developed at MIT or other universities. Stanford has been even more fruitful. The $2.7 trillion in revenues of the 40,000 still-active companies created by its alumni and faculty equal the GDP of the 10th-largest economy. Their employees totaled 5.4 million people (Roberts and Eesley 2011; Eesley and Miller 2012).

Furthermore, the trend is accelerating. Each year in the 1990s, MIT alumni created 900 new companies. And 17% of those companies grew to at least 100 employees within 15 years. With each passing year, there are more entrepreneurs in each graduating class, and they are starting their first companies sooner. They've become gazelle-producing factories.

These results did not spring spontaneously, like wildflowers in an untended field, but from determined efforts over decades to cultivate a garden.

While MIT grads had long been creating new companies, the university had no formal entrepreneurship course until 1961 and no organized effort to develop entrepreneurs. Then, in 1969, a small group of alumni organized the MIT Alumni Entrepreneurship Seminar Program. Attendance reached 300 before the group had to close applications. Over the next three years, 3,000 alumni attended similar sessions in eight US cities. After attending one of these sessions, Bob Metcalfe, MIT class of 1969, resigned from Xerox's Palo Alto Research Center and established his company with two other engineers. He would go on to invent the Ethernet and found 3Com, which he sold to HP for $2.7 billion in 2010.

Not until 1990 did MIT create its Entrepreneurship Center, and it still had just one class on "New Enterprises." Soon, it created an entrepreneurship "track" within its master's degree program. By 2011–2012, there were 47 different courses with a total enrollment of 2,500.

It's hard to imagine Silicon Valley in the absence of Stanford. One of every four technical innovators and founders in the Valley had taken an entrepreneurship course at the university. More than a third of innovators and founders participated in competitions, mentorship programs with faculty, and the like. A growing number of faculty members serve on the boards of startups. Stanford professors Terry Winograd, Jeff Ullman, and Rajeev Motwani moved from informal roles advising two graduate students—Larry Page and Sergey Brin—to formal roles on their company's technical advisory board in its early years. It's called Google.

Certainly, university efforts could never have succeeded without other elements of a nurturing ecosystem that also took decades to build, from a fluid labor market to financial institutions like VC and PE funds, not to mention law firms. At the same time, those other elements would never have been as fertile without Stanford's intensive efforts.

Only in the last couple of decades has Japan even begun to create entrepreneurship programs in its universities. The failure to do so is among the reasons for the very different career paths of MIT graduates from those of Japan's most prestigious college, Tokyo University, known as Todai (Ishii et al. 1993). Created in 1877 as a national university, Todai's mission was to train the country's leaders. To this day, most senior government officials and many leading business leaders are Todai grads.

As of 1993, the most recent study, only 10% of those from Todai reported wanting to create their own firm, compared to 26% of MIT grads. Counting graduates from 1960, 1970, 1980, and 1985, only 11% of Todai graduates in

1993 worked at a firm with less than 300 employees, compared to 33% of MIT grads. Only 16% of Todai graduates had changed jobs even once during their careers, compared to 70% of those from MIT; 28% of the MIT grads had changed jobs at least three times, but less than 1% of Todai graduates did.

Most of this difference results from the varying environments in the two countries, not from distinctions between the two universities. But universities can be a vital ingredient in the needed national changes.

Entrepreneurship Courses, University Spinoffs

Looking at America's results, the Japanese government tried to create Japan's own versions of MIT and Stanford. Beginning in the 1990s, it encouraged universities to create entrepreneurship classes. In 1999, it changed Japanese law to emulate America's 1980 Bayh-Dole Act, which allows universities to own and commercialize research done by their faculty in order to foster spinoff companies (sometimes known as "spinouts"). Many universities have created their own VC funds to finance these startups. By 2000, 140 colleges were offering a total of 330 classes on entrepreneurship, a number that grew to 261 colleges and 1,140 courses by 2010 (MEXT 2007, 2010).

Whether or not they take classes in entrepreneurship, more students are finding it attractive to work at a startup. An article in *Nikkei* (Kobayashi 2020) reports changing preferences: "Take the large trading companies. They still rank high as popular destinations for graduates from top schools. Yet their middle managers lament, with an air of disbelief, that twenty-somethings are freely forgoing the prestige to join startups instead." Each year, the Todai newspaper ranks companies by how many of its grads they hire. Japan's three megabanks usually fill the top three slots. Still, software developer Works Applications came in 11th in 2017. Rakuten came in 15th. Others start off at a prestigious firm and then, feeling unfulfilled, switch jobs. The three-year attrition rate for college hires rose to 33% for the class of 2018, up eight points from the class of 2009. Even at companies with at least 1,000 employees, 25% of new graduates quit within three years (Jiji 2021).

The number of university spinoffs is still small, but it is growing. Whatever the value of the firms as such, the process also helps to create a community of entrepreneurs at the university, giving students a chance to take classes and get mentorship from a professor-entrepreneur.

One of the most famous cases is that of Euglena Corp., the biotech brainchild of Mitsuru Izumo, a 2002 Todai graduate. As detailed in the Introduction, he developed Euglena to solve the problem of malnutrition in countries like Bangladesh and was advised to do so by creating his own company when he attended Stanford for a year. After a year of working for the Bank of Tokyo–Mitsubishi Bank to accumulate money, he quit to form his own enterprise. In 2014, Euglena became the first company coming directly out of university research that went public on the stock market, and as of early 2023, it was valued at ¥110 billion ($846 million), with almost 880 employees and ¥44 billion ($341 million) in sales. Kotosaka is on Euglena's board as well.

Izumo had first learned about the algae euglena from Kengo Suzuki, a fellow agriculture major who was one year ahead of Izumo. Both were in a university club that created business planning contests. Suzuki, who earned his doctorate, became a co-founder of Euglena and heads R&D there. A third co-founder was Takayuki Fukumoto, who, as a former director of sales at a food company, provided the managerial experience (he's five years older than Izumo). He is now head of sales. Euglena still engages in joint R&D with universities.

Euglena's biggest problem was gaining sales, for which it had to line up manufacturers and a big distributor. Finally, at his 501st visit to a big corporation, giant trading company Itochu signed on to promote and sell the product. Itochu has exclusive rights to use euglena powder in its green smoothies and yogurt. Still, the imprimatur enabled Euglena to expand so much that Itochu now comprises just 10% of Euglena's sales.

While Euglena is one of the most famous, as of 2019, there were more than 2,500 university spinoffs listed in METI's database, only some of which have been listed on the stock market as yet. Todai, not surprisingly, was the source for the most at 269, followed by Kyoto University at 191 (METI 2020a).

Most of these spinoffs are still small, with half having no more than five employees and most of the rest between 5 and 20 staffers. At half of these university-initiated startups, the CEO and the CTO (chief technology officer) have a background in academic research in the natural sciences. Importantly, another 18% of CEOs are former managers at larger companies, and an additional 24% had been managers at SMEs. The fact that there were managers willing to take these jobs is encouraging, even if the number is still small (METI 2020b).

The Bifurcated Generation

Not all those who teach entrepreneurship share Kotosaka's experiences or optimism. One of the skeptics is Dimitry Rtischev, who's been running a seminar on entrepreneurship at Gakushuin University for more than a decade.

Few of Rtischev's students see his seminar as a launching pad for their careers. "They know the word venture sounds cool and they're interested in the topic." Still, when the time comes to get a job, "Most of them don't even look at startups. Perhaps one or two in a good year." Rtischev contends that these students are acting in their best interest. "I tell them up front: if you join a big company in Japan, the risks are lower, and the potential rewards are higher than joining a startup" (Interview October 2017).

Interestingly, he argued that the biggest barrier to startups is not finding enough people willing to create new companies, but finding the far larger number of people willing to work for them. "I think there are enough motivated people in Japan to want to start a new venture and they're not typical individuals, either here or in America." The bigger challenge, he said, is getting good, bright, motivated people to turn down big company jobs and instead work at a startup when the risks are so high and the rewards so small. Not only are incomes higher at the big companies, but their employees are more attractive catches in the marriage market.

Rtischev was very skeptical that anything would change the risk-reward ratio. "The system is self-reinforcing. It benefits both the employer and the talented ones who have secured lifetime employment at the big firms. Neither side has an interest in changing it." This book contends that the evidence leans the other way. Labor market rigidity no longer benefits either employers or employees as much it used to do. Therefore, the system is in a process of change that may be slow, but it's still enough to enable startups to recruit staff more easily than in the past.

When I asked Higashide and Takiguchi of Waseda why different teachers of entrepreneurship had such different experiences, they spoke of the bifurcation among the younger generation. On the one hand, three decades of economic stagnation and poorer career prospects have caused the majority of young adults to become even more cautious and conservative than a few decades back. Among survey respondents in their twenties, 55% agreed with the idea of spending their entire lives at one company in 2017, up from 34% in 2004. Nearly 90% supported the idea of lifetime employment, up from 65% in 2004. Similarly, fewer students are studying abroad, in part because companies don't reward overseas experience when it comes to promotion (Cislo and Takahashi 2017; McCrostie 2017). Conversely, a small, but growing slice of young people have become more adventuresome than in the past. It is the latter whom Higashide, Takiguchi, and Kotosaka of Keio see in their classes. Perhaps that is related to the fact that Keio and Waseda are among the places to go for those with entrepreneurial ambitions; these two universities are tied at 8th for the most spinouts, with 85 each in 2019.

Immobile Star Scientists

The "traitorous eight," they were called in 1957, the star scientists who left Shockley Semiconductor Laboratory to create their own new firm, Fairchild Semiconductor. All they did was to set up a firm that competed with their former employer. One of the so-called traitors, Robert Noyce, went on to invent the integrated circuit at Fairchild in 1960. Then, in 1968, Noyce and Gordon Moore left Fairchild to create Intel, while others founded AMD, LSI Logic, National Semiconductor, and dozens of others. By 2014, there were 92 "Fairchildren" on the stock market, with a combined value of more than $2 trillion. Two of the first VC companies—Sequoia and Kleiner Perkins Caufield & Byers—were Fairchildren. Within a few years, Santa Clara Valley in northern California had gained the moniker Silicon Valley.

The tale of the traitorous eight is just the most dramatic and earliest of what has now become commonplace, as in the case of my cousin. The creation of new companies via knowledge spillovers has created a highly fertile ecosystem. Participation in the system produces gains for both the individuals and the system as a whole that far outweigh the losses any individual firm might suffer from losing talent. This is creative destruction at its best. It is the opposite of what is sometimes seen these days when giant tech companies like Amazon, Facebook, or Google have been the subject of antitrust cases accusing them of buying up, or otherwise stifling, new companies that might compete with them.

Unfortunately, at least so far, Japan has not availed itself of the benefits of mobility among top researchers. On the contrary, star scientists mostly work for very big firms, rarely leaving their employer to create a startup or to join one. That's a major reason there are so few knowledge-intensive gazelles in Japan compared to other countries. Labor market rigidity is far more severe among top scientists than in general.

One study looked at mobility among top scientists and inventors in the laser diode industry, whose most well-known uses are in CDs, DVDs, and optical fibers. The top scientists are measured by those whose patents and papers are most often cited by others. Among the top laser diode 50 scientists in each country, only five of the Japanese transferred to another company. By contrast, 26 of the Americans transferred at least once and some did two or three times. In another list of 83 top Japanese laser diode inventors, only one left his employer to move to a startup. By contrast, among 134 top American inventors, 108 moved to startups (Shimizu 2019: 210–211). This is hardly unique to this sector. In the 1990s, the proportion of R&D specialists who had changed jobs was 43% in Germany, 38% in the United States, and 35% in the United Kingdom, but a mere 6% in Japan.

In addition to the usual disincentives for labor mobility in Japan, star scientists face another hurdle. A great deal of their knowledge is "implicit learning" as a member of a team and may even be company specific. Unless they leave together with others in the team, they lose that part of their "human capital." On the other hand, if a few teams leave as a group and go together to the new situation—as is common in the United States—that might create a new trend. It's not evident yet, but it should be tracked as a barometer of progress. One wonders whether university spinouts—whose own scientists may have collaborated with those in the private sector—might provide a congenial new home to start the trend.

Shimizu compares the relationship between incumbents and spinouts to a fruit-bearing tree. A tree needs a strong trunk to develop a general technology, whether it be a steam engine or a laser diode. A myriad of useful applications is its fruit. The big incumbents often work on the former, while a variety of fruit depends on having spinouts. If too many top personnel leave the big incumbents too soon, the growth of the trunk will be stunted. If none leave, the variety and abundance of fruit will be constricted. In the laser diode sector, Japan's big incumbents controlled both trunk and fruit, often doing so on the same technological trajectory. When that trajectory no longer suited a changing market and prices dropped, few could adapt, and they exited the sector altogether. What seems rational to each firm, and its star scientists, may not serve them in the long run.

PART IV

OVERCOMING THE BARRIERS TO GAZELLES' GROWTH

11

Overcoming the Recruitment Obstacle

Did you ever wonder why Silicon Valley is in California rather than, say, Microsoft's home state of Washington? One reason is that California has outlawed non-compete contracts. Such contracts temporarily forbid workers from transferring to a competing firm, or from starting their own firm in competition with their former employer. Of course, an employee cannot steal his employer's intellectual property. Washington state, by contrast, enforces non-compete contracts. It was California's stance on non-compete clauses that enabled the "traitorous eight" to catalyze the development of Silicon Valley (DeVore 2016).

Japan's lifetime employment system for regular workers acts like one big non-compete clause, especially at the largest companies. A design engineer leaving Toyota cannot expect to be hired by Honda, nor even by non-competing top manufacturers.

While many workers can, and do, leave their firms, Japan stands out as having one of the least fluid labor markets in the OECD. Out of 27 OECD countries, Japan has the third-largest share of men who work for the same employer for more than 10 years: 55% (see Figure 11.1).

This figure greatly understates the tenure, since, at many companies, the first five years are often a kind of probation, in which employer and employee see whether they're a good fit. Among full-time male regular workers who were hired in the 1980s and continued for more than five years, a third stayed with the same employer for as long as 30–34 years. At larger companies, the ratio is even higher (Kambayashi and Kato 2017[1]).

Unless qualified managers, technicians, and other talent flow to new innovative firms, how are the latter to get off the ground? Hence, one test of a country's ability to foster gazelles, and innovation in general, is seeing how much of its labor flows to firms generating new patents. Out of nine OECD countries, Japan comes in dead last. Among American firms, a 10% hike in their stock of patents leads to a 2.2% hike in their labor force. It's 1.5% in the

---

[1] The authors graciously provided updated data for their paper's charts.

The Contest for Japan's Economic Future. Richard Katz, Oxford University Press. © Richard Katz 2024.
DOI: 10.1093/oso/9780197675106.003.0012

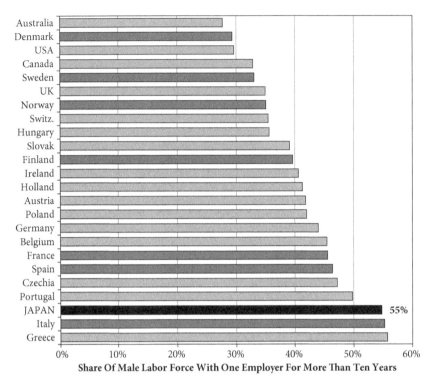

Figure 11.1 Japan has third-longest male job tenure in OECD.

Source: OECD (2020e).

Note: We look at men because the majority of women are non-regulars and a large share temporarily drop out of the labor force while their children are young.

United Kingdom, 1.3% in France, 0.8% in Germany, and just 0.5% in Japan. Behind this relative immobility stands the lifetime employment system (Andrews et al. 2014: 30).

The bad news is that policymakers have made a bad situation even worse. In the name of labor flexibility, they deregulated labor regulations so as to enable more industries to use non-regular workers, those who work part-time or under temporary contracts. That would have been fine if those workers were paid the same wages as regulars, as required by Japanese law, and in line with the practice in some other countries like France. Instead, flexibility was a pretext for wage austerity. Had the law mandating equal pay for equal work been enforced, then people with regular jobs would have been far less hesitant to create, or work for, a startup. They'd know that, if the startup failed, they'd be able to get a good-paying job again.

The good news, as will be detailed below, is a shift in attitudes among today's workers, as well as some shift in company behavior. Today's employees are far more willing and able to shift companies in mid-career than their parents were. In response, more companies acquiesced to hiring more people in mid-career in order to accommodate them. At the same time, companies whose internal staff lacks the requisite digital skills are being compelled to hire experienced specialists. The trends are in the right direction. To give them critical mass, policymakers need to take action. Specific recommendations will come at the end of the chapter.

Lifetime Employment and Seniority Wages: Pros Turn into Cons

A fundamental premise of this book is that social institutions do not arise and endure unless they serve some important function. Unfortunately, institutions can maintain themselves long after becoming obsolete. For decades, Japan's labor system on average provided more benefits than costs to both employers and employees. That was the case when the labor force was both young and growing, the economy was growing rapidly, and giant, capital-intensive corporations provided the lion's share of innovation (i.e., the "Schumpeter Mark II" innovation model discussed earlier). For example, workers who do not fear being laid off will gladly accept labor-saving technology that can raise company revenue and thus their wages. At the same time, companies are more willing to invest in training workers that they expect to stay with them.

Now that the labor force is shrinking, the economy lethargic, and knowledge-intensive gazelles are increasingly pivotal to innovation (Schumpeter Mark I), the costs of lifetime employment increasingly outweigh the benefits. If a firm has to downsize because its market is shrinking and the law prevents mass layoffs of regular workers—only allowing shrinkage via attrition—then not only will it have many redundant workers, but their average age will rise. Due to Japan's seniority wage system, the average wage per worker will also rise. In their initial response, all too many companies created make-work projects that often lost money, but less money than if the workers just sat at the window. Amusement parks were Nippon Steel's scheme. If a turnover of the labor force takes a generation, that makes it harder for a company to shift when its management is used to a certain way of thinking and who may be loath to let disagreements stand in the way of harmony with their longtime friends. No wonder older companies get less benefit from their investments in modern equipment, which often requires changing company habits.

This system became unsustainable, and so it was not sustained. Tokyo changed the law to enable increased use of low-paid, easily dismissed non-regular workers, who now number nearly 40% of the labor force.

Lifetime employment began during the rapid industrialization following the Meiji Restoration when new manufacturers suffered a scarcity of skilled manufacturing workers. Workers switched jobs when offered a higher wage, and companies regularly poached talent from each other. For instance, a textile mill would send its agents to another mill where, disguised as employees, they would spread the word that the mill from which they'd been sent had better wages and working conditions. "But it would soon become evident that the new factory had no better wages or working conditions than the one the deserters had left. From such . . . emerged the factory dormitories—virtual prisons for detaining workers and preventing them from escaping" (Taira 1962: 153–154).

In the 1910s, as many as 80% of blue-collar workers switched jobs every year. To halt this, beginning around 1910, employers began a movement for employment stabilization, later called lifetime employment. It included a no-poaching pact among the employers. Part of this process was convincing workers that the feeling of "company as family" was an age-old facet of Japanese culture. In reality, the post–World War II practice of "a lifetime commitment is no more strongly rooted in the sociocultural values of Japan than the universal practice of labor piracy and exploitation in the early days of Japan's industrialization" (Taira 1962: 158).

During World War II, Tokyo imposed laws preventing workers from leaving a job in certain industries without government permission. Lifetime employment became even more prevalent after the war, but, in a reversal of needs, now the impetus came from labor. In the early postwar era, labor was abundant, which reduced workers' bargaining power. Hence, it was the unions that demanded job security. Court decisions over the 1960s–1970s made it very difficult for employers to resort to mass dismissals.[2] It took until the 1970s for labor turnover to decline to its current low rate.

---

[2] In 1979, the courts established four conditions to be met before regular employees could be dismissed: (1) employers should be faced with compelling and unavoidable necessity for dismissals; (2) they should have made every effort to avoid dismissals (e.g., transfers to affiliated companies,

In the first few decades, the system worked. Not only did companies and workers have a stake in technological improvements, but learning within a long-lasting team is greater than the sum of learning by individual members of the team.

Indeed, during the same period that lifetime employment became entrenched in Japan, it also prevailed in many of the large American firms, albeit less rigidly and with a different flavor. The resemblance should not be surprising because, in the prevailing Mark II technological regime, that approach was adaptive, as were other practices misperceived as characteristically Japanese. In fact, until the 1980s, US large corporations resembled what we now think of as the traditional Japanese large-firm model. Lifetime employment was the norm at large blue-chip companies such as IBM, HP, AT&T, General Electric, oil companies, and the Big Three auto companies, for example. "The innovation models were based on in-house R&D, with AT&T's Bell Laboratories leading the way in basic and applied research. . . . Companies tended to be vertically integrated, controlling most aspects of their supply chains themselves" (Kushida 2015: 17).

Over time, seniority pay became part of the labor system, once again something the unions pushed for after World War II. A worker would start off with relatively low wages but would earn more and more the longer he stayed, until a certain age (currently around 60). So, there was an incentive to stay. Adding to these carrots, there was a stick: if a worker left a big company, few other companies, particularly in the same industry, would hire him at comparable pay. Over time, other carrots and sticks evolved that not only incentivized workers to stay, but also let them share in the prosperity of their employers. Twice-yearly bonuses adding up to a third of annual income act as a kind of profit-sharing, another reason for workers with secure jobs to embrace technology that enhances profits. While some companies provide portable pensions, most still provide a lump sum retirement payment, which a worker loses if he switches jobs. That's a big deal since at companies large and small, the payment averages about three years' worth of pay. Finally, the 1950s brought the triumph of enterprise unions, whereby a union represents just the workers at one firm, rather than all workers in a given industry.

terminating employment of temporary and part-time workers, facilitating early retirement, reducing overtime, and suspending new hires); (3) they should consult with trade union representatives and employees about dismissals; and (4) they should establish reasonable standards and apply them fairly when selecting workers for dismissal.

Workers at Toyota are incentivized to align their interests more with their employer than with fellow workers at Nissan or Honda.

Just as an economy needs a balance among mice, gazelles, and elephants, so economies need a balance among various lengths of job tenure. For some companies and workers, a kind of lifetime employment may be quite suitable. However, in today's situation, there are fewer such companies and such workers than a few decades ago, as detailed below. Not surprisingly then, the situation is changing in both positive and negative ways.

Generational Shift

Unless a venerable print media company could up its game in online media, its president knew, it faced steady decline. Unfortunately, his in-house staff lacked the capabilities. So, he broke with tradition, reached a delicate accommodation with the company union, and, for the first time, the company engaged in some mid-career hiring. That was the only way to gain expertise in website design, web marketing, advertising, analysis of readers' clicks, and so forth. The move saved the company.

One day, one of these bright twenty-something mid-career hires greeted the CEO, saying, "Thank you so much for the opportunity; now I'm moving to my next job." Stunned, the CEO asked why. "Well, a couple of firms were following my career here and one offered me a good job." The CEO couldn't believe his ears; he had given this fellow a chance, exciting work, and good pay. Was he bargaining for more money? "No, it's not the money," came the reply. "Working for you was a great adventure. And now I'm off to my next adventure" (Interview October 2019).

Harry Hill at Shop Japan recounted a similar experience. Given the severe shortage of ICT-related professionals, the competition among companies to recruit, and retain, these staffers has become much more intense. In fact, one day, a group of his data engineers came to him, saying that they wanted to spin off their own company. Oak Lawn would have an equity stake, but they wanted to act independently. If Oak Lawn did not agree, they'd leave. He agreed willingly.

Just 21% of young adults have even heard of terms said to describe attitudes allegedly held by Japanese employees, terms like *kigyo senshi* (corporate soldier) and *moretsu shain* (fiercely devoted employee). That compares to 55% of those in their forties (Murai 2015).

The myth portrays Japanese salarymen as loyal workaholics who buy into the myth of the company as family, and are happy to sacrifice time with their real family for the sake of the company. The reality, according to cross-country polls, is that Japanese employees are more dissatisfied with their work life than employees in other rich countries and are increasingly dissatisfied with each passing year (Inoue 2022; Reuters 2008). Korn Ferry found that just 56% of Japanese employees felt "engaged" at work, 10 points below the 23-country average. The source of the dissatisfaction is not just the long hours, but also "the narrow range of originality and ingenuity that individuals are permitted as well as delays in empowering them in many workplaces" (Inoue 2022). Moreover, despite all the disincentives for switching jobs, the majority of job-switchers say they made the right choice (Kyodo 2021). In short, many of those who stay at their firms do so, not because they feel happy or loyal, but because the lifetime employment system and government policies provide too many disincentives to switch jobs. Moreover, companies with less job satisfaction also show less growth in sales and profits. The system is no longer optimal for either employees or employers.

Even those employees who are content to stay at the elite companies say they no longer feel that they owe it to their employer to sacrifice family life and personal fulfillment. The demand for shorter days is just the beginning. A few decades ago, employees would regularly go out drinking with colleagues or clients 10–15 times per month as part of team-building rituals. Those who'd rather spend time with their families feared losing out on promotions. Today drinking nights are down to fewer than 5 per month. Whereas job-switchers were once regularly criticized as disloyal, now only 22% of male regulars say switchers would face such criticism from their co-workers (Holbrow 2022).

Even at the Ministries—once among the most sought-after job in Japan—the new restiveness can be felt. One in seven officials age 30 or younger told the Cabinet Personnel Bureau in 2020 that they will leave their Ministry within a few years. "I want a more attractive job," explained half of the respondents. Joining, or even founding, a startup has become a trend among some of these younger bureaucrats, particularly those who have spent time in an overseas posting (Suzuki 2020; Sato 2018).

The growing pursuit of personal fulfillment is hardly limited to work life. Before the 1990s, divorce was primarily initiated by men. Women, who were dependent on their husbands for income, resisted. Today, it's the other way around (Alexy 2021). A few decades ago, socially acceptable reasons for women to initiate divorce were things like abusive behavior or the husband seeking a new wife. Now, women divorce because they find the marriage unfulfilling, lacking in intimacy, or damaging to their sense of self. Allison Alexy added that people in Japan speak very often about how this is a generational shift. She also noted that this paralleled similar changes in other countries.

The Japanese equivalent of fulfillment or raison d'être, *ikigai*, is spoken of more often these days, but in a new way (Ozawa-de Silva 2020). For older generations achieving a sense of *ikigai* was more about fulfilling oneself within the context of the standard norms of family and company. These days, it's more about finding meaning in one's own individual desires.

The year 2020 saw the birth of a new company named Project MINT (Meaning, Ikigai, Network, Transform) devoted to teaching people how to achieve *ikigai* via a 10-week course. Its founder, Tomoe Ueyama, left SONY after eight years and, like many other entrepreneurs, she recharged her mental batteries by going abroad. "After I left SONY, I wanted to be a part of a change in Japan's educational system so that it could harness more individual creativity. So, I moved to San Francisco, freelanced in education innovation, and reported on the trend to Japanese educators" (Interview May 2022).

It had never occurred to her to create her own company until she saw a social problem, particularly among the aged, that she felt she could help address. As Japanese society becomes more accepting of individual diversity, it is becoming more common to belong to various organizations or communities. For example, not only working in a company but also doing *pro bono* work at an NGO (nongovernmental organization) or joining a learning community. "Older Japanese women are naturally good at building networks in various communities because of their life experience in family, friends, and assorted organizations. Most male salarymen have not been good at this because they spent so much of their time just within the company environment. After they retire, they tend to feel lonely."

In less than two years, her company reached 16 staffers (Ueyama plus 15 part-time contractors), and she hopes to keep expanding. Eventually, Ueyama would like to bring it to other Asian countries, like South Korea and Singapore, where people's careers give them less fulfillment than elsewhere.

Desire versus Feasibility

What has most changed vis-à-vis careers is not people's preferences, but their feeling that it's now more feasible to act on those preferences. Surveys over the two decades have consistently shown that just half of respondents preferred to work at one firm and become a manager there, while 31% preferred to work at many firms, eventually becoming a manager somewhere else (Takahashi 2019: 14).

Fewer people believe that companies can still fulfill promises of lifetime employment, so the security that kept people at a boring job is disappearing anyway (Kashiwagi 2018). In a 2015 survey by Dentsu, Japan's biggest advertising firm, just 18% believed they would work for one company for their entire careers, whether they wanted to or not (Murai 2015).

For a long time, there was a big gap in Japan between those dissatisfied with their jobs, and those willing to act on that feeling. A 1999 survey found that just 60% of job holders in Tokyo were satisfied with their job, but only 27% wanted to change jobs (Yashiro 2011). Often, what people "want" is constrained by what they think is attainable. In some situations, people "dream small." However, as Tsusaka pointed out, as generations and economic conditions changed, so did expectations and behavior.

By now, job-switching has grown enough to show up in the statistics. This came through in a pioneering study that compared the tendency to stay at the same employer among workers of successive cohorts and ages, such as those age 25–29 or 30–34, and those who entered the workforce in 1982 versus 1997 (Kato and Kambayashi 2016; Kambayashi and Kato 2017). Far more of those born 15 years later switched jobs at the same age (see Figure 11.2).

Let's go through the data since the chart is a little complicated. Among those who had already worked for the same employer 10–14 years, how many stayed with that employer for another 10 years, or more? Among 25–29-year-olds who had already put in 10 years as of 1982, 70% stayed another 10 years. However, among those who came of age 15 years later, the share staying on dropped a hefty 18 percentage points to 52%. A similar pattern can be seen in the 30–34-year-old cohort. In older cohorts, there's also a change, but not to the same degree.

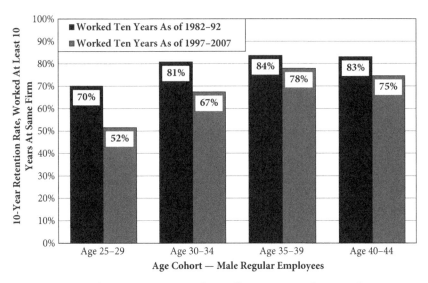

Figure 11.2 Workers age 25–44 were less willing to stay at the same firm after 1997.

Source: Kambayashi and Kato (2017), updated with data emailed by Kato.

Supply and Demand Show Their Power

Giving even greater force to the attitudinal change is a growing shortage of labor, particularly in very skilled areas. In 2016, METI projected that, as demand grew, the shortage of ICT professionals would rise from 170,000 in 2015, to 370,000 by 2020, and 790,000 by 2030 (Kogure 2019). In this and other occupations, companies have started bidding against each other to hire experienced staffers. This goes very much against the postwar practice of hiring people straight out of high school or college as blank slates and molding them in the firm's image. They've also been compelled to pay some specialists premium wages. In 2019, NEC offered a starting salary of ¥10 million ($77,000) to the best R&D recruits, which would often mean giving them a higher salary than those hired years earlier. SONY offered a 20% pay hike for specialists in AI and other fields. Premium pay for a particular occupation goes against the postwar tradition of pay based primarily on seniority. Most stunning of all, by 2019 the salaries of mid-career salarymen who switched from a large firm to some domestic startups increased by 40%, which exceeded the pay jump they could get from switching to a listed company (Schaede 2020: 201).

Persol Holdings—a staffing agency founded in the 1970s by Yoshiko Shinohara, who would become Japan's first female self-made billionaire—not only helps companies find mid-career ICT pros; it also offers training programs in ICT.

The percentage of firms engaging in mid-career hiring almost doubled from just 35% in 1994 to 70% by 2019. The shift included firms with at least 1,000 employees, where lifetime employment was traditionally most prevalent. Two-thirds of the firms said that they adopted mid-career hiring to replenish employees when experienced employees retired, while 17% said it was to gain employees with various sorts of experience and skills that the firm needed (Abe and Hoshi 2007;[3] MHLW 2022a).

One encouraging sign of the change in the supply-demand situation is that the need for companies to offer wage premiums to job switchers has broadened to all sorts of occupations. Back in 2009, just 15% of men switching jobs got a salary hike of more than 10%. As of 2017, the share almost doubled to 27%. The biggest hikes were among younger workers. For example, among those age 25–29 of both sexes, the share of job-switchers getting pay hikes of more than 10% doubled from 18% to 35%, while those getting pay hikes of more than 30% tripled from 4% to 13% (see Figure 11.3).

This is good news for entrepreneurship. With more employers willing to hire people in mid-career, and at a premium to boot, more staffers will feel they have a fallback option if they start, or work for, a new company and it fails. Still, labor-market fluidity will need to increase even more if Japan hopes to create gazelles on a European or even American scale.

Is What's Good for Japan Good for Toyota?

Just because some trend benefits the economy as a whole does not mean it benefits the dominant incumbent firms. If labor mobility hurts them, they will resist the needed change. Fortunately, some research shows that individual companies can also benefit. One study documented that firms with conventional Japanese employment practices can raise profits by raising labor turnover (Yamamoto and Kuroda 2016). Of course, firms with excessive turnover can run into trouble, but most Japanese corporate elephants are far below the optimal rate of turnover.

---

[3] Updated data graciously provided by the authors.

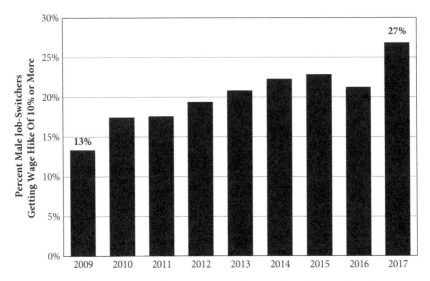

Figure 11.3 Companies need to pay more to lure workers from other firms.
Source: MHLW (2017d, other years).

In the past, the benefit of a low level of turnover outweighed the costs in Japan, but not anymore. In the lifetime employment system, workers tend to develop company-specific skills, rather than either occupation-specific or more generalized skills. In a stable technological environment, that can work very well. However, in a situation of rapid and uncertain technological change, firms need to bring in fresh thinking and new skill sets via mid-career hiring. Consequently, say Yamamoto and Kuroda, the optimal level of employee turnover has changed in the Japanese labor market, and as a result, "business performance is improving in companies that are changing their behavior accordingly." They calculate that the profit-maximizing turnover rate in Japan is now 20% per year. But the actual average turnover rate is just 6.7%. Similarly, the average mid-career hiring rate of 4% is too low. They conclude that "firms with conventional Japanese employment practice can earn profits by raising labor turnover" (1).

If companies find the Yamamoto-Kuroda conclusions borne out by their own experiences, then firms with optimal turnover and mid-career hiring would likely be able to take market share away from firms that do not. Their share of the labor force would also grow. Other big firms, seeing their success, would emulate them.

What Should the Government Do?

The government can give economic selection a nudge by reversing a host of policies that have hitherto penalized workers who switch jobs.

Japan has already begun taking one very important step: making pensions more portable (i.e., a worker still gets his pension benefits if he switches firms). Most of Japan's 56 million employees are in the national pension plan, which is already portable. However, 17 million are in an additional corporate pension plan. Many of the latter also receive a hefty lump sum retirement package averaging about three years' pay. While the lump sum payments are not portable, Japan began making some of the corporate pensions portable beginning in 2005. As of 2018, the 7.2 million workers in defined *contribution* plans can transfer their pension benefits. The remainder transferring from a firm with a defined *benefit* plan can only transfer their benefits if the new company chooses to accept them. (MHLW 2020a, 2020b).

The most important measure is to end the enormous difference in wages between regular and non-regular workers. That way, regulars would feel they had a fallback option if they took a chance on a new firm, and it failed. At the same time, companies would retain the flexibility to adjust payroll sizes and non-regulars would get a living wage. All Tokyo needs to do is to enforce its own laws. The 2008 Part-Time Workers Act mandates equal pay for equal work, and explicitly outlaws paying non-regular workers or women lower wages if they are doing the same job as regular full-time male workers (Katz 2015a). As is the case with laws forbidding discrimination against female employees, the government takes no responsibility to investigate and prosecute violations. So far, Tokyo has shown no interest in moving on this, despite frequent and futile calls on companies to raise wages.

Since courts interpret the current labor law as virtually forbidding mass layoffs of regular workers until a company is at death's door—when earlier downsizing might have reduced the number of eventual layoffs—it would help to modify those laws.

Japan's publicly financed social safety net is like an umbrella designed for a climate where it never rains; it's full of holes. On paper, as of 2019, unemployment compensation looks generous. Unemployed get 70% of their previous wage for the first six months and 35% for the next six months for workers above age 45 with long job tenure (even if at different companies). However, the eligibility rules are so strict—most non-regulars are ineligible—that only

20% of the unemployed actually get compensation. Consequently, the ratio of unemployment compensation to lost income of all the unemployed is a truly dismal 10%–15% (OECD 2018a). One of the biggest sources of growing long-term unemployment has been young adult men.

Finally, Japan needs to pursue "active labor measures" that use retraining and job-matching to help workers transition to new jobs. Currently, the government subsidizes firms to keep redundant workers on their payrolls, and Japan spends only one-third as much as the typical OECD country on active labor measures.

The rigid labor system and lack of a strong social safety net comprise the greatest impediment to public toleration of creative destruction. Japan needs a new lodestar: one that protects the worker, not the job. The flexicurity alternative, and its suitability to Japan, will be the subject of Chapter 17.

12

Overcoming the Digital Divide and R&D Gap

To a famished wanderer, a banquet is no banquet if it lies across a river he cannot ford. So it is with SMEs and the feast unleashed by digitization.

On one side of the digital divide stand companies like Nitori, a leading furniture retailer sometimes likened to IKEA. It has started to expand its e-commerce business using a visual tool called "augmented reality" (AR). Via a smartphone app, its customers can experiment with different types of furniture. Its sales more than doubled from 2012 to 2022. Many of Japan's SMEs get just crumbs from the table since most cannot afford to hire new staffers with the required skills, cannot find enough SME-oriented consulting companies to service their needs, and, worst of all, have no idea how much ICT could help them. They truly do not know what they are missing.

With each passing year, the digital divide between Japan and other countries, as well as between Japan's giants and its SMEs, becomes an ever-larger chasm. Among 63 countries, Japan ranks a dismal 29th in overall digital competitiveness (IMD 2022: 83, 102–103, 109). Its biggest handicap was what IMD called the agility of companies, a measure of how much companies are able to benefit in sales and profits from their digital investments by changing the way they operate. Japan ranked dead last at 63rd, despite ranking 41st in its spending on digital technologies. While Korea and Germany were somewhat higher than Japan on how much they spent, both ranked much higher on company agility, 16th and 34th, respectively.

SMEs employ 70% of Japan's labor force but conduct just 5% of spending on R&D, compared with 30% in the average OECD country. In the era of COVID, where telework becomes a necessity, 74% of Tokyo SMEs had no plans for remote work. Of those who had none, a third said that they lacked the proper equipment (Economist 2021).

The Contest for Japan's Economic Future. Richard Katz, Oxford University Press. © Richard Katz 2024.
DOI: 10.1093/oso/9780197675106.003.0013

Government action to overcome the digital divide would be a huge boost to both gazelle-formation and overall productivity growth. Yet, leaders continue to be distracted by the "shiny objects." In former days, it was exotica like superconductivity and nanotechnology. Today, it's AI and cryptocurrencies. Softbank CEO Masayoshi Son called for AI to be a *mandatory* subject for college entrance exams (meanwhile, Son's own $100 billion Vision Fund has invested almost entirely in overseas startups). Prime Minister Abe talked of producing 250,000 college students proficient in AI each year by 2025.

Should mandatory AI really be the priority when, out of 63 countries, Japan came in second-to-last in the digital skills of its population (IMD 2022: 105)? One reason is that, while Japan's high school students rank at or near the top among 80 countries in math and science tests as well as collaborative problem-solving, the schools come in dead last in several digital areas, such as teachers' knowledge of ICT skills, ability to teach them, and resources to train these teachers (OECD 2020j: 265–270). How is that possible? The reason, explained an advisor to the government on education reform, is that these skills are not included in university entrance exams. So, teachers feel no incentive to teach them (Suzuki 2022: minute 43:05 to 45:00). The exam will include ICT-related questions beginning in 2025, but that still leaves the question: Who will teach the teachers?

Beyond that, Japan suffers a severe shortage of professionals in the foundations of ICT needed by its companies. So far, Tokyo's digitization efforts have focused on small goals like having government agencies use email instead of FAX machines, getting rid of the *hanko* (stamp) that officials now have to use to sign documents, or letting citizens fill out government forms online.

What Japan really needs is the prosaic work of reducing the digital divide. A good start would involve training more students in everyday commercial ICT, making low-cost consulting available to SMEs, and providing tax relief for startups investing in ICT and R&D. Without such efforts, Raksul's recent move to set up a tech center in Bengaluru (Bangalore), India, could be a harbinger. Raksul wants to create 10 business lines to transform conventional industries, as it is doing in parcel delivery. One of those business lines will be in ICT, and the Bangalore facility will be the hub of its global effort. Raksul's Chief Technology Officer Yusuke Izumi explained that, given the competition within Japan for scarce IT professionals, Raksul would not be able to recruit enough staffers to base the project in Japan.

The High Cost of Free Technology

Most people can appreciate that it costs several percent of GDP to produce new knowledge, from R&D expenditures to the costs of running a research university. What's often less appreciated is how much more it costs for a country to *absorb* even freely available knowledge, like teaching children 2 + 2 = 4. American universities spend nearly $160,000 to transfer free knowledge from professors to each engineering student through graduate school.

How much, then, does it cost the companies who need to hire these specialists? Even if all the software and hardware were free, the SME would still need to pay staffers or outside consultants capable of assimilating new knowledge and of advising executives on how to use it well.[1]

Given their limited resources and understanding, it's no wonder that Japan's SMEs spend so little on ICT. While large companies devote 10% of their total investment to software, the ratio is just 4% at firms with fewer than 300 employees. Only one in four SMEs invested in IT equipment or software in 2017. But one cannot run 2022 software on a 2012 computer. Back in 1993, the average age of equipment was nearly the same at large companies and SMEs, just 4.4 and 4.9 years, respectively. By 2015, the average age had risen to 6.4 years at big companies and 8.5 years at SMEs (METI 2017a: 14–15).

The digital divide is part of the reason that Japanese SMEs have a bigger productivity gap with larger companies than exists in the rest of the OECD. In Japan, output per worker at firms with 10–49 workers—not counting the micro enterprises with fewer than 10 workers—is just 42% of productivity at firms with at least 250 workers. That's 10 points lower than in the typical OECD country (see Figure 12.1). As the OECD put it, low SME productivity in Japan stems in part from "less investment in new technology and digitalization, reflecting their weaker financial position, lack of human capital and the advanced age of many owners" (OECD 2019e: 52).

---

[1] One of the criticisms of endogenous growth theory is that, despite its other contributions, it assumes that knowledge can be absorbed at no cost. Some later generations of the model remedied this shortcoming (Braunerhjelm et al. 2010; Audretsch 2007).

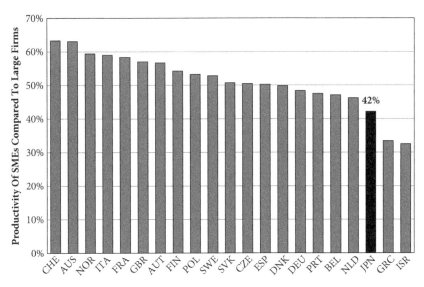

Figure 12.1 The productivity gap between SMEs and big firms is worse in Japan.

Source: OECD (2019e: 79).

Note: Compares enterprises with 10–49 employees to those with 250 or more; see country code pg. 12 for abbreviations.

How Do I Use This Stuff?

Perhaps even more pivotal is that too many SMEs have no idea how to get the best out of ICT. This shortcoming afflicts not only SMEs, but also many of Japan's biggest companies. Virtually all SMEs use computers and the Internet, but most just rationalize tasks they already undertake (e.g., using email to receive customer orders). This cuts labor costs but does not expand sales. Others know how to use ICT to expand sales, profits, productivity, and jobs by improving their product line, enhancing data analysis of their customer behavior, conducting better inventory management, developing new partnerships with other firms, and utilizing e-commerce. Recall the beer and diaper story from Finland.

Among SMEs using e-commerce for B-to-B business, its biggest use in Japan, 31% said the main purpose was cutting costs. Coming in fifth was increasing sales, named by just 20%. The pattern was very different among SMEs doing B-to-C e-commerce, a much smaller use of these tools. Increasing sales came in first at 40%. When METI asked SMEs that had not yet invested in IT why not, the biggest reason, at 43%, was "a lack of personnel who can introduce IT." A close second at 40% was "The effects of introducing IT are unclear or are not sufficient" (METI 2016a: 116–157).

If more of these SMEs had the financial and personnel resources to make the proper decisions about ICT investment and usage, they really could exploit its potential. Unfortunately, even among those SMEs already investing in ICT, only 4% say that they have sufficient personnel on staff to get the best out of it. What's really surprising is that 40% of *large* enterprises need to use external consultants in addition to internal staff to help design strategic use of ICT. Given the shortage of ICT pros in Japan, this is going to become an increasingly severe problem unless remedies are undertaken (METI 2016a: 116–157).

How Problems Give Rise to Solutions

Solutions to one problem always create new problems that often give rise to new companies that can envision yet another solution. The rise of advanced software is producing a shortage of software engineers. And, in this case, one of the needed new companies is Monstar, which taps overseas software talent. Having evolved from an earlier startup launched by the 30-year-old Hiroki Inagawa and a few of his friends, Monstar undertakes software projects outsourced to it by companies unable to do it themselves. So far, the Monstar firm has already carried out more than 2,000 projects.

Monstar owes its existence to a combination of new technologies and globalization. The latter goes far beyond founder Hiroki Inagawa getting his MBA at Australia's Bond University and working for seven years at US-owned consulting firms like PwC. "I tried to create a new platform so that Japanese companies could work with developers from overseas. We launched that in 2013" (Interview June 2018). At that point, he was 37. Clients hire Monstar to create the software they need and Monstar provides it using engineers all over the world, mostly in Asia. Of its 1,000 employees, 700 are in foreign countries. Inagawa requires the latter to come to Japan to learn Japanese, so as to better communicate with clients.

Interestingly, one of the big investors getting Monstar off the ground was Pasona, a recruitment firm that, as of 2022, had revenues of ¥366 billion ($2.8 billion). "Because of the shortage of engineers in Japan, Pasona finds it can only fill 10%–20% of their clients' needs. So, Pasona talked to us about hiring overseas engineers and performing work for their clients," explained Inagawa. Another early investor was Digital Garage, a Japanese VC firm started in 1995. Initially, it was medium-sized companies that utilized Monstar, but over time big companies became clients as well, some of them introduced by Pasona. Often, they hire Monstar to accomplish software tasks that the in-house staff is not equipped to handle. Inagawa's goal is revenues of $1 billion by 2025. One Monstar is not enough.

What Is the Government Doing?

What are policymakers doing to address the problem? The short answer is not enough. All too often, what the government gives with one hand, it takes away with the other.

In 2020, Prime Minister Yoshihide Suga proposed what he called a big campaign of digitization, including the creation of a new Digital Agency, to begin in 2021. However, this was almost entirely about putting online various sorts of government forms, from inter-agency communication to people's taxes. Very little has been said about aiding SMEs to overcome the digital divide.

METI has requested a budget of ¥39 billion ($300 million) in fiscal 2020 to aid businesses, a drop in the ocean compared to the $11.3 billion the European Union has budgeted for 2021–2027 to help its SMEs exploit digital technologies. The European Union had begun pilot projects in 2016 and found a high level of satisfaction among SMEs that used them (European Entrepreneurs CEA-PME 2020).

The governmental Japan Finance Corporation (JFC) does provide loans to buy IT equipment and software, some at standard interest rates and some lower. However, the government cannot substitute for banks. In 2016, the JFC lent money to 88,000 of Japan's 3.8 million SMEs; 90% of them were micro firms with fewer than nine staffers (BOJ 2017). More helpful would be well-designed tax breaks, like accelerated depreciation allowances, as well as improving SME access to bank loans (details in the next chapter).

METI's Organization for Small & Medium Enterprises runs its own low-cost consulting program for SMEs, a program called the CIO Development Support Program. This is another case of the government trying to fill a gap in the private market, rather than stimulating the private market to do the task.

Just as in JFC lending, the government cannot provide aid to even a fraction of the firms that need it. More helpful would be measures to aid the hiring of private consultants, encouraging more foreign ICT pros to work in Japan, encouraging more private firms like Monstar, and stimulating universities to offer practical courses to SME executives.

Just as SMEs need to meet certain qualifications to get CIO development support, so must any financial aid (METI 2016a: 156).

Ninety Percent of Government Aid to R&D Goes to Large Companies

There are, unfortunately, serious doubts about how earnestly the government wishes to dimmish the digital divide. Consider how it handles subsidies to R&D, a related issue.

Japanese SMEs of all ages that invest 2.5% of their revenue in R&D are more than twice as profitable as those who do no R&D. Those profits give them a lot more funds to plow back into expansion (METI 2017a: 399). Moreover, as noted above, the connection between innovation and growth is even stronger for younger, smaller firms than for older, larger firms.

Like most other rich countries, Japan provides government aid to company R&D. That makes a lot of sense, since technology is a primary source of growth and, as most economists agree, market forces alone would not provide a sufficient amount. As a share of GDP, Japan is in the middle of the pack among 26 OECD countries in giving financial aid, about 0.15% of GDP. Unfortunately, only 12% of that aid goes to companies with fewer than 500 employees, those most in need of such aid. This compares to 26% in the United Kingdom and 52% in Germany (OECD 2020h). Only 8% goes to companies with fewer than 250 workers, the lowest rate in the OECD (see again Figure 2.3 in Chapter 2).

The primary reason is that most government aid comes via tax credits on company profits, rather than direct subsidies. A tax credit, however, only helps firms already earning profits. The very nature of a knowledge-intensive gazelle is that, in its early years, it is very likely to be losing money as it spends money to develop its product. Hence, the tax credit does it no good. In a survey of nearly 400 university spinoffs, half spent more than ¥10 million ($77,000) per year on R&D, but only 40% were already earning any profit, and of the latter, the majority had profits of less than $50,000. Nonetheless, as noted above, as the years go on, R&D-intensive SMEs end up being far more profitable.

The direct subsidy, by contrast, helps both profitable and not-yet-profitable firms. Of course, it also helps firms that never become profitable. But that is one of the ways societies generate more experiments when there is no way to tell in advance which one will succeed. For this reason, several countries provide all, or almost all, of their aid via direct subsidies. In Germany, university-based analysts screen the subsidy applications for worthiness.

In 2015, Japan added a 30% tax credit for R&D conducted in collaboration with a university or public research institution. This, too, inordinately helps the incumbents because they are the most likely to be invited to such collaboration. Qualified newcomers need to be invited, not only because they are more likely to come up with fresh ideas that will help everyone, but also because it would help these potential gazelles find customers and expand (Kneller 2007: 165, 203; Rtischev 2016).

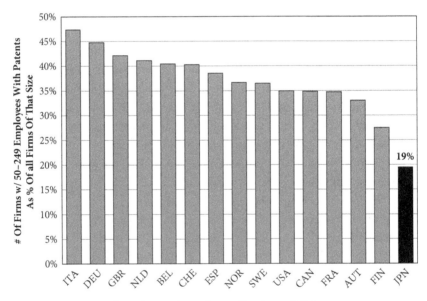

Figure 12.2 Japan places last in SME share of business R&D.

Source: OECD (2013a: 195).

Note: The number of firms with 20–249 employees conducting R&D as a share of all firms with 20 or more employees; see country code pg. 12 for abbreviations.

If the government is truly interested in promoting gazelles, it should use a policy common in other countries: long "carry-forwards" of the tax credit. A carry-forward means that, if a firm earns, say, a $20,000 tax credit in 2020, but has no profits that year, then it can carry the credit forward to, say, 2025 or 2030, when it does earn profits. The OECD recommends long carry-forwards to avoid favoring incumbents. After warning that subsidies to incumbents that delay the exit of less productive firms might slow the reallocation of resources from less to more productive firms, it lists as an example, "fiscal measures that favor well-established firms, such as R&D tax credits that do not have carry-forward provisions" (OECD 2015c: 79).

A few OECD countries do provide long carry-forwards (e.g., 20 years for the US and Canada and forever in the UK), but Japan is not one of them. It used to offer a trivial one-year carry-forward, but, as of April 2015, had abolished even that in the name of fiscal discipline. Despite talk of promoting high-growth startups, the Abe administration moved in the opposite direction (OECD 2010, 2019h: 1).

Government tax policy is not the only reason that Japan comes in dead last in the OECD in the share of business R&D done by SMEs (see Figure 12.2) and SMEs' share of patents. However, instead of ameliorating the problem, government policy has aggravated it. It's giving tax breaks to cash-rich elephants while denying them to the potential gazelles who really need them.

13

Finance for New Firms

Finance is the lifeblood of capitalism. It decides who gets to produce what, and how much. All day and all through the night, going back and forth across borders, it shifts capital from one company to another. If it's working well, it dispenses credit to firms likely to use it well and withdraws it from those that no longer do so. The process not only raises living standards but also the financial returns to capital (i.e., whether ¥1,000 of capital earns 2% or 5%). That, in turn, is how the system provides better returns to the nation's households, whether through bank accounts, pensions, or the stock market. Unfortunately, for at least four decades, Japan's financial system has done its job poorly, handing out money to zombies and denying it to potential gazelles.[1]

In all rich countries, it's hard for startups to get funding in their earliest years. So, most get their start via the assets of the founder, family, and friends. Some max out their credit cards or take a second mortgage on their house. In Japan, however, the lack of access to bank credit is not only more severe, but it also goes on for far longer in an SME's life. In a survey of 1,600 Japanese companies less than seven years old, 67% said fundraising was their biggest problem during the preparation stage, 57% at the founding and initial years, and 35% during the growth stage (Yamori et al. 2019: 56). Other surveys show similar results.

Why is credit so pivotal to gazelle formation? It's because, as detailed earlier, firms that have the funds to start off bigger are more likely to survive, and the survivors have a better chance of becoming high-growth gazelles (Audretsch 2012: 21). And access to external funds is the key to starting off big enough and expanding quickly enough.

---

[1] No American should speak of Japanese finances without acknowledging that the 2008–2009 global calamity was the result of catastrophic malfeasance and widespread criminality by financial conglomerates in the United States and elsewhere, *not* including Japan. Still, the causes and consequences of America's financial meltdown are very different from the long, slow corrosion in Japan (Katz 2009a; Rakoff 2014).

The Contest for Japan's Economic Future. Richard Katz, Oxford University Press. © Richard Katz 2024.
DOI: 10.1093/oso/9780197675106.003.0014

Young firms in Japan find it more difficult to get credit, as do younger people, those most likely to create innovative and ambitious firms. That's one reason only 25% of Japanese SMEs are under 10 years old, the lowest share in the OECD (Criscuolo et al. 2014: 28).

Most of the reason for this lies in problems with the banking system, and a dearth of venture capital and angel investments. Other obstacles include assorted easy-to-remedy regulations. For example, some government measures unintentionally created barriers to growth by giving SMEs an incentive not to expand too much lest they lose their eligibility for assorted government benefits. Until 1999, the government limited SMEs to no more than ¥100 million ($770,000) of equity capital before they lost their SME status and thus eligibility for all sorts of benefits. When the government tripled that limit to ¥300 million ($2.3 million), many SMEs raised more capital. That increased their financial cushion in case of bad times, thereby lowering the odds of default, which made banks willing to extend a larger amount of loans to them. That, in turn, enabled them to invest more in plant and modern equipment and thus expand.

The Need for Angel Investment

Professional angel investors play a critical role in getting potential gazelles off the ground. They offer not only initial-stage seed money, but also all-important mentoring. They do so long before a firm is ready for venture capitalists or private equity firms or banks to jump in. Many of the best angels are former entrepreneurs. In Japan, reported Toshio Sugioka of Nomura's Institute of Capital Research, 30% of startups fail within 12 months, mainly due to a lack of outside financing and insufficient managerial experience. More angel finance would help solve both of these problems, he argued (Sugioka 2002).

In the United States, startups funded by angels are not only more likely to survive, but they hire 40% more people in the first few years and are able to gain more follow-up financing from banks and others. In 2019, angels invested a total of $24 billion in 63,730 companies, an average of $376,000 per company. That's 20 times the number of companies who received VC money, although each of the latter received millions of dollars in investments. Equally important, well-designed tax breaks increased the volume of angel investments. Twenty-six states in the United States have enacted tax credits.

After Wisconsin enacted a 25% tax credit in 2005, total angel investments jumped 10-fold (Center for American Progress 2020). A very positive case, and one studied by Japanese policy advocates, is the United Kingdom's Enterprise Investment Scheme (OECD 2016: 88–89).

Angels, unfortunately, are scarce in Japan. For example, consider the dearth of angel investments in <u>university spinoffs</u>. During 2015–2019, Japanese universities launched about 180 spinoffs per year, about a fifth of the US rate. Most start with too little capital: a quarter with just ¥10–50 million ($77,000 to $384,000). Only a third were capitalized at more than ¥50 million ($384,000). Moreover, almost all of the funding had to come from the company founder(s), friends, family, and employees. In only 1% of the cases were angels the largest shareholders (*Nikkei* 2014; METI 2020b). Many of these firms failed to reach their potential and others never got off the ground in the first place.

A dearth of funding keeps startups too small to reach <u>minimum efficient scale (MES)</u>. In 2019, the average 1–3-year-old Japanese startup received a paltry $91,000 in funding, while 5–7-year-old startups received $2.5 million (Arnold-Parra 2021). This compares to a global average of $7 million in VC "seed money" for a new startup, an average investment of $20 million in the first post-seed money round, called Series A, a few years later, and then a few years after that the Series B round averaging $58 million (Graham 2019: 5). With such limited funding, no wonder Japan has so few gazelles and even fewer <u>unicorns</u>.

Chapter 18 will show the battles within the government—including during the Kishida era—over what should be an easy reform: providing effective tax incentives for more angel investment.

Starved of Growth Capital from Banks

Only two of every five Japanese SMEs under 10 years old have been able to get bank loans, and less than half among firms 10–20 years of age. The older the firm, the more willing are banks to lend to it (see Figure 13.1).

To make matters even worse, when banks do condescend to lend to younger firms, they charge an interest rate up to 2 percentage points higher than the rate for a firm that is 50 years old (see Figure 13.2).

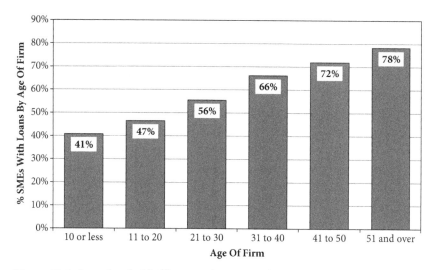

Figure 13.1 Less than half of firms under age 20 obtained loans.
Source: METI (2016a: 338).

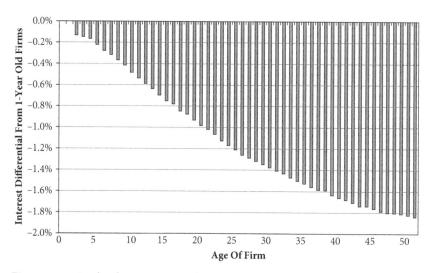

Figure 13.2 Banks charge younger firms higher interest rate.
Source: Sakai et al. (2010: 1975).

Note: The borrowing cost is measured as the difference in interest rate from youngest firms, put at zero. Data from 1995–2002.

The banks have their reasons, of course. Upwards of 80% of loans to SMEs require some sort of collateral, and startups have little collateral to offer. The banks also prefer lending to firms with which they have a long relationship, because this gives them soft information on the quality of management. Since startups by definition have little track record, banks say they lack any sound basis for making a credit evaluation. Moreover, given the high failure rate of new firms, it's better to be safe than sorry (Masaji et al. 2006).

While all this sounds reasonable, it surely cannot be the whole story. Why, for example, does a firm's age play a much bigger factor in a loan's interest rate than that firm's creditworthiness scores? SMEs in the most creditworthy decile averaged a cash flow equal to more than eight times their interest bill, while those in the worst decile couldn't even pay the interest on their old loans without borrowing more money. Yet, the gap in lending rates between these two deciles was much less than the gap in rates between old and young SMEs (IMF 2012a: 42).

Nor do the hurdles seen in Japan pose as big a problem in other countries. The IMF has compared borrowing conditions among SMEs in Japan, France, and Germany, using a measure called the Kaplan and Zingales (KZ) index. That index measures the degree to which a lack of credit prevents firms from investing enough or hiring enough people compared to firms with sufficient credit. A third of Japanese SMEs are considered credit constrained, compared to 26% in Germany and 18% in France (IMF 2017a: 33).

Lack of credit for new SMEs is one of the primary reasons that just 15% of Japanese SMEs are five years old or younger, less than half the OECD median of 36% (see again Figure 8.3 in Chapter 8).

The age of the founder matters at least as much as the age of the firm. Entrepreneurs in their twenties were able to get only half as much credit as their counterparts in their thirties. METI (2002: 54) concludes: "The younger the age of the entrepreneur, the greater the probability that the chief factor determining whether an individual starts up in business is . . . the inability to raise sufficient funds at the time of startup." Among founders in their twenties and thirties, 40% report difficulty in raising outside funds from banks, compared to just a quarter of those in their fifties (Higuchi et al. 2007: 180).

Meanwhile, 40% fewer female founders of SMEs got loans from private banks compared to men, while 16% fewer obtained them from government lenders. This is another reason why it's harder to spot female entrepreneurs in Japan (Higuchi et al. 2007: 180).

The Dreaded Personal Guarantee

If all this were not enough, Japan's banks impose yet another hoop for newcomers to jump through: a demand for collateral and/or a personal guarantee far beyond the rate of such demands in other OECD countries. METI reports that among firms with fewer than 100 employees, 80%–85% had to post collateral to get a loan (METI 2002: 143). In fact, banks depend far more on collateral than on evaluating the cash flow potential of a firm, particularly a small or new one (Masaji et al. 2006). They also rely on collateral far more than their counterparts elsewhere: 72% for Japan versus 45% for the median OECD country (see Figure 13.3).

By definition, startup companies have little collateral to offer. Consequently, the banks also require a "personal guarantee," not only for new companies, but for upwards of 85% of all SMEs. While collateral pledges the assets of the company, a personal guarantee entangles the personal assets of the owner (e.g., one's house and financial assets). Contributing to the complexity is the fact that many owners of unincorporated SMEs comingle their personal and business assets. It gets worse. Masahiro Ito protested that, even when he sold 80% of his business to investing partners, his personal guarantee still applied to 100% of the loan.

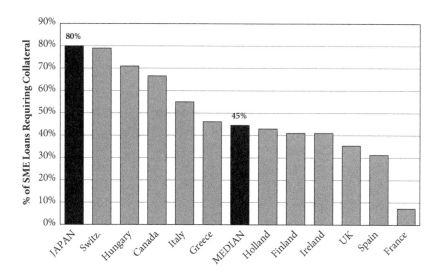

Figure 13.3 Japanese banks are outliers in collateral requirement.
Source: METI (2002: 143) for Japan; OECD (2018d: 39) for other countries

Yes, personal guarantees are common elsewhere, but nowhere near to the same degree as in Japan. In 2017, reported the IMF, banks in the average rich countries insisted on personal guarantees in 22% of the loans to SMEs; in the United Kingdom, it was 35%, but in Japan, a whopping 84%. The IMF commented on the drawbacks of reliance on collateral and the personal guarantee. It not only limits credit for newer, more innovative, and fast-growing SMEs, but it also weakens banks' incentives to do credit screening and risk-based lending. "Banks may not necessarily lend to the most productive firms, but instead lend to those with sufficient collateral" (IMF 2017a: 32–33, 45).

In effect, these loans to SMEs are more like personal loans than business loans, and, when banks lend to the SME founder rather than the SME itself, they do less screening of the business, and business performance is worse. Professor Roberta Cole and her colleague compared 5,000 American startups. They found that those who had to use personal loans had a 46% lower level of revenue over three years compared to those getting business loans (Cole and Sokolyk 2018).

The banks contend that collateral and personal guarantees impose discipline on the borrowers because they have "skin in the game." While that has some truth, the bigger impact is that it makes the borrowers overly cautious. Yes, SME borrowers posting collateral and/or personal guarantees do have higher rates of profit. But why? The borrowers, fearful of losing their house if they defaulted, cut costs to the bone in ways that hurt growth (e.g., lower rates of investment, less modern machinery, etc.). Consequently, a study found that sales growth was lower in the firms having to post collateral or personal guarantees. "The increase in profitability of collateralized borrowers is driven by cost reductions rather than by sales growth" (Ono et al. 2008: abstract).

METI finally recognized the problem of excessive collateral and personal guarantees in 2008, saying, "For SMEs that have no assets . . . and yet possess promising innovations or capabilities, establishing an environment in which funds can be borrowed smoothly from financial institutions is extremely important [to] the vitality of Japan's economy" (METI 2008: 179). However, it was the Financial Services Agency (FSA) that had jurisdiction over the issue, and it took until 2013 for anything to happen. The FSA and METI's own SME Agency issued guidelines for the banks to reduce personal guarantees based on their own self-regulation. Traditionally, such guidelines, while not bearing the formal power of law, are obeyed. In the few years since implementation began at the end of 2014, the portion of new SME loans (by number, not value) that required a personal guarantee has gradually diminished, from 88% in 2015 to 70% in early 2022 (FSA 2022).

It is unclear what this really means for credit availability for young firms. Banks are adept at meeting the numbers sought by the government while evading their intent. The data refer to more than 1 million new loans, but that actually includes both rollovers of loans to existing loans and loans to new customers. It is possible that most of the reduction was simply to the former, and that does not help younger companies. It also does not tell us whether the banks will continue lending to young firms if there is no longer a guarantee, or if they'll replace that with greater demand for collateral or a government guarantee. It may take a few years to sort out the real impact.

Draconian Personal Bankruptcy Laws

Roger Eberhart and his colleagues have shown that more lenient bankruptcy laws not only promote more entrepreneurship. They also improve the quality of startups by inducing individuals with more education, experience, and talent to take the now-lessened risk. Moreover, they calculate that the assorted reforms of *firm* bankruptcy law have produced this result in Japan (Eberhart et al. 2017).

However, *personal* bankruptcy law remains very harsh. If an SME owner chooses the bankruptcy option, his home will be seized. He may keep furniture along with 3 months' living expenses, to an amount equal to about $10,000. He may keep his car, and a life insurance policy up to a maximum of about $2,000. In the United States, the SME owner's home cannot be seized, he can keep some land, as well as savings up to about $30,000 (this varies by state).

In 2013, the Abe administration vowed to reform the Civil Code, including the parts governing personal bankruptcy. When the code was amended in 2017, the promised change regarding personal insolvency was absent (Jones Day 2017).

The Consequences

If a country's financial system limits entrepreneurial opportunities to men over age 40 with abundant financial assets, collateral, and income, is it any wonder that so few people even try to create high-growth firms, or that those who do try are more likely to fail?

SMEs younger than 10 years who cannot get bank loans expand their capital stock by 3.8% per year, compared to 4.8% for those with loans (see again Figure 8.6 in Chapter 8). After 10 or 20 years of compounding, this differential results in a big difference. Importantly, the inability to get bank loans affects the investment by younger firms more than older ones since the latter are generating more profits to reinvest.

When Kyoji Fukao and his colleagues investigated why the productivity gap between SMEs and larger firms is so much larger in Japan (see again Figure 12.1 in Chapter 12), they calculated that two-thirds of the gap was explained by lower investment rates at the SMEs (METI 2016a: 68).[2] That difference in investment rates was largely due to financial constraints. The same problem applies to investment in R&D.

A potentially viable gazelle can fail because lack of credit prevents it from reaching MES quickly enough. Due to path dependency, others may find themselves locked into a suboptimal strategy that cannot be corrected later. Those who fear being unable to survive rough times for lack of credit are even more likely to avoid the risky path required to thrive.

Government Loans and Credit Guarantees: Help or Hindrance?

The government was hardly blind to the dearth of credit. It sought to fill the credit vacuum by making direct loans through the Japan Finance Corporation (JFC), as well as providing fee-based government guarantees for private loans. In the latter program, in case of default, a government-backed entity would reimburse the bank for 70%–90% of the value of the loan (during the financial crises of the late 1990s and early 2000s, it reimbursed 100%). Unfortunately, these actions have done more harm than good. Help to potentially dynamic startups has been dwarfed by measures shoring up inferior firms, even outright zombies.

As discussed earlier, shoring up inferior firms hinders the entry of newer, more efficient and innovative firms (see again Figure I.1 in the Introduction).

---

[2] Some economists would contend that a greater share of the gap is the efficiency with which firms use their capital and labor. Still, there's no question that financial constraints have yielded suboptimal levels of investment.

The resulting adverse selection is, along with the lack of finance for newcomers, one of the biggest obstacles to Japan having more gazelles.

These programs are mammoth. From 1997 through 2019, the combined figure for direct loans and credit guarantees averaged a staggering 21% of the value of all loans to SMEs and 11% of GDP each year (see Figure 13.4). Few other OECD countries even have direct government loans to SMEs. While most have loan guarantee programs, none, except for Korea's, is sizable. In the median OECD country in 2018, the figure was a tiny 0.13% of GDP.

Over the past two decades, a staggering 40% of Japan's SMEs have used credit guarantees each and every year (JFC 2021: 17). Almost as many also borrow directly from the JFC. Credit guarantees are particularly vital at the regional banks and credit unions that have traditionally been the main source of SME credit (e.g., 17%–21% of all loans at the regional banks) (IMF 2012b: 30).

The JFC does have a program focused on newcomers, but they focused on shoring up mom-and-pop shops, not nurturing gazelles. In 2016, about a fifth of all new SMEs received such loans. Half went to those employing just one or two people; 93% had less than 10 staffers. Even years later, when the JFC surveyed the recipients, the average firm added just 1.3 more people. Altogether, the companies receiving these loans generated just 96,000 jobs, less than 0.2% of all jobs in Japan (BOJ 2017).

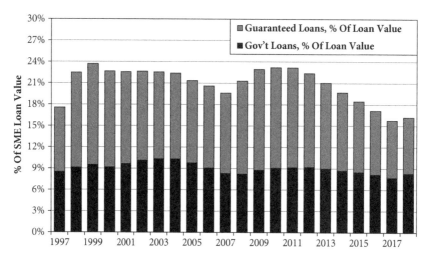

Figure 13.4 Government loans and government-guaranteed private loans, % of all SME loans.
Source: OECD (2019a: 144; 2016: 311).

Rather than filling a gap in the financial system, the primary purpose of JFC loans seems to have been funding the "disguised unemployment" that results from a flawed labor market, as well as shoring up marginal, or even zombie-like, SMEs that provide financial support to the elderly. Although there seem to be no data on loans by the age of either the borrowers or the enterprises, in all likelihood, the majority went to the mom-and-pop retail stores, restaurants, hair salons, and so on, that provide a second career for those who've been forced to retire from their jobs as early as 55–64 years of age, but who cannot get a private or governmental pension until age 65. In recent years, 70%–80% of all owners of unincorporated wholesale and retail SMEs, restaurants, and so on, were over 60 years old (Statistics Bureau 2017, 2018).

It was not always thus. In the 1950s–early 1960s, private banking was unable to mobilize the enormous amount of capital required. Hence, government loans financed a third or more of investment in such critical areas as steel, machinery, coal, electric power, and agriculture. As time went on, private savings rose and banks became stronger, government loans were increasingly devoted to helping out industries fading into the sunset (like coal), segments of society vulnerable to changes in the economy (farmers) or the rigidities of labor markets (those over 55 years old), as well as groups vital to the electoral success of the ruling Liberal Democratic Party (LDP), from farming and construction to SMEs (Katz 1998: 85, OECD 2019a: 143).

These days, however, as Ulrike Schaede points out, the government lenders are performing a disguised welfare function (Schaede 2005: 152, 171–172). Even the agencies that carry out the lending recognize that they serve only to prevent or postpone the SME's bankruptcy rather than to turn it around. Because the Japanese government does not offer a full-fledged welfare program for the structurally unemployed, it strives to keep overt unemployment as low as possible. Moreover, she adds, "To the extent that shame is associated with going on welfare in Japanese society (as anywhere else) providing government loans to bankrupt firms is an elegant way to arrange for welfare while preserving the appearance of an economic contribution." The government has built a trap for itself, Schaede points out. "As long as the government has insufficient alternative routes to provide welfare to very small firms, curtailing or abolishing these loan programs may cause severe social hardship."

The credit guarantee program seems to serve the same welfare function, however constructive it may have been when it began in 1948. The borrower pays a fee to governmental credit guarantee corporations. It is the bank, not the borrower, which decides whether an SME must use the credit guarantee to get the loan. Until 2006, every borrower paid the same insurance premium, no matter the level of risk.

The ostensible rationale is that credit evaluation is labor intensive and therefore too expensive to perform for an SME borrowing only $100,000 or so. What is more likely is that, in the past few decades, the banks have become so dependent on collateral that, in training their staff, they have "focus[ed] skill creation on collateral evaluation rather than borrower credit risk assessment" (Schaede 2005: 154).

It took until 2011 for the government to attempt a remedy by stimulating the formation of a Credit Rating Database (CRD). The idea was that banks could share information so that the cost of credit evaluation was spread around. Unfortunately, the CRD has not been as effective as hoped, even though it collects and distributes data on about 3 million of Japan's 4 million SMEs. While several credit registries are available, over half of the surveyed financial institutions said these agencies do not provide enough information in a timely fashion to enable them to properly evaluate credit risk. Moreover, financial institutions often fail to share credit information through credit registries, partly because of what should be easily correctable problems, such as the lack of a unique identification system for each borrower in the absence of a unique tax identification number (IMF 2012: 46). In the face of public resistance, the government began issuing such numbers in 2015 but, as of 2021, only 40% of citizens had signed up for such numbers.

A well-designed credit guarantee program focusing on young SMEs with growth potential would be very helpful if it enabled carefully screened applicants to get more private bank loans and if the government tracked the performance of the users. That is not what Japan does. Instead, the borrowers using credit guarantees are similar to those borrowing from the JFC: older people running mice. Moreover, the banks don't bother monitoring borrowers with guaranteed loans as much as those without guarantees. As a result, most of the SMEs using the guarantees suffered "*subsequent* lower profitability, and higher probabilities of falling into financial distress" (Uesugi et al. 2010: 19).

Pressuring Private Banks to Shore Up Zombies

The government loan and guarantee programs are part and parcel of the same policies that have pressured private banks to give unending life support to zombie SMEs via sub-market interest rates as well as evergreening of the loans (essentially lending new money to enable the borrower to repay the old loan, or the interest on it). The IMF reported (Lam and Shin 2012: 10) that borrowing costs for SMEs with low creditworthiness have fallen below banks' breakeven rate, and today borrowing rates are even lower. As for the latter, evergreening refers to a bank lending a failing SME the money to pay its interest, so it does not have to write down the value of its books. That makes nonperforming loans look smaller than they really are (OECD 2015a: 31).

In 2009, during the global financial crisis, the Diet passed a temporary law called the Financial Facilitation Act, which required financial institutions, in response to requests by SME borrowers, to grant grace periods for payments of interest and principal, and even some reduction of interest and debt obligations. All the SME had to do was to *say* it had a plan to make those loans performing within 5 to 10 years. In return, the banks could reclassify nonperforming loans as performing. That relieved the banks of the financial burden of having to write down, or write off altogether, trillions of yen in bad and dubious loans. During fiscal 2009–2013, the years when the temporary law was in force, the banks approved 97% of the 4.1 million applications on loans totaling ¥120 trillion ($9.2 trillion)—a flabbergasting *half of the value of all SME loans*, an amount equal to a fifth of Japan's GDP (Ono and Uesugi 2014).

As if this were not lax enough, Takeo Hoshi reports that, in 2009, the FSA changed its Inspection Manual so that "on condition that a company simply claimed to have a prospect for the formulation of a business reconstruction plan, the company's loan could be classified as normal" (Hoshi 2011: 4).

Even after the law expired in 2013, the FSA continued to pressure banks to continue forbearance. Consequently, the banks approved a total of 9.5 million cases during 2009–2019. Since there were less than 4 million SMEs, many of the applicants restructured several agreements several times. To top it all off, 40% of the SMEs whose loans received all this forbearance did not even bother to formulate turnaround plans, let alone fulfill them (Endo 2013; Yamori et. al. 2019: 8; FSA 2018).

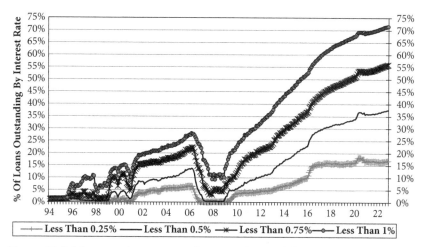

Figure 13.5 Near-zero interest rates keep zombies on life support.
Source: BOJ (2023b).

The excess capacity in assorted markets created by keeping the zombies afloat reduces the profits for healthy firms, which discourages their entry and investment. Consequently, industries dominated by zombies exhibit less job growth and lower productivity. Depending on the share of zombies in an industry, investment was depressed between 4% and 36% per year compared to a baseline level[3] (Caballero et al. 2008: 1943, 1946).

What used to manifest itself as a crisis of nonperforming loans at the banks has been transferred by this accounting ploy as deepening corrosion of the economy.

Zero Interest Rate Policy Further Atrophies Bankers' Skills

At this point, perhaps the biggest distortion of the financial markets is the government's decision to fight economic stagnation primarily via monetary stimulus—that is, a near-zero interest rate policy. As of early 2023, 16% of all loans charged less than 0.25%; 37% charged less than 0.5% (see Figure 13.5). At this rate, even the most zombified borrower can appear able to pay its debts.

---

[3] Although the study covered listed corporations, the point applies to SME zombies as well.

Removing the main pricing tool for credit—charging higher interest rates to less creditworthy borrowers—is like charging the same price for filet mignon and ground chuck. Pound after pound of chuck would lie unbought, while, as in the former Soviet Union, lines would form for the filet mignon. Stores might even ration the filet: only so much per customer. The same thing happens in Japan's loan market. With credit no longer rationed by risk-based interest rates, banks need other methods: collateral, personal guarantees, and government credit guarantees.

The whole syndrome further atrophied bankers' skills. What need for smart employees who knew their clients intimately or could evaluate the prospects of a new business, when the main criteria for lending was collateral and/or a personal guarantee? What need for the skills to set the proper interest rate when banks are given FSA guidance to lend to troubled SMEs at sub-market rates? How many bank officers would take the risk of recommending a loan to a new company with good prospects at banks that still use the *genten shugi* promotion system? Even if the government did away with all of its counterproductive policies in a flash, the banks could not act like proper banks until the skill set of credit approval officers is improved. That will be neither simple nor quick.

How sad to see this level of deterioration when, back in the high-growth era and beyond, Japan's main bank system was widely lauded as one of the secrets to the country's phenomenal success. Assessing the creditworthiness of borrowers is the most important function of banks, but it's also difficult and costly. Just relying on collateral is far less costly, but nowhere near as effective in allocating a nation's savings to their most productive use in promoting growth. Back in its heyday in the high-growth era, Hugh Patrick concluded that Japan's banking system "combined the use of collateral with intensive monitoring . . . seeking to distinguish between potential borrowers with excellent growth prospects, but little collateral, and those simply with sufficient assets" (Patrick 1994: 39–40).

In those days, distressed firms with close ties to a main bank recovered more quickly than other firms, as measured in sales or investments. One reason was that banks played an important role in forcing out the incumbent managers of distressed firms. Moreover, firms with bank executives as managers or directors were more likely to experience turnovers in top executives depending on performance (Hoshi et al. 2017: 3).

The system worked well—until it didn't. Due to a number of changes in the financial environment, in the late 1970s and 1980s the use of collateral more and more supplanted credit evaluation. That led to the 1980s stock and property bubble, due to a vicious cycle. Companies used their stock and property as collateral to borrow from the banks, then used that money to buy even more stocks and property, which then increased their collateral, leading to even more borrowing and buying. As far as the banks were concerned, each borrower had good collateral, but they ignored the systemic distortion. When this bubble met its inevitable popping, there ensued the bad loan crisis of the 1990s–early 2000s, and, finally, a quarter century, so far, of near-zero interest rates. In the end, banks intervened less and less in borrowing companies to rehabilitate them and were less effective when they tried (Hoshi et al. 2017: 1).

MOTHERS Market Proves a Disappointment

If banks have failed to open opportunities to potential gazelles, so has the stock market. In 2000, the Japanese government tried to promote superstar gazelles by midwifing the creation of a stock market for new companies on the Tokyo Stock Exchange. It's called MOTHERS (Market Of The High-growth and Emerging Stocks). Officials at the time exuded great confidence that this would replicate US success with the NASDAQ stock market. Investors on NASDAQ had funded the explosive growth of world-famous superstars like Apple, Cisco, Starbucks, Amazon, -T-Mobile, and Tesla. MOTHERS never even came close. Unlike the First Section market, which is dominated by professional and institutional investors, MOTHERS is dominated by retail investors. This has led to a very low ceiling on how much money a newcomer can raise via either its initial public offering (IPO) or later offerings. As of 2020, not a single one of the nearly 400 companies on MOTHERS had sales exceeding $1 billion, and just four independent firms have sales exceeding $500 million. By contrast, Starbucks alone takes in $26 billion. Of the companies that have graduated from MOTHERS to the First Section of the Tokyo Stock Exchange, only six have sales above $1 billion, and most of these are firms that have grown, not by challenging the big incumbents—in the mold of Amazon, Cisco, and Tesla—but by focusing on markets where the incumbents have little presence, such as web-based services, cell phone gaming, online flea markets, or social networking (SPEEDA 2021; Japan Securities Research Institute 2018).

Finance, the SME Succession Crisis, and the Rise of New Financial Institutions

Sometimes it takes a crisis to drive change. In the case of finance, the needed driver may be what is widely called the SME succession crisis, a product of both aging and generational change. Without a big change, the social dislocation could be very unforgiving.

If, in the 1990s–early 2000s, everyone worried that too many zombie firms were being kept on life support, now is an added worry in the opposite direction: that too many healthy SMEs will fail for lack of a successor. Every year as many as 70,000 successful SMEs—60% of them profitable—go out of business simply because aging owners cannot find a successor (Kamei and Dana 2012: 61). By 2028, according to METI, 2.45 million SMEs will be led by a president over age 70, of which about half have no successor in place (Tsuji 2017; METI 2018a: 357). As many as 6.5 million jobs could disappear (IMF 2019: 15–16; Nihon M&A Center 2020: 57). Among incorporated SMEs, only 3% want to close when the CEO leaves the scene. They want a successor to keep it going, but the majority cannot find one (METI 2017b: 10).

This is a relatively new problem caused by generational change. As late as the 1980s–early 1990s, approximately 95% of the owners of SMEs passed the firm to a son, daughter, son-in-law, or other family member, no matter the desires of the younger relative. Not anymore. Younger relatives uninterested in taking over are far more willing to resist their parents. By 2012, only 42% of SMEs with a successor found that person in a family member. Another 33% of the successors were employees (METI 2014: 253).

While this crisis reflects a clear generational change in attitudes, it also reflects the gaps in Japan's financial system and, in small ways so far, it is beginning to evoke change in finance. One financial flaw is the banks' demands for a personal guarantee. As noted before, many potential successors among employees are unable or unwilling to take on the burden of the personal guarantee. A second flaw is the dearth of firms advising retiring CEOs on various options and/or engineering enough mergers to keep these businesses alive.

Such services and institutions are beginning to arise: 14% of SMEs accepted a new owner-CEO recommended by their bank, tax accountant, local business association, or a similar partner; 9% by recruiting a new owner-CEO from the outside by themselves, sometimes with advice from a bank or accountant; and a tiny 1.5% sold their SME to another firm or outside investor (see Figure 13.6). Unfortunately, these alternative measures remain far

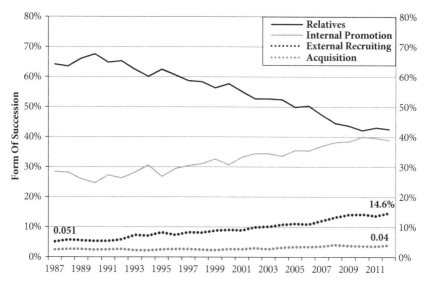

Figure 13.6 Change in forms of business succession.
Source: METI (2014: 253).

too small to fill the gap. Consequently, firms without successors either close down, or else the incumbent stays as long as he can (METI 2018a: 357).

SMEs that previously disdained selling themselves to another firm are now reassessing. A third of medium-sized firms told a survey that they'd consider a merger or acquisition to ensure continuation of the business. To whom do the SMEs look for referrals? One would think this is a job for the firm's bank. The problem, however, is that, while SMEs usually have a main bank, they don't have a main bank*er*, since loan officers are often transferred from branch to branch, or job to job at the same bank, every few years. So, 69% said their first choice was their tax accountant, typically an individual who has worked for them for decades and would also know potential partners (Uchida 2011; METI 2017a: 266, 295).

The situation has given rise to new sorts of independent specialized companies, matchmakers like Nihon M&A Center, Strike Co., and M&A Capital Partners. The number of matches arranged by them tripled between 2013 and 2018, with Nihon M&A Center alone reached more than 3,000 deals during 2017–2020, 80% of which were for succession mergers. In a fifth of the deals, the sales price topped ¥1 billion ($7.7 million) and the target had more than 50 employees. This is still a drop in the ocean compared to the need. In 2021, government agencies and M&A companies were able to find buyers from only 2,400 SMEs, and so 44,000 of them closed down, of which 24,000 were still profitable (METI 2017a: 345; Japan Times 2019; Dooley and Ueno 2023).

Nihon M&A Center was formed in 1991 by a group of tax accountants. Like so many other founders of gazelles, its creators have international experience. Nihon M&A's founder and current chairman, Yasuhiro Wakabayashi, had been a salesman at Olivetti Japan, where he built a network of contacts at regional banks and accounting firms. They now feed him information on inquiries from both buyers and sellers. Half the company's stock is held by foreign shareholders. In 2017, *Forbes* included Nihon M&A on its list of the best 200 companies in Asia with less than $1 billion in revenue. In 2022, its revenue reached ¥44.4 billion ($340 million).

One of Japan's newest billionaires as of 2023, Shunsaku Sagami, founded the M&A Research Center in 2018 at the age of 27, where he uses AI to link profitable SMEs facing a succession crisis with potential buyers. For example, one of M&A Research Institute's past deals included the sale of an IT firm with ¥200 million in revenue) but no successor to a ¥1.5 billion ($11 million) competitor seeking to expand. Sagami had a strong motivation, having seen his own grandfather's SME close for lack of a successor. Sagami himself became a billionaire when his company went on the stock market. Yet, Japan needs a lot more firms like this since, in the final quarter of 2022, he closed just 33 deals and had another 427 in process (Lee 2023; n.p.).

In addition, there is a small, but growing number of private equity (PE) firms buying up good SMEs with succession problems (Lee and Takezawa 2019; Wada 2020). Almost all of NSSK's deals, which are reportedly in the $100–200 million range, involve succession issues.

In the past, PEs were dismissed in Japan as "vulture funds," and, while some certainly fit the label, it is being increasingly recognized that many dealing with SMEs in countries like the United States do, in fact, help firms improve their health and their expansion. However, Japan has too few PE firms, and many of them can only handle 15–20 deals at a time. In 2018, there were reportedly just 686 PE and VC deals with a Japanese target. The targets include both large giants spinning off divisions and SMEs. As of 2021, there were 52 full members of the Japan Private Equity Association and 66 supporting members. Many of these are PE operations of big banks and investment banks, which have a very different culture, set of goals, and performance rates from independent PE firms. This compares to about 2,000

PE firms in North America and 1,000 in western and northern Europe as of 2014.

Even global PE funds are now recognizing the opportunities. There are about 170 global PE firms investing in Japan, but they may be channeling their money through Japan-based funds, and only a portion of this is for succession issues. The majority is for corporate spinoffs. So far, the scale is small. In 2021, for example, Bain Capital announced the creation of a $1 billion fund to invest in SMEs with succession issues. However, at an average of $50 million per deal—about the same size as deals for foreign purchases of unaffiliated firms in Japan—that's just 20 deals. It would take tens of billions of dollars to make a real impact. As of 2020, foreign PE funds had invested less in Japan than in China, India, Australia/New Zealand, and South Korea, but the amount being invested in Japan is rising fast (*Nikkei* 2021; Suzuki 2021).

METI has set up a Business Succession Support Center to help SMEs that feel they cannot get proper advice from others. In 2016, it handled nearly 7,000 consultations, which resulted in about 400 successions (METI 2018a: 361). In 2019, it announced a plan to expand the program so as to create 1,000–2,000 matches per year.

The best thing for Japan would be if banks and Japan's giant trading companies—which often arrange all sorts of deals for SMEs—joined the trend. That is beginning. Regional banks are rapidly increasing their consulting business on SME succession, handling nearly 30,000 consultations in 2016, triple the number in 2012 (METI 2018: 319). However, so far Japan's leading financial institutions have not geared up for this task and often refer their customers to the Nihon M&A Center, as do some regional banks.

The succession crisis could cause such social dislocation as to bring to the fore the need for a more fundamental overhaul of finance. Achieving that will not be easy, but failure to address it will heighten human suffering and political stress.

No Obvious Silver Bullet in Banking

It's easy to say get rid of evergreening loans to zombies, or to train bankers to be better in credit evaluation, including in regard to promising startups. Getting from here to there without excessive social disruption is extremely difficult. The plethora of chicken-and-egg dilemmas can leave policymakers paralyzed. Banks have no incentive to train their personnel to assess business prospects as long as personal guarantees, collateral, and government guarantees play such an outsized role in lending decisions. On the other hand, if all these props evaporated tomorrow, the banks would not have enough trained personnel to handle the new environment. Similarly, it's hard for interest rates to play their role in allocating credit as long as almost all loans charge less than 1%. However, if the BOJ raised rates too abruptly, the GDP might tank.

Finance is the thorniest impediment to making Japan a place where gazelles may safely graze. Given the generational and technological changes that are stimulating additional flexibility in the labor market, it is very likely that, if a way were found to make substantially more funding available for potential gazelles, a flood of successful gazelles would emerge. The first step is using tax incentives to promote more angel and venture capital investment to give potential gazelles a start. But unless banks do a better job, gazelles will lack the growth capital they need.

14

The Butterfly Effect in Finding Customers

Can the force of a tornado in Kansas really be altered by the flapping of a butterfly's wings two weeks earlier in Kanagawa? In certain kinds of systems, seemingly tiny changes can yield startlingly large differences, a phenomenon termed the "butterfly effect." In the economic sphere, a set of fairly limited reforms in India in the early 1990s rapidly ramped per capita GDP growth from just 2% during the three pre-reform decades to 5% over the following three decades. Prior to the reforms, such growth was seen as impossible; instead, India was said to be doomed to a slow "Hindu rate of growth." And yet, comparably little change yielded outsized results.

We may not see a full-scale butterfly effect in the increased access of Japanese startups to customers. Nonetheless, large ripple effects in this direction have resulted from changes in foreign exchange rates, reforms of retail laws, declining competitiveness of Japan's multinationals, and, most of all, the onset of e-commerce.

No business can survive, let alone grow, without the ability to access customers. In Japan, however, the growing power of incumbents during the 1970s–1990s made it difficult for new *independent* SMEs to get a fair chance at getting new customers. This obstacle hindered those in both the business-to-business (B-to-B) world and those selling consumer goods. Along with the dearth of external funding and difficulty in recruiting staff, limited access to customers was one of the most important reasons Japan had so few gazelles.

On the B-to-B side, bigger companies preferred to buy from suppliers with whom they'd worked for years or decades. The suppliers seen as most reliable were those in their corporate groups, or subcontractors who produced components based on the parent's specifications and sold most of their output to just that one customer, or fellow members of the six big horizontal *keiretsu* like Mitsubishi or Sumitomo. Beyond that, there are illegal cartels of assorted producers that keep out newcomers, activities to which the Japan Fair Trade Commission turned a blind eye (Katz 1998: 45, 176–177). Auto parts makers

The Contest for Japan's Economic Future. Richard Katz, Oxford University Press. © Richard Katz 2024.
DOI: 10.1093/oso/9780197675106.003.0015

have been particularly notorious, and several have been sent to jail as a result of investigations by the US Justice Department (DOJ 2012, 2018).

Given Toyota's famous just-in-time system, whereby components arriving too early pose as big a headache as those landing too late, automakers said they didn't want to take a chance on a new supplier. Both trust and tacit knowledge grow from repeated interaction. At the same time, smaller suppliers realized that, unless they hitched themselves to the corporate giants, their chances of finding customers were limited. Consequently, small producers were increasingly reduced to mere subcontractors. At the peak, three of every four manufacturing enterprises was a subcontractor, as was one of every two services companies (Whittaker 1997: 35).

On the business-to-consumer (B-to-C) side, in the 1970s small retailers were given the legal power to block large retailers from a neighborhood, so most retailers were tiny. That increased the leverage of large producers and their distributors over what retailers put on their shelves. They would sometimes violate the Anti-Monopoly Law with impunity, threatening to cut off supply to stores or distributors also offering goods from a newcomer, foreign or domestic. How can newcomers grow if consumers can't even see their products?

The system began to unravel when the yen's value rose sharply in the mid-1980s, which raised the price of Japanese goods in export markets. Hence, Japan's big multinationals started producing overseas, not just to reach foreign customers, but also to make products they'd import back to Japan to sell there. Japan's automakers, for example, now produce 80% as much outside Japan as within Japan. As of 2019, overseas production by Japan's multinationals in all industries was almost 60% as high as these companies' domestic output and a third as much as total domestic manufacturing—up from almost nothing in 1985 (METI 2020d: 6). Multinationals in other countries also produce a lot overseas, but that has not prevented them from expanding production at home. This shift by parent companies reduced their need for domestic subcontractors, many of whom went out of business. Those remaining responded by diversifying their customer base.

Reforms of the Large-Scale Retail Store Law began in the early 1990s, prompted by an alliance between big Japanese retailers and Washington, helping American retailers tap the market. This shifted some of the bargaining power from producers to big retailers who were more open to products from newcomers. The biggest blow to the big incumbents trying to keep newcomers out of the retail business has been the rise of e-commerce. E-commerce enabled them to bypass the incumbent-dominated distributors and address customers directly, as will be detailed shortly below. It's a perfect example of how technology can change the power balances in society.

The decline in competitiveness of Japan's elephants in the digital era compelled them to work with companies who had the expertise that they lacked, initially big companies, but with time a growing number of newcomers. Those competitiveness problems, in turn, resulted from a closed corporate group system that often left the parents in the dark about changing technologies. Akira Mitsumasu, author of a book on the vertical *keiretsu* (Mitsumasu 2015), told me, "Many Japanese affiliates who mostly trade within their corporate group have no idea what's happening in the rest of the world. So, they are not catching up with the latest technologies" (Interview June 2018). Even Toyota, as detailed below, had to take on new ICT suppliers because their traditional group members were not up to the task.

The decline of subcontracting has opened opportunities for independent SMEs to have more success on the B-to-B front.

Vertical *Keiretsu*: The Rise of Subcontracting

Japan's vertical *keiretsu* are sprawling behemoths encompassing hundreds of legally separate companies. As of the early 2010s, SONY had 1,227 companies in its corporate group. The comparative numbers were 913 for Hitachi, 511 for Toyota, 578 for Sumitomo Trading Company, and 784 for Orix financial services. Among the top 200 firms on the stock exchange, the average number of subsidiaries per firm rose from 45 in 1990 to 108 in 2005. These group members are legal subsidiaries or affiliates of the parent (Mitsumasu 2015).[1]

In the early 2000s, 26,000 corporate groups and their 56,000 subsidiaries employed 18 million people, a third of all employees. Half of them worked at just the biggest 290 groups. Within manufacturing, more than half of all employees worked for a corporate group, and a quarter were employed at the top 40 groups (Mitsumasu 2015: Kindle location 274). These figures do not include the much larger category of subcontractors. While Toyota has 1,000

---

[1] In a subsidiary, the parent has majority ownership share; in affiliates, the parent has less than a majority but still enough to exert control.

subsidiaries and affiliates, it has almost 40,000 suppliers, of which the majority are subcontractors. At the peak of subcontracting in the early 1980s, an estimated 80% of all factory workers were employed by a legal group member or subcontractor (METI 2018b). "The share is gigantic. You don't see this in other countries," Mitsumasu told me.

In those days, subcontracting often meant complete domination by the parent. That's because the majority relied on one customer for a majority of their sales and made products based on parent specifications. A fifth conducted 90% of their sales with just one customer (METI 2016a: 89).

The rise of vertical *keiretsu* and subcontracting was promoted by METI beginning in the 1960s as a way to modernize the economy, in accordance with a 1963 strategy document called Basic Policy for SMEs and the 1970 Subcontracting Promotion Law. The vision was partnerships between superiors and subordinates, not the creation of gazelles that might challenge incumbents. It's not that METI disparaged competition altogether. On the contrary, unlike many countries in Europe, METI never created a single national champion in any key exporting industry.

In those days, subcontracting's benefits to the economy were widely seen as outweighing any downside. By the late 1950s and early 1960s, large Japanese producers faced difficult challenges in manufacturing complexity, and small firms were constrained by technical and financial resources (Nishiguchi and Brookfield 1997: 92). To meet these challenges, large manufacturers began to invest heavily in their subcontractors and to upgrade the complexity of the work they performed under parent company guidance.

Unfortunately, METI continued to promote this system even as the net benefits to the economy became net losses. "By the 1990s, the subcontracting system no longer increased profits for either the parent or the subcontractor relative to manufacturers without this relationship" (Kimura 2001: 7, 11, 168).

Surviving versus Thriving

All too many of the SMEs in Japan who conduct B-to-B sales are given a terrible dilemma. If they try to thrive without ties to a corporate group, they are more likely to fail altogether. Partly that's because potential customers tied up in the *keiretsu* have been notoriously reluctant to buy from newcomers (a trait now eroding, as detailed below). Moreover, unlike the subcontractors, whom the parent will support in rough times, independents may not have a reliable financial cushion in rough times if they cannot get bank finance.

On the other hand, if independents manage to break into markets and survive, they will then enjoy faster growth and higher profitability than a subcontractor. Evolving from a firm founded in 1926, the independent Nakashima Propeller has become Japan's biggest propeller maker with a 30% global share in large propellers. President Motoyoshi Nakashima stressed, "The future is not bright if one . . . becomes a mere servant" to a particular customer. "We do not limit ourselves to supplying one or two companies . . . [or] to Japan" (EIU 2013: 27; Nakashima Propeller 2019).

Subcontractors find themselves trapped in a dependency relationship that limits their expansion. Few of them export. "For a young firm to run a business as an exclusively subcontracting firm possibly could mean sacrificing the chance of growth for the sake of stability" (Yasuda 2005: 12). Analysts liken this sacrifice to an insurance premium that subcontractors pay to maintain their life span. When METI asked subcontractors in 1991 their main reason for accepting that status, the top answer (57%) was the stability of work volume. Coming in next, at about 25% each, were difficulties in developing their own products or in marketing and securing customers (Whittaker 1997: 88).

That insurance premium is high. For one thing, they face a lot of pricing pressure from their main customer (Asanuma 1988: 19). Beyond that, the big firms regularly used their monopsonistic bargaining power to shift costs and risks to their subcontractors (van Kooij 1991: 149). Beyond that, parent companies regularly transferred redundant employees to subsidiaries where the pay and benefits were lower. Some experts contend that the monopsonistic power of the parents has diminished over time, at least for some subcontractors with technological or other advantages (Whittaker 1997: 97).

Importantly, dependence on their parents for technological input leaves many subcontractors without either the technological or marketing expertise needed to graduate from that dependence. An estimated half of independent SMEs conduct R&D, and that averages 2.6% of their total sales. Among subcontractors, just 28% do R&D and, of those that do, it averages just 2.0% of sales (Kimura 2001: 10). Moreover, because so many subcontractors have to rely on their parent companies for designs, a large number of them are unable to market to an additional company, and that increases their dependence (van Kooij 1991: 149).

Many of the subcontractors who believe that they, too, have technological prowess resent the parents who won't let them be "lords of their own castle." In a 1983 study, subcontractors said they developed 80% of new technologies in process rationalization, half in die-making, and a third in machines. Yet just a fifth owned the patents involved in these new technologies (Nishiguchi and Brookfield 1997: 93). Professor Chesbrough contends that parents may deliberately "constrain the operations of new spin-offs in ways that reduce their chances for success. One type of constraint is to limit the markets for the venture to those deemed 'strategic' by the corporate parent" (Chesbrough 2006b: 137).

Japanese giants are hardly unique in imposing on SMEs a trade-off between surviving and thriving. What differentiates Japan is the pervasiveness of subcontracting. In the European Union, just 16% of all manufacturing SMEs were subcontractors in the early 2000s (EIM Business & Policy Research 2009: 24). In the 1980s, the top three customers accounted for 85% and 95%, respectively, of the entire revenue of Japanese subcontractors doing high-tech work and assembly work (Nishiguchi and Brookfield 1997: 100). In Britain, the comparable figures were just 50%–60%.

While many SME owners genuinely prefer security to growth, many others, if circumstances allowed, would have taken a different path. Many subcontractors speak of the hope that they could escape from being "like rats on a treadmill" if they could improve their bargaining power by upgrading their technical capacity. *Datsu shitauke* (escape from subcontracting) is a common hope (Whittaker 1997: 137). As we'll soon see, when circumstances changed, so did the bonds of subcontracting.

Subcontracting and Its Implicit Social Contract Unravel

Companies make their own decisions, but only from the options available on the menu. As circumstances change, some favorites drop off the menu. So it has been with subcontracting.

As early as 1991, Eric van Kooij argued that "[t]he classic model of subcontracting fits an industrial society better than an information society, and so it is being replaced in Japan by a new model of networking" (van Kooij 1991: 153). An additional reason for the decline of subcontracting is ironic: the upgrading of SME capabilities catalyzed by subcontracting led more of these subcontractors to feel confident that they could finally escape from subcontracting.

As in all mature economies, manufacturing's share of the labor force plunged. This happens for the same reason that, with modern farm technology, a small sliver of the population can feed the entire country. Modern machinery enables one factory worker to produce what used to require two or three. Moreover, unlike in other rich countries, the absolute level of Japanese manufacturing stopped rising. From 1990 to 2019, domestic plus foreign demand for made-in-Japan manufactured goods fell 7%, compared to a 38% rise in demand for those made in Germany and 66% for those made in the United States (Federal Reserve Bank of St. Louis 2020).[2]

Added to this factor is the impact of the yen rise, as noted above. As a result of these two factors, manufacturing SMEs halved from 314,000 in 1997 to just 167,000 in 2014 (latest available) (METI 1997, 2014).

From a political standpoint, this represents a break in the sense of mutual obligation between parent and subcontractor. Subcontractors had paid their "insurance premium" year after year, but now when aid was needed, it was not there. It may have been unavoidable for the parents to downsize or to move offshore, but it rents the social fabric. Some giants also opened procurement to subcontractors who had previously mostly served their competitors (e.g., Toyota and Nissan buying from each other's subcontractors). While this greater flexibility does help the economy as a whole, it creates political friction that can become a driver of reform as well as resistance.

For years, Toyota insisted it would produce no less than 3 million vehicles in Japan in order to support its system of almost 40,000 suppliers, which it viewed as key to its competitive edge. That's one reason Toyota has so far lagged in the production of battery-based electric vehicles (EVs). The latter need just half the 30,000 parts of a conventional car. Some analysts contend that Toyota will eventually do what it must and sacrifice its suppliers. Time will tell.

By contrast, consider tiny auto startup FOMM, which is dedicated to producing floatable EVs for the market in flood-prone Thailand. It was begun in 2013 by three middle-aged managers at major auto firms. CEO Hideo Tsurumaki had worked for 15 years at Suzuki (a Toyota affiliate) and

---

[2] Demand for manufactures here is measured by gross output rather than the value-added measure used in GDP tables.

then at Toyota Auto Body. He got the idea when he saw how many people drowned in Japan's 2011 tsunami while trying to drive away, only to have their cars sink. "I knew I could not make this car if I stayed in that company" (Interview June 2018). FOMM began production in Thailand in 2019 and started marketing on a small scale in Japan in 2022. Tsurumaki was not fettered by ties to old suppliers; his car has just 1,600 parts.

It is telling that a Japanese giant with foreign ownership took a different path from Toyota. Nissan had put out an EV, the Leaf, starting in 2011, when Carlos Ghosn was in charge, and Honda announced in early 2022 that it would cooperate with GM in producing by 2027 an EV priced at $30,000. However, as of 2020, Toyota President Akio Toyoda was still dismissing battery-powered EVs as "over-hyped" (Landers 2020).

For all these reasons, the subcontracting system has already become a pale shadow of its former self. From 1981 onward, subcontractors plunged from 66% of all manufacturing SMEs in 1981 to just 45% in 1997 (latest data available) and undoubtedly much lower today (METI various years; Kogyo Jittai Chosa (Manufacturing Current Status Investigation) in Japanese; Whittaker 1997: 35). In addition, the tradition of subcontractors selling to just one or two customers also frayed. In 1991, only 23% of subcontractors sold less than 30% of their output to their top customer; by 2014 the share had nearly doubled to 40% (METI 2016a: 89).

The Rise of e-Commerce

Nothing has given a greater boon to independent SMEs accessing customers and challenging the incumbents than the rise of e-commerce. Rakuten is, of course, the poster child, helping 56,000 ordinary SMEs enjoy rapid expansion.[3] As *Forbes* wrote (Frazier 2011: n.p.), "Going online is just about the only way a new retailer can crack the Japanese market. A welter of local restrictions, license requirements and exclusionary distribution agreements make Japan one of the least hospitable settings for new stores. The country's big cities are rife with small boutiques . . . but they are unlikely to mount a challenge to the department store giants."

---

[3] Rakuten ran a big loss in 2022 due to an ill-advised move into mobile phones, and in late 2022, S&P reduced its bond rating to junk status. But that does not detract from its achievements in e-commerce.

About 90 million of Japan's 126 million people buy goods and services online, and, by 2022, their spending had reached nearly 8% of retail sales, triple the 2.8% share in 2010 (METI 2020d). E-commerce lets consumers do price comparisons, and that puts downward pressure on prices. Still, as a share of total retail sales, Japan does not make the list of the top 10 countries (the 10th being Canada at nearly 14%).

Apparel is one of the biggest products for online sales. The leader is Zozotown, an outgrowth of online retailer Start Today. Launched in 1998 by the 23-year-old Yusaku Maezawa—Japan's 22nd richest person in 2020—Start Today began life as an importer of CDs and books. Upon graduating from high school, Maezawa moved to the United States to avoid becoming a typical Japanese salaryman, "after seeing all the tired faces on my morning commutes" (Yamamoto 2016: n.p.). A member of a rock band, he started collecting CDs of his favorite musicians. Then, upon returning to Japan, he started a mail-order business importing CDs in 1995. Start Today moved to online sales in 2000, added Zozotown in 2004, and, in 2014, changed its name to Zozo Inc. Finally, in 2019, Maezawa sold Zozo to Yahoo Japan for $3.7 billion, enabling the 43-year-old to create his life's next chapter.

B-to-C e-commerce in Japan is dwarfed by B-to-B commerce, peaking at ¥270 trillion ($3.5 billion) in 2019 before falling 5% in the following year due to COVID (METI 2021a). It is still mostly conducted among firms in the same vertical *keiretsu*, often using closed corporate networks like EDI rather than the Internet. By 2017, the value of B-to-B transactions conducted online reached almost a third of all B-to-B transactions (METI 2018c).

Japan is a long way from reaching its potential (METI 2006). As of 2006 (latest data available) only 12% (184,000) out of Japan's 1.5 million incorporated enterprises conducted any type of e-commerce—marketing, making orders, accepting orders, arranging delivery, providing services, and so on—via the Internet (as opposed to a closed network like EDI). Tellingly, retailers founded after 1995 used e-commerce almost twice as much as those established earlier. As the size of the enterprise rises, so does the use of e-commerce.

Antitrust Concerns about e-Commerce Giants

There is one fly in the e-commerce ointment: accusations that big companies dominating e-commerce in Japan—Rakuten, Amazon, and Yahoo—do what many oligopolists do: abuse their power. There are accusations of forcing costs onto vendors, unilaterally changing contracts, dropping vendors, and in the case of Amazon, setting up its own products in direct competition with its vendors using the data it has gained from their activities on Amazon's site. In a METI survey in October 2018 of 2,000 vendors, a vast majority of respondents expressed dissatisfaction with how they were treated by Japan's giant Internet malls. The Japan Fair Trade Commission (JFTC) set up a procedure in January 2019 to solicit further comments and concerns (Takeuchi and Sugihara 2019).

The JFTC raided Rakuten's headquarters in February 2020, investigating accusations by its vendors. However, the JFTC is notoriously weak and often accepts a company's "business improvement plan" rather than punish it, even in cases of repeated violations. Lacking confidence in the JFTC and feeling that it treats domestic e-commerce giants more leniently than foreign-owned ones like Amazon, 276 of Rakuten's vendors set up their own "union" in October 2019 to negotiate with Rakuten and pressure JFTC into more active intervention. Within two months, 2,800 of Rakuten's 40,000 vendors had signed the union's petition. Yuki Katsumata, Rakuten Union's leader, said he had endured Rakuten's "frequent, one-sided changes of terms of business for five years," because he relies on the platform for 80% of his revenues. "But his patience has run out" (mLex 2019: n.p.). According to the JFTC's 2019 interim report, 93% of Rakuten's vendors and 73% of Amazon's have lodged similar complaints (JFTC 2020).

The accusations against Amazon—second in sales to Rakuten in Japan— are very different. That's because Amazon sells its own brands; Rakuten does not. Both the United States and the European Union have launched antitrust investigations on whether Amazon competes by illegal means. The European Union filed charges on November 10, 2020. Amazon denies the charges. California has already launched antitrust charges, and the US FTC is preparing a suit as of February 2023 (Reuters 2019; Chan 2020; Mattioli 2020).

The JFTC raided Amazon's headquarters in 2018. Its investigation of Amazon has so far been primarily focused on accusations that it has unfairly pushed financial burdens onto vendors. According to a JFTC survey of vendors, 41% of vendors reported that Amazon sold similar or identical goods after they did. In those cases, 83% were sold at a lower price and 57% were sold under more advantageous conditions. In November 2020, the JFTC said it would look at the EU investigation to see if any results could be utilized within Japan. While the JFTC has reached a settlement with Amazon on other complaints, this one appears to be unresolved as of early 2022 (JFTC 2019).

An antitrust lawyer, Kentaro Hirayama, commented in January 2022, "Since the [various cases vis-à-vis Rakuten and Amazon] resulted in no clear recognition of illegal acts, it is difficult to refer to them in future lawsuits and other cases. . . . The JFTC's response seems not necessarily riding the global tide and is peculiar" (Okuno 2022: n.p.).

To be sure, e-commerce is allowing tens of thousands of SMEs to thrive, but not as well as they could in the absence of alleged anticompetitive practices. For markets to perform well, they must be embedded in healthy market institutions, and fair competition is one of the most important. If e-commerce is to play its needed role in promoting gazelles, the JFTC needs to be given the budget, staffing, and political support to be more aggressive. That, however, is something critics have advocated for years; progress has been glacial.

Elephant-Gazelle Collaboration

It was a milestone in Japan's supply chain system. In 2018, for the first time, the number of software vendors exceeded traditional parts makers among the top 5,000 of first-tier and second-tier suppliers to Toyota and its 16 core group companies. But it was a milestone in another way as well. Most of the software vendors are new to the Toyota supply chain, and few wanted to join Toyota's vertical *keiretsu*. They cherish their independence, their ability to supply anyone, and to engage in technological collaboration with anyone. Toyota had to accept these conditions because it and its group companies lack the required expertise. There are wildly varying estimates of the software and electronics cost of a car—a Deloitte analysis put it at 40% up from 18% in 2000 (Tingwall 2020). In any case, Toyota chieftain Akio Toyoda has acknowledged that, without mastering digitization, Toyota cannot survive (Fujimoto and Kamada 2019).

All of this means a second route for potential gazelles to access customers: selling directly to the elephants and even engaging in joint development with them via open innovation. Toyota, for example, has made investments in some of Japan's leading software startups, including a ¥10 billion ($77 million) investment in Preferred Networks (PF), a specialist in AI.

PF is a 2014 spinoff from a search engine company founded in 2006 by two graduate school students at Todai. It is one of Japan's very few unicorns. PF seeks clients and partners far and wide, collaborating with companies in a wide variety of fields and receiving major investments from some of them. Examples include JXTG Holdings (oil), Fanuc (industrial robots), Hitachi (heavy machinery), Kao (cosmetics), Gree (online gaming), Mizuho Bank, and Mitsui Trading Company.

Back in 2016, I spoke about the ability of new companies to supply elephants with Takahiko Ono, the founder of Oscar Technology (OscarTech). Despite being just three years old, it had recently managed the difficult task of becoming a supplier to Denso, one of Japan's biggest parts makers and a member of the Toyota Group. OscarTech developed software that automates something called parallel processing for multi-core computer processors. Hitherto, that software required human engineers to write code. Autos are just one of many potential applications. We met at the offices of WERU, the Waseda University–based venture capital firm that was funding OscarTech. At that time, OscarTech had sales of just $1 million in a $20 million market that Ono envisioned rising to $3 billion by 2025. Even though OscarTech was new, it had unusual leverage: Waseda University, where Ono did some teaching, owned the patents. More importantly, he had developed a technology that the elephants could neither create nor even reverse engineer. "Sometimes people who have worked together in the same corporation for 30 years have difficulty in understanding something very different. Sometimes a company's parts department would say that they could do this themselves, but they can't," he explained.

In March 2020, OscarTech was acquired by Fixstars, a software company begun in 2002, which is now listed on the First Section of the Tokyo Stock Exchange. It includes among its clients such big names as Toshiba, Canon, Hitachi, and Mizuho Securities. Hopefully, elephants seeing the need for gazelles like OscarTech and Fixstars will also support reforms that can spawn more of them.

In talking with a friend in the Japanese pharmaceutical industry, he noted that most of Japan's successful new gazelles were, in one way or another, based on the Internet and/or software, whether they be retailers, like Rakuten and Aksul, matchmakers like Raksul and LINKERS, assorted creators of business and personal services, like Monstar and Preferred Networks, or inventors of machinery using advanced software like OscarTech. There are at least two reasons for that. First, existing markets in Japan are so dominated by incumbents that most newcomers have adopted a "blue ocean strategy," entering a field with few entrenched leaders or stifling regulations. They seem to avoid a "red ocean strategy," where they can't grow without going toe-to-toe with the elephants and their bureaucratic protectors. Second, given the difficulty of raising funds, newcomers are focusing on computer- and software-intensive fields where the initial costs are a lot lower than those requiring expensive equipment, such as biotechnology and pharmaceuticals. These two issues limit the sectors in which Japan will see gazelles, at least for a while.

One exception is EV car manufacturer FOMM because fewer parts mean much lower costs. It, too, has been able to secure collaboration deals with long-established companies. In 2017, FOMM reached a pact with Yamada Denki, one of Japan's largest retailers of consumer electronics, to begin both sales of FOMM's EV and a sharing service. As of 2019, Yamada Denki and six other investors, mostly big corporations, have injected a total of ¥4.9 billion ($38 million) into FOMM. In 2018, giant computer and electronics producer Fujitsu reached an agreement with FOMM to co-develop a battery cloud service for EVs. The service will help manage and provide information on driving conditions, battery conditions, information on the vehicle user's battery usage, and the need for replacement. In 2018, the Exedy group—a leading producer of parts for transmissions and the rest of the drive train, invested in FOMM as part of its effort to transition its product line to a world fighting climate change. Battery-powered EVs do not need transmissions.

Can Japan's Elephants Master Open Innovation?

Open innovation is a critical pathway for would-be gazelles to penetrate the B-to-B market in most countries, but especially in Japan because it can help overcome the traditional reluctance to buy goods or services from a new firm. Unfortunately, not only are most Japanese giants resistant to open innovation, but just because a company wants to practice open innovation doesn't mean its internal business culture permits it to do so. Henry Chesbrough pointed this out in a report on his work with 30 managers in the Silicon Valley outposts of leading Japanese companies: "Many internal changes will be required to Japanese firms' organizational processes in order to use open innovation to work more effectively with Silicon Valley," and, we would add, with others as well (Chesbrough (2013: 4).

The first step is understanding that open innovation is not simply licensing technology developed by others, nor is it a one-way street. It means genuine joint development. That does not come easy for companies used to going it alone. It's even harder to treat Japanese SMEs as equal partners since these companies have long treated them as subordinates.

Panasonic is a good case study (Nakazono et al. 2014). Like so many other of Japan's elephants, Panasonic has had an enormous amount of experience in open innovation of a sort, but only between itself and its 600 subsidiaries and affiliates. It was open to members of the group but closed to non-members. After Panasonic was hit hard in the dot.com bust of the early 2000s, it committed itself to digitization, hitherto not its forte. As part of that, it tried and failed, to embrace open innovation.

When I visited Panasonic in 2019 and spoke to the person in charge of open innovation within the R&D Department, his answers were telling. All his examples of open innovation turned out to be members, or former members, of the Panasonic group, or else cases of cooperation with researchers at universities. He added that Panasonic had been doing that sort of cooperative effort for three decades; it just didn't call it open innovation. He did not seem to feel that something different was required.

By contrast, Osaka Gas established an Open Innovation Office in 2008 and designated specific employees in charge of open innovation at individual R&D departments. In 2011, for instance, when individual R&D departments of Osaka Gas requested 54 different technologies from outside of the company, the Open Innovation Office successfully found partners for all 54 (Nakazono et al. 2014: 258).

Overall, according to a 2015 METI survey, just 45% of 195 listed companies said they were engaging in more open innovation than years earlier. Even among the latter, 70% of R&D was still being conducted within the firm or corporate group. When elephants do engage in open innovation, their favorite partners are other giants, Japanese or foreign. According to METI, only 0.7% of large-firm innovation activities was based on collaboration with startups (Schaede 2020: 168). A study reported, "Entrepreneurs and startup companies are unlikely to be chosen as a partner for open innovation. Companies rather choose suppliers, universities, customers and even competitors" (Japan Intellectual Property News 2018: n.p.).

Why, I asked Masatoshi Ueno at the Silicon Valley office of Asahi Glass, could Japanese elephants work with startups in Silicon Valley, but not those in Japan? "Most of the big Japanese corporations look down on Japanese SMEs as mere suppliers," he replied. "They cannot treat them as equal partners." Traditionally, in technical cooperation within the corporate group, the direction, goals, and so forth are dictated by the parent. "So, even when they say they are doing open innovation with non-group smaller companies," he continued, "they are really just outsourcing, rather than actively collaborating, Culturally, these companies are able to treat non-Japanese startups as partners but act as if Japanese SMEs should be subordinates. Also, within Japan, these companies act 'in the Japanese way,' but, outside of Japan, they accept the necessity of doing things differently" (Interview March 2018).

One possible transition belt toward more open innovation is working with matchmakers like LINKERS. At meetings with big incumbents, I was surprised how many times LINKERS was mentioned. Fukata of Panasonic's Game Changer Catapult had used LINKERS on two projects. When asked why his experience seemed so different from others at Panasonic, Fukata replied, "Existing divisions are very conservative, so they can't really work with these startups. We, as an 'edge' division working on creating new products, and even our own new startups, have to work with outside SMEs" (Interview October 2019). Japan needs many more companies like LINKERS, but founder Maeda told me in 2019 that so far, no other company in Japan does what LINKERS does.

In 2016, Keizai Doyukai, a more forward-looking business organization than Keidanren, issued a policy proposal for expanding open innovation. Among other things, it recommended such steps as: increasing the number of coordinators in public research institutes that can connect parties; expanding tax incentives for open innovation; creating a position with an enterprise in charge of open innovation independent from R&D departments; strengthening of VC funds within the national universities (akin to Todai's Edge Capital Partners which, as of 2020, had invested in more than 70 startups). The Keizai Doyukai proposal suggests that companies not only have internal political problems regarding control of R&D but, even with the best efforts, have difficulties in finding the right partners. The Kishida administration included the notion of tax incentives for open innovation in its 2022 Five-Year Plan, but as noted above, no concrete measures were included in the December 2022 tax proposals.

It remains to be seen whether the open innovation successes at some elephants will become harbingers or remain exceptions.

15

The Importance of Being Global

> International opening of the economy is the sine qua non of the
> overall reform process.
>
> —Jeffrey Sachs et al. (1995: 3)

Japan stands apart. In the rest of the world, countries seeking to boost growth encourage foreign companies to set up new facilities on their soil or buy domestic companies, ventures known as inward foreign direct investment (FDI). China is the most spectacular success story for this strategy, but many other countries—from India to the new market economies of eastern Europe—enthusiastically court foreign enterprises. By enabling the fresh ideas of foreign companies to spill over into the broader economy, inward FDI boosts the performance of local suppliers, business customers, and sometimes even their own competitors.

Among major countries, only one has said "no, thank you" to these benefits: Japan. In the last pre-COVID year, 2019, the United Nations Conference on Trade and Development (UNCTAD) ranked 196 countries in terms of cumulative inward FDI as a share of GDP. Japan came in dead last at 196, just ahead of North Korea, which was getting investment from China (UNCTAD 2022).

Inward FDI is not the only measure of globalization, but it's one of the most impactful. Long ago, economists discovered that countries with more trade and more inward FDI grew faster.

Rich countries are so much more integrated than they used to be, whether it comes to trade, FDI, technology transfers, or the interchange of people. In 27 OECD countries, the median ratio of trade (exports plus imports) to GDP doubled from 42% in 1970 to 81% in the pre-COVID year of 2019. Meanwhile, the median stock of inward FDI exploded from a mere 6% of GDP in 1980 to 44% in 2019.

The Contest for Japan's Economic Future. Richard Katz, Oxford University Press. © Richard Katz 2024.
DOI: 10.1093/oso/9780197675106.003.0016

Trade, FDI, and other forms of globalization have been intensely criticized by both the left and the right. Some of the beefs are legitimate—like concerns about "hot money" flows disrupting newly liberalized financial systems, as in 1997–1998—but most scapegoat globalization for problems caused by other factors. Globalization, like technology, is a powerful force for lifting per capita GDP. But, as with labor-saving automation, some people are hurt in the process, and many governments stand back from helping the latter. The fault lies not in globalization per se, but in the political power balance within that society.

Progress Report on Japanese Globalization

On some fronts, Japan is far more globalized than a generation ago. A few decades back, one rarely saw foreign-branded PCs on office desktops. Today, two of every three PCs and laptops in Japan run on Windows and another 15% are Apples. One can hardly walk a few blocks in a big city without seeing a Starbucks or KFC.

For a long time, few talented Japanese were willing to take a chance on working for a foreign firm, partly due to fear that the company might one day lay them off. Today, young graduates flock to them. When LinkedIn surveyed its few million members in Japan, 19 of the 25 companies ranked highest in job satisfaction were foreign ones; eight of the top ten were American (Gilchrist 2019).

During 1970–2000, not just imports, but also exports were far lower than was typical for a country with its population, per capita, and GDP. Today, the ratio of trade (exports plus imports) to GDP ratio has risen to around 35%, far more in line with international norms (see Figure 15.1).[1]

Back in the early 1980s, only 4% of Japanese stocks were owned by foreign investors. There were restrictions on Japanese corporate fundraising via global bond markets. Then came a series of reforms—some prompted by US-Japan talks beginning in 1984, others by Japan's "financial big bang"

---

[1] Back in the 1970s and 1980s, Japan was justifiably criticized for the low levels of manufactured imports, just about 20% of all imports. In recent years, the share has risen to around 60%. However, nearly 60% of Japan's total manufactured imports are produced by Japanese affiliates overseas, double the ratio of the late 1990s. This pattern limits a main benefit of trade: exposing companies to the force of international competition.

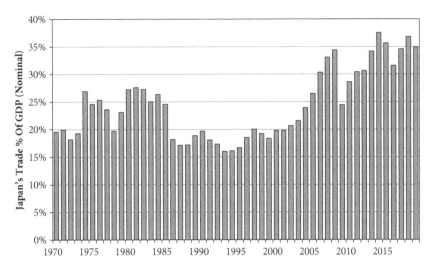

Figure 15.1 Japan's increasing openness to international trade.
Source: World Bank (2022).

in 1998. The change was dramatic. By 2020, foreign investors owned almost a third of all shares on the First Section of the stock market (Japan Exchange Group 2021b) and, by 2021, 14% of Japanese government bonds (MOF 2022b).

On other fronts, however, Japan lags far behind, including the vital person-to-person contacts that broaden one's horizons.

I remember walking into the offices of Scopis, a Berlin-based medical device startup. It had developed augmented reality (AR) software to guide surgical instruments for delicate procedures like brain surgery. Most of its dozens of employees seemed to be from countries other than Germany, with English as the common language. Perhaps that's one reason that, although only a decade old, it has sales in more than 50 countries. Similarly, Silicon Valley would be unthinkable without the 70% of its technicians who hail from outside the United States, mostly Asia. In Japan, as of 2017, only a trivial 0.7% of all employed people were permanent residents from foreign countries (Japan Macro Advisors 2020c).

We have repeatedly seen how many of Japan's new entrepreneurs have some overseas experience, typically college study abroad. On this vital front, Japan is backsliding. While language is a factor, that does not explain the plunge in the past couple of decades. The number of Japanese studying abroad almost quadrupled from 18,000 in 1986 to 65,000 in 2003. Then the numbers fell back to only 30,000 in 2016 (UNESCO 2022: n.p.). Moreover, only a couple thousand spent at least a year abroad (McCrostie 2017). Among 27 OECD countries, Japan comes in second-to-last in the share of students who get a college degree from a foreign university, just ahead of the United States (OECD 2020i: 231).

In the United States, 12% of college professors were foreign citizens in 2017, not including foreign-born immigrants. In Japan, by contrast, as of 2019, just 4% of faculty at Japanese universities were foreigners, with China as the biggest source, followed by the United States and South Korea (Kakuchi 2019).

Nor do Japanese professors enhance their mental palette by teaching overseas or by engaging in collaborative research across borders. Among professors in 18 rich and middle-income countries, those in Japan came in second-to-last both in teaching abroad and in international research collaboration (Rostan 2014: 5). Despite similar language issues, Japan is topped by faculty from China and Korea. Moreover, very few Japanese scientists work overseas or cooperate on papers with scientists from other countries (Katz 2023b: n.p.).

All across North America and Europe, one finds leading CEOs who are citizens of a foreign country. In the United Kingdom's top 100 companies, 40% of CEOs are foreigners. The comparable figure for France's top 40 is 10%, and for Germany's top 30, it's 20%. In Japan, over the 26 years from 1996 to 2012, only 13 CEOs of Japan's top 2,000-plus companies have been foreigners (Pandey and Rhee 2015: 204).

Admittedly the primary reason for this dearth is that most Japanese CEOs are chosen from the firm's lifetime employees. So, few people who are new to the company, Japanese or foreign, can become CEO. However, that does not explain the lack of foreign career experience among those who do rise to the top.

These days, any European or North American hoping to secure a chair in the executive suite had better get some experience working in a foreign country. That's true for 88% of Europe's leading companies and 86% in North America. One of every 10 Fortune 500 CEOs was born outside the United States; some are citizens now, some not. But in Japan, only 17% of CEOs of the country's multinationals have ever even worked in another country. Booz & Company, which conducted the survey, commented, "It will be difficult for a company headed by a senior executive who has not had to make tough decisions about subsidiaries and overseas operations to compete globally" (Ghemawat and Herman Vantrappen 2014: n.p.). If attending a foreign university or having an overseas posting does not aid promotion even in a multinational firm, where's the incentive to gain any cosmopolitan experience?

For decades, scholars have known that companies perform better if their top executives have worked overseas and have learned there are many ways to skin a cat. That helps them strategize more fluidly, not just in regard to other countries, but at home as well. Indeed, the more time spent overseas and the wider the variety of national cultures, the more it helps performance (Le and Kroll 2017: 577). Similarly, having foreign companies and individuals studying or working in a country broadens the mindset of its citizens. That's why Japan's relative lack of business and educational globalism is so injurious.

Why the Personal Touch Matters

In an open world, no nation need reinvent the wheel when it can import technology invented elsewhere. That includes the technology of training young people to become entrepreneurs. With the likes of MIT and Stanford having spent decades learning how to churn out entrepreneurs en masse, Japanese universities can avail themselves of their techniques for doing so.

That's just what the Tokyo University of Science (TUS) did in 2014 when it was becoming de rigueur for Japanese universities to offer classes in entrepreneurship. The chairman of the board, former software industry executive Shigeru Nakane, invited MIT professor Michael Cusumano to help relaunch TUS's School of Management with a new focus on entrepreneurship, making him special vice president and dean of entrepreneurship and innovation. He was also asked to redesign and relaunch the Management of Technology Program aimed at mid-career businesspeople. Cusumano is not only a veteran at teaching management and entrepreneurship but is fluent in Japanese and has lived in Japan for a total of eight years. He worked on this from 2014 to 2017 and has continued as a consultant.

Cusumano had to start from scratch. "TUS is Japan's largest science and engineering university, with almost 20,000 students, and yet had no entrepreneurship course until then" (Interview July 2021). The lodestar of Cusumano's strategy was integrating technological and commercial innovation. Japan is a world leader in new patents but has lost much of its prowess in turning top-notch technologies into must-have products and in generating new companies to do so.

This problem is not unique to Japan. "The biggest reason for startups failing is weak connections to the customer. In fact, the best predictor of the success of a startup coming out of MIT is that someone on the founding team is an expert in sales or marketing." Before Cusumano's arrival, the university had never tracked how many of its graduates had created new companies.

Given that approach, Cusumano created a new institution devoted to entrepreneurship activities, the Tokyo Entrepreneurship and Innovation Center, with some help from MIT's Regional Entrepreneurship Acceleration Program. At the same time, he orchestrated the merger of the Graduate School of Innovation with the School of Management. For the first time, TUS students could learn from faculty with expertise in each area. He also redesigned the Management of Technology curriculum for mid-career students to emphasize either technological innovation (the traditional emphasis) or MBA-type training (a new specialty). The university also established a new investment management company and a fund to invest in startups as well as help manage some of the entrepreneurship promotion activities.

Enrollment in the newly merged school rose to nearly 2,000 in 2021–2022. The female share rose from just a sliver to about a third. It is also noteworthy that, in 2017, around 900 students took at least one entrepreneurship class, with half of those students taking the "Startup School" course.

It may take a while before this program bears fruit in new companies since founders typically first work for several years at a larger company to gain experience. While perhaps a half-dozen startups have emerged, much of the early effect may be seen in the students' employers (two-thirds of the grad students are sent by their employers). "The graduates may not become entrepreneurs, but I think they'll become better employees because of the program," explained Cusumano. "Down the road, an opportunity may arise for them to spin out their own company from their employer." Cusumano is trying to instill the notion popular at American business schools that all MBAs need to learn about innovation management and entrepreneurship, even if they never become an entrepreneur. Both new and old companies must be able to commercialize new technologies and products.

An idea whose time has come is a lot more powerful if the person with the idea has access to movers and shakers. That's the case with Daniel Okimoto, a Stanford professor of political science. Having just retired in 2015, he was preparing his move to New Zealand when a conversation with his nephew, a senior vice president at Google, changed not just his life but the digital strategy of a couple dozen top Japanese elephants. The nephew was part of a team that built the AlphaGo computer program, the first to beat human masters of the Asian game of "go." It is built on the AI expertise of DeepMind, a British venture acquired by Google. With "go" said to have more board configurations than there are atoms in the known universe, this was a major milestone.

Okimoto assumed that technologists from Japan were flying in to learn the ramifications of Google's achievement and asked his nephew. "Almost none," came the reply. Chinese technologists, on the other hand, came in droves. An alarmed Okimoto gathered a handful of five former students working in the Valley and told them, "Unless we do something, in 10 years Japan is going to find it's become a has-been country" (Interview April 2022).

Trapped in their focus on digital developments in Japan rather than globally—a mindset the Japanese have nicknamed the Galapagos syndrome, akin to the isolated evolutionary path on that island—most Japanese companies presumed they were doing fine, blissfully unaware of what they were missing. Even those with outposts in the Valley lacked deep personal networks. "They thought that they had it under control," Okimoto recalled. "So, we decided to start a nonprofit organization that would bridge this chasm, calling it the Silicon Valley Japan Platform (SVJP). We had no manpower and no money apart from $30,000 donated by one of the six."

What they did have was decades-long friendships with Japanese CEOs at 28 flagship companies. The group spent a year in talks on what was needed for a successful digital transformation, bypassing corporate bureaucracies to go straight to the top. They were given a boost when Prime Minister Abe accepted SVJP's invitation to visit Silicon Valley in 2015 and called for more cooperation between Japan and the Valley.

When Tokio Marine Insurance, a property and casualty insurer, joined SVJP in 2015, it had no serious office in the Valley. However, Tsuyoshi Nagano, its CEO then and now its executive chairman, had spent eight years in Orange County in southern California and connected with Silicon Valley–type companies there. "That predisposed him to be very aggressive in transforming Tokio Marine," said Okimoto. He appointed one of their rising young managers to a new department of digital technology. Today, it has 100 staffers. "Some of them will be senior executives, even CEOs, one day. The company has now built this internal division to train, and expose to international trends, their top upcoming managers."

Once the SVJP was established, it brought the Japanese CEOs to the Valley every pre-COVID year. They visited top firms, spoke with their American counterparts, and also visited Stanford University. "They've been astounded by the advancements in digital technology and what it means for their business sectors."

Others who joined the SVJP—such as Mitsubishi UFJ Bank, JR (Japan Rail) East, Fast Retailing, and NEC—now have a major presence in the Valley. They have spent billions of dollars investing in or acquiring startups, in collaborating with mid-size startups, and in technological agreements with giants like Google and Microsoft.

Most importantly, among some—but only some—of the SVJP members, promotion criteria have been modified. "Employees have to have Silicon Valley experience to get ahead." That's not something Okimoto and his colleagues discussed with these CEOs, but a natural outgrowth of their epiphanies. This is the type of internal organizational change that Chesbrough had deemed necessary in the case of open innovation.

Initially, none of the Silicon Valley giants wanted to join SVJP, but now they are working actively with the Japanese companies in SVJP. "Google has been the engine of growth for collaboration because all of our Japanese member companies have signed agreements with Google." Fast Retailing, for example, contracted Google to construct its data platform for inventory, production, storage, delivery, and customer data, along with its "big data" programs. Japan is now one of Google's biggest clients.

Moreover, in a victory for open innovation, the CEO of a major financial services company instructed his technical people to find a way to collaborate with a certain electronics giant even though hitherto the companies had no relationship. When the technicians asked what they should work on, the CEO replied, "It doesn't matter. You go and decide after you meet with their chief technology officer." As a result, said Okimoto, "They ended up working together for two years to create a state-of-the-art cybersecurity platform, which they are both using and selling to the international market."

Okimoto had stressed open innovation. "I was often advocating open architectures and open systems for new technologies and, of course, that was anathema to the Japanese. Now, however, they are beginning to think about how to do that." Okimoto is hardly the first to preach the doctrine of open innovation to Japanese companies; what made SVJP so impactful was the personal bonds with CEOs. As for the future, Okimoto mused, "Whether or not they really embrace it is yet to be seen. But I think they going to have to adapt to it."

If Eastern Europe Can Reform Its Economy, Why Not Japan?

Back in 1995, GDP per work-hour in eight former Soviet bloc countries[2] was just 39% of the US level, while Japan's was more than twice as high, at 70%. By 2019—prior to COVID and the invasion of Ukraine—eastern Europe had grown to 59% of the US level. Conversely, Japan was unable to keep up and dropped to just 61%. If these trends continue, surpassing Japan is just a matter of time (OECD 2022a).

How did eastern Europe catch up so quickly? When the Berlin Wall fell in 1989, few people under age 65 had ever seen capitalism during their working years. Many aspiring business founders could not even define profit.

Eastern Europe imported managerial talent, mentorship for would-be businesspeople, and the most modern machinery via inward FDI. Companies from OECD nations either bought up old state-owned enterprises or started new ones from scratch and sent some of their own managers. As employees moved to other firms or started their own, the imported knowledge diffused throughout the economy. From just 5% of GDP in 1992, the total cumulative amount of FDI mushroomed to 55% by 2019. In Japan, by contrast, inward FDI, a negligible 0.4% of GDP in 1992, had risen by 2019 to a measly 4.4%, the lowest of 196 countries (UNCTAD 2022).

While FDI is hardly the only factor in eastern Europe's progress, it's been indispensable. Trade and FDI exert not just economic impact, but political influence as well. Competition breaks up domestic cartels, formal or informal, and so an abundance of competing imports is just as important as exports. It breaks up domestic alliances that obstruct all sorts of reforms. In addition, foreign business executives in the host country often create alliances with pro-reform domestic forces. FDI, like trade, "not only establishes powerful direct linkages between the economy and the world system but also effectively forces the government to take actions on the other parts of the reform program under the pressures of international competition" (Sachs et al.

---

[2] Czechia, Estonia, Hungary, Lithuania, Latvia, Poland, Slovak Republic, and Slovenia.

1995: 2). Unfortunately, the results regarding political democracy in eastern Europe are mixed.

Rich countries likewise benefit from these economic and coalition-busting effects. Not until Japanese automakers set up their factories—so-called transplants—on US soil using American workers did Detroit take seriously the measures that enabled their competitors to seize market share. In response, they finally upped their own game on issues like quality and durability.

Before Renault took over faltering Nissan in 1999 and brought it back to life, the company had run huge losses year after year, including $7 billion in 1999 alone. Until 1996, Nissan never had a chief financial officer (CFO), as had become standard in most American and European corporations. No mere bookkeeper, the CFO is a strategist who advises on the financial viability of undertaking—or failing to undertake—assorted investments, marketing strategies, pricing, and so forth. Many CFOs have gone on to become CEOs. Even when Nissan finally created a CFO, he did not have access to all the necessary information (Paprzycki and Fukao 2008: 2766–2768 on Kindle). As a result, Nissan did not know whether a particular model was profitable or not, a problem that is said to be pervasive at some of Japan's corporate giants that produce hundreds, or even thousands, of unrelated products. Nissan did not know it was paying more than Renault for identical parts. No wonder Ghosn was able to return the company to profitability in just one year.

A study of 19 OECD countries confirmed that FDI improved economic growth in rich countries, mainly by raising the level of labor productivity (Alam et al. 2013). Productivity, in turn, was improved partly via better technology and partly through enhancing managerial skills.

Most importantly, FDI's benefits not only help the foreign-owned company, but spill over to competitors, suppliers, customers, and even unrelated companies in the same region (Chung and Yeung 2003). Via knowledge spillovers, other firms learn about new technology and managerial approaches at the foreign-owned firms that, for one reason or another, did not exist in the domestic market (e.g., the managerial changes that Ghosn instituted at Nissan or the low-defect production strategies that Japanese transplants brought to the United States). Competitive pressures force good companies to up their game and drive laggards out of business, thereby raising the average productivity level of those that remain in business. The improved managerial techniques diffuse as managers and other employers switch from firm to firm. It is these spillover effects that provide the greatest benefits. For example, as Japanese auto assemblers increased their production volume in the United States, efficiency rose not just at those who supplied the transplants, but at other parts makers as well.

Finally, foreign firms can spawn a host of domestic entrepreneurs, as does Geodesic, a VC firm run by John Roos, who served as President Obama's ambassador to Japan. Among other activities, Geodesic funds American high-tech firms to start operations in Japan. One of these is Salesforce, a global leader in customer relations management (CRM) software that now has a major presence in Japan. Roos sits on its Board. A subsidiary VC firm, Salesforce Ventures, funds new firms in related areas. "Salesforce Ventures had a young guy," Roos explained, "and he ended up starting his own venture fund in Japan in Software-as-a-Service enterprises. He's been able to raise a fair amount of money because the Japanese now want to find ways to really support and invigorate the system through digitization" (Interview March 2022).

Japan's massive internal market has been both a blessing and a curse, continued Roos. The market is so big that new companies can succeed without engaging the global market and therefore may be late in seeing new developments overseas. "Ten years ago, the concept of cloud software was foreign. And now there's incredible movement. Foreign cloud-based firms have done very well in Japan." Similar developments are taking place in areas like automation, business intelligence, data, development tools, messaging, security, and online meetings, for both business-oriented and consumer-oriented uses. One company in this area, called UiPath, has a frontier technology for automating assorted robotic processes. It's a new technology in Japan, and even though Japan is a world leader in robotics, big companies there are buying UiPath's product. "Fast-growing startups from here are going to Japan. Japanese professionals go to work for these companies, and then they leave to start their own."

The Benefits to Japan of Inward FDI

Although measuring the all-important spillover effects is impossible because the amount of FDI is still too small, the data for Japan does show the benefits that FDI brings to foreign-owned firms. Compare, for example, the impact on Japanese companies when a foreign company bought a domestic manufacturer (a mere 67 cases during 1994–2001) versus an acquisition by another domestic firm (1,362 cases). Within three years of the purchase, firms purchased by foreigners improved substantially more than those bought by another Japanese firm. Total factor productivity (TFP) improved twice as much. Also, the profit:sales ratio increased with foreign acquisition but not with domestic acquisition (Paprzycki and Fukao 2008: Chapter 5).

One of the big reasons for these results is that inward FDI introduces firms to global innovations in ways of doing things of which they had previously been unaware. Moreover, when foreign-owned firms in Japan conduct R&D, they generate seven times as much spillover productivity benefits at other firms (suppliers, customers, even competitors) than do domestic firms spending the same amount. One scholar concluded that this is "probably because knowledge of foreign firms is often new to domestic firms" (Todo 2006: 998).

A more recent paper covering manufacturers during 1995–2013 reported that "companies that break through the traditions of Japanese governance and have some foreign ownership exhibit greater export and innovation activities" (Okubo et al. 2017: 1). It is notable that the benefits of FDI were substantially higher for unlisted firms than for those on the stock market. The greater the share of foreign ownership in a firm, the higher that firm's spending on R&D, the number of patents generated, sales growth, exports, profitability (return on assets), and productivity (TFP). One reason for better profitability is that, in some companies, FDI led to a decrease in capital investment on tangible items but an increase in knowledge-based capital, in tune with the global trend discussed earlier.

A firm's ability to benefit from FDI hinges on its absorption capacity. Companies that are already doing some innovation, whose corporate culture is open to fresh ideas, and who tend to pay higher wages, have greater absorption capacity. They are therefore more likely to choose FDI as a path to further improvement. At the same time, foreign companies prefer to buy companies that are already superior performers and then make them even better.

One of the most important findings is the snowball effect. A company is more likely to accept some foreign investment if it sees other companies in the same industry in the same prefecture with foreign investment. It's akin to people being more likely to become entrepreneurs if they personally know some entrepreneurs.

When FDI comes in, the better competitors within the country up their own game. Inferior competitors downsize or even go out of business. In short, FDI not only makes good firms better, but also helps national growth by culling the herd.

Japan's Main Impediment to FDI: The Vertical *Keiretsu*

Given all these benefits, why did Japan come in dead last among 196 countries?

It's not because Japan is unattractive. On the contrary, in survey after survey, multinational companies list Japan as a top target due to its large, affluent market, a well-educated workforce and customer base, and high technological levels. Japan came in fourth out of 27 rich countries in an "FDI Confidence Survey" of senior executives around the world (A. T. Kearney 2020).

Moreover, former public antipathy has virtually evaporated. In surveys conducted in the early 2000s, 47% of respondents said the impact of foreign companies on the Japanese economy was positive, whereas only 8% thought it was negative. Only 4% held the once-common view that foreign firms and financiers were "vultures" who wanted to buy Japanese companies on the cheap and then sell them to make a quick buck. Twenty percent of respondents said that they'd like to work for a foreign company, while another 20% said that they would not do so (Paprzycki and Fukao 2008: Kindle location 4408).

Despite all this, Japan is way behind global norms. Hoshi and Kiyota (2019: 28) calculated that inward FDI would have already reached a very impactful 35% of GDP by 2015 if Japan performed like other countries based on factors known to influence the level of FDI: per capita GDP, population, distance from other countries, Free Trade Agreements, technological capacity, and so forth. FDI from the US alone would have amounted to 13% of Japan's GDP.

In reality, the main hurdle is Japan's structural impediments to carrying out the primary form of FDI: foreign firms buying healthy companies so as to gain a built-in labor force, customer base, brand name, and suppliers. In the typical rich country, 80% of inward FDI takes the form of mergers and acquisitions (M&A) (Carril-Caccia and Pavlova 2018), but in Japan, inbound

M&A has been rare, except for a few spectacular rescue operations in recent years, such as Foxconn's purchase of Sharp.

The essential obstacle is that Japan's most attractive companies are largely off-limits to foreign purchasers. The press covers the dramatic exceptions where foreign companies rescue fallen stars like Nissan, Sharp, and Toshiba. In reality, as noted above, most foreign investors seek out superior companies that can not only help their sales within Japan but offer resources enhancing the parent's global expansion. Why are these attractive firms off limits? Some factors are legacies from the past; others are due to ongoing impediments.

Unlike postwar Europe, which welcomed FDI as an alternative to imports, Tokyo for years legally restricted both imports and FDI. In 1964, when Japan joined the OECD, it was obliged to phase out most restrictions. The process did not finish until 1976 and was not codified into law until 1980. M&A was not liberalized until the end.

During this process, METI set up a Capital Transactions Liberalization Countermeasures Special Committee. One of these "countermeasures" was promoting cross-shareholding among corporations so as to protect management from unwanted purchases. Rather quickly, the shares held by "stable shareholder" allies leapt, leaving as few as 15%–25% of the shares publicly traded. Consequently, unlike in other countries, there were not enough shares on the market for any would-be acquirer to acquire a majority.

For four decades now, there have been few overt governmental restrictions to inward FDI beyond the sort seen in other countries. Nonetheless, lingering impediments like the cross-shareholding system keep inward M&A low.

Things have changed somewhat as a result of the banking crisis of the 1990s–early 2000s and the three lost decades. There has been a substantial increase in both domestic M&As as well as cases of foreigners acting as white knights for failing Japanese giants. Nonetheless, protectionist and nationalist attitudes remain. A few years back, the government tried, and failed, to stop Taiwan's Foxconn from rescuing Sharp. Various rules, such as tax policies surrounding the "triangular merger" mechanism for stock-for-stock swaps, make acquisitions more cumbersome and expensive than they ought to be. Stable shareholding has declined, but not enough to entirely alter the situation.

The biggest factor of all is that most of Japan's appealing companies are entangled with the huge corporate groups discussed earlier. In some cases,

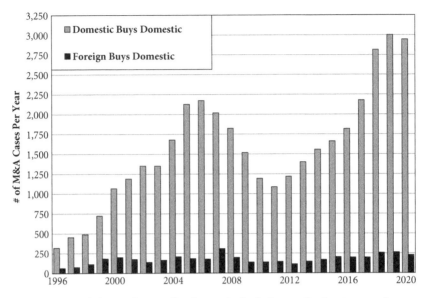

Figure 15.2 M&As mushroom for domestic deals, less so for foreign purchases.
Source: RECOF (2021).

these companies are subsidiaries or affiliates of Japan's corporate giants. In other cases, the SME is not officially an affiliate but is a subcontractor dependent on the giant. As a matter of business culture, unless they are forced by financial dislocation, parent companies tend not to sell members of their corporate group to any other firm, either a domestic or foreign one.

Following the financial reforms of the 1998 Big Bang and beyond, domestic M&As mushroomed, and companies were more willing to sell affiliates to other Japanese firms. However, the number of purchases by foreign companies stalled out at around 200 cases per year from 2000 onward (see Figure 15.2).

During the quarter century of 1996–2020, foreign companies were only able to buy a negligible 51 companies that were members of a corporate group, as opposed to 3,157 unaffiliated companies. In the couple dozen cases where foreigners could buy a group member listed on the stock market, the average purchase price was a hefty $265 million. However, such companies were rarely on the menu at Chez Nippon. By contrast, Japanese parents bought almost 19,000 members of their own corporate group, or someone else's, plus another 38,000 unaffiliated companies (see Figure 15.3).

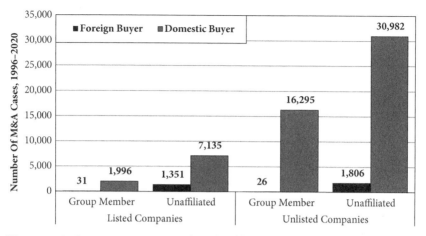

Figure 15.3 Group companies not for sale to foreigners.
Source: RECOF (2021).
Note: See text for explanation.

Ambiguous Government Policy

Tokyo claims to desire more inward FDI, and the Japan External Trade Organization (JETRO), a METI affiliate, has various "Invest in Japan" programs. The fact, however, is that, when countries are truly determined to lure more inward FDI, they succeed. Consider Korea, whose business system resembles that of Japan in so many ways. When reformer Kim Dae Jung became president in 1999, he truly welcomed FDI because he saw it as part of the democratization process. As a result, inward FDI leapt from less than 3% of GDP in the decade before Kim's arrival to 14% today. Similar leaps occurred when Taiwan democratized, when Deng Xiaoping embraced globalization as the route to China's modernization, and when India undertook reforms in the early 1990s (see Figure 15.4).

For a while, during the reign of Prime Minister Junichiro Koizumi (2001–2006), it looked as if Japan might be launching a similar shift. In January 2003, Koizumi set a goal for inward FDI to reach 2.5% of GDP by 2006, and in 2006, he raised the target to 5% of GDP by 2011. He achieved results: FDI quadrupled from 1% of GDP the year before Koizumi took power to 4% by 2008. Since then, however, the rise has stalled out.

Under Koizumi—with input from American Chamber of Commerce (ACCJ) leaders like Nicholas Benes and despite the resistance of

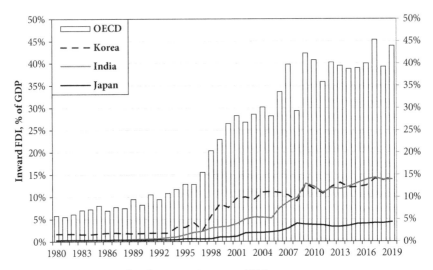

Figure 15.4 Korea and India versus Japan on FDI.
Source: UNCTAD (2022).

Keidanren—Tokyo reformed the company law in 2007 to make inward M&A easier. For the first time, foreign companies were allowed to use cash in so-called triangular mergers to buy 100% of the stock of Japanese firms, and for the first time, they could use their own stock to pay for a company using a triangular merger. In either case, they could squeeze out small holders of stock. In a triangular merger, the foreign buyer sets up a Japanese subsidiary as a vehicle for the purchase and that subsidiary must meet certain conditions. Would-be buyers still face some unwieldy rules and unfavorable tax treatment, including the way capital gains are counted and taxed on stock swaps. The good news is that, over time, many of these formal hurdles in the M&A rules have been ameliorated, or else firms have found a way to outflank them, according to Benes and the current co-chairs of the ACCJ's FDI Committee, Ken Lebrun and Bryan Norton. Both Lebrun and Benes in their professional careers have represented companies involved in inward M&A.

While progress is slow, Benes commented, "The difference from 2005 is like night and day. Domestic M&A is common, and, in some cases, shareholders have forced management's takeover defenses to be dismantled. This new atmosphere may be the biggest reason to expect more FDI via M&A in the future. Still, the floodgates will still open more slowly than is optimal for Japan" (Interview July 2021).

When Shinzo Abe succeeded Koizumi in his first, one-year term in 2006, he endorsed the 5% goal, and yet that goal has never been met. In 2015, when the Abe administration released its "Five Promises for Attracting Foreign Businesses to Japan" in 2015, the difficulty in buying existing firms was not even mentioned.

One would think that, as part of JETRO's "Invest in Japan" program, it would solicit foreign buyers, but forces inside the government have so far prevented it. For example, to help ameliorate the SME succession crisis, a 2020 interim report of the cabinet-level Council for Promotion of Foreign Direct Investment in Japan (2020: 3) advocated helping these SMEs find suitable foreign partners and to "facilitate business transfer between third-parties (merger & acquisition)." The final report, published in June 2021, purged all talk of inward M&A. Clearly, someone feared foreign purchases more than the closure of hundreds of thousands of healthy firms, and those in a position to know are not saying who did it. Still, the fact that the proposal even made it to the interim report is something new.

To make matters worse, the government hides from itself how badly it has failed. The Ministry of Finance (MOF) reported that inward FDI climbed to ¥40 trillion ($310 billion) in 2020. In reality, the 2020 figure was just ¥24 trillion, according to the IMF, OECD, and UNCTAD (see Figure 15.5).

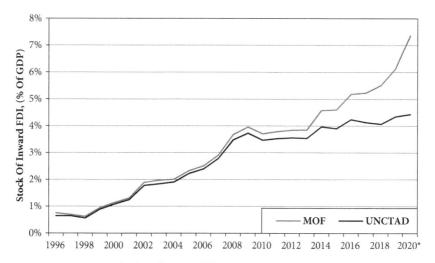

Figure 15.5 Japan is hiding from itself how low inward FDI is.
Source: MOF (2022a); UNCTAD (2022).

How is such a huge discrepancy possible? Two sets of numbers are approved by the IMF, but only one of them—called the "directional principle"—is authorized for looking at a country's FDI over time or for comparing countries. The MOF, by contrast, highlights the other set, called the "asset/liability principle." The latter has its uses, but it includes items having nothing to do with real FDI (e.g., loans from overseas affiliates back to their parents in Japan). A spokesman for the MOF confirmed that such loans accounted for most of the discrepancy. Asked about the MOF's choice of numbers, an OECD official replied, "The directional principle is better suited to analyze the economic impact of FDI. It is the recommended presentation for FDI statistics by country and industry" (Interview October 2021). If solving a problem requires recognizing that you have one, Tokyo is in trouble.

Corporate Reform and Inward FDI: The Role of the ACCJ

American business leaders in Japan point to another trend they believe will increase inbound M&A: corporate governance reform. Under Abe, Japan's stock market and the government's Financial Services Agency (FSA) promulgated respectively the 2014 Stewardship Code and the 2015 Corporate Governance Code. These codes sought to have companies place more emphasis on the rate of profit—seen as a reflection of efficiency—not just size and market share. The governance code was directed toward the operating firms while the stewardship code addressed institutional investors in those firms. The Governance Code was proposed to the government by Benes, who at the time was an ACCJ governor. Beginning in 2013, he had conversations with people like Yasuhisa Shiozaki, Prime Minister Shinzo Abe's chief cabinet secretary, as well as a leading official at the FSA. He not only persuaded them of the need for the code but helped shape its content.

Many ACCJ leaders believe that greater stress on profitability will not only raise Japanese growth, but also promote more FDI. One noted that, "Ten years ago, when I used the term return on equity (ROE), many Japanese executives asked me what I was talking about. Not these days" (Interview August 2021). To improve profitability, he contended, corporate giants will increasingly have to focus on core competencies. That requires hiving off non-core divisions and subsidiaries. Some analysts see as harbingers companies like Hitachi and Shiseido which sold healthy divisions to foreign private equity (PE) firms so they could focus on their most lucrative activities.

Lebrun noted that "the stock market has certainly rewarded companies that are taking these steps" (Interview July 2021).

Eventually, this logic may bear fruit, but the results so far are disappointing. Hitachi and Shiseido are the kind of globally active firms that are most likely to improve efficiency without outside pressure. Hitachi, in fact, began divesting before either the promulgation of these two codes or pressure from activist investors (Stevenson and Inajima 2022). While "select and focus" was a big buzzword in boardrooms during the past decade, it's hard to find data confirming whether very much has taken place, and there are reasons to wonder. The total number of subsidiaries and affiliates in 2017 was more or less the same as in 2007. Japan offers a tax break for conglomerates divesting themselves of inefficient divisions or affiliates, but few companies seem to have taken advantage of it (METI 2020e).

In anticipation of a boom in carve-outs, KKR, Bain Capital, CVC, and about 80 other domestic and foreign PE firms are building up their war chests. The anticipated upsurge has yet to emerge. Since 2004, there have only been about 10–20 domestic divestitures above ¥10 billion ($77 million) to PE firms per year, a figure that has not increased over time. The typical sale has been priced at around ¥50 billion ($385 million), with the notable exception of 2017, when a group led by Bain Capital paid $18 million for 40% of Toshiba's memory unit. Nor has there been any trend increase in the total value of deals (see Figure 15.6).

The delay is caused by still "insufficient pressure on corporates to sell quality assets," and the fact that "boards and shareholders do not yet push for strategic divestitures" (Bain & Company 2018: 5). Instead, Bain added, corporations are taking easier routes to show better ROE numbers, such as stock buybacks and selling low-quality assets (i.e., those that are unprofitable, and/or suffer declining sales and a worsening competitive position). While the latter sales are necessary, they are just the low-hanging fruit and are insufficient. Companies need to sell operations that, while still profitable, no longer fit within a firm's overall core strategy and thus bring down overall profitability and efficiency. In many cases, those operations might be even more profitable in another company where they add some synergy to existing operations.

By 2022, there were some signs that the situation may be changing, albeit slowly, according to Bain & Company (Ohara 2022). Among the top 50 M&A deals where corporations divested parts of themselves, eight were what Bain & Company called "transformative" (i.e., an effort to shed non-core activities

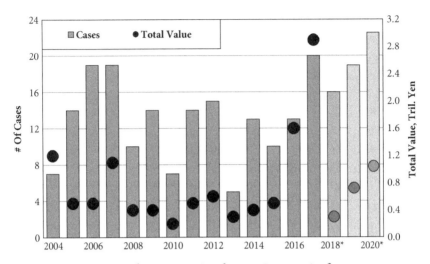

Figure 15.6 Corporate divestitures via sales to private equity firms.

Source: Bain & Company (2021 and previous years); 2018–2020 author estimates based on data provided by Bain & Co.

Note: Includes only domestic divestitures; from 2018 onward (*), Bain no longer provided annual breakdowns; 2019–2020 is author's rough estimate based on the historical ratio of carve-outs to total PE activity.

even if they were profitable). That's up from just two a couple of years earlier. This is one of the most important barometers of genuine corporate reform, but 8 cases out of 50 does not yet a trend make.

Foreign PE funds have also helped to spawn Japanese PE companies. Take Taisuke Sasanuma, who co-founded Japan's first PE firm, Advantage Partners, in 1992, together with an American, Richard Folsom. Both men had learned the ropes at Bain & Company. Then there's Jun Tsusaka, who in 2014 founded NSSK. Tsusaka had worked for America's PE giant, TPG. Having spent years in the semiconductor field, mostly in Japan, Richard Dyck is now a director at a Japanese PE firm called Japan Industrial Partners. Specializing in buying non-core parts of Japan's big conglomerates, it purchased Hitachi Chemical, part of the Hitachi Group, and Dyck became a director.

Regardless of any rules on paper, shareholders' power over management is limited by a simple financial fact: Japan's 5,000 biggest corporations have little need to raise money on the equity markets since their internally generated cash flow regularly surpasses their investments in new plant and equipment. The overall decline in stable shareholders should be a force for improving shareholder power. However, as Benes points out, FSA rules make it hard for minority shareholders to act collectively in making suggestions to management, as they can in the United States and the United Kingdom.

Besides, firms can make financial measures look better without any real improvement. For example, if firms use *current* profits (i.e., profits *after* interest payments) to measure ROE or return on assets (ROA), then the BOJ's continual lowering of interest rates makes profit rates look better. However, when ROA is measured by *operating* profits (i.e., profits *before* interest), improvement has been just marginal. At the 5,000 biggest corporations, operating profits rose only a smidgen from 3.5% during 1996–2012 to 3.8% during 2013–2019 (i.e., prior to COVID) (see Figure 15.7). Worse yet, as we saw earlier, these firms increased their profits primarily by cutting wages, rather than via efficiency. Unless shareholders care how profit numbers are achieved, then it's not clear why increased shareholder power would lead to more productive corporate strategies.

The magnitude of change required in inward FDI will require a concerted policy effort by the government and business leaders. And they are divided. In the Koizumi era, recalled Benes, the biggest business federation, Keidanren, successfully lobbied METI to make the tax treatment for cross-border stock swaps as "burdensome and difficult as possible." In contrast, the more progressive Keizai Doyukai has welcomed FDI as part of overall reform. In 2005, it called for increasing inward FDI to 10% of GDP, and in

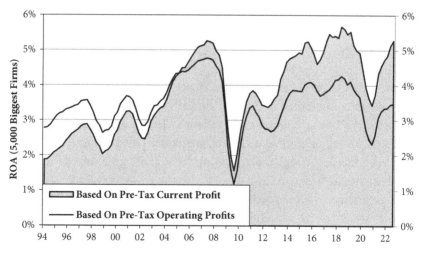

Figure 15.7 ROA, based on current versus operating profits.
Source: MOF (2023a).

2005 and again in 2015, it advocated better tax treatment of inbound M&A. Unfortunately, Keidanren continues to have much more clout.

In fact, suspicion about resistance to inward FDI by parts of the government and big business are so embedded that one prominent American business executive noted how Toshiba's management and METI used the pretext of "national security concerns" in a failed attempt to block a shareholder vote against management in 2021. He feared that the same thing might occur in other cases.

Without concerted policy action, when 2030 arrives, Japan might still be little better than 196th.

America's Stake

One of the greatest foreign policy challenges of our era is handling the rise of an increasingly powerful and ambitious China without falling into a war. Integrating China into a rules-based world order will be a lot easier if Japan has the ability and the will to act as an economic counterweight in the Pacific. China's alliance with an aggressive Russia adds to the challenge.

China is not only acting aggressively in seizing Pacific islands, but it is using its enormous economic size to create a web of dependencies: ties of foreign aid, of investment, of imports, and of technology. Even US multinational giants find themselves cooperating with Beijing in order not to lose the Chinese market, whether it be high-tech firms cooperating with Beijing's internal security efforts or motion picture producers changing plots or blackballing certain actors.

The world at large benefits from a prosperous China that not only plays by the rules but helps shape them in a responsible manner. At the same time, China's stake in global stability can conflict with its territorial aggrandizement and tactics of economic intimidation. That gives other nations some leverage. To the extent that a vibrant, technologically advanced Japan plays a heavier role in the region via its companies, FDI, and assorted Free Trade Agreements, an improved balance of economic power may limit what China can do and increase the possibility of Beijing returning to something closer to its past stance of a "peaceful rise."

So far, Japan's economic travails have reduced its influence in Asia, hence its ability to act as a counterweight to China. The Asia Power Index reported that, in 2021, across all dimensions of power, Japan has "for the first time dropped below the major power threshold of 40 points and is now considered a high-performing middle power," and by 2023 was down to 37.2. When it comes to economic relationships, that is, "the capacity to exercise influence and leverage through economic interdependencies" within Asia, like trade, investment, and technological leadership, Japan's score fell from 56 in 2018, when the index was launched, to only 40.1 by 2023. By contrast, China's score is 98.3 (Lowy Institute 2023: n.p.).

It is civil society, not Washington, that will be the prime locus of American activities that aid Japanese entrepreneurship. When it comes to economic issues, America has turned inward in recent years. That trend escalated under Donald Trump and continued when Joseph Biden became president (e.g., the latter's emphasis on "Buy America" procurement and trade policies). The Biden term is the first time in three decades that a president has lacked authority from Congress to negotiate any new trade pacts. As of this writing, there is no initiative by the Biden administration to ask for renewal of that authority.

Although former US ambassador to Japan John Roos agreed that most of the American measures that help Japan's economy would come from businesses and universities, rather than the government, he suggested one possible exception to this picture, the security implications of China's advances in technology. "Japan and the US need to do a better job of collaborating. That will happen in the private sector, but Washington can and should do more of that kind of collaboration with Tokyo."

PART V
THE POLITICS OF REFORM

16

The Values of Japan's Postwar Political Economy

The political economy that developed in the postwar era emerged out of a tumultuous past, one marked by the need of the ruling conservatives to respond to bitter, sometimes violent class-struggle moves by the increasingly popular Socialist and Communist parties. Unlike Europe's Social Democrats, Japan's Socialists were dyed-in-the-wool Marxists who opposed Japan's alliance with the United States during the Cold War. Not until after the fall of the Berlin Wall in 1989 would the Left decline and any relatively Center-Left pro-capitalist parties arise to oppose the conservatives.

In this crucible, a political economy emerged with certain core values: equality, opportunity, stability, and protection of the weak. How these values were translated into policies determined whether they promoted growth or undermined it. As will be seen, the focus on job security rather than income security lies at the heart of many of the obstacles to creative destruction. What is needed today is not a change in values, but yet another of Japan's innumerable transformations in how they are used. Illustrating how Japan's political values developed and manifested themselves in the past several decades will demonstrate that the reforms proposed in this book are quite compatible with those values.

It's vital to remember that Japan began the postwar era as a poor agricultural economy. Even though it's now known that the economic miracle had already taken off by the early 1950s, as late as 1957 Harvard's preeminent Japanologist Edwin Reischauer still wondered whether Japan would ever export enough to pay for indispensable imports of food and raw materials (Reischauer 1957: 316–317).

The ruling Liberal and Democratic parties—both conservative despite their names—had two desires: to catch up to the West and to ensure enough popular support to remain in power. Since rapid industrialization rapidly shrank the rural population, the conservatives' prime voter base, and the Left often had majorities in the growing cities, serious analysts raised the specter

The Contest for Japan's Economic Future. Richard Katz, Oxford University Press. © Richard Katz 2024.
DOI: 10.1093/oso/9780197675106.003.0017

of a Socialist-Communist majority in the Diet. To forestall this threat, the Liberals and Democrats merged in 1955 to form the Liberal Democratic Party (LDP). More fundamentally, the conservatives had to solve the central political problem of growth led by creative destruction: that it creates losers as well as winners. Unless the losers, from farmers to textile workers to mom-and-pop shops, could somehow be appeased, they could unleash a backlash.

Often, the LDP's two goals—fending off the Left and appeasing the victims of rapid development—coincided, most dramatically in the case of coal. By the 1950s and early 1960s, imported oil had become much cheaper than domestic coal. The modern industries being promoted by MITI, the precursor of METI, had a great desire to switch. And yet, this would mean severe job losses for several hundred thousand coal miners. In 1959–1961, when mine owners decided to reduce the workforce, a long and violent strike by a Socialist-led coal miners' union coincided with Left-led riots against the 1960 renewal of the US-Japan Security Treaty. So alarming were the protests that President Dwight Eisenhower canceled his trip to Japan and Prime Minister Nobusuke Kishi, formerly imprisoned for three years as a Class A war criminal suspect, had to step down.[1] The backlash against shutting down the mines had begun earlier, and was so threatening that, in 1955, MITI restricted the number of new oil-fired electricity plants. It did so even though other bureaus within MITI were promoting a domestic petroleum refinery industry. Since, until 1964, all foreign exchange for imports required MITI's approval, MITI's price for granting foreign exchange to steelmakers and utilities was their purchase of domestic coal at high prices. To all of this, MITI added direct state subsidies, which lasted until 1986.

When former MOF bureaucrat Hayato Ikeda replaced Kishi, he put economic betterment for all—combined with the protection of society's losers—at the center of politics. He launched an Income Doubling Policy so successful that it overshot its goals, thereby beginning to remove the Left's raison d'être. By the mid-1960s, talk of class struggle evaporated as surveys increasingly showed upwards of 90% of the population began calling itself middle class, a self-conception pushed in the media.

Coal mining was just one of innumerable fading industries where the government used subsidies, import protection, and other tactics to slow the setting of the sun on those industries. Japan's political leaders felt the situation required that they placate some sunset sectors in order to retain

---

[1] Kishi was the grandfather of Prime Minister Shinzo Abe, and the latter's hero.

enough public support to carry out their pro-growth program. In the terms of political scientist Kent Calder, they juggled a balance between "strategy and "compensation" (Calder 1988). Strategy referred to the array of policies and institutions devoted toward rapid economic and technological catch-up. Compensation referred to the methods used to slow, or even arrest, the downsizing of declining sectors while bolstering the income of people hurt by creative destruction.

During the high-growth era, any losses to growth from compensation measures were dwarfed by the success of pro-growth policies. Besides, with GDP growing 9%–10% a year, there were plenty of new jobs to absorb the declines in sunset sectors. Over time, fewer of the 30% of factory workers who lost or left their jobs every year complained since it was easy in that era to find new, and better, ones (Moriguchi and Ono 2006: 153). Compensation made Japan politically safe for creative destruction.

Compensation politics shaped the political ethic that equality and security should include not just the individuals working in sunset sectors but the sectors themselves, as in coal mining. Not for Japan was the neoliberal economic model.

It would be a mistake to think it was only compensation politics which embodied the values of equality and security. A wide range of measures providing equality and security actually served to accelerate growth.

Equality, Security, and Growth

A few decades ago, economists, even liberal ones, believed that equality must come at the expense of growth. The "big trade-off" it was called. Today, however, orthodoxy understands that equality, *if achieved in the right way*, can actually enhance growth, primarily by improving the human capital of the lower half of the population. The OECD has published myriad reports along this line, including one subtitled *Why Less Inequality Benefits All* (OECD 2015b). One study calculated that, had Japan not suffered increased inequality during 1990–2010, its cumulative per capita growth over that period would have been 21% rather than 17% (Cingano 2014: 18). The real issue is that equality can be produced in ways that enhance growth, as in Scandinavia's flexicurity system, or in ways that hamstring it, as in today's Japan.

Aside from the limited use of standard redistribution measures—from progressive taxes to social security for the aged—Japan has employed several other growth-enhancing measures to achieve equality and security. The top three were: universal healthcare; high educational achievement for all; and high intergenerational mobility. There is a serious risk that these achievements are being undermined by low growth, aging, rising income inequality, and chronic budget deficits.

Not only does Japan offer universal care, like all rich countries other than the United States, but "[i]n most respects, Japan has one of the most egalitarian health care systems in the world" (Ikegami and Campbell 1999: 70). Compared to other countries, Japan exhibits surprisingly little difference between rich and poor in health outcomes like illness and life expectancy. Moreover, rich and poor alike spend the same portion of their household income for insurance premiums and out-of-pocket expenses combined: a range of 7.6% to 8.5% (Statistics Bureau 2020c). Universal healthcare was accepted by both the Right and the Left and finally began to be achieved in 1961 under Ikeda, and then expanded, partly because the LDP had to compete with the rising leftist parties.

An egalitarian healthcare system pays off in better growth and income equality. Children whose parents put off eye exams due to money woes end up doing less well in school, lifetime incomes, and productivity. Without affordable universal healthcare, a single devastating incident, or a chronic physical or mental malady, can cause a family to become unable to work or have to deny their children a college education. Every year, 2.6% of Japanese households suffer a catastrophic health crisis, much less than the median of 8% among 20 rich OECD countries (OECD 2019i: 113). Still, over the course of a decade, this adds up to a considerable share of households. While the poorest 40% suffer 80% of these incidents, no one ever knows if they will be among the victims.

What Japan wrestles with now is whether it can sustain this exemplary situation. Per capita expenditures for seniors are several times higher than for younger people (Ikegami 2014: 35). As a result, by 2018, nearly 40% of all healthcare spending was devoted to those over 75 (MHLW 2018a). Ultimately the ability to finance care is determined by GDP per capita and the cost of care. Back in 1980, there were only 17 seniors to be supported by every 100 working-age people. By 2020, the figure had risen to 50, and it's projected to hit 72 by 2050.

In response, the government has cut public healthcare spending per senior by 15% during 1999–2019. That has kept government spending on healthcare fairly flat at around 2.6%–2.7% of GDP since 2013 (Cabinet Office (2020). Total healthcare spending, after rising from 6% of GDP in 1990 to 10.6% in 2011, has remained fairly flat since then, as of 2019 (OECD 2022i). One result is that inequalities in health are beginning to show up. For example, part-time workers now have a higher risk for mortality than regular workers (Inoue et al. 2016: 4).

One of Japan's proudest achievements has been equity in education, where a child's opportunity is not limited by the parent's socioeconomic status. Such equity is vital to income equality, social mobility, and economic growth. And it's self-reinforcing. The more equality there is in educational achievement, the greater the equality in incomes down the road, which, in turn, reinforces equality in educational achievement for the next generation.

In the famous PISA (Program for International Student Assessment) tests of 15-year-olds run by the OECD, not only does Japan rank high among 77 countries—sixth in the combined reading, math, and science scores in 2018—but student scores hinge less on their parents' socioeconomic status than elsewhere. This is due to deliberate efforts by the government to produce such equity. In 2018, only 8% and 9% of the variance in student scores in math and science, respectively, were due to the socioeconomic status of their parents, compared to an average of 13% and 14% in the other rich countries (OECD 2019j: 4–5). Not only do Japan's top students perform better than most, but so do its poorest performers. Japan's achievement is not a product of low immigration rates. Only 1% of the variation in scores among countries was caused by differences in immigration (OECD 2012: 47).

Unfortunately, the rise in income inequality over the last couple of decades has begun to translate into educational inequality. In 2009—when median household income was just ¥2.8 million ($22,000) per year—only a third of families with income below ¥4 million ($31,000) could send their children to university, compared to half of those earning between ¥4 million and ¥6 million ($31,000–46,000), and almost two-thirds of those earning more than ¥10 million ($77,000) (Jones 2011: 34). One of Japan's saddest statistics is that nearly a third of *high-achieving* disadvantaged students say they do not expect to be able to complete college versus 10% among of advantaged students with similar scores (OECD 2019j: 5). While that is no worse than the typical OECD country, Japan used to be better.

To make a bad situation even worse, the vicious cycle is perpetuating itself across generations. By their late thirties, male university graduates in Japan earn 36% more than a high school graduate, and by their early fifties, when it comes time to send their own children to college, they are earning 56% more than a high school graduate (Research Institute for Higher Education, Hiroshima University 2020).

The OECD reports, "As household income rises from less than ¥2 million ($15,000) annually to more than ¥15 million ($115,000), the proportion of correct answers by sixth-grade primary students in math rose from 63% to 83%, with a similar improvement in the Japanese language test" (Jones 2011: 34). Why does income matter so much? Because, despite the Constitution's mandate of free compulsory education, public schools cost families a great deal of money. There is no tuition in elementary and middle school, but there are fees, incidental expenses, and uniform costs. High schools charge tuition, and since 2011, the government has subsidized this, but just for the poorest families. The upshot is that a family with two children that sends both to public schools has to shell out about $8,000 per year for 12 years. Half of that is for the private cram schools (*juku*) and/or tutors preparing students for the exams that determine which school they attend at the next level (MEXT 2019). College is another $24,000 per year. Job prospects often depend on the school one attended. Among 25 OECD countries, Japan shows the lowest level of public spending on education from primary school to college. So, parents have to make up the gap (see Figure 16.1).

It need not be this way. Japan could make high school tuition free for all. It, like Korea, could offer quality public after-school classes instead of *juku*. The MOF contends that Japan cannot afford to spend more on education. In reality, it cannot afford not to do so.

If Japan wants to overcome its demographic age crunch, one of the most effective steps would be to lower the financial burden on families. Around 80% of couples in the 25-to-35 age group identified the high cost of education and childcare as a reason why they had fewer children than they would have liked (Jones 2011: 32).

Ever since the 1868 Charter Oath, a foundational document in Japan's modernization, Japan has vowed to enable each person to pursue his own calling, to have the opportunity to rise in income and status. A key test of whether a nation is really a land of opportunity is intergenerational mobility. Does the family of one's birth write a person's story, or can an individual write their own story by dint of brains, talent, and drive?

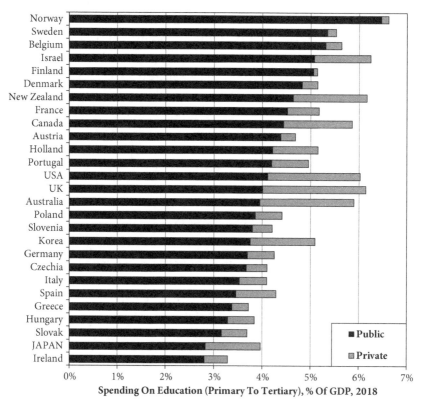

Figure 16.1 Japan lowest in public spending on education.
Source: OECD (2021d: 247).
Note: Primary to tertiary.

Intergenerational income mobility measures how much of a child's in-come is determined by his own actions, as opposed to being set at birth by his parents' socioeconomic status. Japan's figure is 65%, 11th out of 22 countries (Jones (2018: 196). In other words, in Japan, two-thirds of someone's lifetime income is determined by his own actions and circumstances, and just one-third by his parents' station in life. In the United States, the American Dream is not what it used to be: the figure is 59%, 16th out of the 22.

The question now is whether Japan's social mobility will be eroded by growing inequality, low growth, and rigid labor markets. Across countries, the more equal incomes in one generation, the greater the ability of their chil-dren to rise (or fall) by their own actions. About half of the intergenerational mobility in OECD countries can be explained by the equality of income within a generation (Jones 2018: 196). Given how much parents' income matters so much for college, growing income inequality is a danger sign for both individual opportunity and national welfare (Corak 2016).

Discussing healthcare, education, and social mobility may seem to have taken us far afield. But, across the rich world, we can see how the erosion of the social contract has generated a populist backlash against creative destruction. Japan has not seen the rise of populism, but the problems discussed here can either spur reform or reinforce resistance.

The Social Contract Deconstructs

In the past, equality and security in labor practices became an essential part of the social contract. Beginning in 1955, the union federations and leading companies undertook nationwide wage negotiations in preparation for which unions ran short-term strikes called the *Shunto* (spring offensive). Eventually, the *Shunto* became ritualized but, for years, they were used to intimidate employers prior to the negotiations. The number of work-days lost to strikes averaged 2–4 million per year. Over time, companies came to feel that fairly uniform wage hikes across industries and firms were more conducive to labor peace. Wage dispersion among companies of the same size decreased substantially during the 1960s (Moriguchi and Ono 2006: 163). During the 1950s and early 1960s, the system of lifetime employment, seniority pay, and large semi-annual bonuses spread throughout big business and, to some degree among SMEs as well.

The government expanded measures for equality and security when the LDP felt most at risk of the opposition taking power by capturing the urban vote, as in expanding universal healthcare and clamping down on pollution in the 1970s. Conversely, it has implemented policies eroding equality and security, and living standards—such as expansion of non-regular work—when it felt less of a challenge.

The social contract gave Japanese workers both equality and security of income without the kind of overt governmental social safety net seen elsewhere. Instead, the safety net was job-based. That, as will be seen, eventually eroded the growth upon which the social contract depended.

Table 16.1 Three Models of Capitalism in the Mid-1980s

	Market Income Gini		Post-Govt Income Gini		Gov't Impact	
1	Norway	0.29	Finland	0.20	Holland	−0.14
2	Denmark	0.30	Denmark	0.22	France	−0.12
3	Finland	0.31	Norway	0.22	Sweden	−0.12
4	**Japan**	**0.31**	Sweden	0.22	UK	−0.11
5	Sweden	0.35	Holland	0.23	Germany	−0.11
6	Germany	0.36	Germany	0.25	Finland	−0.10
7	New Zealand	0.36	New Zealand	0.26	New Zealand	−0.10
8	Canada	0.37	France	0.27	Italy	−0.09
9	Holland	0.37	**Japan**	**0.28**	Australia	−0.09
10	USA	0.38	UK	0.28	Canada	−0.08
11	Australia	0.39	Canada	0.29	Denmark	−0.08
12	UK	0.39	Australia	0.30	Greece	−0.08
13	France	0.39	Italy	0.31	Norway	−0.07
14	Italy	0.39	USA	0.33	USA	−0.05
15	Greece	0.40	Greece	0.33	**Japan**	**−0.03**

Source: Förster and d'Ercole (2005: 25).
Note: Working age people 18–65; the Gini coefficient is a measure of inequality, with a higher number meaning greater inequality; see text for further explanation.

Three Models of Capitalism

To see Japan in context, let's look at three models of capitalism along the axis of income equality for working-age people age 18–65 in Table 16.1. The data is from the mid-1980s. The measure of income inequality is the Gini coefficient which goes from 0 to 1 and where a higher number means more inequality.

The Nordic Model in the 1990s

Income equality (wages and other personal income) is produced by the market. Among 15 OECD countries, Norway, Denmark, Finland, and Sweden take four of the five top spots. Moreover, government redistribution (taxes and transfer payments) makes it even more equal. There is a governmental safety net in case of job loss or ill health.

The American Model Post-Reagan

Income distribution produced by the market is unequal and government redistribution only modifies this a little. The United States came in 10th in market-determined income but second from the bottom in post-government income equality because it also came in second from the bottom in government redistribution measures. The labor market is very flexible, but there is much less social protection in case of unemployment or a healthcare crisis, or aging.

The Japanese Model Pre-Lost Decades

Income distribution *apparently* produced by the market is more equal than elsewhere. Japan comes in fourth out of the 15. Hence the government does little directly to redistribute income; Japan comes in last in redistribution. The labor market is less flexible, and the society-wide social safety net is so thin that workers are dependent on the continuation of their jobs, and therefore the survival of their employer.

As late as the 1980s, Japan felt little need for a robust governmental safety net. Not only was unemployment low, but so was poverty, just 11% for working-age people prior to any government measures. The government had virtually no measures to lower the rate further. Social welfare measures were aimed at the elderly.

In place of overt measures, Japan put even more stress on compensation methods to sustain zombies and transfer income covertly. While the public believed that equality and security were being produced by the market, the market itself was being manipulated to sustain an illusion. Via subsidies and assorted anticompetitive devices, like recession cartels, supply and demand—and therefore prices—were twisted like pretzels. Distorted prices, in turn, served as the conveyer belt of a hidden redistribution of income from the economy's efficient sectors to the inefficient. Efficient manufacturers paid domestic firms higher prices for inputs from inefficient domestic providers than they could have obtained on the international market via imports. The automakers' association, for example, bargained with the associations of construction firms, glass producers, and others on price. A BOJ study showed that this transfer pricing was a significant part of the economy (Oyama

1999: 3–4). During this period, Japan was notorious for having high prices by international standards for all sorts of items.

The secret of its political success was precisely that the transfer was hidden. It let beneficiaries hide from themselves the artificiality lying behind their welfare so that, in the words of economist Takashi Kiuchi, "Society's losers don't feel like losers" (Interview 1996).

As interest groups became increasingly dependent on these measures, they gained a constituency demanding their continuation. The problem was that, by preventing creative destruction, the system undermined growth and therefore sowed the seeds for its own demise.

The most well-known example of income redistribution has been in agriculture, where the measures were more overt and became the subject of international trade conflicts. Rural votes have always been pivotal to the LDP, and, for a few decades, it had to compete with the Socialists and Communists for those votes. To do so, the LDP offered mammoth subsidies. By the 1980s, more than 75% of all farm income came from subsidies and price-support programs—a percentage far higher than in any other industrial state. Moreover, less than a third of those calling themselves farmers, and getting these subsidies, are full-time farmers. Many supposed farmers also do construction work and much of public works construction, exemplified by the notorious "bridges to nowhere," which were built, not to aid transportation, but to provide jobs in swing districts. That's one reason Japanese food prices are so high, and consumers have to spend more of their money on food than those in other rich countries (see again Figure 3.4 in Chapter 3). So, what looks like income distribution determined by market prices is really disguised redistribution via price manipulation.

Then there are the taxes and land-use laws that make the majority of farms too small to be efficient, while also making it well-nigh impossible to convert "farmland"—whether it's actually farmed or not—to other, more productive uses. As a result, by 2015, a stunning 15% of all farmland outside of Hokkaido had been abandoned by its owners (Statistics Bureau 2016).

In the late 1960s to early 1970s, the LDP feared losing another bastion of support, small business, which had become twice as large as the farm vote. Previously, when the conservative majority seemed secure, the government had favored larger modern companies over small businesses with tax breaks, subsidies, government loans, and low (regulated) interest rates. Supermarket chains started edging out mom-and-pop shops. In response, small business owners started turning to the Left. By 1971, one of every six small business owners was involved with the Communist-affiliated small business federation, Minsho, and even more were voting for the Socialists or Communists in local assemblies in prefectures and cities.

The LDP fended off this threat with a redistribution of income disguised as government loans to over half the nation's small businesses (see again Figure 13.4 in Chapter 13). At the same time, the Finance Ministry overlooked large-scale tax evasion by small businesses on as much as 60% of their income.

The Large-Scale Retail Store Law was only one of the anticompetitive laws appealing to mom-and-pop shop owners. The LDP banned pharmacies from opening branch stores. When the Supreme Court declared this unconstitutional, the Health and Welfare Ministry—the bailiwick of Ryutaro Hashimoto, a future prime minister and, earlier, of Hashimoto's father—issued a sub rosa directive for the drug producers not to sell to any such pharmacies. Drug companies that didn't wish to see their license approvals drag on for years obliged (Katz 1998: 82). Despite lobbying by the banks, one of the LDP's biggest contributors, the government delayed for almost two decades efforts by the banks to issue revolving credit cards, which would have hurt credit facilities already being run by small stores. This all turned the tide. Socialist and Communist support declined and, in the aftermath of the fall of the Berlin Wall, they no longer had any electoral power.

Apologists claimed that, for ancient cultural reasons, Japanese preferred these small stores for their personalized service. In reality, once the law was lifted, customers abandoned the tiny shops and their number plummeted, from 1.1 million in 1987, before the legal change, to just 374,000 in 2012 (Statistics Bureau 2016).[2] The argument against creative destruction is that society cannot absorb the disruption, but the drastic drop in mom-and-pop shops suggests that it can, as long as it's done in the right way.

It would have cost the economy much less just to give cash to the beneficiaries of this shadow play. When income is transferred via these anticompetitive measures, the loss to consumers and productive industries is greater than the gain to those being cosseted. The result was declining growth.

---

[2] Data since 2012 is not commensurate with 1988–2012 figures and so is not shown.

In the end, the economy could no longer support the economic burden. This is what produced the lost decades beginning after the 1990 crash in stock and property prices.

The resulting slow growth in per capita GDP led to a decline in living standards for much of the population. The sad irony is that policies enacted in the name of equality, security, and rising incomes have ended up eroding all three. As discussed earlier, real median per capita income among working age people fell by 2% during 1995–2018. However, this is not a case like the United States of the rich getting richer at the expense of everyone else. In Japan, the income share of the top 0.1% in 2012 was 2.4%, no higher than in the early 1960s (Moriguchi 2015: 22). In Japan, rich and poor alike have been getting poorer; it's just that the rich are getting poorer at a slower pace. Working-age Japanese at the 90th percentile of incomes (i.e., those with incomes greater than 90% of their compatriots) endured a 2% fall during 1995–2018, while those at the 10% percentile suffered a whopping 16% drop (OECD 2022j).[3]

Japan is the only OECD country where the level of "absolute poverty"[4] rose between 1995 and 2015: from 12% of working-age people in 1995 to 19% (this is after government redistribution measures). Much of this is due to the increase in non-regular workers. It's not just those below the poverty line that are affected. As of 2018, the income of people at the 20th percentile equaled just 16% of those at the 80% percentile, the fifth-lowest out of 28 OECD countries, far below the OECD average of 21% (OECD 2022j). In 2018, 7.4 million people (11% of the entire workforce) were part-timers who had to work two different part-time jobs to make ends meet (Van 't Veld 2020).

Giving up equality and income did not gain Japanese workers any more security. On the contrary, the lack of a robust social safety net means that much of the middle class is vulnerable to a long-term illness, the loss of a non-regular job by one spouse in a two-income family, the closing of one's employer, and so forth. Over the course of any four-year period, 36% of Japanese in the middle-income quintile (41st to 60th percentile) descend to

---

[3] The OECD's nominal figures were adjusted for CPI inflation/deflation. Some readers may wonder how median personal incomes could fall when average per capita national income (GDP) rose. That's because personal income is only part of national income, which also includes corporate cash flow and government taxes. If taxes are hiked, personal income takes a hit. If corporations rake in cash flow but don't spend it on hiring more workers and/or raising wages, that also detracts.

[4] The usual measure—called "relative poverty"—is the share of people living below 50% of the median income in any given year. A rise in absolute poverty means that, in 2015, there were more people below the *1995* poverty line than there were in 1995 itself, 19% vs. 12%.

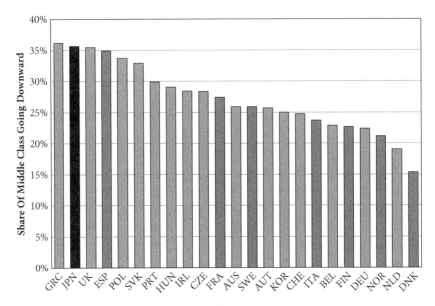

Figure 16.2 Japan 2nd highest in % middle class moving downward.
Source: Jones (2018: 51); see country code pg. 12 for abbreviations.

a lower rank, the second-worst figure in the OECD (see Figure 16.2). Even those currently enjoying satisfactory incomes and a regular job have a justifiable fear that these incomes are not secure.

Unfortunately, even as this situation changed, the Japanese government persisted in denying the need for an overt government social safety net or claiming that budget deficits meant the nation could not afford it. Among 25 OECD countries in the latter half this century's first decade, Japan came in third lowest, raising incomes of the poorest 20% of working-age households by just 13% versus an OECD average of 50% (OECD 2013c).

The government was spending more money on social welfare, but almost all of it went to social security for the elderly and healthcare for all. Since Japan lacked an overt social safety net for the poor, but still needed the follow the political imperative to do something, it continued to run a policy of covert adverse selection, extending government loans and credit guarantees to zombie firms. Because this lowered growth, it also eroded the tax base and worsened budget deficits, making the MOF stance counterproductive even by its own criteria.

Unfortunately, the anxiety resulting from all this can make people even more leery of the only real cure: creative destruction plus a governmental social safety net. A look at Scandinavia in the next chapter suggests how Japan can reduce both the dislocation and the anxiety—in ways harmonious with Japan's social ethic—once again making the country politically safe for creative destruction.

17

Flexicurity

A Third Way

Japan is not a country where it will be persuasive to claim the solution is a dog-eat-dog, winner-take-all economy à la Reagan and Thatcher. And yet, for the past quarter century, all too many reformers in Japan have spoken as if that is the only alternative to the current regime. In response, Japanese opponents of reform in Japan point to adverse consequences of Anglo-American methods to argue against needed changes in Japan. To bring back equality, security, and rising living standards, Japan needs to find a different way of realizing its values, one that coheres with growth. Fortunately, there is such an alternative, and one that's also harmonious with Japanese political-economic culture. It's the flexicurity model developed in the four Nordic countries. This brings us back to the three models of capitalism explored in Table 16.1 in Chapter 16.

The post-Reagan-Thatcher Anglo-American model, the neoliberal model, lets the locomotive of creative destruction roll on, even if a lot of people get ground up in the wheels. The United States is the only major country that fails to provide significant government-funded retraining and job-finding programs for workers who lose their jobs regardless of cause. Instead, it provides meager assistance, but only for those who lose their jobs due to trade.[1]

A second model, popular in some of the southern European countries, such as Italy and Spain, to some degree in France—and increasingly in Japan—stands across the railroad tracks commanding the engine to slow lest creative destruction be too destructive. Strict employment protection rules reduce layoffs, but proponents forget that barriers to exit also create barriers to entry. That, in turn, can lead to higher unemployment and slower

---

[1] This incentivizes unions to blame trade for jobs actually lost due to other reasons. The fact that US factory workers forced out of their industry by imports suffer a 20% pay cut in the next job versus just 3% in Europe (OECD 2005: 47) helps explain why voters in the "Rust Belt" sent Donald Trump to the White House in 2016 (Katz 2017).

The Contest for Japan's Economic Future. Richard Katz, Oxford University Press. © Richard Katz 2024.
DOI: 10.1093/oso/9780197675106.003.0018

productivity growth. As in Japan, regular workers are protected from mass dismissals, while the remainder live a precarious existence, suffering both lower wages and longer periods of unemployment or underemployment.

The Nordic model—given the name "flexicurity" (a portmanteau of flexibility and security) by a Danish prime minister in the 1990s—tries to marry the best of both worlds. It drives growth by giving fairly free play to market capitalism, while providing income equality and security by actively helping people transition from job to job and providing income support as they do so. This includes high levels of income replacement during periods of unemployment and substantial spending on active labor measures. Rather than trying to provide job security, protecting a worker's current job, they provide income and employment security. As a result, long-term unemployment (more than a year out of work) is far less pervasive than in the southern European model: just 1% in Sweden and Denmark during the pre-COVID years of 2016–2019, compared to 4% in France and more than 6% in Italy and 7% in Spain (OECD 2021c).[2]

Japan has ended up with a hybrid: the thin social safety net of post-Reagan America with the rigid and bifurcated labor market of the southern Europeans.

What makes the Nordic countries particularly illuminating is that many of Japan's political values and experiences have more in common with the Nordics than with the Anglo-Americans. Japan and the Nordics share a communitarian, egalitarian political-social ethic, and, for a long time, the Nordics had been one-party democracies. Like Japan, the Nordics suffered from mounting structural flaws—including anti-competitive practices like those in Japan—that finally culminated in big macroeconomic and banking crises in the early 1990s. Then, under a series of alternating Social Democratic and center-right governments, these countries instituted reforms. They cured macroeconomic instability and dealt with growth-hindering structural flaws, but still maintained the traditional emphasis on equality and security. Even parties that had once preached neoliberalism changed, realizing they had to keep the fundamentals of the Nordic model.

The political and economic success of flexicurity has drawn interest from all over the world. Ministers from France and Spain, company chiefs

---

[2] While total unemployment among native-born Swedes was just 4% in 2019, it was close to 15% among immigrants, many of whom came as refugees from the Middle East. This difference has fed anti-immigrant populism.

258 THE POLITICS OF REFORM

from China, and labor unions from Hungary have all flocked to Stockholm and Copenhagen to learn from their practices. The European Union has recommended flexicurity to its members (EU Commission 2007). It's encouraging that Japan's Ministry of Health, Labour and Welfare commissioned Danish experts to write a paper on the potential advantages to Japan of flexicurity (Bredgaard and Larsen 2007). During the Democratic Party of Japan's brief tenure in power during 2009–2012, it, too, conducted a study of the Scandinavian labor system. It's discouraging that these studies have not yet impacted Japanese policy.

"Our tradition is that we protect people, but not jobs," former Swedish Social Democratic finance minister Par Nuder explained to me. "Being a small country, depending on exports, we can't even think of trying to protect our industry. We have to be very competitive." The secret, he says, is that "[w]e have created social bridges from old conditions that are no longer competitive jobs to new conditions. If you want to have a strong capitalism, you have to have a strong social safety net" (Katz 2009b: 24).

In the flexicurity model, social protection and market dynamism are not alternatives, but partners. Active labor measures, income security, and the like provide social insurance that makes populations willing to accept creative destruction. In turn, creative destruction provides the higher growth that finances the social welfare measures. In fact, such a mutual reinforcement is carried out in the private marketplace every day in all sorts of countries. For example, because the commodity futures market enables farmers to get a guaranteed price for their products months ahead of the harvest—and shifts the price risk to someone else—they are more willing to grow more food. The result is cheaper food for everyone else. "We spread the risk to everyone through a publicly funded social welfare system," explained Swedish State Secretary of Finance Hans Lindblad. "In Japan, the risks are kept within each company, which we think is riskier" (Katz 2009b: 25).

Back in the 1940s, two economists from Swedish Trade Union Confederation argued that wage equality for people in the same occupation would help efficient firms make higher profits, enabling them to expand. Inefficient industries and firms would have to either improve or downsize. The result would be a flow of workers from low-productivity industries and companies to higher-productivity ones. That, in turn, would expand GDP and raise average wages. Their notion was adopted, and it worked. Equality and efficiency reinforced each other (Hibbs and Locking 2000: 775).

It is cheaper and easier to lay off redundant workers or even close down a plant in Scandinavia than in Germany or France. A third of Danes change jobs every year, the highest in the OECD. Two-thirds of them quit to find better jobs. Denmark, Sweden, and Finland top the charts in how much of their GDP they spend on active labor measures (2% for Denmark and 1.25% for Sweden) (OECD 2022g). In the latter part of this century's first decade, a third of Danish and Swedish adults were in some sort of government-financed adult education and training program, the highest share in Europe. While generous unemployment insurance replaces up to 75%–90% of a low-income worker's wage, active labor market programs help those workers transition to a new job quickly.

The countries that spend the most on such active measures see the lowest share of middle-income workers suffering downward mobility (Jones 2018: 51). Unfortunately, Japan spends a miserly 0.15% of GDP on active labor market measures, the 20th of 23 rich countries (OECD 2022g). The United States is the 21st. That's one reason why Japan has the OECD's second worst case of downward mobility (see again Figure 16.2 in Chapter 16).

In Japan, during rough times, instead of laying off regular workers, the pain is spread around by reducing hours and compensation for all of the regular workers. The ethic behind this practice is admirable, and the system worked well when regular workers comprised most of the workforce and when applied to temporary rough patches. It doesn't work when 40% of workers are non-regulars or when companies need to downsize if they are to survive at all.

No wonder Scandinavians don't fear losing or leaving their jobs. On the contrary, 80% of Swedes and 75% of Danes say they benefit from shifting positions, compared to just 40% in the rest of the European Union.

A Rigidly Segmented Labor Force

In the southern European model, it is not the worker, but the current job that is protected. That means the employer, no matter how inefficient, must also be protected. However, that protection applies only to regular workers, those with open-ended employment contracts, as in Japan. The share of these protected workers is 55% in France, 62% in Japan, and similar numbers in Italy and Spain. The problem is not that people have part-time or tempo-rary contracts, assuming that they want such work. Rather, it's the difficulty non-regular workers have in ever gaining regular status and the potential for advancement that comes with it.

The segmentation is severe. In Spain, only 30% of non-regular workers can transition to permanent status after three years, and only half for as long as 10 years. In France and Italy, just 40% and 45%, respectively, of temps can attain permanent jobs after three years (Eurofound 2019; OECD 2015d: 188).

Japan is now as segmented as southern Europe (Nippon.com 2016; Gordon 2017), a violation of the egalitarian ethic once so valued in Japan. Only a few decades ago, non-regular jobs were mostly for women who genuinely desired part-time work once their children had grown or pensioners who wanted to supplement their income. By 2021, their share was up to 37%. Even when they do the same work side by side with regulars, they suffer much lower pay and far fewer benefits like bonuses and pensions (Osawa and Kingston 2022: 128; Statistics Bureau 2022b).

Among these non-regulars are 15 million Japanese workers on fixed-term contracts—rather than the open-ended contract of regular workers. A third of these temporaries have worked for the same employer for more than five years. Consequently, many have assimilated the company-specific skills that improve their productivity. Their temporary contracts keep getting renewed, but they never advance to regular status. A law that went into effect in 2018 requires employers to grant them permanent status after five years if they request the change. Otherwise, they must be let go. So far, its impact does not seem promising. A loophole says the five years must be continuous, and there are already reports of employers refusing contract renewals and then rehiring them after a time so as to prevent them from ever reaching five-year continuity (*Japan Times* 2018). Others have simply been let go and new non-regulars—who lack the tacit learning of their predecessors—hired in their place. Moreover, in a 2018 decision, the Supreme Court reinforced pay gaps via its new definition of what constituted "reasonable discrimination" (Okunuki 2018).

As in southern Europe, the longer one labors as a non-regular, the lower the likelihood of ever becoming a regular (Osawa and Kingston 2022: 133–135). Most transitions into regular employment happen for workers in their early twenties. Among those age 25–44, just 14% of non-regulars ever gain regular employment.

In short, a policy advertised as offering worker protection actually protects just one part of the labor force.

Flexicurity Works

Across a host of dimensions, the flexicurity model does a far better job of serving the income and security of workers than either the southern European model or the current Anglo-American model.

Without sustained growth in labor productivity, increases in living standards are not possible. Back in the 1970s, both Japan and the Nordic countries were in the process of catching up to the United States. By 2018, the flexicurity countries exceeded living standards in the United States by 5%. Japan, as we've seen, fell back. The southern European countries also performed worse than the Nordics (OECD 2022a).

Productivity growth enables higher living standards, but it does not guarantee that the fruits of growth will go to the workers who produce that growth. Among 23 OECD countries, Sweden and Norway came in first with a cumulative total real wage hike of 63% during 1995–2019. Japan and Italy came in last with 2% and 3%—basically zero growth over a quarter century—and Spain, at 8%, was almost as dismal (OECD 2022b). In the United States, during 1979–2018, real wages of the median worker rose a dismal total of just 6% over three decades (Congressional Research Service 2019: 4).

How about income equality among working-age people? Out of 29 OECD countries in 2018, the United States and the United Kingdom came in dead last, followed closely by Italy and Spain at 25th and 26th and Japan at 22nd. France was in the middle of the pack (OECD 2022h). The four Nordic countries ranked fifth through eighth.

People need not just good income, but the security of that income. Among 22 OECD countries, Denmark, Norway, and Finland come in first, third, and fifth in having the lowest share of people in the middle class falling into the bottom 20% of income. Japan comes in 21st, just ahead of the United Kingdom; there are no data for the United States (see again Figure 16.2).

The Politics of Flexicurity

How have the Nordics achieved widespread public support for flexicurity? One of the vital ingredients, they believe, is the universality of benefits. They are provided to everyone, not just to the "deserving poor." Former Swedish finance minister Nuder explained to me: "Even the wealthiest Swedes can take benefits from the system. We don't want a system where you have to pinpoint those who need others' charity. The rich and the middle class would start to question why they should pay high taxes if they don't get the benefits." When I asked a Swedish business executive whether he resented paying such high taxes, he replied, "We pay high taxes, but we're also the ones who get the benefits. We all get sick. We all need education. We all risk losing our job. We all get old" (Interview December 2007).

Workers with rising income, equality, and security make few demands to keep zombie firms alive or to block growth-enhancing open trade. "We are pro-free trade," declared Lena Westerlund, senior international economist at the Swedish Trade Union Confederation. "Sweden would not have achieved at this level of per capita income if we didn't have an open economy. But we want to have security for the workers" (Interview December 2007). On the other hand, given the lack of security in the United States, she contended, it is rational for American workers to fear globalization.

In fact, globalization drove the upgrading of the Nordic economies and therefore living standards, which reinforced support for open trade. When Sweden, Norway, and Finland joined the European Union in 1995 (Denmark had joined in 1973), both trade and inward direct investment soared, explained Stefan Folster, chief economist of the Confederation of Swedish Enterprise. At the same time, Sweden upgraded its human capital, rapidly increased the number of PhD-level engineers, and expanded adult education for ordinary workers. The result was a technological transformation of the country. Back in the 1970s–1980s, Sweden's biggest exports were resource-intensive and medium-technology products. But by the 1990s, Sweden had begun turning itself into a high-tech power, both on the export market and at home.

The philosophy behind flexicurity did not always exist. On the contrary, just a few decades ago, the Scandinavians shared some of Japan's flaws. Their ability to change gives hope that Japan can do likewise. Sweden, like Japan, allowed cartels that stifled creative destruction, reported Folster. "Cartels were legal. They would divide up the country and companies would have monopolies in their region. They were quite common." Just as in Japan, Sweden and Denmark imposed regulations—from limits on large-scale stores to regulations concerning hours—aimed at protecting mom-and-pop shops. Joining the European Union required ending these growth-stifling practices.

One of the reasons that the Nordic countries recovered from their 1990s crisis was that, as noted above, decades of one-party rule—in their case the Social-Democrats—was replaced by the alternation of parties. This led both the Social Democrats and the conservatives to respond to the crisis by moving to the center and realizing that previously beneficial practices no longer worked. It is hard to see how the ultimately successful reforms would have gone so well had these countries remained one-party democracies. The lesson is that, while Japan can still make many of the needed reforms under LDP rule, it will be much harder than if the LDP faced a greater risk of losing power by failing to solve Japan's problems. And the amount of reform will likely be less than it otherwise would have been. Recall that it was the fear of losing power in the 1970s that elicited firm LDP action on issues ranging from pollution to universal healthcare.

It all sounds like a wonderful example from which to learn, but not so easy to emulate. How does a country like Japan go from its current system to something more like flexicurity? Claus Hjort Frederiksen, Danish minister for employment, explained, "I don't believe in the 'one size fits all' approach. Each country has to adopt the practices that suit it best. . . . But it is possible to learn from our experience. . . . You could start with making sure that certain benefits are not tied to a single employer. If that system exists, you cannot create flexibility." Sweden's Hans Lindblad, at the time state secretary of finance, explained it this way: "Just as you buy insurance to spread risk, here we spread the risk to everyone through a publicly funded social welfare system" (Interview December 2007).

Will Japanese voters accept the higher taxes that come with flexicurity? Some say no, but much of voter resistance to taxes exists because, with some justification, voters don't trust Tokyo to use the money well. On the other hand, Japan's universal healthcare and social security rely on government spending. No one expects Japan to "go Scandinavian," nor should it. But adapting parts of the flexicurity package step-by-step, thereby building up its credibility, is not an impossible task. The good news is that, ever since the 1871 Iwakura Mission,[3] Japan has shown its skill in learning about the best practices of other nations and then adapting them to Japanese conditions and values.

---

[3] As part of the new Meiji government's effort to learn about all the developments in the West it had missed out on during Japan's more than 200 years of self-isolation, it sent a group led by Tonomi Iwakura to foreign countries. Among other purposes, the mission devoted itself to learning about Western ways in science and technology, economics and politics, and culture, so that Japan could adopt, and adapt, the practices it felt would be most helpful in becoming a strong, modern country It was the most famous of several such missions.

18

A Political Scenario for Successful Reform

The shift of tectonic plates is excruciatingly slow, but inexorable. Eventually, the tension becomes irresistible, the earth gives way, and the landscape is no longer the same. There is in Japan at this moment a quiet, tectonic shift in the foundations of society. Unlike the earth's plates, however, their force is hardly irresistible. On the contrary, fear of disruption makes resistance powerful and determined. And the process in Japan will hardly be as abrupt as an earthquake. However, we do know that stasis is not on history's menu. If Japan cannot resurrect its past entrepreneurialism, the economy will continue to corrode, with all the attendant stresses on people and politics. While generating more gazelles is by no means the only step required for full-scale economic revival, no recovery is possible without it.

Japan's tectonic tension arises from a fundamental conflict of interests. The policy preferences of Japan's ruling elites—the so-called iron triangle of the LDP, conservative leadership in the powerful Ministries, and the Keidanren big business federation—contradict the needs of the broad sociopolitical coalition whose support the elite has relied upon for decades. For more than a quarter century, the iron triangle has tried to resolve that contradiction by applying various tweaks. The effort has failed because policymakers recoil from the more fundamental reforms that real recovery requires, shying away even from some of the simple reforms that would seem to pose little threat to their power or status. On the contrary, as detailed above, it has made things worse by transferring huge portions of national income from households to corporations, for example, raising taxes on households while lowering them on companies, from household savers to corporate borrowers via the BOJ's zero interest rate policy, and from consumers in general by pushing down the value of the yen. This transfer suppresses consumer purchasing power and forces the government to run chronic deficits to keep the economy afloat and it keeps zombies alive via negligible interest rates (see again Figure 13.5 in Chapter 13).

The Contest for Japan's Economic Future. Richard Katz, Oxford University Press. © Richard Katz 2024.
DOI: 10.1093/oso/9780197675106.003.0019

The LDP was not always so inept at adaptation. In the past when economic conditions changed, it deftly changed with them. In the 1970s, it was threatened with losing power due to the decline of its main base, hosts of farmers. So, it shifted policies to attract the urban vote. It lured new supporters without alienating its old base by rapidly implementing universal healthcare, strong anti-pollution laws, laws protecting small retailers against more efficient large stores, and upping farm subsidies. Some of these policies were economically beneficial; others laid the groundwork for eventual economic decay. While unions were never included in the LDP's support base, the LDP reached over the heads of the unions to attract blue-collar workers, elevating its vote share among industrial workers from just a quarter in 1965 to half by 1985 (Pempel 1998: 7–10).

Today, the LDP has so far found itself incapable of a similar course correction, even when it seems to try. It retains power, not because it has the support of the population but because the opposition parties seem so feckless and those disenchanted with the LDP simply do not vote. Turnout keeps dropping.

As T. J. Pempel has explained, political regimes do not change, or fall, simply because they no longer rule well, conditions worsen, and they lose popularity. They change because dilemmas over how to respond to that deterioration create fissures within the socioeconomic support base, and within the leadership group itself (Pempel 1998). Mikhail Gorbachev once remarked that the Communists fell from power primarily because those charged with running the system, people like him, stopped believing in it. A similar trend began emerging among Japan's elite bureaucrats in the mid-1990s as a seeming mere rough patch turned into the lost decades. Among the first to perceive the severity of the economy's downshift were some of the most talented officials in METI and the MOF. Low growth is producing splits not only *among* various interest groups in the LDP support base, but also *within* each of them. As detailed earlier, assorted protectionist measures for farmers cause high food prices for consumers. While such economic tensions seemed relatively minimal to people under conditions of good growth, they became far less tolerable when low growth meant fighting for shares of a shrinking pie.

New technology divides big business, which was once seen as monolithic. Some firms and sectors benefit from the onset of the digital era, while other, less adaptable firms and sectors, like many in electronics, are hurt by it. Under the leadership of Rakuten's Mikitani, Internet-based companies set up their own lobbying group called the Japan Association of New Economy (JANE). Some of them left Keidanren, which is heavily tilted toward old-line heavy industry firms. It now regularly meets with government officials and Diet members to lobby for its issues, one of which is entrepreneurship.

Even such fissures are not sufficient to effect what Pempel calls a regime shift, when a new leadership group arises, has a better policy profile that meets the changing needs of the population, and organizes itself around a different socioeconomic coalition. The rise of Franklin Roosevelt's New Deal coalition and later Ronald Reagan's conservative coalition are prime examples of a regime shift. No regime disappears until there is something to replace it. In Japan, that new alternative is still in the process of formation. Almost a quarter of a century ago, Pempel presciently wrote, "Far more fragmentation, realignment, and false starts are likely before any new equilibrated regime can be identified. Indeed, there is no guarantee that such clarity will emerge for some time" (Pempel 1998: 205).

Nor can an alternative leadership arise without a political-economic program that can actually solve Japan's economic problems, and the ability to create a coalition in support of that program. The good news here is that solutions are arising. Many of the ideas in this book have been informed by a new generation of academics producing truly superb analyses and policy proposals. Approximately 100 policy-oriented academics are fellows with METI's policy think tank, the Research Institute for the Economy, Trade, and Industry (RIETI), founded in 2001. Many others work at Japan's few independent think tanks (e.g., about 50 at the Canon Institute for Global Affairs). Creating more independent policy-oriented think tanks would be a big step forward. The biggest obstacle to reform is not lack of good ideas, but of political will to put them into action.

While it may seem that a regime shift is a powerful moment, like a crucial election, it is actually a long process that can sometimes culminate in a pivotal moment. From the standpoint of entrepreneurship, the priority today is to introduce piecemeal reforms that would trigger the creation of more gazelles. This would not only provide a direct economic payoff, but also enlarge the presence and clout of interest groups with a stake in further reform. Examples of measures that combine low political and budgetary costs with outsized economic and institutional benefits include changing the tax code to provide more R&D aid to new firms, tax incentives that could spawn more angel investors, and additional steps that help universities incubate, or cooperate with, new firms. While some of these measures will injure this or that incumbent group of companies, there are also lots of incumbents who would benefit (e.g., giant pharmaceutical companies that need open innovation with new biotech firms).

What is needed are a few far-sighted, strong-willed officials who can ally with policymakers in the prime minister's office, Diet members, and assorted powerful companies. Motivations will vary. Some pro-entrepreneurship reformers in the LDP will simply be trying to get the party to adapt in order to prolong its dominance. Others in the LDP and bureaucracy would be seeking to raise Japan's potential growth, or to solve some particular problem, or even serve some particular interest group. Some in opposition parties will be seeking a way to finally win an election. As the Japanese proverb says, they sleep in the same bed, but dream different dreams. The variance in dreams does not matter. What matters is that progress on the ground will stimulate a snowball effect in society. Success can build on success. Already, for example, companies like Recruit and Rakuten have already become so huge that many of their employees have founded their own new gazelles. And recall how the 1986 Equal Employment Opportunity Law ended up reducing gazelles' difficulties in recruiting talented staff because it led to an upsurge in the number of educated ambitious women. In 2022, Prime Minister Kishida came out with a proposal, albeit a flawed one, aimed at creating 100,000 new high-growth innovative startups in the coming five years or so. Reformist officials are still trying to use Kishida's call to improve the content of the measures (see Chapter 19).

It is impossible to tell whether the long process of regime shift in Japan will culminate in the LDP splitting, as in 1993, or being ousted in an election, as in 2009, with Japan entering a new era in which parties alternate in power, or even the LDP shifting its policies, as American Democrats did under Roosevelt and the Chinese Communist Party did under Deng Xiaoping. What we do know is that, in the absence of some sort of a shift, Japan will continue to flounder indefinitely. What we also know is that the fissures within the LDP support base are growing, and elements of a social and intellectual support base for a very different policy profile are emerging.

This ferment creates an opportunity for change that did not exist a decade or two ago. The focus of this chapter is to examine those fissures and realignments, starting with the political parties and moving on to the bureaucracy, big business, labor, and SMEs.

Politicians Promise Structural Reform, Fail to Deliver

It's not as if Japanese voters don't feel the need for change. Three times this century—2005, 2009, and 2012—the Japanese electorate overwhelmingly chose politicians who claimed to champion reform. All three times, the winners failed to deliver. That has led to an all-too-common fatalism, the sense that failure of reform is inevitable. Excessive pessimism, however, is just as damaging as unwonted euphoria, a topic to which we'll return in the final chapter.

In 2001, Junichiro Koizumi rode to the prime ministership on a pledge to overwhelm what he called "the forces of resistance" in the "old" LDP. "There is no growth without reform," he declared, but, in his view, economic reform required that political reform come first. His slogan was "Change the LDP to change Japan." When in 2005 he purged from the LDP Diet members who opposed assorted political reforms, he was given an overwhelming mandate in the ensuing election. Unfortunately, because of his politics-first orientation, his only lasting economic achievement was, in cooperation with Minster Heizo Takenaka, ending the long banking crisis. Worse yet, once he left office, party politics looked almost as if he had never been there. His designated successor, Shinzo Abe, even returned to the LDP those whom Koizumi had purged. Despite all these shortcomings, he made one invaluable and lasting change in the public mindset: no growth without reform. Even those most opposed to reform were compelled to call themselves reformers.

The next step came in 2009, when for the first time since 1947, voters ousted the ruling party via an election (as opposed to the LDP split in 1993). Like Koizumi, the opposition Democratic Party of Japan (DPJ) triumphed on the banner of transformation. Had the DPJ been able to rule well enough to last more than one term, that may well have been the end of one-party dominance. More serious competition for votes would make Tokyo more responsive to people's needs, as in the 1950s–1970s.

Unfortunately, hopes for a new era where parties regularly alternated in power failed. The DPJ not only faced relentless undermining by the LDP-allied bureaucracy, the press, and Washington, but also proved unbelievably feckless. Its first prime minister, Yukio Hatoyama, was widely derided as "the Alien." His successor, Naoto Kan, was the stuff of Greek tragedy. First, during the European debt crisis of 2010, Kan fell for MOF propaganda that Japan risked a similar crisis and made a tax hike the centerpiece of his 2010 Upper House election campaign. Almost no parties ever win by promising tax hikes, so, not surprisingly, the DPJ lost. Control of the Upper House enabled the LDP to block any legislation passed by the DPJ in the Lower House, the House that chooses the prime minister.

Then, in 2011, when a horrible tsunami that killed 20,000 people also caused a serious nuclear accident, the bureaucrats and press succeeded in blaming Kan for problems that were the fault of the alliance of utilities, pro-nuclear bureaucrats, and LDP politicians, disparaged by critics as "the nuclear village." Kan ended up stepping down.

Kan's DPJ successor then pushed the unpopular tax hike through the Diet and the DPJ lost the 2012 Lower House election in a landslide. The LDP-MOF alliance had gotten the DPJ to suffer the political cost for passing its own tax agenda. Shinzo Abe returned to power in a campaign focused on reviving the economy through Abenomics. He, too, failed to deliver.

More fundamentally, the DPJ had no credible policy program. To be sure, the DPJ was more modern and reformist in its outlook, as well as less corrupt. However, to a voter asking exactly how Japan would differ under a DPJ regime, it had no clear-cut answer. I found this out as early as 1997 when I asked DPJ leader Hatoyama that very question.

What would have made a lasting DPJ victory important was not the virtue of the DPJ per se, but the prospect of a new system of truly contested elections. Competition is as essential to healthy politics as to a healthy economy. Japan has lacked that. For the 75 years since the end of World War II, the LDP and its precursors have ruled the entire time, with just three very short interruptions (1947–1948, 1993–1994, and 2009–2012).

Voters who were willing to give the LDP second and third chances would not do the same for the DPJ. The DPJ no longer exists in its 2009–2012 form. It split and then partially remerged. Eventually, a credible opposition party will likely emerge. It would be strange if Japan could permanently remain the only rich democratic country with permanent domination by one party. However, there are certainly no guarantees about when this might happen.

The upshot is that the political system is less stable and static in the face of economic instability than it appears. Those who see Japan in stasis use the language of inevitability: the DPJ failed because it was bound to. In their eyes, the Japanese people as a cultural trait prefer one-party dominance and will for decades to come. I see this history through the prism of contingency: the DPJ fell because of the combination of self-inflicted wounds and chance events like the nuclear disaster. My view is that, without sufficient growth, the LDP can no longer rule as it always has: by being a catch-all party that can satisfy all of its constituencies. Hence, the search for ways to revive growth will remain a political imperative. Already, that imperative is opening the door to some necessary pro-gazelle measures as well as shifts in socioeconomic alignments.

What is the incentive for either the dominant LDP or the opposition parties to make Japan safe for creative destruction? LDP dominance is threatened by public dissatisfaction. In 2009, when the voters ousted the LDP—a political earthquake no one had predicted a couple years earlier—the turnout rate was a very high 69%. In 2012, when the LDP returned to power, it received two million *fewer* votes than it had garnered in its 2009 drubbing. In ensuing elections, turnout has continued to fall. In fact, the four lowest turnout rates in the past few decades have all come in the elections since 2012.

Back in the 1960s, independent swing voters—known in Japan as floating voters—comprised just 6% of the electorate. Since the 1990s, their share has at times risen to 40% or more. Many of these floaters are very interested in politics and, compared to party supporters, tend to be younger, more urban, and greatly interested in issues ranging from long-term economic performance to the environment to childcare access (Tanaka 2012). It was Koizumi's ability to attract these voters that led to his ascension in 2001 and a huge mandate in the 2005 election, another unforeseen shakeup. The DPJ attracted them in 2009 when it soundly defeated the LDP.

The LDP has not recaptured these voters, nor has the opposition. They are staying home. If the LDP cannot provide a genuine road to recovery, it has to fear that it could once again be ousted by an opposition that finally gets it act together. Meanwhile, if the opposition has any hope of taking power, it must offer a credible solution that gives these floating voters a reason to take a chance. In any case, there will be no end to political pressure for a solution to low growth and falling living standards for large parts of the population.

Of course, there are, and will continue to be, countervailing electoral pressures favoring the status quo. Thirty million regular workers, mostly males, do enjoy job security, even if it comes at the expense of wages, and many are unwilling to risk this in the effort at improvement. Many incumbent elephants have much to fear from a system of creative destruction, as do poorly performing SMEs. Most of all, as we've seen in the rise of populism in the United States and Europe, when voters see the social contract unravel, many try to tighten their grip on what they fear losing. Nonetheless, the most successful election campaigns since 2001 have been ones in which the victors promised thoroughgoing reform, even if, once in power, they offered more rhetoric than action.

Disputes among the Government Ministries

With the best will in the world, it would be neither easy nor quick to make the labor market more fluid or to get banks to do better credit screenings. On the other hand, once political obstacles are overcome, the government can, with a stroke of a pen, alter taxes, budgets, and regulations.

Every year, Ministries put together proposals for tax revisions. Although some of the required changes could involve a hard fight with the MOF, the latter is hardly all-powerful. Some simple changes involving little loss of revenue would help a great deal and would, by promoting growth, raise tax revenue down the road. One needed tax change that is both simple and impactful would multiply R&D by potential gazelles via the tax credit carry-forward system described earlier.[1] Yet, it was not even included in Kishida's 2022 proposals. One official who favored such a measure explained that pro-startup reformers in assorted agencies and Ministries decided to limit how many tax changes they sought in hopes of getting something substantial past the MOF Tax Bureau and the LDP Tax Commission.

Japan should also use more direct, but carefully screened, R&D subsidies, as other countries do, because it gives immediate cash to not-yet-profitable firms. In 2015, Japan added a 30% credit for R&D conducted in collaboration with a university or public research institution. At present, it is almost always just the big established corporations that get invited to such research consortia, not startups. The latter need to be invited, not only because it would help them, but because they would bring new ideas to the table (Rtischev 2016).

A couple of years ago, I asked serial entrepreneur Jeffrey Char what the government could do to stimulate more entrepreneurship. He immediately pointed to the government's procurement budget, a huge 16% of GDP (OECD 2019j: 135). Currently, the government favors *small* companies with a big "set-aside" (i.e., a certain portion of its overall procurement that

---

[1] A carry-forward helps startups which tend to be unprofitable in their early years. It means that the tax credit granted to a corporation for doing more R&D would apply not just to the year in which the R&D investment was done, but for 10 or 20 years down the road until the firm makes profits and can thus benefit from the tax break.

it will buy from qualified SMEs). What it needs to do, stressed Char, is to also have a "set-aside" for *new* companies, since the latter are more likely to become gazelles. Such a set-aside would immediately increase new firms' revenue. That creates ripple effects. Banks would be much more willing to finance the expansion of SMEs that have bigger, reliable revenue flows. Bigger corporations would be more willing to take on new suppliers that had met government standards.

As it turns out, the year before I spoke with Char, METI's SME agency added a set-aside for companies under 10 years old, and in 2018, set a goal of raising the share of national contracts awarded to these young SMEs to 3%. However, the government has not come anywhere close to reaching its announced targets. In fiscal 2020, it amounted to a barely visible ¥78 billion ($600 million), just 0.8% of all national procurement (METI 2021b). As part of Kishida's "new capitalism" initiative, some pro-startup officials proposed raising the procurement target for startups from 3% to 10%, and Keidanren included this goal in its startup proposals (Keidanren 2022: 15). In the end, however, Kishida's five-year plan limited itself to simply reaching the 3% goal (Cabinet Office 2022c: 16).

Still, no one came up with concrete proposals on how to reach the procurement target. In many countries, it is difficult for qualified SMEs to take advantage of the procurement opportunities, partly due to insufficient awareness, and also insufficient legal and technical expertise to prepare bids, not to mention impediments created by the digital divide. So, most OECD countries provide capacity-building workshops and other forms of training to enable SMEs to participate. Japan is not among them (OECD 2018b: 106–107).

Suppose, however, that all levels of government awarded to new SMEs contracts equal to 2%–3% of their procurement. In 2019, that would have provided a market worth ¥1.6 to ¥2.7 trillion ($12 to $21 billion) for new would-be business-to-business SMEs who find incumbent corporations resistant to trying a new supplier. That's 10 times what the government actually did. If that proved successful, the set-aside could be expanded. If the average new SME got a contract for $10 million, that would cover 2,700 new companies each year.

Keep in mind that Char's notion grew out of his own entrepreneurial experience. The greater the number of such entrepreneurs, the greater the number of new, concrete proposals. And the more such proposals are put into action, the more successful entrepreneurs there will be. That, in turn, means more individuals and trade groups with the ability to lobby officials and Diet members, to push for inclusion in government advisory councils on relevant issues, and to find powerful companies willing to back their proposals.

Today, there is a battle within the bureaucracy between those who want more set-asides for new companies and those who still wish to prop up old, inefficient SMEs. This division belies the notion that the bureaucracy is simply a monolith that stonewalls reform. The many cases of such obstructionism lie behind this perception. Nonetheless, there is a surprisingly large number of officials who often feel as frustrated as other citizens by the obstruction of their own Ministries. Even successes on their part that may seem marginal and arcane can add up to a critical mass if there are enough of them.

The best of these reformist officials tend to be in their forties or early fifties. They're old enough to have authority, but not so senior as to have become jaded. They tend to have good contacts in the Diet, academia, and the press, and know how to push through reforms without stirring up too much resistance.

One of them is a METI veteran named Yoshiaki Ishii, a man with a deceptively unassuming demeanor who takes very seriously the bureaucracy's image of itself as "guardians of the nation" (Corbin 2014). He started his career in 1992 at METI's Agency for Small and Medium Enterprises and has devoted his career to promoting new, innovative firms. When I first met him in 2016, he was director of the New Business Policy Office at METI's Industrial Policy Bureau, the bureau devoted to strategic thinking about the economy as a whole. This Bureau tends to suffer from far less clientelism than Bureaus devoted to specific industrial sectors.

Back in 2006, when Ishii was the project leader for the ambitious revision of Japan's Company Law, he succeeded in making registration of a *godo kaisha* (limited liability company, LLC) easier and almost cost-free. Creating LLCs—beginning in 1988 in the United States and earlier in some other countries—has bolstered the launching of high-growth SMEs, because of two benefits. As with a standard corporation, the owners don't lose their house or other personal property if the LLC defaults on its debt. Unlike a standard corporation, however, the LLC is immune from double taxation in the United States and other countries with a similar tax law. Double taxation refers to profits being taxed at the corporate level and again at the individual level when the latter receives dividends.

Recognition of the LLC for tax purposes on the federal level unleashed a flurry of gazelle creation with 59% of "high-growth innovative enterprises" in the United States in 2013 having been created in the five years after 1988, another 27% during 1993–2013, but just 24% in all the years before that (Tachiki 2013: 66).

In Japan, unfortunately, while the LLC law was passed by the Diet, the MOF used its regulatory power to block the LLC from having the tax advantages that LLCs—or their equivalent—enjoy elsewhere. Reflexively, the MOF Tax Bureau argued that Japan could not afford to lose the revenue. My sense from conversations with officials is that the Tax Bureau is so much not worried about the small (and perhaps only temporary) revenue loss from this or that provision per se. Rather, it fears that setting too many precedents would cause the dam to break. Double taxation remains in place as of early 2022, and ending it was not even mentioned in Kishida's 2022 proposal. Nor did METI officials with whom I spoke in late 2022 include it in their goals. The reason was their strategy of focusing on just a few matters in the hopes of breaking through the resistance from fiscal hawks, and even there they got less than they had hoped for. A classic case of the hung jury phenomenon reinforcing the status quo.

Another of Ishii's efforts was an improved tax break for professional angel investors, who are rare in Japan. In 2014, Ishii tried to remedy this short-fall by expanding Japan's minimal tax breaks for qualified professional angels investing in certain types of firms. Some incentives had been created back in 1997 by Tatsuya Terazawa, an earlier reformer who went on two decades later to become vice minister for international affairs of METI, the second-highest career post within the Ministry. Those incentives applied to business angels investing in R&D-intensive startups and for startups entering new fields. But limits placed on it by the MOF Tax Bureau rendered it almost in-effective. There were limitations on the age of the firm (no more than three years) and a maximum tax deduction of a piddling $100,000 for an angel's *total* investments (rather than in each company). That maximum is dwarfed by the typical size of angel investments in the United States, which in 2019 was $400,000 per startup. Not surprisingly, at its 2008 peak, angel invest-ment in Japan equaled just 1% of the amount in Britain. Despite these lim-itations, it elevated the concept of angel investments for many in Japan to see. One of them was Ishii, who strove to break through the limitations. He proposed that angels be able to invest in firms of different ages, that they be able to deduct up to 40% of their investment from their personal income tax, that losses be subject to a loss carry-forward, and that the ceiling on total deductions be raised (Nikkei 2014).

While parts of his proposal were adopted, the MOF blocked a raising of the ceiling. Like the denizens of Dickens's "Circumlocution Office," the MOF Tax Bureau can always patiently explain "why it cannot be done." Yet, they exercised no objection when it came to VC investments by corporations. The latter can deduct 25% of the invested amount in qualifying startups (BDO Tax News 2020: n.p.). Worse yet, the MOF-LDP proposed reducing the maximum deduction for angels to ¥8 million ($61,000) (Deloitte 2019: 14).

Favoring corporate VCs (CVCs) has a decidedly negative effect on the birth of gazelles, not to mention the thinner slice of Silicon Valley–type startups. Independent angels and VCs have a direct financial stake in the financial success of the venture firm. That's how they make their money. Moreover, they are often former entrepreneurs and thus provide not just money but also vitally needed mentoring. On the other hand, the staff at CVCs are employees of the parent company, who have little background in entrepreneurship, will only be at the CVC for a few years, and their salary does not depend on the success of their investment choices. Moreover, the interests of the parent and the startup do not necessarily coincide. If, for example, the corporate VC is mostly interested in gaining information about trends in technology that it can exploit, it is not likely to invest enough money to make the venture firm grow.

In the United States, independent VCs invest about 75%–80% of all VC money, whereas they have typically invested only a minority in Japan. The good news in Japan is that the independents' share of all VC money in Japan has risen from just 21% in 2008 to 33% in 2020 (Kushida 2022: table 1). Whether they will become dominant as in other countries remains to be seen, but this would be a big barometer of progress.

In 2022, the Kishida administration unveiled a new tax incentive for investing in startups. Retail investors who sell up to ¥2 billion ($14 million) worth of stock in either a listed or unlisted company will not have to pay the 20% capital gains tax as long as they reinvest their profits in a qualified startup under five years old. Unfortunately, the tax incentive's poor design means it's not likely to fulfill its mission of providing abundant startup funds.

One problem is that Japan's plan requires retail investors to bet their money on individual companies rather than professionally managed angel funds that have a diversified portfolio of startups. Few ordinary investors will take that risk; nor should they. Here's why. While the average American angel fund got back a terrific 2.6 times its initial investment in just 3.5 years, it lost money on half of the startups in which it invested. The other half earned enough to produce outsized overall returns. If experts lose money in half the cases, then requiring Japanese laymen to pick and choose a firm is ill-advised. The real tragedy is that Tokyo missed a simple fix: it could have copied the very successful French plan which offered a hefty tax incentive to invest in angel funds (see discussion of this in Chapter 19). Like investing in a mutual fund in the stock market, this reduces the risk.

Worse yet, it's not easy for ordinary investors to place their money in an angel fund because Japanese law allows no more than 49 investors, called limited partners (LPs), to invest in any single fund. Moreover, in an effort to protect ordinary people, these LPs are limited to institutional investors or very wealthy individuals, those who've already invested at least ¥100 million ($770,000) in stocks or bonds. This limitation is a major constraint on generating more angel funds.

Splits in the Corporate World

One might expect the elephants to resist pro-gazelle reforms. All too many of their executives prefer the quiet life, spending their career in markets where their dominance is rarely disrupted. So it might seem natural for them to shudder at the specter of a new generation of self-styled disrupters. However, just as in the Ministries, the forces of technological, demographic, and generational change are creating divisions not only among different corporations, but also within them.

To the extent that a supposedly monolithic "Japan Inc." ever existed, it exists no longer. There is a growing number of relatively new companies, especially in newer industries, whose founders and executives are cut from a different cloth. Among older firms, there is a gap between internationally oriented companies and those limited to the domestic market. There are rifts by industry and by the level of foreign ownership.

Some elephants adapt by accepting practices that help their own firm, such as open innovation with startups, at the expense of the ability of elephants as a group to fend off possible future challengers. In some cases, firms are divided internally, as in the case of Asahi Glass discussed above, where some senior executives were pushing for open innovation and the R&D management was trying to preserve its hierarchical role. As has been known for decades, the interests of a firm and its assorted managers are not identical.

Stresses in the system can suddenly torpedo even those corporate institutions that once seemed indestructible pillars of the economy, such as the famous horizontal *keiretsu* like Mitsui and Mitsubishi. The banking crisis, ongoing economic stagnation, and declining global competitiveness have laid them low, forcing cross-*keiretsu* mergers not just in banking but across the spectrum (Lewis and Inagaki 2016). While *keiretsu firms* still rake in cash, the *keiretsu* as collective associations no longer determine the trajectory of the overall economy. Today, the most dynamic firms, like Toyota and Hitachi, even if they have historic ties to the horizontal *keiretsu*, dance to their own tune with their own corporate groups.

These stresses are already creating substantial splits within the corporate community, not only regarding their own corporate strategy, but also in terms of broad policies. A think tank named InfluenceMap has documented this divergence on the issue of climate change (InfluenceMap 2017, 2020).

Following the 2011 nuclear meltdown, the country launched a campaign to build 40 new coal-burning electric plants. Some are already built, others are in process. In addition, Tokyo has spent taxpayer money to finance the export of coal plants. The focus on coal, says the think tank, is "misaligned with the strategic interests of Japan Inc." Among the top 100 companies on the stock market, 53% "have business models that would prefer proliferation of renewable electricity generation, both in Japan and globally, compared to coal" (InfluenceMap 2017: 3). Focusing on coal has hindered companies' ability to compete in a market for renewable energy projects that Bloomberg New Energy Finance says will be worth $10 trillion between 2020 and 2040. Having a strong market at home can enable firms to reach economies of scale, as well as rise on the learning curve. Coal is just one of the tacks in the road, along with a refusal by METI, the patron of the utilities, to pressure the latter into erecting transmission lines connecting solar fields or windfarms to the main transmission lines.

How did Tokyo come to adopt a policy that hurts the majority of leading firms? Just seven sectors representing less than 10% of Japan's GDP not only dominate internal Keidanren policymaking on this issue, but also determine which industries get to send representatives to METI's advisory councils on energy (InfluenceMap 2020: 5). The sectors include iron/steel, electric power, automotive production, cement, electrical machinery, oil/petrochemicals, and the coal value chain, including the machinery companies making coal-fired plants. Left out of policymaking are sectors comprising 70% of GDP, such as retail, financial services, logistics, construction, and real estate. The latter two are interested in developing zero-emissions buildings. Not once has the chair of Keidanren been the CEO of a services company.

As a result, the companies left out have created their own lobbying groups on climate change, such as Japan Climate Initiative (JCI). In early 2021, when Prime Minister Yoshihide Suga was making plans to upgrade Japan's commitment to fighting climate change, 300 companies in the JCI, including many heavy-hitters, called on the government to reach for 40% renewable electricity by 2030. Not a single automaker or leading producer of heavy machinery signed on (Japan Climate Initiative 2021; Katz 2021b).

Additional pressure came from environmental nongovernmental organizations (NGOs), as well as activist investors focusing on ESG (Environmental, Social, and Governance) agenda. Particular pressure was applied to Japan's three megabanks (Mizuho, UFJ Mitsubishi, and Sumitomo Mitsui). These megabanks have been the world's top three financiers of new coal plants, mostly in developing countries, and account for 32% of all such finance globally (Rainforest Action Network 2019).

In March 2020, an NGO named Kiko Network filed a shareholder motion at Mizuho's annual meeting to force the megabank to rein in lending to coal companies. Similar pressure was exerted on the other two. A month later, the three megabanks, as well as the government, announced that, in principle, they would no longer fund new coal plants. Then, Toshiba announced it would take no new orders to build coal-fired utilities. Environmental groups welcomed the change, while warning about all the caveats the banks put in. Nor have they yet committed to stop funding existing projects. In 2020, Mizuho and UFJ Mitsubishi said it would take until 2050(!) to stop completely their financing of coal-related activities. There will undoubtedly be further pressure (Yamaguchi 2020).

Until recently, the notion that an NGO like Kiko could have impact was laughable. Not until a 1998 change in the law did Japanese NGOs exist in their modern form. They couldn't even open a bank account. Their rights were further expanded in 2006, when people saw that, in the 2005 Kobe earthquake, voluntary organizations often performed better than the government.

And yet, it's hard to assess their real clout—at least so far. For example, an individual close to Mizuho's management downplayed Kiko's role, contending that the Board was moving in that direction already.

Nonetheless, the rise of socially conscious NGOs—and their ability to ally with activist investors interested in better financial returns—opens the door to previously inconceivable coalitions. One does not imagine people whose hearts race when they dream of saving the rainforest or ending nuclear power to ally with activist investors stirred by hopes for higher dividend payouts or tax credit carry-forwards for R&D investments. Yet, the two groups work together in setting the ESG agenda. The ability of professional politicians to combine such seemingly unlikely partnerships into even broader socioeconomic coalitions is an essential part of the process leading to a pro-gazelle policy shift.

Policy fissures among companies, and within them, can be exploited by policy entrepreneurs, from both companies and NGOs, to take steps that nourish new gazelles. For example, Japan's big pharmaceutical companies would benefit from an R&D tax loss carry-forward that helps the small biotech firms with whom they need to partner.

Not even the stodgy Keidanren has been immune to this change. In June 2021, Keidanren appointed as one of its 19 vice chairs Tomoko Namba, the founder and executive chairman of Tokyo-based online services firm DeNA Co. The press has emphasized that she is the first woman to become vice chair, but just as important is that she is an entrepreneur who created a successful firm in the Internet world when she was 37. Many Internet-based firms have refused to join Keidanren because of its conservativism. Rakuten's Mikitani quit in 2010 for that reason. Namba authored Keidanren's recommendations on the startup ecosystem, which called for a 10-fold jump in annual venture capital investments as well as the number of new startups in Japan by 2027 (Appell 2022). It also called for 100 unicorns by 2027 and 100,000 startups overall (Keidanren 2022; Sugihara 2022).

Assessing this is a half-full versus half-empty matter. On the one hand, Keidanren's issuance of this report was helpful, played a positive role in the Kishida administration's call for the same goals, and legitimized the notion that Japan needs a lot more startups. On the other hand, the actual measures proposed by Keidanren, like those of the Kishida administration, were rather limited. However, even if only Keidanren's three substantive proposals were implemented well, it would be a great step forward. It called for raising the share of set-asides for startups in public procurement from 3% to 10%, for an expanded angel tax, and a more user-friendly stock options tax to make it easier to recruit talented staff. It mentioned minor changes in the R&D tax, but nothing about the R&D tax credit carry-forward, or the double taxation of LLC profits (Keidanren 2022:15,19,35,49). Unfortunately, there is little indication that Keidanren lobbied vigorously in the 2022 debate over the governmental measures needed to make the 2027 goal come true.

Shifts in the Labor Movement on the Regular versus Non-Regular Split

Imagine what it would mean for entrepreneurship if Japan's labor market became far less rigid, mid-career hiring became even more widespread than now, and hourly wages between regular and non-regular workers were equalized. In that case, anyone leaving a regular job to start a new firm, or to work for one, would have a reliable fallback option in case the venture failed, as so many do. The penalty for failure would be far less severe than it is now, when anyone leaving a regular job has a difficult time finding a new job at anything close to their previous wage. Reducing that risk would produce a Japan with far more entrepreneurial experiments and thus far more successes.

At the same time, imagine if those who lost their jobs because their employer downsized or closed knew that they had a chance at getting a new good job at good pay. That would reduce pressure on the government to keep zombie firms alive just to preserve current jobs. More zombies would exit and, as shown in Figure I.1 in the Introduction, the more that inferior firms exit, the greater the room for new firms to enter.

The rigidity of Japan's labor system lies at the root of why Japan has so many policies that hobble creative destruction. Unfortunately, both employers and unions—as well as many of Japan's 30 million regular workers who are not union members—have opposed the needed reforms, and so change of attitude is required in both camps. Under the rubric of flexibility, employers have wanted the ability to dismiss regular workers without being required to offer a healthy severance package and to hire non-regulars at low pay in an evasion of equal pay laws. Unions, in response, see every policy aimed at flexibility as a pretext for wage-cutting and therefore distrust and reject almost all proposals aimed at reducing rigidity, even if on paper they appear to assure the prevention of wage-gouging. A few years ago, academics on an advisory council to the government tried to break this standoff, but to no avail (see details above).

Moreover, unions have a narrow view of their constituency. They mostly represent only regular workers and have been willing to let their employers hire non-regular workers at lower wages as long as the regulars have security against layoffs. Hence, unions have, for the most part, been complicit in the bifurcation of the labor force and the protection of zombies. The good news, as this chapter will explore, is that we are seeing some positive shifts on this front. A small, but growing, minority of unions have begun serious efforts to not only to bring part-time workers into their union, but also to bargain for equal wages for equal work.

Some argue that the labor market is already fixing itself, with a decline in lifetime employment and its corollary, seniority pay. But lifetime employment has not declined. Rather, the portion of the labor force involved in the system has shrunk, but for most of Japan's 30 million workers, many of whom prize the security that the system appears to provide, little has changed.

Consider seniority pay, which gives regular workers a big incentive not to switch jobs. In Japan, more than in any other rich OECD country except Korea, a worker's salary depends on his years with the same employer. In 2017, a full-time male employee with 30 years at the same employer saw his pay almost double compared to his starting pay. By contrast, in Germany the same worker would see his pay rise 50%, and in the United Kingdom, France, and Italy just 30%. Their pay rises of course, but due to other factors, not just seniority (Nishimura 2020: 18).

Repeatedly, over the past few decades, the press has prematurely proclaimed that Japanese companies are moving from seniority-based pay to merit-based or occupation-based pay. For example, 58% of Japanese firms had adopted merit-based pay as of 2018, up from 18% in 1999 (Japan Productivity Center 2020). However, the data show that this just reflects some additional merit-based adjustment to seniority-based pay. From 1990 to 2010, there was almost no change in the seniority wage curve. From 2010 to 2018, there was some decrease in the wage peak in a worker's 50s, but this has more to do with wage austerity than a shift to merit pay (see Figure 18.1). There has always been some variation of wages within a particular age group, based on educational levels, size of the company, and the industry, but occupational variation has been a much weaker factor. But their importance shows no increase during the past couple of decades (MHLW 2020c). A 2019 OECD report handed down its verdict: "The seniority-based wage system in Japan remains strong" (Jones and Seitani 2019: 10).

Seniority pay is one reason that, among regular workers, job switching is still far less frequent than elsewhere. Among all workers in the 50–59 age group who were hired at graduation from high school or college by large

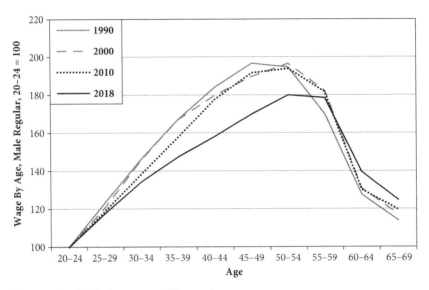

Figure 18.1 Seniority wages still prevail.

Source: Statistical Yearbook (2012); MHLW (2018b).

Note: Covers regular male workers at establishments with at least 10 employees.

companies, 46% of those in factory jobs had never changed employers, and 36% in other occupations (Jones and Seitani 2019: 11–12). However, as detailed above, as part of the generational change in attitudes, workers in their thirties and forties, particularly those in high-skilled occupations, are changing jobs far more than their parents did.

Moreover, there are some breaches in the system, mainly because the bargaining power of those with special talents has increased. In 2020, Fujitsu began offering an annual salary as much as ¥30 million ($230,000) for high-tech engineers, while keeping average annual pay at around ¥8 million ($61,000) for its 32,000 employees. It had no choice if it wanted to keep its younger skilled workers from shifting to other firms, even to some operating outside Japan. Toyota's union has accepted occupational pay differentials in light of global competition and the shortage of ICT professionals and the like. "We need to support our company to secure workers amid labor shortages," is how spokesman Takayuki Furukawa explained the union's change of heart (Kajimoto and Nakagawa 2020: n.p.).

While these are still tantalizing exceptions, more common so far are cases where attempts to downplay seniority pay evoke strong resistance from those at the age where they benefit from the system. Many unions, with some justification, see the call for merit-based pay as yet another way to impose pay cuts. One century-old firm, with about 200 workers, brought in a group of youngish IT specialists as mid-career hires. Without a shift to digitalization, it would have been doomed. Still, the company union rebelled. Why, it complained, did some of these younger newcomers get paid even more than long-term, older employees? Why weren't the veterans trained in the technology and given those positions, they asked (as if this were easy to do)? It caused quite a headache and slowed mid-career hiring. In the end, the company was able to work out a solution with the union regarding pay scales that enabled the mid-career hiring.

The hold of lifetime employment on regular workers' minds is rooted in the history of Japan's labor-management relations. Contrary to later myths, Japan was hardly characterized by labor harmony. Japanese unions began the postwar era with a huge upsurge in both membership and militancy as the US-led Occupation gave workers, for the first time, the right to bargain collectively and to strike. Half of all workers joined unions, which were mostly led by the newly legalized Socialist and/or Communist parties. Meanwhile, employers were equally militant in fighting union demands. That's why the employers' organization, Nikkeiren, called itself "fighting Nikkeiren" in those days. From 1946 to 1976, Japan ranked sixth out of 18 industrialized countries in the number of workers on strike per year (Pempel 1998: 152).

Gradually, employers gained greater bargaining power, unions were tamed, and strikes turned barely perceptible. Rising living standards dampened dissatisfaction, the Socialist and Communist leadership lost popularity, and so-called enterprise unions increasingly replaced militant unions. In 1989, these splits finally resulted in a new, conservative labor federation called Rengo, which includes about 70% of all unionized workers. In the process, unions became increasingly toothless. Union membership plunged to just one out of every six workers these days (OECD 2020b). There are now almost no strikes except symbolic ones lasting less than a day (Statistics Bureau 2020a). A low rate of strikes when wages are rising signifies a welcome era of labor-management peace. This is what characterized the 1960s during the high-growth era. On the other hand, a low rate of strikes when wages are falling signifies labor weakness. It is not unique to Japan.

The creation of enterprise unions by employers poses one of the biggest institutional obstacles to labor market reform. As opposed to industrial unions, like the United Auto Workers in the United States, which represents hundreds of thousands of workers across many companies, enterprise unions represent only the workers in a specific company. For example, the Federation of All Toyota Workers' Unions consists of 312 separate unions. Across the economy, the average union has just 400 members (MHLW 2017a, 2017b; *Reuters* 2013).

The result is that workers at a given enterprise have interests more in common with their employer than with workers in a competing firm or even non-regulars at their own firm. If their employer is more profitable, they'll get a higher bonus (which can amount to as much as a third of annual income). If hiring non-regular workers at low pay helps their employer boost sales by cutting costs, ensures its survival, or even just avoids downsizing, then union members feel their jobs are more secure. Because lifetime employment makes finding a new regular job so hard, job security has for a long time been a top priority, a goal for which workers have been willing to sacrifice wages and, after some initial resistance, to tolerate the hiring of non-regulars. Unions at exporting companies were among the first to endorse the hiring of non-regulars.

Rengo initially opposed deregulation allowing more non-regulars, seeing it as a ploy that would lead to the end of <u>court decisions</u> enforcing the no-layoff policy for regulars. It eventually acquiesced to the inevitability of deregulation measures and moved its lobbying effort to the protection of regulars' job security in the new deregulated environment. Importantly, most unions insisted on the segmentation between regular and non-regular workers. Indeed, nearly 70% of unions still ban non-regulars from membership (Oh 2012). That has helped employers play divide-and-conquer.

The rise of non-regulars has decreased the share of union members at companies. Unlike in many European countries, non-members are not covered by the terms of a contract that the union negotiates. As a result, just 17% of Japan's workers were covered by the terms of union contracts. That compares to 57% in the median OECD country (OECD 2020b). The upshot is that while regular workers at an individual firm may believe that they benefit when their employer prospers by hiring non-regulars, in reality, it weakens the bargaining power of labor as a whole. It's a big contributing factor to the stagnation of real wages even among regular workers.

Ironically, the legal restriction on contract coverage has given unions a reason to organize non-regulars, and that has led to some new, more positive moves by some unions. Unions without a majority of workers in a company lose their bargaining rights on certain issues, such as overtime work. Many unions now have to recruit part-timers in order to maintain those rights.

In 2019, part-timers amounted to a fifth of all employees (Statistics Bureau 2020b). Reportedly, at least one-third of workers with part-time status actually work full-time (Ishii 2018: 477). Meanwhile, temporary workers are ineligible to join a union under Japanese law. Given that millions of temporaries work for years at the same company, often doing the same job as full-time regulars, the law should be changed.

In the past 20 years or so, however, a new tendency has arisen, an effort to recruit part-timers to the unions and, in some cases, to negotiate equal pay for equal work as well as equal promotion opportunities. The share of unions organizing part-time workers rose to 24% in 2010 (Oh 2012: 513). By 2017, part-timers comprised 12% of all union members, triple the 4% rate in 2005, while the percentage of part-timers who are union members doubled to 8% (Rengo 2019). The year 2010 saw the founding of UA Zensen, a federation of industrial unions. As of 2019, half of its 1.7 million workers were part-timers.

It is not easy to attract part-timers to the unions, to convince regular workers to admit them, or employers to accept this. Success has come most often when the union and management agree that unionizing part-timers, and equalizing wages and conditions between regulars and part-timers, can improve productivity, lower employee turnover, improve worker skills, and enhance competitiveness (Oh 2012). In one case study, a company admitting non-regular workers to the union and equalizing pay and promotion opportunities greatly reduced turnover. This boosted profits since turnover costs can add up to as much as two or three month's pay in the cost of finding and training replacements and waiting for them to do their job well.

Over the years, even in giant companies like the Aeon supermarket chain and Bank of Tokyo-Mitsubishi UFJ, the company and the union have agreed to accept non-regulars into the union.

To the extent that this trend grows and equal pay for equal work becomes a reality rather than an unenforced law—even if some other distinctions between regulars and non-regulars remain—new companies will have less trouble recruiting experienced, talented staff.

Dilemmas for SMEs

Reforming the SME sector is at once both one of Japan's most necessary reforms and one of the hardest to achieve.

With SMEs employing 70% of the labor force, Japan cannot have an overall productivity revolution without reforming them. Today, they are woefully unproductive compared to SMEs elsewhere. As noted earlier, in Japan, output per worker at firms with 10–49 workers is just 42% of productivity at firms with at least 250 workers. It's 51% in the rest of the OECD. The gap would be even worse if data were available on the micro mom-and-pop shops.

Moreover, as discussed as the outset, the host of lackluster SMEs and outright zombies act as a barrier to the entrance of newer, superior SMEs in a case of adverse selection, adding yet another drag to Japan's economic performance (see again Figure I.1).

Because many of the most moribund SMEs serve as disguised welfare for those over age 60, one cannot simply drive them out of business with a neoliberal economic policy. It requires having a far more substantial overt governmental social safety net. In the absence of one, the SMEs have constituted an important bloc of support for the status quo.

What opens the door to change is that the ability of the state to preserve the status quo is falling apart before the very eyes of these SMEs. In the past few decades, offshoring and automation have halved manufacturing SMEs, while reform of the Large-Scale Retail Store Law and the rise of convenience stores reduced mom-and-pop retailers by 70%. In coming years without a solution, hundreds of thousands of profitable SMEs will close for lack of a successor, threatening several million jobs.

Meanwhile, the zero-interest rate policy has eroded the ability of the regional banks to provide life support for moribund SMEs. With rates so low, the regional banks in aggregate can no longer cover their operating expenses via their core function (i.e., income earned on loans minus interest paid on deposits) (BOJ 2016; IMF 2017b). The situation will become increasingly worse as older loans with higher interest rates mature. Data through 2021 show that the regional banks have so far managed this situation by cutting operating expenses and increasing fee income.

No wonder Japan has seen the disappearance of half of the smallest and often the least efficient SMEs, the individual proprietorships (mom-and-pop shops) with just 1–4 employees. Back in 1986, Japan hosted more than 4 million individual proprietorships with a total of 12 million employees—one out of every four private-sector employees. These are primarily family businesses with family employees, many of them created by retirees from regular jobs. By 2014, both the number of such enterprises and the number of employees had been cut in half. While six million jobs disappeared from the proprietors, the number of jobs at corporations, large and small, rose by 14 million (Economic Census for Business Frame, assorted years; Economic Census Basic Survey, assorted years).

If the status quo—or, we should say, the status quo ante—cannot be sustained, then these SMEs need a better solution. Some of the SMEs, those who are more efficient, have reason to become part of the reformist bloc. For one thing, as discussed above, supporting the zombies has driven somewhat healthier SMEs out of business. Second, without financial reform, the succession crisis would remain unmanageable. Might not some of those facing closure due to succession issues prefer reform to the end of their business dreams?

Where to Start

In political-economic reform, getting the sequencing right is indispensable. Doing the right things in the wrong order can be disastrous both politically and economically. The genius of the successful reforms in China beginning in the late 1970s and in India in the early 1990s was starting with steps that combined a manifest economic payoff with relatively little economic or political costs.

In Japan's case, it would seem that the best place to start is with reforms that remedy the dearth of external finance and the difficulty in acquiring initial customers. On the one hand, better conditions on these two fronts would make a huge difference in the number of successful high-growth startups. On the other hand, they have little budgetary or political cost.

This effort could start with the items discussed earlier: improved tax breaks for professional angels; genuine implementation of bigger procurement set-asides for new companies; the loss carry-forward for R&D; ending all double taxation for LLCs; and implementing, and improving, the proposed open innovation tax incentive discussed in 2022. At the same time, the FSA should issue guidelines against banks that charge firms 10 years old higher rates than older ones with a bad credit rating (see again Figure 13.2), disproportionately denying loans to women and demanding excessive personal guarantees.

As these policies catalyze more gazelle formation, the gazelles will have a greater weight in the economy and thus greater lobbying power vis-à-vis the bureaucracy and Diet members.

These measures lack the political explosiveness of some truly far-reaching policies that are indispensable to full economic revival, like equal pay for equal work or ending financial life support for zombies. None of these financial proposals challenges LDP rule, though they may step on some toes of assorted interest groups. Few voters would even be aware of the measures.

The main obstacle is the Tax Bureau of the MOF, and some officials within the FSA. A concerted alliance of reformers within METI and the Cabinet Office, as well progressive sections of the business world, could defeat obstructionism from the "Bureau of Why It Cannot Be Done." It would help if reformers got Diet members to question MOF officials about the research showing that their failure to loosen the credit tourniquet on new ventures is lowering Japan's growth—hence its future tax base.

There have already been some changes within the LDP in regard to startups. This is mainly because the party's big business base has recognized that they need ICT-based gazelles to help them solve technological challenges they cannot solve on their own, as seen in the case of Toyota software suppliers, the growth of LINKERS, and Keidanren's 2022 policy statement. In a major speech in London, Prime Minister Kishida declared, "It is therefore my earnest wish to create the next startup boom in Japan" (Kishida 2022). Of course, previous prime ministers have talked of splendid goals without offering the measures needed to turn goals into reality, and so far, Kishida has not been markedly different. But his statement of these goals creates an opportunity for reformers to push for more measures to implement them.

As part of the Kishida effort, the LDP, for the first time, created a "study group" devoted to promoting startups, called the Startup Parliamentary League. Like Keidanren, it called for a 10-fold increase in VC funding to ¥10 trillion ($77 billion) by 2027, as well as a 10-fold increase in venture companies. It is noteworthy that the head of the League, Takuya Hirai, the first head of the new Digital Agency in 2020, spoke on a panel with Rakuten's Mikitani at a JANE conference in 2021.

It would be a big help if pro-entrepreneurship members of the LDP formed a permanent "policy tribe" (*zoku*)—and if other parties established analogous caucuses and formed cross-party study groups. This could really give the entrepreneurial community and its allies greater ability to exert influence within the Diet and the bureaucracy. As opposed to a mere "study group," the LDP *zoku* are groups of Diet members who have made themselves experts in a particular area of policy. Foreigners are familiar with the role of the farm *zoku* in trade negotiations. The *zoku* are usually led by senior Diet members, often include Diet members who formerly worked at a Ministry with juris-diction over that topic, and, importantly, often have discussions with the relevant Ministry before a proposal is made to the Cabinet and the Diet. Even if they cannot impose their own ideas, they can often veto or water down proposals antithetical to the interest group or ideas they represent. Even though the power of the *zoku*, in general, has declined in recent years, it would be a step up in the influence of the entrepreneurial community.

The main hurdle to reviving Japanese entrepreneurship is not a lack of feasible solutions; it is getting Japan's political leadership to implement them.

19

Japan Can Do It, But Will It?

Back in the 1990s, Mark Bivens, a co-founder of a Japanese venture capital firm called Shizen Capital, explained, "If you told your parents you wanted to start a company, they would banish you or you'd never get married. If you had the misfortune of starting a company and it failed, you'd have a black check mark at [the bank] and be ineligible to get a mortgage for 10 years. Failure was stigmatized" (Interview June 2022).

It was not Japan, but France, that Bivens was describing. He had worked there as a venture capitalist before moving to Japan. So ingrained was the sense of France as culturally anti-entrepreneurial that it fit the stereotype when it was falsely reported that George W. Bush had said, "The French don't even have a word for entrepreneur." Today, just a couple of short decades later, France feels like a different country. Since 2000, it has created almost 38,000 new startups, valued in mid-2023 at $293 billion, up from just $11 billion in 2010 (Dealroom.co 2023). About 2,500 of the startups are involved in deep tech (i.e., solutions based on profound scientific or technological breakthroughs). In 2023, the country now boasted 36 unicorns. There were none just a dozen years ago. By contrast, only six unicorns inhabited Japan, far from the 20 that, in 2018, Shinzo Abe had promised to have by 2023.

France's VC investment quadrupled to 0.14% of GDP from 2009 to 2022 and ranked 9th highest among 28 OECD countries. Japanese VC has also grown, having tripled to 0.06% by 2021, but still ranked just 18th (OECD 2023b).

Why has France succeeded so much more than Japan? The surprisingly simple answer is that, in the late 1990s, out of fear that, despite its world-class giants, France was falling behind in global competitiveness, the government put into place programs for innovative newcomers that were well-designed and executed.

On a visit to Silicon Valley, Prime Minister Lionel Jospin left impressed by startups' spillover benefits for the entire economy. The government also recognized that external finance was indispensable and yet, as in Japan, there was almost no seed money to get startups off the ground. Consequently, in

The Contest for Japan's Economic Future. Richard Katz, Oxford University Press. © Richard Katz 2024.
DOI: 10.1093/oso/9780197675106.003.0020

1997, the government created a Mutual Fund For Innovation (FCPI) aimed at catalyzing new private financiers. Under the FCPI scheme, ordinary people could receive huge tax benefits from investments in startups via venture capital and angel firms.

Far from being forced to take a high-risk gamble on a single company, as in Japan, they could place their money in a diverse portfolio chosen by professionals who were licensed and scrutinized by the government. Moreover, instead of VC funds being limited to just 49 investors as in Japan, they could have thousands. That gave them the economies of scale needed to finance expensive research on the target startups. The startups themselves had to meet the criteria for being knowledge-intensive innovators with growth potential, having devoted at least one-third of their revenue over three years to research, having less than 500 employees, and being headquartered in the European Union.

During 2000–2017, citizens who invested in firms no older than seven years could reduce their income tax bill every year by 25% of the amount they invested up to a maximum deduction of €12,000 ($13,000)—€24,000 for a married couple—as long as they held the investment for five years. They could reduce their misnomered "wealth tax"—which caught many middle-class people—by half of the amount they invested up to a maximum of €50,000 ($54,000). On top of that, profits were exempt from the capital gains tax.

As a result, in a typical year, more than 100,000 people invested a total of €1 billion ($1.08 billion) into these programs, an average of €10,000 ($11,000) per household. This does not count the funds invested outside of this program. In 2017, the French government declared that the initiative had achieved its goal of "transforming the mental software of the French populace" to appreciate the importance of startups, and reduced the size of the incentives.

Although the initial years were difficult and details had to be refined, the program hit its stride and now provides excellent returns. For example, the median fund launched in 2008 returned to investors cash adding up to five times their initial investment. The median fund began in 2014 provided a stunning 12-fold return on the investment. A virtuous cycle ensued. The availability of funding lured talented people; consequently, new startups now grow around 20% a year. At the same time, the influx of talented founders has, in turn, encouraged more professionals to invest. By 2015 (the latest number available), the number of professional business angels reached 8,000.

Bivens, who was skeptical when the FCPI program began, was one of those professionals before he moved to Japan. In 2021, total external funding raised by startups reached a record €12.4 billion ($13.4 billion). Bivens's verdict: "France's high-tech ecosystem has now grown into a tremendous success, and I assert that government support via tax policy was the key catalyst" (Interview June 2023, Katz 2023c: n.p.).

It seems counterintuitive that such outsized impact could spring from such a simple technical measure. But it happens more than people realize. Once upon a time, depression-creating bank runs, as in the 1930s, were seen as an inherent and unavoidable feature of capitalism. Then, governments instituted deposit insurance. Today, that's one of the major reasons why recessions, not depressions, now characterize capitalism.

If France can succeed in overcoming its anti-entrepreneurial habits and mindset through concrete policy measures, why not Japan?

The immediate answer is that France's program was well-designed and executed, whereas Kishida's was both narrowly focused and poorly designed. But that just begs the question of why Kishida didn't offer something better. Again, the immediate answer is Kishida's personality. Rather than acting decisively, he styled himself as a good listener who let different factions work it out, and fiscal hawks shorted-sightedly blocked better measures. And yet, when Kishida chose to, he could be decisive, for example, abandoning the long taboo against defense spending being no more than 1% of GDP and creating a plan to double such spending in just five years. Certainly, no one can accuse Shinzo Abe of being indecisive, and yet he chose to exercise his clout on security issues rather than economic goals. So, personality alone does not tell the tale.

The deeper answer seems to be that, on economic issues, Japan has given veto power to so many players that watering down of measures, sometimes even immobilism, often prevail. For example, while Kishida was able to end the 1% defense-spending taboo, the assorted players were completely unable to agree on how to pay for this. So, they simply kicked the can down the road for at least a couple of years. Kishida did not insist upon the tax hikes he had advocated.

For decades after the experience of a militaristic dictatorship from the late 1930s through World War II, Japan's political system was run as if decisiveness by a prime minister was somehow undemocratic. Until Junichiro Koizumi came to power in 2001, the tradition was that legislation was not drafted by the prime minister's office or its satellite agencies, but by the Ministry whose turf and clients the legislation affected. The Ministries could therefore sabotage, or even defy, the prime minister's desires. There was a similar and parallel process inside the LDP itself. Gaining consensus to make a big course correction was therefore difficult. A personally strong prime minister could prevail by putting his foot down on this or that priority matter, but he could not do so for more than a few measures. The default option was inertia. For that reason, the Japanese prime minister was considered one of the weakest heads of government among the rich democracies.

Imagine Japan's policymaking process to be like a jury in which all decisions must be unanimous or nearly so. Then imagine that the jurors have personal, and conflicting, stakes in the outcome as each Ministry tries to protect its clients or its right to veto initiatives on issues that come under its bailiwick. There'd be hung juries most of the time. Now take it a step further and imagine that the same jury meets on issue after issue. Participants would hesitate to push their views too forcefully lest it create acrimony with those they have to keep dealing with. No wonder there's such immobilism. To take just one example, for almost a quarter of a century, reformist bureaucrats in METI have tried to create an effective tax incentive for angel investment and the MOF and LDP Tax Commission keep watering it down.

This analogy is, of course, a gross exaggeration, but it captures some of the flavor of the system. It also ignores all the exceptions: those issues on which policymakers have effected great economic and social change, sometimes even greater change than they anticipated. The 1986 Equal Employment Opportunity Law led millions of women to go to four-year colleges and get real careers, even if nowhere near as many as could have happened had Japan enforced its laws on equal pay and promotion. The 1991 reform of the Large-Scale Retail Store Law enabled bigger, more efficient stores to come into neighborhoods and displace mom-and-pop shops, leading not only to greater productivity in distribution and retail but the reduction of these shops by two-thirds as elderly shop-owners retired and fewer new elderly replaced them. This reform caused far less hardship than critics had predicted. Prior to the 1998 financial Big Bang, foreigners owned almost no corporate shares or government and corporate bonds. Japan's capital markets were insulated from global trends. Now, foreigners own more than a third of corporate shares and 15% of government bonds. In the same year, the Diet took control over banking issues away from the MOF and created a new entity, the Financial Services Agency (FSA) in response to the MOF's gross mishandling of the bank's bad debt crisis. In 2003, the Koizumi administration began resolving the stupefying debt crisis without the magnitude of harm to debtors that opponents of reform had predicted.

Effective governance requires making such exceptions more of the rule. In an effort to overcome that systemic logjam, Koizumi, and later Abe, began to shake up the system. On several issues, Koizumi insisted that the prime minister's office and its satellite agencies, not the Ministries, would not only decide on issues, but also write the legislation. From the beginning, he was called dictatorial and even fascistic by critics within his own party, just for doing what happens as a matter of course in other major democracies. In 2005, Koizumi went even further. When Koizumi's postal reform failed to pass in the Upper House because of opposition by members of the LDP, he dissolved the Diet, called an election, and expelled the dissidents from the LDP (his successor Abe invited them back in).[1] From then on, the prime minister's power kept increasing, with zigs and zags depending on the prime minister's personal abilities and approval ratings.

Still, on many economic reform issues, the veto power has remained. The upshot is incredible frustration, even cynicism, expressed in the common lament: "everyone knows something must be done, experts know what to do, politicians wax eloquent about their goals, and, in the end, no one actually does very much."

Japan is not the only state afflicted by immobilism. So intense has partisan rancor become in the United States that, as the years pass, Congress passes fewer and fewer substantive bills. In Japan, this situation has engendered big swings between hope—as shown in the three elections where politicians talking of reform won big victories—and fatalism, when those hopes are dashed. That fatalism is captured by the popular Japanese expression *shikata ga nai* (it cannot be helped).

Such defeatism is understandable, given the track record of the past few decades. But unwarranted defeatism is just as corrosive as irrational optimism. It blinds one to the amount of progress that has already occurred, as illustrated in this book. It ignores the ways in which politicians' dilemmas and incentives are being changed by social, economic, demographic, and technological developments, like the succession crisis at SMEs, the loss of

---

[1] The mammoth Japan Post, which also runs one of the world's largest banking and insurance organizations, is a major locus of patronage, money for pork barrel projects, and power among LDP Diet members. Koizumi's limited success in completely privatizing and reforming it was a keystone in his effort to reform the LDP itself.

competitiveness among elephants in the digital era contrasting with the rise of new companies due to e-commerce, the growth of new companies as an interest group, and the impact on government budgets of aging. Moreover, assorted reforms are happening all the time, such as the corporate governance reforms instituted in the past decade, or the FSA's directive to reduce the role of the personal guarantee in bank lending. The problem is that, on so many matters, the pace and magnitude of reform are so constrained that Japan is always behind the curve vis-à-vis the forces of economic decay, like aging. More importantly, defeatism blinds people to the levers for accelerating future progress. Demoralization paralyzes the will. Defeating this defeatism is necessary to the success of the reform.

Japan's tragedy is that the country need not change that much in order to set recovery into motion. The payoff from some of the tax incentives proposed here would be very impactful while causing little disruption. In too many cases, even obvious reforms are blocked by ideological blinders and inertia, even when they do no harm to any vested interests. In fact, Japan's problems are, in many ways, much easier to solve than some of the problems troubling, for example, the United States, with its bitter partisan animosity, threats to democracy, the existence of a large underclass, and the poor educational achievement of large parts of the population. So many of the initial measures I've suggested could easily be adopted and implemented if the political will were there. Seeing greater-than-expected economic payoff and less-than-feared social pain from these measures would make it easier to take more difficult steps. It would go a long way to counter fatalism and demoralization.

To be sure, the ability of the LDP to stay in power despite its failure to solve problems does let its leaders think they can substitute rhetoric for reality. More punishment of do-nothing incumbents by voters would help a great deal. Nonetheless, LDP rule does not preclude serious action. Some other one-party states, like China and India, have implemented substantial reforms.

There's no assurance that change will be in the right direction. Though Japan has so far been spared the rise of populism, aside from an Osaka-based regional party, that could change. In North America and Europe alike, many formerly left-of-center workers who've lost jobs or suffered wage cuts due to the impersonal forces of automation and productivity have fallen for right-wing demagogues who point the finger at the very personal figures of corporate elites bringing in imports and immigrants or engaging in offshoring

(Frey et al. 2018; Guriev 2020). The best inoculation against destructive populism is a cure for the economic ills which feed it.

In showing drafts of this book to colleagues, I've found little resistance to the notion of how the megatrends are impacting Japan in powerful and positive ways. Nor have I faced pushback on my proposals for reform: their benefits, their political and economic feasibility, and the fact they reflect already existing indigenous trends. What remains in question is whether all this is enough to overcome resistance to reform. Why won't Japan simply miss this opportunity, as it has missed so many previous ones?

I readily admit there is no guarantee. Nor can I deny that wholesale reform remains an uphill climb, mainly due to lack of political will. What I do contend is that the hill is a lot less steep than it used to be and therefore the chances for reform far, far greater. I also contend that the initial steps to catalyze a quantum leap in entrepreneurship are well within the capacity of an LDP government. And this even serves their interests, because pulling off economic revival would certainly help its popularity. While it does require that Japan's political leaders overrule some hidebound and powerful factions and organizations within the LDP, the Ministries, and the private sector, the initial reforms need not harm any of the important interest groups within society. Beyond that, if the initial steps are done well, the process can snowball both economically and politically with far less hardship than is already being caused by low growth.

What is the source of my cautious hopefulness? Partly, it stems in part from the logic of the megatrends, which are gaining more traction than ever before. Beyond that, it stems from a gut feeling, a judgment call arising out of my experience in researching this book. For most of my career, I have primarily met with Japan's elite: officials, politicians, and business executives. I have seen the striving of brilliant reformers, the hurdles they face, their successes, their disappointments. By contrast, for the past several years, I have spent my time with another Japan, the Japan of the young and not-so-young entrepreneurial layer. What a breath of fresh air. It resonated with past episodes of economic and social elan in Japan, from Meiji era modernization to the post–World War II economic miracle. Just how different was this side of Japan really struck me when I met with a 50-ish manager at one of Japan's corporate giants, the kind of person I had dealt with most of my career. I was overwhelmed by my reacquaintance with the atmosphere of tedium, the sense of someone counting the days until retirement. It brought home to me why Japan had missed so many past opportunities and why today's generational change is so encouraging, even inspiring. The Japanese people have shown in their votes that they yearn for some sort of reform, even if they cannot articulate exactly what that should entail. The cohort of younger entrepreneurs is bringing about business reform one company at a time. All that is needed is for policymakers to nurture the positive trends and to bring them to critical mass.

Japan has so much to gain by doing the right things, and so much to lose by failing to do so. And because of trends that no one planned—shifts in generational attitudes and technology, aging, and the political stresses caused by low growth—doing the right things would cause far less initial hardship and resentment than Japan's leaders have feared. And surely much less than trying to maintain the status quo. That's what makes this Japan's greatest opportunity in a generation. What a tragedy it would be if Japan were to throw away its best shot at doing again what it used to do so well: generating tens of thousands of new, innovative companies that propel above-par growth.

Acknowledgments

You never know what can result from a simple luncheon conversation. Some years back, Columbia Professor Hugh Patrick asked me: if a member of Japan's Diet or an official asked you to suggest 5 or 10 specific measures—tax changes, regulatory reforms, expenditures, laws—that would help promote economic recovery, what would you recommend? I felt that what Japan most needed were more contestable markets and far more startup companies. But what exactly could the government do? That question sent me down a path of obsessive investigation whose end product is this book.

While the investigation began in Japan, it soon led me to Berlin, where Professor Verena Blechinger-Talcott of the Free University of Berlin had invited me to come for a couple of weeks to research any topic I wanted. I chose to look at the startup upsurge in Berlin, and Verena and her associates were immensely helpful in arranging meetings. I was hooked. For the first time in years, the thought of writing another book grabbed me, this time about what specific measures the government could do to generate more new, innovative, high-growth companies in Japan. However, I was still involved in other activities, including my 20th year of publishing a monthly newsletter on Japan called *The Oriental Economist*—the continuation of a magazine founded in the 1930s by Toyo Keizai's legendary editor, Tanzan Ishibashi. I could not do this and write a book at the same time.

The answer came in another lunch, this time with MIT Professor Richard Samuels, who was a visiting professor at the Free University every summer. He observed that I clearly wanted to do the book and advised me to find a way. When I got home and spoke to my wife, Linda, she agreed with him and so I took a leave of absence from *TOE*, and the latter has now returned in the form of a blog called *Japan Economy Watch*.

To finance the project, I approached Allan Song, of the Smith Richardson Foundation (SRF), who encouraged me to apply for a grant. Devin Stewart of the Carnegie Council for Ethics in International Affairs arranged for the Council to be my institutional sponsor for the SRF grant. After a peer review, the Foundation provided a very generous grant, and the Council has been very gracious to me in administering it. Devin also introduced me to quite a few entrepreneurs and experts on entrepreneurship in Japan.

To get a good publisher, I needed an agent, and, for that, I needed introductions from colleagues. I hit gold when Taggart Murphy introduced me to Hamish Macaskill, chief of the English Agency in Tokyo. Hamish not only believed in the book, he also believed it could find both an audience and a great publisher. He also helped me reframe the Introduction so as to bring out its message in even sharper focus. And he found me a great publisher in Oxford University Press.

My editor at Oxford, James Cook, provided exactly what I sought in an editor. Passages that I thought were perfectly clear, James pointed out, did not communicate as well as I thought they did. He improved the balance between points I was making and the details I used to make those points. He helped me sharpen the overall message. His suggestions turned this book into what I had hoped it would be.

In the process of writing, I had sought feedback from colleagues who generously provided advice, none more so than Columbia Professor Gerald Curtis. He pointed out the need to translate the discussion of the positive megatrends into a plausible scenario by which the suggested reforms had a good chance of being realized. The last couple of chapters benefited greatly from his advice. Meanwhile, Yuichiro Yamagata, the former editor-in-chief and then president at Toyo Keizai, suggested ways to strengthen the message, especially to Japanese readers. Others who provided invaluable feedback include Greg Noble, Aurelia George Mulgan, Richard Solomon, Taggart Murphy, Christina Ahmadjian, John Campbell, Naoki Ikegami, and Jake Schlesinger. Yoshiaki Ishii introduced me to a host of entrepreneurs in Japan, while Laurence Greenwood introduced me to key sources of insights in Silicon Valley.

Over the several years of research, I received enormous help from several university students who served as research assistants: Che Chung Hsu, Toshimitsu Ueta, Chung-Yu Lu, Kazuki Yokota, and Tetsuya Aoki. I found a wonderful interpreter in Yuri Nambu Stoyanov.

Most of all, I thank my wife, Linda, and daughter, Laura. Linda not only urged me to follow my dream, but graciously bore with me as I went through a writer's all-too-common obsessiveness, not to mention repeated rides on the emotional roller coaster. Laura was the first to provide valuable, and encouraging, feedback on early drafts of the initial chapters. I could not have completed this book without them.

Bibliography

Accounting Intelligence (2018). "Angel Investment Taxation in Japan." http://accountingi ntelligence.jp/en/2018/11/22/angel-investment-taxation-in-japan/.

Acemoglu, Daron, Ufuk Akcigit, and Murat Alp Celik (2014). "Young, Restless and Creative: Openness to Disruption and Creative Innovations." NBER Working Paper 19894. http://www.nber.org/papers/w19894.

Acs, Zoltan, Pontus Braunerhjelm, David B. Audretsch, and Bo Carlsson (2009). "The Knowledge Spillover Theory of Entrepreneurship." *Small Business Economics*, Vol. 32, No. 1 (January 2009), pp. 15–30.

Acs, Zoltan, William Parsons, and Spencer Tracy (2008). "High-Impact Firms: Gazelles Revisited Small Business Research Summary." *Small Business Research Summary*, No. 328 (June 2008). https://www.researchgate.net/profile/Zoltan-Acs-2/publication/267 218946_High-Impact_Firms_Gazelles_Revisited/links/546160f40cf27487b4527453/ High-Impact-Firms-Gazelles-Revisited.pdf

Acs, Zoltan, and Attila Varga (2005). "Entrepreneurship, Agglomeration and Technological Change." *Small Business Economics*, Vol. 24, No. 3 (April 2005), pp. 323–334.

Agarwal, Rajshree, and David B. Audretsch (2001). "Does Entry Size Matter? The Impact of the Life Cycle and Technology on Firm Survival." *The Journal of Industrial Economics*, Vol. 49, No. 1 (March 2001), pp. 21–43. http://terpconnect.umd.edu/~rajshree/resea rch/10%20Agarwal,%20Audretsch%20-%202001.pdf.

Alam, Abdullah, M. Usman Arshad, and Wasim Ullah Rajput (2013). "Relationship of Labor Productivity, Foreign Direct Investment and Economic Growth: Evidence from OECD Countries." *Journal of Business and Management Sciences*, Vol. 1, No. 6, pp. 133–138. http://pubs.sciepub.com/jbms/1/6/3.

Alexy, Allison (2021). *Ezra Vogel Lecture*, November 9, 2021. https://youtu.be/abGD HiZXDwo.

Alon, Titan, David Berger, Robert Dent, and Benjamin Pugsley (2017). "Older and Slower: The Startup Deficit's Lasting Effects on Aggregate Productivity Growth." NBER Working Paper 23875, September 2017. http://www.nber.org/papers/w23875.

Ambrose, Brent, Larry Cordell, and Shuwei Ma (2015). *The Impact of Student Loan Debt on Small Business Formation*. Federal Reserve Bank of Philadelphia, July 2015. https:// www.philadelphiafed.org/the-economy/the-impact-of-student-loan-debt-on-small- business-formation.

Kobayashi, Nobuko (2020). "Japanese Companies Can No Longer Expect Lifetime Loyalty from Workers." *Nikkei*, April 3, 2020. https://asia.nikkei.com/Opinion/Japan ese-companies-can-no-longer-expect-lifetime-loyalty-from-workers.

Anelli, Massimo, Italo Colantone, and Piero Stanig (2019). "We Were the Robots: Automation and Voting Behavior in Western Europe." BAFFI CAREFIN Centre Research Paper 2019-115. https://www.econstor.eu/bitstream/10419/202831/ 1/dp12485.pdf.

Aoyagi, Chie, Giovanni Ganelli, and Nour Tawk (2016). "Minimum Wage as a Wage Policy Tool in Japan." IMF Working Paper WP/16/232. https://www.imf.org/en/Publications/WP/Issues/2016/12/31/Minimum-Wage-as-a-Wage-Policy-Tool-in-Japan-44412.

Appell, Douglas (2022). "Japan Plots Path to Venture Capital Relevance." *Pensions and Investments*, April 11, 2022. https://www.pionline.com/alternatives/japan-plots-path-venture-capital-relevance.

Arcese, Gabriella, Serena Flammini, Maria Claudia Lucchetti, and Olimpia Martucci (2015). "Google and Open Innovation." R&D Management Conference, Pisa, July 2015.

Arnold-Parra, Samuel (2021). "Japan's Tech Competitiveness: Why the Decline?" *Global Risk Insights*, March 7, 2021. https://globalriskinsights.com/2021/03/japans-tech-competitiveness-why-the-decline/

Asahi Shimbun (2023). "Nonregular Workers Feel Left Out of Measures to Lift Birthrate." May 17, 2023. https://www.asahi.com/ajw/articles/14898453.

Asanuma, Banri (1988). "Japanese Manufacturer-Supplier Relationships in International Perspective: The Automobile Case." Kyoto University Working Paper Number 8, September 1988. https://repository.kulib.kyoto u.ac.jp/dspace/bitstream/2433/37903/1/08.pdf.

Audretsch, David (2007). "Entrepreneurship Capital and Economic Growth." *Oxford Review of Economic Policy*, Vol. 23, No. 1 (Spring 2007), pp. 63–78. https://doi.org/10.1093/oxrep/grm001.

Audretsch, David (2012). "Determinants of High-Growth Entrepreneurship." Report prepared for the OECD/DBA International Workshop on High-Growth Firms: Local Policies and Local Determinants, Copenhagen, March 28, 2012. https://search.oecd.org/cfe/leed/Audretsch_determinants%20of%20high-growth%20firms.pdf.

Baily, M. N. (2003). "The Sources of Economic Growth in OECD Countries: A Review Article." *International Productivity Monitor*, No. 7 (Fall 2003), pp. 66–70. https://www.researchgate.net/profile/Martin-Baily/publication/24051661_The_Source_of_Economic_Growth_in_OECD_Countries_A_Review_Article/links/558c54b208ae591c19d9fc2f/The-Source-of-Economic-Growth-in-OECD-Countries-A-Review-Article.pdf.

Bain & Company (2018). "Japan Private Equity Report."

Bain & Company (2021). "Japan Private Equity Report."

BDO Tax News (2020). "Japan World Wide Tax News Issue 55—June 2020." https://www.bdo.global/en-gb/microsites/tax-newsletters/corporate-tax-news/issue-55-june-2020/japan-new-open-innovation-tax-incentive%E2%80%9D

Birch, David (1987). *Job Creation in America*. New York: Free Press.

BOJ (2016). "Chart IV-5-3: Ratios of Banks for Which Loan-Deposit Income and Other Income Falls Short of Expenses and Distribution of Their Income-to-Expenses." *Financial System Report*, October 2016. https://www.boj.or.jp/en/research/brp/fsr/fsr161024.htm.

BOJ (2017). "Support for the Establishment of Japan Policy Finance Corporation." https://www.boj.or.jp/announcements/release_2017/data/rel170630b4.pdf (in Japanese).

BOJ (2023a). "Bank of Japan Accounts/Assets/Japanese Government Securities/Japanese Government Bonds." https://www.stat-search.boj.or.jp/index_en.html.

BOJ (2023b). "Loans and Discounts Outstanding by Interest Rate." https://www.stat-search.boj.or.jp/index_en.html.

Bosma, Niels, Erik Stam, and Sander Wennekers (2010). *Intrapreneurship: An International Study*. EIM SCALES Research Report H201005. Zoetermeer, Netherlands: EIM.

Braunerhjelm, Pontus, Zoltan J. Acs, David Audretsch, and Bo Carlsson (2010). "The Missing Link: Knowledge Diffusion and Entrepreneurship in Endogenous Growth." *Small Business Economics*, Vol. 34, No. 2 (February 2010), pp. 105–125. https://link.springer.com/article/10.1007/s11187-009-9235-1.

Bredgaard, Thomas, and Flemming Larsen (2007). "Comparing Flexicurity in Denmark and Japan." Japan Institute for Labour Policy and Training (JILPT).

Brown, McLeod (2018). "States with Most Non-Citizen College Professors." *Zippia the Career Expert*, April 11, 2018. https://www.zippia.com/advice/states-non-citizen-college-professors/

Brown, R., S. Mawson, and C. Mason (2017). "Myth-Busting and Entrepreneurship Policy: The Case of High Growth Firms." *Entrepreneurship and Regional Development*, Vol. 29, No. 5–6 (February 2017), pp. 414–443. http://dx.doi.org/10.1080/08985626.2017.1291762.

Broz, J. Lawrence, Jeffry Frieden, and Stephen Weymouth (2021). "Populism in Place: The Economic Geography of the Globalization Backlash." *International Organization*, Vol. 75, No. 2 (2021), pp. 464–494. doi:10.1017/S0020818320000314.

Brüderl, Josef, Peter Preisendörfer, and Rolf Ziegler (1992). "Survival Chances of Newly Founded Business Organizations." *American Sociological Review*, Vol. 57, No. 2 (April 1992), pp. 227–242.

Bureau of Economic Analysis (2015). "GDP by Industry." https://www.bea.gov/data/gdp/gdp-industry.

Bureau of Economic Analysis (2019). "Measuring the Digital Economy: An Update Incorporating Data from the 2018 Comprehensive Update of the Industry Economic Accounts," April 2019. https://www.bea.gov/media/5481.

Bureau of Labor Statistics (2020). "Job Openings and Labor Turnover Survey." https://www.bls.gov/data/#employment.

Bureau of Labor Statistics (2021). "The U.S. Productivity Slowdown: An Economy-Wide and Industry-Level Analysis." *Monthly Labor Review*, April 2021. https://www.bls.gov/opub/mlr/2021/article/the-us-productivity-slowdown-the-economy-wide-and-industry-level-analysis.htm.

Bureau of the Census (2016). "Firm Characteristics Data Tables." https://www.census.gov/data/tables/2016/econ/bds/2016-firm-and-estab-release-tables.html.

Bureau of the Census (2021). "Business Dynamics Statistics: Firm Age: 1978–2018." https://data.census.gov/cedsci/table?q=BDSTIMESERIES.BDSFAGE&tid=BDSTIMESERIES.BDSFAGE&hidePreview=true.

Business.com (2022). "The 10 Largest E-commerce Markets in the World by Country." https://www.business.com/articles/10-of-the-largest-ecommerce-markets-in-the-world-b/.

Caballero, Ricardo, Takeo Hoshi, and Anil K Kashyap (2008). "Zombie Lending and Depressed Restructuring in Japan." *American Economic Review*, Vol. 98, No. 5, pp. 1943–1977. https://www.aeaweb.org/articles/pdf/doi/10.1257/aer.98.5.1943.

Cabinet Office (2020). "Transfers from General Government to Households (Social Security Transfers)." Annual Report on National Accounts for 2019. https://www.esri.cao.go.jp/en/sna/data/kakuhou/files/2019/tables/2019s9_en.xlsx.

Cabinet Office (2022a). "Quarterly Estimates of GDP." https://www.esri.cao.go.jp/en/sna/sokuhou/sokuhou_top.html.

Cabinet Office (2022b). "GDP Gap and Potential Output Growth Rate." https://www5.cao.go.jp/keizai3/getsurei/2131gap.xls.

Cabinet Office (2022c). "Startup Development Five-year Plan." https://www.cas.go.jp/jp/seisaku/atarashii_sihonsyugi/pdf/sdfyplan2022en.pdf.

Calder, Kent (1988). *Crisis and Compensation: Public Policy and Political Stability in Japan.* Princeton, NJ: Princeton University Press.

Carril-Caccia, Federico, and Elena Pavlova (2018). "Foreign Direct Investment and Its Drivers: A Global and EU Perspective." *ECB Economic Bulletin*, April 2018. https://www.ecb.europa.eu/pub/economic-bulletin/articles/2018/html/ecb.ebart201804_01.en.html.

Castellacci, Fulvio, and Jinghai Zheng (2010). "Technological Regimes, Schumpeterian Patterns Of Innovation And Firm-Level Productivity Growth." *Industrial and Corporate Change*, Vol. 19, No. 6, pp. 1829–1865. http://nrl.northumbria.ac.uk/11936/1/castellacci_technological_regimes.pdf.

CB Insights (2022). "The Complete List of Unicorn Companies." https://www.cbinsights.com/research-unicorn-companies.

Center for American Progress (2020). "Mobilize More Angel Investors through a Federal Tax Credit." https://startupsusa.org/issues/capital/.

Chan, Kelvin (2020). "EU Files Antitrust Charges against Amazon over Use of Data." *Associated Press*, November 10, 2020. https://apnews.com/article/eu-files-antitrust-against-amazon-8e0222555df76c36bfbeed3289222d94.

Chang, Sea-Jin (2011). *Sony vs Samsung: The Inside Story of the Electronics Giants' Battle for Global Supremacy.* New York: Wiley.

Chesbrough, Henry (2006a). "New Puzzles and New Findings." In Henry Chesbrough, Wim Vanhaverbeke, and Joel West (eds.), *Open Innovation: Researching a New Paradigm*, pp. 15–34. Oxford: Oxford University Press.

Chesbrough, Henry (2006b). "The Open Innovation Model: Implications for Innovation in Japan." In D. H. Whittaker and R. E. Cole (eds.), *Recovering from Success: Innovation and Technology Management in Japan*, pp. 129–144. Oxford: Oxford University Press.

Chesbrough, Henry (2013). "Open Innovation: Implications for Japanese Innovation." Report to NEDO, March 10, 2013.

Chesbrough, Henry, Wim Vanhaverbeke, and Joel West, eds. (2006). *Open Innovation: Researching a New Paradigm.* Oxford: Oxford University Press.

Christensen, Clayton (1997). *The Innovator's Dilemma: When New Technologies Cause Great Firms to Fail.* Cambridge, MA: Harvard Business Review Press.

Chung, Wilbur, W. Mitchell, and B. Yeung (2003). "Foreign Direct Investment and Host Country Productivity: The American Automotive Component Industry in the 1980s." *Journal of International Business Studies*, Vol. 34, pp. 199–218. http://www.rcmewhu.com/upload/file/20150528/20150528154644_5498.pdf.

Cingano, F. (2014). "Figure 3. Estimated Consequences of Changes in Inequality on Cumulative per Capita GDP Growth (1990–2010)." In Trends in Income Inequality and its Impact on Economic Growth, OECD Social, Employment and Migration Working Papers, No. 163. http://dx.doi.org/10.1787/5jxrjncwxv6j-en.

Cislo, Connor, and Maiko Takahashi (2017). "Japan's Millennials Tend to Sacrifice Higher Earnings for Job Security, Thwarting BOJ's Economic Reforms." *Bloomberg*, July 7, 2017. https://www.japantimes.co.jp/news/2017/07/21/business/japans-millennials-tend-sacrifice-higher-earnings-job-security-thwarting-bojs-economic-reforms/#.XoDt73J7lc8.

Clayton, Richard, Akbar Sadeghi, James R. Spletzer, and David M. Talan (2013.) "High-Employment-Growth Firms: Defining and Counting Them." *Monthly Labor Review*, June 2013. https://stats.bls.gov/opub/mlr/2013/06/art1full.pdf.

Cole, Rebel, and Tatyana Sokolyk (2018). "Debt Financing, Survival, and Growth of Start-Up Firms." *Journal of Corporate Finance*, Vol. 50, pp. 609–625.

Cole, Robert (2004). "Capturing Value from Technology Assets: Strategic Approach to Standards: The Telecom Case." Speech to Kokusai Keizai Kenkyujo.

Cole, Robert (2005). "Telecom Deregulation and Telecom Competition in World Markets: Understanding Japan's Decline." Institute for Technology, Enterprise and Competitiveness, Doshisha University, Research Paper 05-03. https://www.researchg ate.net/publication/228991835_Telecom_Deregulation_and_Telecom_Competition_ in_World_Markets_Understanding_Japan's_Decline.

Cole, Robert (2006). "The Telecommunication Industry: A Turnaround in Japan's Global Presence." In Hugh Whittaker and Robert Cole (eds.), *Recovering from Success: Innovation and Technology Management in Japan*, pp. 31–46. Oxford: Oxford University Press.

Cole, Robert, and Yoshifumi Nakata (2014). "The Japanese Software Industry: What Went Wrong and What Can We Learn from It?" *California Management Review*, Vol. 57, No. 1 (November 2014), pp. 16–43.

Cole, Robert, and Hugh Whittaker (2006). "Introduction." In Hugh Whittaker and Robert Cole (eds.), *Recovering from Success: Innovation and Technology Management in Japan*, pp. 1–281. Oxford: Oxford University Press.

Congressional Research Service (2019). "Real Wage Trends, 1979 to 2018." https://digital commons.ilr.cornell.edu/cgi/viewcontent.cgi?article=3116&context=key_workplace.

Cooper, Arnold, F. Javier Gimeno-Gascón, and Carolyn Woo (1997). "Initial Human and Financial Capital as Predictors of New Venture Performance." *The Journal of Private Equity*, Vol. 1, No. 2 (Winter 1997), pp. 13–30.

Corak, Miles (2016) "Inequality from Generation to Generation: The United States in Comparison." IZA Discussion Papers, No. 9929, Institute for the Study of Labor (IZA), Bonn. https://www.econstor.eu/bitstream/10419/142368/1/dp9929.pdf.

Corbin, David (2014). "Meet Yoshiaki Ishii, the Government Official Who Can Save Startups in Japan." TechInAsia website, July 30, 2014. https://www.techinasia.com/ yoshiaki-ishii-meti-save-japan-startups.

Corrado, Carol, Jonathan Haskel, Cecilia Jona-Lasinio, and Massimiliano Iommi (2013). "Innovation and Intangible Investment in Europe, Japan, and the United States." *Oxford Review of Economic Policy*, Vol. 29, No. 2 (Summer 2013), pp. 261–286.

Corrocher, Nicoletta, Franco Malerba, and Fabio Montobbio (2003). "How Do New Technologies Emerge? A Patent-Based Analysis of ICT-Related New Industrial Activities." *Innovation, Organization and Management*, Vol. 5, No. 2–3.

Council of Economic Advisers (2001). Economic Report of the President, January 2001. https://www.govinfo.gov/content/pkg/ERP-2001/pdf/ERP-2001.pdf.

Council for Promotion of Foreign Direct Investment in Japan (2020). "Policy for Formulating a Medium and Long-Term Strategy for Promoting Foreign Direct Investment in Japan 2021." July 28, 2020. http://www.invest-japan.go.jp/documents/ pdf/en_2021_strategy.pdf.

Criscuolo, C., P. N. Gal, and C. Menon (2014). "The Dynamics of Employment Growth: New Evidence from 18 Countries." *OECD Science, Technology and Industry Policy Papers* no. 14, OECD Publishing. http://dx.doi.org/10.1787/5jz417hj6hg6-en.

Dealroom.co (2023). https://app.dealroom.co/companies.startups/f/company_status/ not_closed/launch_year_min/anyof_2000/slug_locations/anyof_france?showStats= true&statsType=value-valuation.

Decker, Ryan, John Haltiwanger, Ron Jarmin, and Javier Miranda (2014). "The Role of Entrepreneurship in US Job Creation and Economic Dynamism." *The Journal of Economic Perspectives*, Vol. 28, No. 3 (Summer 2014) .

Delbridge, Rick, Takahiro Endo, and Jonathan Morris (2019). "Entrepreneurs or Employees? The Emergence of 'Disciplining Entrepreneurialism' in Subsidiary Organizations at Cyberagent." In *Managing Inter-organizational Collaborations: Process Views*. Emerald Publishing Limited.

Deloitte (2019). "2020 Tax Reform Proposals Announced." *Japan Inbound Tax and Legal Newsletter*, No. 49 (December 2019). https://www2.deloitte.com/jp/en/pages/tax/artic les/bt/japan-inbound-tax-legal-december-2019-no49.html

Department of Justice (2012). "Acting Assistant Attorney General Sharis A. Pozen Speaks at the Briefing on Department's Enforcement Action in Auto Parts Industry." https:// www.justice.gov/opa/speech/acting-assistant-attorney-general-sharis-pozen-speaks- briefing-department-s-enforcement.

Department of Justice (2018). "Japanese Auto Parts Company Pleads Guilty to Antitrust Conspiracy Involving Steel Tubes." https://www.justice.gov/opa/pr/japanese-auto- parts-company-pleads-guilty-antitrust-conspiracy-involving-steel-tubes.

Deshpande, Rohit, Amir Grinstein, Sang-Hoon Kim, and Elie Ofek (2013). "Achievement Motivation, Strategic Orientations and Business Performance in Entrepreneurial Firms." *International Marketing Review*, Vol. 30, No. 3, pp. 231–252. https://www.resea rchgate.net/profile/Amir_Grinstein/publication/263495208_Achievement_motiva- tion_strategic_orientations_and_business_performance_in_entrepreneurial_firms_ How_different_are_Japanese_and_American_founders/links/54ccc9c70cf24601c 08b0d96.pdf.

Desvaux, Georges, Jonathan Woetzel, Tasuku Kuwabara, Michael Chui, Asta Fjeldsted, and Savador Guzman-Herrera (2015). *The Future of Japan: Reigniting Productivity and Growth*. New York: McKinsey & Company.

DeVore, Chris (2016). "Silicon Valley Keeps Winning Because Non-Competes Limit Innovation." *TechCrunch*, February 18, 2016. https://techcrunch.com/2016/02/18/sili con-valley-keeps-winning-because-non-competes-limit-innovation/.

di Lampedusa, Giuseppe (1958). *The Leopard*. New York: Pantheon.

Dooley, Ben, and Hisako Ueno (2023). "Japan's Business Owners Can't Find Successors: This Man Is Giving His Away." *New York Times*, January 3, 2023. https:// www.nytimes.com/2023/01/03/business/japan-businesses-succession.html

Dore, Ronald (1987). *Taking Japan Seriously: A Confucian Perspective on Leading Economic Issues*. Stanford, CA: Stanford University Press.

Dore, Ronald (1996). *The End of Jobs for Life? Corporate Employment Systems: Japan and Elsewhere*. London: Centre for Economic Performance.

Eberhart, Roger, Charles E. Eesley, and Kathleen M. Eisenhardt (2017). "Failure Is an Option: Institutional Change, Entrepreneurial Risk, and New Firm Growth." *Organization Science*, Vol. 28, No. 1, pp. 93–112. https://pubsonline.informs.org/doi/ 10.1287/orsc.2017.1110.

Economic Census for Business Frame (2014). "Table 3: Enterprises, etc., Establishments and Persons Engaged by Sex, by Industry Major Groups, Size of Domestic Regular Employees (11 Groups), Legal Organization (5 Groups) and Single or Multi-Unit Enterprises within Japan (2 Groups)." https://www.e-stat.go.jp/en/stat-search/ files?page=1&layout=datalist&toukei=00200552&tstat=000001072573&cycle=0&tcla ss1=000001074966&tclass2=000001077017&result_page=1&cycle_facet=cycle.

Economic Census for Business Frame (various years). "Tabulation of Establishments" and "Economic Census-Basic Survey 2014 for Employees." https://www.e-stat.go.jp/dbv iew?sid=0003134144.

Economist (2021). "A Reluctant Japan Inc at Last Enters the Digital Age." https://www. economist.com/business/2021/03/13/a-reluctant-japan-inc-at-last-enters-the-digi tal-age.

Edwards, Linda (1992). "The Status of Women in Japan: Has the Equal Opportunity Law Made a Difference?" Working Paper No. 71, Columbia University Center on Japanese Economy and Business. https://academiccommons.columbia.edu/doi/10.7916/ D8HH6SJT/download.

Eesley, Charles, and William Miller (2012). "Impact: Stanford University's Economic Impact via Innovation and Entrepreneurship." https://engineering.stanford.edu/sites/ default/files/stanford_innovation_survey_exec_summary_updatedmarch2013.pdf.

EIM Business & Policy Research and Ikei Research and Consultancy (2009). "Graph 4. Presence of SME Subcontractors and Contractors by Sector, EU-27, 2009." EU SMES and Subcontracting.

EIU Economist Intelligence Unit (2013). "Japan's Middle Market: Crucial. Competitive. Concerned," p. 27. https://www.slideshare.net/economistintelligenceunit/japans-mid dle-market-crucial-competitive-concerned-24041300.

Endo, Toshihide (2013). "Post-Crisis Regulation of Financial Institutions in Japan." Presentation at ADBI-JFSA Joint Conference, March 8, 2013. https://www.fsa.go.jp/ frtc/kenkyu/event/20130425/19.pdf.

Ernst & Young (2011). "Nature or Nurture? Decoding the DNA of the Entrepreneur."

EU Commission (2007). Towards Common Principles of Flexicurity, Draft Council Conclusions.   https://eur-lex.europa.eu/LexUriServ/LexUriServ.do?uri= COM:2007:0359:FIN:en:PDF

Eurofound (2019). "Labour Market Segmentation: Piloting New Empirical and Policy Analyses." Publications Office of the European Union, Luxembourg. https://ddd.uab. cat/pub/estudis/2019/215471/ef19033en.pdf.

European Entrepreneurs CEA-PME (2020). "Enabling the Digital Transformation of European SMEs: EU Commission (2020) Digital Innovation Hubs (DIHs) in Europe." https://ec.europa.eu/digital-single-market/en/digital-innovation-hubs.

Evans, David, and Boyan Jovanovic (1989). "An Estimated Model of Entrepreneurial Choice under Liquidity Constraints." *Journal of Political Economy*, Vol. 97, No. 4 (August 1989), pp. 808–827.

Farquhar, Brodie (2019). "Wolf Reintroduction Changes Ecosystem in Yellowstone." https://www.yellowstonepark.com/things-to-do/wolf-reintroduction-changes-ecosystem.

Federal Reserve Bank of St. Louis (2020). "Production of Total Manufacturing." https:// fred.stlouisfed.org/.

Foreign Correspondents Club of Japan (2015). "Banzai, Green & Bancel: JA and International Group on Abe's JA Reform Plans," February 12, 2015. https://www.yout ube.com/watch?v=p1gE_CxGmJw.

Förster, Michael, and Marco Mira d'Ercole (2005). "Figure 10. Trends in Inequality of Market and Disposable Income among the Working-Age Population." *Income Distribution and Poverty in OECD Countries in the Second Half of the 1990s.* Paris: OECD. https://www.oecd-ilibrary.org/income-distribution-and-poverty-in-oecd-countries-in-the-second-half-of-the-1990s_5lgsjhvj7422.pdf?itemId=%2Fcont ent%2Fpaper%2F882106484586&mimeType=pdf.

Foster, Lucia, John Haltiwanger, and Chad Syverson (2005). "Reallocation, Firm Turnover, and Efficiency: Selection on Productivity or Profitability." NBER Working Paper 11555, Table 7. http://www.nber.org/papers/w11555.

Frazier, Donald (2011). "Japan's Newest Billionaire Racks Up Online." *Forbes*, April 6, 2011. https://www.forbes.com/forbes/2011/0425/features-yusaku-maezawa-japan-harajuku-billionaire.html?sh=292a3a0e47ec.

Frey, C. B., T. Berger, and C. Chen (2018). "Political Machinery: Did Robots Swing the 2016 US Presidential Election?" *Oxford Review of Economic Policy*, Vol. 34, No. 3, pp. 418–442. https://www.oxfordmartin.ox.ac.uk/downloads/academic/Political_Mach inery_July_2018.pdf.

Frid, Casey, David Wyman, and Bentley Coffey (2016). "Effects of Wealth Inequality on Entrepreneurship." *Small Business Economics*, 47, pp. 895–920. https://link.springer.com/article/10.1007/s11187-016-9742-9.

Financial Services Agency (2018). "Changes in Lending Conditions at Financial Institutions." https://www.Financial Services Agency.go.jp/news/30/ginkou/20190628-3/02.pdf.

Financial Services Agency (2022). "About the Utilization Record of 'Guidelines for Management Guarantee.'" https://www.fsa.go.jp/news/r3/ginkou/20220623-3.xlsx.

Fuckup (2022). https://fuckupnights.com.

FuckUp Nights Tokyo (2022). https://fuckupnightstokyo.doorkeeper.jp/.

Fujimoto, Hidefumi, and Noriko Kamada (2019). "Toyota's Mighty Keiretsu System Has Met Its Match: Digitization." *Nikkei*, December 1, 2019. https://asia.nikkei.com/Busin ess/Automobiles/Toyota-s-mighty-keiretsu-system-has-met-its-match-digitization.

Fukada, Shiho (2018). "Japan's Prisons Are a Haven for Elderly Women." *Bloomberg*, March 16, 2018. https://www.bloomberg.com/news/features/2018-03-16/japan-s-pris ons-are-a-haven-for-elderly-women.

Fukao, Kyoji, and Hyeog Ug Kwon (2005). "Why Did Japan's TFP Growth Slow Down in the Lost Decade? An Empirical Analysis Based on Firm-Level Data of Manufacturing Firms." RIETI Discussion Paper Series 05-E-004. https://www.rieti.go.jp/jp/publicati ons/dp/05e004.pdf.

Fukase, Atsuko, Takashi Mochizuki, and Eric Pfanner (2016). "Japan Inc.'s Message to Foreign Buyers: Hands Off." *Wall Street Journal*, January 23, 2016. https://www.wsj.com/articles/japan-inc-s-message-to-foreign-firms-keep-out-1453441206.

Futagami, Shiho (2010). "Non-Standard Employment in Japan: Gender Dimensions." ILO, International Institute for Labour Studies, Discussion Paper 200, February 15, 2010. https://www.ilo.org/inst/publication/discussion-papers/WCMS_192841/lang--en/index.htm

Gelb, J. (2000). "The Equal Employment Opportunity Law: A Decade of Change for Japanese Women?" *Law & Policy*, Vol. 22, No. 3–4, pp. 385–407.

GEM, Global Entrepreneurship Monitor (2013). "GEM Special Report on Employee Entrepreneurial Activity." https://www.researchgate.net/profile/Maribel_Guerrero/publication/258643022_Global_Entrepreneurship_Monitor_Special_report_on_entrepreneurial_employee_activity/links/5614372308ae983c1b405fbf/Global-Entre preneurship-Monitor-Special-report-on-entrepreneurial-employee-activity.pdf.

GEM, Global Entrepreneurship Monitor (2018–2019). "Global Report." https://www.gemconsortium.org/report/gem-2018-2019-global-report.

Gender Equality Bureau (2021). "Numerical Targets and Updated Figures of the 4th Basic Plan for Gender Equality." https://www.gender.go.jp/about_danjo/seika_shihyo/pdf/numerical_targets_2021.pdf

Gender Equality Bureau (2022). "List of Numerical Targets of the Fifth Basic Plan for Gender Equality at Gender Equality Bureau." https://www.gender.go.jp/about_danjo/seika_shihyo/pdf/numerical_targets_2022.pdf.

Ghemawat, Pankaj, and Herman Vantrappen (2014). "Japan Slow to Attract Foreign Executive Talent." *Nikkei*, April 24, 2014. https://asia.nikkei.com/Business/Japan-slow-to-attract-foreign-executive-talent.

Gilchrist, Karen (2019). "These Are the Best Companies to Work for in Japan in 2019, According to LinkedIn." *CNBC*, April 2, 2019. https://www.cnbc.com/2019/04/03/linkedin-top-companies-to-work-for-in-japan-2019-flipkart-amazon-oyo.html.

Glen Royal of Scotland Journal (2022). "The Lawyer's Dulles Bag: A Timeless Success in Three Careers." http://glenroyal.global/journal/interview-09-motoe-taichiro/.

Gordon, Andrew (2017). "New and Enduring Dual Structures of Employment in Japan: The Rise of Non-Regular Labor, 1980s–2010s." *Social Science Japan Journal*, Vol. 20, No. 1, pp. 9–36. https://academic.oup.com/ssjj/article-pdf/20/1/9/10852601/jyw042.pdf.

Graham, Alex (2019). "State of the Venture Capital Industry 2019." https://www.toptal.com/finance/venture-capital-consultants/state-of-venture-capital-industry-2019.

Guriev, S. (2020). "Labor Market Performance and the Rise of Populism." *IZA World of Labor*, July 8, 2020. https://wol.iza.org/articles/labor-market-performance-and-the-rise-of-populism/long.

Halberstam, David (1993). *The Fifties.* New York: Villard.

Harada, Nobuyuki (2003). "Who Succeeds as an Entrepreneur? An Analysis of the Post-Entry Performance of New Firms in Japan." *Japan and the World Economy*, Vol. 15, pp. 211–222.

Hathaway, Ian (2018). "High-Growth Firms and Cities in the US: An Analysis of the Inc. 5000." *Brookings Institution*, February 5, 2018. https://www.brookings.edu/research/high-growth-firms-and-cities-in-the-us-an-analysis-of-the-inc-5000/.

Henrekson, Magnus, and Dan Johansson (2010). "Gazelles as Job Creators: A Survey and Interpretation of the Evidence." *Small Business Economics*, Vol. 35, pp. 227–244. https://link.springer.com/content/pdf/10.1007/s11187-009-9172-z.pdf.

Hibbs, Douglas, and Håkan Locking (2000). "Wage Dispersion and Productive Efficiency: Evidence for Sweden." *Journal of Labor Economics*, Vol. 18, No. 4 (October 2000), pp. 755–782.

Hicks, J. R. (1935). "Annual Survey of Economic Theory: The Theory of Monopoly." *Econometrica,* Vol. 3, No. 1 (January 1935): pp. 1–20.

Higuchi, Yoshio, Yoshiaki Murakami, and Masaaki Suzuki (2007). *The Growth and Exit of Startups.* Tokyo: National Life Finance Corp. (in Japanese).

Hiroshima University (2017). "Number of Graduates, Universities (Undergraduates) and Junior Colleges." https://rihe.hiroshima-u.ac.jp/en//?smd_process_download=1&download_id=5313.

Hoefle, Manfred (2017). "Big Company Disease." https://www.managerism.org/topics/size-and-complexity/lesson-no-43.

Hofstede, Geert, and Michael Harris Bond (1988). "The Confucius Connection: From Cultural Roots to Economic Growth." *Organizational Dynamics*, Vol. 16, No. 4 (Spring 1988), pp. 5–21.

Holbrow, Hilary J. (2022). "Changing Employment Norms and Women in Japanese Workplaces." Presentation to the Japan Forum for Innovation & Technology, University of California, San Diego, April 5, 2022. https://www.youtube.com/watch?v=mELdHiZjeWI.

Hoshi, Takei (2011). "The Hidden Risks in Japan's Financial System." https://www.nira.or.jp/pdf/e_opinion4.pdf.

Hoshi, Takeo, Anil Kashyap, and David Scharfstein (1990). "The Role of Banks in Reducing the Costs of Financial Distress in Japan." NBER Working Paper 3435. https://www.nber.org/papers/w3435.pdf.

Hoshi, Takeo, and Kozo Kiyota (2019). "Potential for Inward Foreign Direct Investment in Japan." NBER Working Paper Working Paper 25680. http://www.nber.org/papers/w25680.

Hoshi, Takeo, Satoshi Koibuchi, and Ulrike Schaede. (2017). "The Decline in Bank-Led Corporate Restructuring in Japan: 1981–2010." NBER Working Paper 23715. http://www.nber.org/papers/w23715.

Huston, Larry, and Nakkil Sabab (2006). "Connect and Develop: Inside Procter & Gamble's New Model for Innovation." *Harvard Business Review*, March 2006. https://hbr.org/2006/03/connect-and-develop-inside-procter-gambles-new-model-for-innovation

Ikeda, Naoshi, Kotaro Inoue, and Sho Watanabe (2017). "Enjoying the Quiet Life: Corporate Decision-Making by Entrenched Managers." NBER Working Paper 23804, September 2017. http://www.nber.org/papers/w23804 (abstract).

Ikegami, Naoki, ed. (2014). *Universal Health Coverage for Inclusive and Sustainable Development: Lessons from Japan.* Washington, DC: World Bank.

Ikegami, Naoki, and John Campbell (1999). "Health Care Reform in Japan: The Virtues of Muddling Through." *Health Affairs*, Vol. 18, No. 3, pp. 56–75. https://www.healthaffairs.org/doi/pdf/10.1377/hlthaff.18.3.56.

IMD (2022). IMD World Digital Competitiveness Ranking 2022. https://www.imd.org/centers/world-competitiveness-center/rankings/world-digital-competitiveness/.

IMF (2012a). "Japan: Selected Issues." IMF Country Report No. 12/209, p. 46. https://www.imf.org/~/media/Websites/IMF/imported-full-text-pdf/external/pubs/ft/scr/2012/_cr12209.ashx.

IMF (2012b). "Table 6. Japan: Estimated Share of Credit Guarantees for SMEs, by Bank." Japan: Financial Sector Assessment Program—Technical Note on Credit Intermediation IMF Country Report No. 12/262. https://www.elibrary.imf.org/view/IMF002/13088-9781475510454/13088-9781475510454/13088-9781475510454.xml?rskey=YJLMs8&result=1&highlight=true.

IMF (2017a). "Financial Sector Assessment Program." IMF Country Report No. 17/283, pp. 32–33. https://www.imf.org/en/Publications/CR/Issues/2017/09/18/Japan-Financial-Sector-Assessment-Program-Technical-Note-Long-Term-Challenges-for-Financial-45261.

IMF (2017b). "Japan Financial System Stability Assessment." IMF Country Report No. 17/244, p. 45. https://www.imf.org/-/media/Files/Publications/CR/2017/cr17283.ashx.

IMF (2019). "Productivity Drag from Small and Medium-Sized Enterprises in Japan." Working Paper WP/19/137. https://www.imf.org/en/Publications/WP/Issues/2019/07/01/Productivity-Drag-from-Small-and-Medium-Sized-Enterprises-in-Japan-46951.

InfluenceMap (2017). "Japan's Energy Choices Towards 2020: How Its Shift to Coal Is Misaligned with the Strategic Interests of Japan Inc." November 2017. https://influencemap.org/report/Solving-Climate-Change-Can-Japan-Show-Leadership-ac0c71365ca3e2cf3c6cbbd5ecd1a914.

InfluenceMap (2020). "Japanese Industry Groups and Climate Policy: Corporate Influencing of Japan's Climate and Energy Choices." August 2020. https://influence map.org/presentation/Japanese-Industry-Groups-and-Climate-Policy-899704d00 5cb96359cc5b5e2a9b18a84.

Inoue, Mariko, Mariko Nishikitani, and Shinobu Tsurugano (2016). "Female Non Regular Workers in Japan: Their Current Status and Health." *Industrial Health*, Vol. 54, pp. 521– 527. https://www.jstage.jst.go.jp/article/indhealth/advpub/0/advpub_2016-0105/_pdf https://doi.org/10.1596/978-1-4648-0408-3.

Inoue, Takayuki (2022). "Why Japanese Workers Remain Dissatisfied with Their Jobs." *Nikkei*, May 12, 2022. https://asia.nikkei.com/Sp.otlight/Datawatch/Why-Japanese-workers-remain-dissatisfied-with-their-jobs

Ishii, Masamichi, Yoshiko Yokoo, and Yukihiro Hirano (1993). "Comparative Study on Career Distribution and Job Consciousness of Engineering Graduates in Japan and the US." Science and Technology Agency, March 1993. https://nistep.repo.nii.ac.jp/record/ 4536/files/NISTEP-RM028-FullE.pdf

Ishii, Tomoaki (2018). "Employment Conditions and Emerging Labour Movements of Non-Regular Workers in Japan." *Asia Pacific Journal of Human Resources*, Vol. 56, pp.   474–491.   https://www.researchgate.net/profile/Tomoaki_Ishii2/publication/ 323610796_Employment_conditions_and_emerging_labour_movements_of_non-regular_workers_in_Japan/links/5e1c301d92851c8364c8f8d9/Employment-conditi ons-and-emerging-labour-movements-of-non-regular-workers-in-Japan.pdf.

Japan Climate Initiative (2021). "Calling for an Ambitious 2030 Target for Japan to Realize the Paris Agreement Goal." April 19, 2021. https://japanclimate.org/english/news-top ics/call-for-ambitious-2030-target/.

Japan Exchange Group (2021a). "Summary of Earnings Digests by Listed Companies." https://www.jpx.co.jp/english/markets/statistics-equities/examination/.

Japan Exchange Group (2021b). "Ownership by Investor Category." https://www.jpx. co.jp/english/markets/statistics-equities/examination/01-archives-01.html.

Japan Intellectual Property News (2018). "Japan Still a Developing Nation on Open Innovation." August 3, 2018. http://japanip.blogspot.com/2018/08/japan-still-develop ing-nation-in-open.html.

Japan Macro Advisors (2020a). "Wages and Hours Worked." https://www.japanmacroa dvisors.com/page/category/economic-indicators/labor-markets/wage-and-hours-worked/.

Japan Macro Advisors (2020b). "Demographics." https://www.japanmacroadvisors.com/ page/category/economic-indicators/labor-markets/japan-population/.

Japan Macro Advisors (2020c). "Labor Markets: Immigration to Japan." https://www.jap anmacroadvisors.com/index.php/page/category/economic-indicators/labor-markets/ immigration-to-japan/.

Japan Securities Research Institute (2018). "Securities Market in Japan 2018." https:// www.jsri.or.jp/publish/english/english_09.html.

Japan Times (2018). "Editorial: Job Security for Irregular Workers." February 2, 2018. https://www.japantimes.co.jp/opinion/2018/02/12/editorials/job-security-irregular-workers/#.Xx16g-d7lc8.

Japan Times (2019). "Industry Ministry to Craft Comprehensive Package to Support Third-Party Business Succession." August 24, 2019. https://www.japantimes.co.jp/ news/2019/08/24/business/industry-ministry-craft-comprehensive-package-supp ort-third-party-business-succession/#.Xu0xE-d7lc8.

JEITA, Japan Electronics and Information Technologies Association (2020). "Production Forecasts for the Global Electronics and Information Technology Industries." https://www.jeita.or.jp/english/press/2020/1216.pdf.

JFC (2021). "Guide to Japan Finance Corporation 2021." https://www.jfc.go.jp/n/english/pdf/2021jfc_e_a.pdf.

JFTC (2019). "Press Release Regarding Interim Report of Survey on the Trading Practices of Digital Platformers." April 17, 2019. https://www.jftc.go.jp/houdou/pressrelease/2019/apr/190417.html.

JFTC (2020). Press Conference, November 11, 2020. https://www.jftc.go.jp/houdou/teirei/2020/oct_dec/201111.html.

Jiji Press (2021). "New Graduates' Turn Japan in Japan Shows First Fall in Three Years." October 22, 2021. https://www.japantimes.co.jp/news/2021/10/22/national/graduate-turnover-japan-fall-3-ye–s.

JILPT (2006). "Labor Unions' Efforts in Organizing Part-Time Workers." www.jil.go.jp/english/reports/documents/jilpt-research/no48.pdf.

JILPT (2014). "Survey on Administrative Position." *Career and Compatibility Support for Male and Female Regular Employees*. March 2014. https://www.jil.go.jp/institute/research/2014/documents/0119.pdf.

Jo, Yoon, Misaki Matsumura, and David Weinstein (2019). "The Impact of E-Commerce on Relative Prices and Consumer Welfare," December 2, 2019. NBER Working Paper 26506. https://www.nber.org/papers/w26506.

Johnstone, Bob (1999). *We Were Burning: Japanese Entrepreneurs and the Frontier of the Electronics Age*. New York. Basic Books.

Jones Day (2017). "Civil Code." *Japan Legal Update*, Vol. 25 (May 2017). https://www.jonesday.com/en/insights/2017/05/japan-legal-update--vol25.

Jones, Randall (2011). "Education Reform in Japan." OECD Economics Department Working Papers No. 888. https://dx.doi.org/10.1787/5kg58z7g95np-en.

Jones, Randall (2018). "A Broken Social Elevator? How to Promote Social Mobility." http://dx.doi.org/10.1787/9789264301085-en.

Jones, Randall, and Haruki Seitani (2019). "Labour Market Reform in Japan to Cope with a Shrinking and Ageing Population." OECD Economics Department Working Papers No. 1568, p. 10. https://www.oecd-ilibrary.org/deliver/73665992-en.pdf?itemId=%2Fcontent%2Fpaper%2F73665992-en&mimeType=pdf.

JPC, Japan Productivty Center (2020). https://www.jpc-net.jp/movement/whitepaper.html (in Japanese).

Kahneman, Daniel (2011). *Thinking, Fast and Slow*. New York: Farrar, Straus and Giroux.

Kajimoto, Tetsushi, and Izumi Nakagawa (2020). "Japan's Efforts to Raise Wages Wane as Firms Embrace Merit-Based Pay." *Reuters*, February 11, 2020. https://www.reuters.com/article/us-japan-economy-wages/japans-efforts-to-raise-wages-wane-as-firms-embrace-merit-based-pay-idUSKBN2052SN.

Kakuchi, Suvendrini (2019). "Frustrated International Academics Sense Discrimination." *University World News*, October 5, 2019. https://www.universityworldnews.com/post.php?story=20190930115905942.

Kambayashi, Ryo (2017). "Declining Self-Employment in Japan Revisited: A Short Survey." *Social Science Japan Journal*, Vol. 20, No. 1, p. 79. https://academic.oup.com/ssjj/article/20/1/73/2866301.

Kambayashi, Ryo, and Takao Kato (2017). "Long-Term Employment and Job Security over the Past 25 Years: A Comparative Study of Japan and the United States." *ILR Review*, Vol. 70, No. 2 (March 2017), pp. 359–394. https://journals.sagepub.com/doi/10.1177/0019793916653956.

Kamei, Katsuyuki, and Leo-Paul Dana (2012). "Examining the Impact of New Policy Facilitating SME Succession in Japan: From a Viewpoint of Risk Management in Family Business." *International Journal of Entrepreneurship and Small Business*, Vol. 16, No. 1, pp. 60–70.

Karp, Andrew (2017). "Vision Monday's Top Labs–2017," September 11, 2017. https://www.visionmonday.com/vm-reports/top-labs/article/vision-mondays-top-labs-2017-in-alphabetical-order/.

Kashiwagi, Shigeo (2018). "Young Japanese Must Prepare for an End to Jobs for Life." *Nikkei*, December 4, 2018. https://asia.nikkei.com/Opinion/Young-Japanese-must-prepare-for-an-end-to-jobs-for-life.

Kato, Takao, and Ryu Kambayashi (2016). "Trends in Long-Term Employment Practices since the 1980s" (in Japanese). *Keizai Kenkyu*, Vol. 67, No. 4, pp. 307–325. http://hermes-ir.lib.hit-u.ac.jp/rs/handle/10086/28208.

Katz, Richard (1998). *Japan: The System That Soured: The Rise and Fall of the Japanese Economic Miracle*. Armonk, NY: M. E. Sharpe.

Katz, Richard (2002). *The Long Road to Economic Revival*. Armonk, NY: M. E. Sharpe.

Katz, Richard (2009a). "The Japan Fallacy: Today's U.S. Financial Crisis Is Not Like Tokyo's Lost Decade." *Foreign Affairs*, Vol. 88, No. 2 (March/April 2009), pp. 9–14. https://www.foreignaffairs.com/articles/united-states/2009-03-01/japan-fallacy

Katz, Richard (2009b). "A Nordic Mirror: Why Structural Reform Has Proceeded Faster in Scandinavia than in Japan." Center on Japanese Economy and Business Working Paper Series, No. 265, October 2008. http://academiccommons.columbia.edu:8080/ac/handle/10022/AC:P:15774.

Katz, Richard (2014). "Voodoo Abenomics: Japan's Failed Comeback Plan." *Foreign Affairs*, Vol. 93, No. 4 (July–August 2014), pp. 133–141. https://www.foreignaffairs.com/articles/asia/2014-06-16/voodoo-abenomics.

Katz, Richard (2015a). "To Raise Wages, Enforce The Labor Laws, Part 1." *The Oriental Economist Alert*, August 14, 2015. https://richardkatz.substack.com/p/to-raise-wages-enforce-the-labor.

Katz, Richard (2015b). "The Myth of Currency Manipulation." *The International Economy*, Vol. 29, No. 3 (Summer 2015), p. 40. http://www.international-economy.com/TIE_Su15_Katz.pdf

Katz, Richard (2017). "How to Fight Anti-Trade Populism: Interview with C. Fred Bergsten." *The International Economy*, Vol. 31, No. 3 (Winter 2017), pp. 26–29. http://www.international-economy.com/TIE_Su17_Katz_Bergsten.pdf

Katz, Richard (2020). "How Will Suga Deal with Regional Banks' Perilous Financing?" *Toyo Keizai*, September 20, 2020. https://toyokeizai.net/articles/-/377371 (English) and https://toyokeizai.net/articles/-/376501 (Japanese).

Katz, Richard (2021a). "Korea Has Surpassed Japan in Per Capita GD." https://richardkatz.substack.com/p/korea-has-surpassed-japan-in-per.

Katz, Richard (2021b). "Japan's Looming Climate Showdown." *Foreign Affairs* (April 21, 2021). https://www.foreignaffairs.com/articles/japan/2021-04-21/japans-looming-climate-showdown

Katz, Richard (2021c). "Why Wages Slowed More in Japan than Elsewhere." https://rich ardkatz.substack.com/p/why-wages-slowed-more-in-japan-than.

Katz, Richard (2022a). "The Heisei Economy: Explaining the Lost Decades." In Noriko Miurai, Jeff Kingston, and Tina Burrett (eds.), *Japan in the Heisei Era (1989–2019)*. New York: Taylor and Francis.

Katz, Richard (2022b). "MOF: Crying Wolf for a Half-Century." https://richardkatz.subst ack.com/p/mof-crying-wolf-for-a-half-century?s=w

Katz, Richard (2022c). "Kishida May Raise Corporate Taxes, Part I." https://richardkatz. substack.com/p/corporate-tax-hikes-tokyo-is-thinking.

Katz, Richard (2022d). "Why Kishida Retreated from 'New Form of Capitalism.'" June 11, 2022. https://richardkatz.substack.com/p/kishida-retreats-from-new-form-of.

Katz, Richard (2023a). "Reading the Mind of BOJ Chief Ueda." https://richardkatz.subst ack.com/p/reading-the-mind-of-boj-chief-ueda

Katz, Richard (2023b). "Restoring Japan's Leadership in Innovation, Part II." https://rich ardkatz.substack.com/p/restoring-japans-leadership-in-innovation-466

Katz, Richard (2023c). "Learning from the French Revolution in Startups." https://rich ardkatz.substack.com/p/learning-from-the-french-revolution.

Kauffman Foundation (2011). "Young Invincibles Policy Brief." https://www.kauffman. org/wp-content/uploads/2011/11/millennials_study.pdf.

Kawai, Hiroki, and Shujiro Urata (2002). "Entry of Small and Medium Enterprises and Economic Dynamism in Japan." *Small Business Economics*, Vol. 18, No. 1–3, Special Issue: Small Firm Dynamism in East Asia (February–May 2002), p. 41.

Kearney. A. T. (2020). "Strategy for Promoting Direct Investment in Japan." http://www. invest-japan.go.jp/committee/chuchoki.pdf (in Japanese).

Keidanren (2022). "Startup Breakthrough Vision: Aiming for 10X10X," March 15, 2022. https://www.keidanren.or.jp/policy/2022/024.html (in Japanese).

Kimura, Fukunari (2001). "Subcontracting and the Performance of Small and Medium Firms in Japan." World Bank Institute, June 2001. http://citeseerx.ist.psu.edu/viewdoc/ download?doi=10.1.1.200.9974&rep=rep1&type=pdf.

Kneller, Robert (2007). *Bridging Islands: Venture Companies and the Future of Japanese and American Industry*. Oxford: Oxford University Press.

Kneller, Robert (2010). "The Importance of New Companies for Drug Discovery: Origins of a Decade of New Drugs." *Nature Reviews Drug Discovery*, Vol. 9 (November 2010), p. 867.

Kneller, Robert (2013). "Review of Maki Umemura, The Japanese Pharmaceutical Industry: Its Evolution and Current Challenges." *Journal of Japanese Studies*, Vol. 39, No. 1 (Winter 2013), pp. 235–240.

Kobayashi, Nobuko (2020). "Japanese Companies Can No Longer Expect Lifetime Loyalty from Workers." *Nikkei* April 3, 2020. https://asia.nikkei.com/Opinion/Japan ese-companies-can-no-longer-expect-lifetime-loyalty-from-workers.

Kogure, Noriyasu (2019). "Shortage of IT Human Resources in the Digital Era." *NRI Journal*, July 8, 2019. https://www.nri.com/en/journal/2019/0708.

Krugman, Paul (2014). "Notes on Japan." *New York Times*, October 28, 2014. https://krug man.blogs.nytimes.com/2014/10/28/notes-on-japan/.

Kushida, Kenji (2011). "Leading without Followers: How Politics and Market Dynamics Trapped Innovations in Japan's Domestic 'Galapagos' Telecommunications Sector." *Journal of Industry, Competition and Trade*, Vol. 11, pp. 279–307. https://doi.org/ 10.1007/s10842-011-0104-7.

Kushida, Kenji (2015). "A Strategic Overview of the Silicon Valley Ecosystem: Towards Effectively 'Harnessing' Silicon Valley." Stanford Silicon Valley New Japan Project, March 15, 2015. http://www.stanford-svnj.org/s/Silicon-Valley-Ecosystem-Overview-2015-m8b8.pdf.

Kushida, Kenji (2022). "Japan's Venture Capital Industry: Snapshot of Growth and Transformation." Carnegie Endowment for International Peace, October 17, 2022. https://carnegieendowment.org/2022/10/17/japan-s-venture-capital-industry-snapshot-of-growth-and-transformation-pub-88187.

Kutsuna, Kenji, and Takehiko Yasuda (2005) "Chapter 6: Funding of Startups." Japanese Startups Tokyo: Hakutoushyobo (in Japanese).

Kyodo (2021). "Slightly More than Half Happy with Job Switch in Japan: Gov't Survey," November 21, 2021. https://english.kyodonews.net/news/2021/11/e0e8f20f476c-more-than-half-in-japan-happy-with-job-switch-govt-survey.html.

Fukao, Kyoji (2004). "Why Did Japan's TFP Growth Slow Down in the Lost Decade? An Empirical Analysis Based on Firm-Level Data of Manufacturing Firms." Paper prepared for the 6th Annual CIRJE-TCER Macro Conference, December 11–12, 2004, Tokyo.

Lam, W. Raphael, and Jongsoon Shin (2012). "What Role Can Financial Policies Play in Revitalizing SMEs in Japan?" IMF Working Paper WP/12/291. https://www.academia.edu/download/53670002/wp12291_3.pdf.

Landers, Peter (2020) "Toyota's Chief Says Electric Vehicles Are Overhyped." *Wall Street Journal*, December 17, 2020. https://www.wsj.com/articles/toyotas-chief-says-electric-vehicles-are-overhyped-11608196665.

Landini, Fabio, Keun Lee, and Franco Malerba. 2017. "A History-Friendly Model of the Successive Changes in Industrial Leadership and the Catch-up by Latecomers." *Research Policy*, Vol. 46, No. 2 (March 2017), pp. 431–446.

Layne, Nathan (2013). "Rakuten CEO Slams Abenomics Failings as Quits Japan Panel." *Reuters*, November 6, 2013. https://www.reuters.com/article/us-japan-economy-rakuten/rakuten-ceo-slams-abenomics-failings-as-quits-japan-panel-idUSBRE9A50I920131106.

Le, Son, and Mark Kroll (2017). "CEO International Experience: Effects on Strategic Change and Firm Performance." *Journal of International Business Studies*, Vol. 48, No. 5 (June–July 2017), pp. 573–595. https://link.springer.com/article/10.1057/s41267-017-0080-1.

Lee, Yoojung, Min Jeong Lee, and Komaki Ito (2021). "Entrepreneur Mentored by Rakuten Billionaire Becomes One Himself." *Bloomberg*, September 30, 2021. https://www.bloomberg.com/news/articles/2021-09-30/entrepreneur-mentored-by-rakuten-billionaire-becomes-one-himself.

Lee, Yoojung, and Shiho Takezawa (2019). "Asian Business Bloodlines on Brink as Lack of Heirs Pushes Owners into Arms of Private Equity." *Japan Times*, August 1, 2019. https://www.japantimes.co.jp/news/2019/08/01/business/asian-business-bloodlines-brink-lack-heirs-pushes-owners-arms-private-equity/#.Xm4ldXJ7lc9.

Lee, Zinnia (2023). "Super Active 32-Year-Old Dealmaker Is Japan's Newest Billionaire." *Forbes*, April 28, 2023. https://www.forbes.com/sites/zinnialee/2023/04/28/super-active-32-year-old-dealmaker-is-japans-newest-billionaire/?sh=46552eae4334.

Lewis, William, Hans Gersbach, Tom Jansen, and Koji Sakate (1993). "The Secret to Competitiveness—Competition." *McKinsey Quarterly*, November 1993. https://www.mckinsey.com/featured-insights/employment-and-growth/the-secret-to-competitiveness-and-competition.

Liang, James, Hui Wang, and Edward P. Lazear. (2014) "Demographics and Entrepreneurship." NBER Working Paper Working Paper 20506. http://www.nber.org/papers/w20506.

Lewis, Leo, and Kana Inagaki (2016). "Japanese Companies Bury the Hatchet to Survive." *Financial Times*, November 4, 2016. https://www.ft.com/content/6880b266-a23c-11e6-82c3-4351ce86813f.

Lowy Institute (2023). "Asia Power Index." https://power.lowyinstitute.org/.

M3 Inc (2020). "About M3." https://corporate.m3.com/en/corporate/.

Malerba, Franco, and Luigi Orsenigo (1996). "Schumpeterian Patterns of Innovation Are Technology-Specific." *Research Policy*, Vol. 25, pp. 451–478.

Masaji, Kano, Uchida Hirofumi, Gregory Udell, and Watanabe Wako (2006). "Information Verifiability, Bank Organization, Bank Competition and Bank-Borrower Relationships." RIETI Discussion Paper Series 06-E-003. https://www.rieti.go.jp/jp/publications/dp/06e003.pdf

Mathias (2013). "Solar Cell Efficiency World Record Set by Sharp: 44.4%." *CleanTechnica*, June 23, 2013. https://cleantechnica.com/2013/06/23/solar-cell-efficiency-world-record-set-by-sharp-44-4/.

Mattioli, Dana (2020). "Amazon Scooped Up Data from Its Own Sellers to Launch Competing Products." *Wall Street Journal*, April 23, 2020. https://www.wsj.com/articles/amazon-scooped-up-data-from-its-own-sellers-to-launch-competing-products-11587650015.

McCrostie, James (2017). "More Japanese May Be Studying Abroad, but Not for Long." *Japan Times*, September 8, 2017. https://www.japantimes.co.jp/community/2017/08/09/issues/japanese-may-studying-abroad-not-long/#.XoDwT3J7lc8.

McGrath, Rita Gunther, Ian C. MacMillan, and Sari Scheinberg. (1992). "Elitists, Risk-Takers, and Rugged Individualists? An Exploratory Analysis of Cultural Differences between Entrepreneurs and Non-Entrepreneurs."

McKinsey (2018). "Rethinking Car Software and Electronics Architecture." https://www.mckinsey.com/industries/automotive-and-assembly/our-insights/rethinking-car-software-and-electronics-architecture.

McLain, Sean (2018). "Honda Took Pride in Doing Everything Itself: The Cost of Technology Made That Impossible." *Wall Street Journal*, August 5, 2018. https://www.wsj.com/articles/honda-took-pride-in-doing-everything-itself-the-cost-of-technology-made-that-impossible-1533484840.

McSparron-Edwards, Allison (2016). "Spectacular Growth: Are You a Gazelle." UK: Consultix.

METI (1997, 2014). "Number of Enterprises by Industry, Legal Status, Size of Capital and Number of Persons Employed." Report by Enterprise of the Manufacturing Census. https://www.meti.go.jp/english/statistics/tyo/kougyo/index.html.

METI (2002). "SME White Paper 2002." https://www.chusho.meti.go.jp/sme_english/whitepaper/whitepaper.html.

METI (2006). "Table 25: Enterprises; by Date of Establishment (9 Groups; for Japan), Industry (Major Groups) and Engagement in Electronic Commerce." Enterprise and Establishment Census. https://www.e-stat.go.jp/en/stat-search/file-download?statInfId=000001129840&fileKind=0.

METI (2008). "White Paper on Small and Medium Enterprises."

METI (2010). "Current Status and Issues Facing Japanese Industries," February 2010.

METI (2013). "White Paper on Small and Medium Enterprises." https://www.chusho.
    meti.go.jp/pamflet/hakusyo/H25/download/2013hakusho_eng.pdf.
METI (2014). "White Paper on Small and Medium Enterprises in Japan." https://www.
    chusho.meti.go.jp/pamflet/hakusyo/H26/download/2014hakusho_eng.pdf.
METI (2016a). "White Paper on Small and Medium Enterprises." https://www.chusho.
    meti.go.jp/pamflet/hakusyo/H28/PDF/2016shohaku_eng.pdf.
METI (2016b). "Survey on the Actual Situation of Ventures from Universities" (in
    Japanese). https://www.meti.go.jp/policy/innovation_corp/start-ups/r1venturerepor
    t_r.pdf.
METI (2017a). "White Paper on Small and Medium Enterprises in Japan." https://www.
    chusho.meti.go.jp/pamflet/hakusyo/H29/PDF/2017hakusho_eng.pdf.
METI (2017b). "White Paper on Small Enterprises in Japan." https://www.chusho.meti.
    go.jp/pamflet/hakusyo/H29/download/2017shokibogaiyou_eng.pdf.
METI (2018a). "White Paper on SMEs 2018." https://www.chusho.meti.go.jp/sme_engl
    ish/whitepaper/whitepaper.html.
METI (2018b). "Percentage of Number of Primary Contractors and Subcontractors."
    Preliminary Report on the Basic Survey on the Information and Communications
    Industry, March 7, 2018. https://www.meti.go.jp/english/statistics/tyo/joho/pdf/2017j
    oho.pdf.
METI (2018c). "Infrastructure Development (Market Survey on Electronic Commerce)."
    http://www.meti.go.jp/press/2018/04/20180425001/20180425001-2.pdfa   (in
    Japanese).
METI (2020a). "Report Compiled on Results of Survey on University-Oriented Venture
    Businesses." https://www.meti.go.jp/english/press/2020/0515_002.html.
METI (2020b). "Survey on the Actual Situation of Ventures from Universities" (in
    Japanese). kobayashi-yuki4@meti.go.jp.
METI (2020c). "Overseas Production Ratio of Overseas Affiliates in Manufacturing
    Industries." Survey on Overseas Business Activities. https://www.meti.go.jp/english/
    statistics/tyo/kaigaizi/pdf/h2c413je.pdf.
METI (2020d). "Summary of Market Research on Electronic Commerce," July 22, 2020.
    https://www.meti.go.jp/policy/it_policy/statistics/outlook/ie_outlook.html   (in
    Japanese).
METI (2020e). "Business Restructuring Study Group to be Inaugurated Jan. 29, 2020."
    https://www.meti.go.jp/english/press/2020/0129_003.html.
METI (2021a). "Results of FY2020 E-Commerce Market Survey Compiled July 30."
    https://www.meti.go.jp/english/press/2021/0730_002.html.
METI (2021b). "Basic Policy of National Contracts Regarding SMEs" (in Japanese),
    September 24, 2021. https://www.chusho.meti.go.jp/keiei/torihiki/kankouju/hoshin/
    r3.pdf and updates at https://www.chusho.meti.go.jp/keiei/torihiki/kankoju.htm.
METI (various years). "Kogyo Jittai Chosa (Manufacturing Current Status Investigation)"
    (in Japanese).
MEXT (2007). "For Comprehensive Measures to Promote Entrepreneurial Activities at
    Universities."   https://www.mext.go.jp/a_menu/shinkou/sangaku/08040317/003.pdf
    (in Japanese).
MEXT (2010). "Industrial Technology Human Resource Development Support Project
    (Entrepreneur Human Resource Development Project)." https://dl.ndl.go.jp/view/
    download/digidepo_11241268_po_E001473.pdf?contentNo=1&alternativeNo=.

MEXT (2019). "Survey of Household Expenditure on Education per Student (Annual Amount), 2018." Statistical Abstract. https://www.mext.go.jp/en/publication/statist ics/title02/detail02/1379369.htm and https://www.mext.go.jp/b_menu/toukei/002/ 002b/1417059_00003.htm.

MGI—McKinsey Global Institute (1992). *Service Sector Productivity*. Washington, DC: MGI - McKinsey Global Institute, Exhibit 2E-11.

MGI—McKinsey Global Institute (1993). *Manufacturing Productivity*. Washington, DC: MGI - McKinsey Global Institute.

MGI—McKinsey Global Institute (1996). *Capital Productivity*. Washington, DC: MGI - McKinsey Global Institute

MGI—McKinsey Global Institute (2012). "Trading Myths: Addressing Misconceptions about Trade, Jobs, and Competitiveness, May 2012, pp. 3, 4, 20. https://www.mckin sey.com/~/media/McKinsey/Featured%20Insights/Employment%20and%20Gro wth/Six%20myths%20about%20trade/MGI%20Trading%20myths_Full_Rep ort_May%202012.ashx

MHLW (2002). "Basic Survey on Wage Structure in 2001." https://www.mhlw.go.jp/tou kei/itiran/roudou/chingin/kouzou/z01/ippan8.html.

MHLW (2014a). "Contractual Cash Earnings, Scheduled Cash Earnings and Annual Special Cash Earnings by Type of Employment." http://www.mhlw.go.jp/english/datab ase/db-l/basicsurvey/xls/2014a.xls.

MHLW (2014b). "Survey on Employment Trends." https://www.mhlw.go.jp/english/ database/db-l/employment_trends_2014.html.

MHLW (2016). "Wage Structure Basic Survey." http://www.e-stat.go.jp/SG1/estat/NewL ist.do?tid=000001011429.

MHLW (2017a). "Table 1: Trends in Number of Labour Unions, Labour Union Membership and Estimated Unionization Rate." https://www.mhlw.go.jp/english/ database/db-l/labour_unions.html.

MHLW (2017b). "Table 5 :Trends in Labour Union Membership and Estimated Unionization Rate of Part-Time Employees." https://www.mhlw.go.jp/english/datab ase/db-l/dl/2017table5.pdf.

MHLW (2017c). "Percentage of Workers by Wage Class, Gender, Age Group." Overview of 2017 Basic Survey on Wage Structure. https://www.mhlw.go.jp/toukei/itiran/rou dou/chingin/kouzou/z2017/dl/13.pdf (Japanese only).

MHLW (2017d, other years). "Table 20: Number of Hired Employees by Age Group, Sex and Change in Wages" Yearbook of Labor Statistics. https://www.mhlw.go.jp/english/ database/db-yl/2017/xls/020.xls.

MHLW (2017e). "Survey on Employment Trends." https://www.mhlw.go.jp/english/ database/db-yl/2017/xls/019.xls.

MHLW (2018a). "Handbook of Health and Welfare Statistics 2018." https://www.mhlw. go.jp/english/database/db-hh/xlsx/5-27.xlsx.

MHLW (2018b). "Contractual Cash Earnings, Scheduled Cash Earnings and Annual Special Cash Earnings by Type of Employment." Basic Survey on Wage Structure. https://www.mhlw.go.jp/english/database/db-l/basicsurvey/xls/2018a.xls.

MHLW (2020a). "The 15th Social Security Deliberation Corporate Pension." https:// www.mhlw.go.jp/content/10600000/000677554.pdf and https://www.mhlw.go.jp/cont ent/000520816.pdf.

MHLW (2020b). "Portability between Corporate Pensions." https://www.pfa.or.jp/kanyu/ seminar/setsumeikai/2020/files/setsumeikai_2020_02.pdf

MHLW (2020c). "Variation of Wages for Workers at Companies with More than 1000 Employees." Basic Survey on Wage Structures. https://www.e-stat.go.jp/stat-search/files?page=1&toukei=00450091&tstat=000001011429.

MHLW (2022a). "Table 3: Percentage of Establishments by Industry, Company Size and Mid-Career Hires of Regular Workers." Survey of Labor Trends. https://www.e-stat.go.jp/stat-search/files?page=1&layout=datalist&toukei=00450072&tstat=000001018522&cycle=0&tclass1=000001018558&tclass2=000001018568&stat_infid=000032177559&tclass3val=0.

Ministry of Internal Affairs and Communications (2017). "Table 16: Population (Persons Engaged in Work) by Sex, Marital Status, Education, Age, Number of Persons Engaged in Enterprise, Status in Employment, Type of Employment, Whether Starting a Business for Oneself – Japan." https://www.e-stat.go.jp/en/stat-search/file-download?statInfId=000031738323&fileKind=0.

Mitsumasu, Akira (2015). *Control and Coordination of Subsidiaries in Japanese Corporate Groups*. Singapore: World Scientific. Kindle edition.

mLex (2019). "Rakuten Faces Japanese Vendors' Protest as They Form Union," December 4, 2019. https://mlexmarketinsight.com/news-hub/editors-picks/area-of-expertise/antitrust/rakuten-faces-japanese-vendors-protest-as-they-form-union.

MOF (2022a). "Table 6d-1-1: International Investment Position." https://www.mof.go.jp/policy/international_policy/reference/iip/6IIP.xls.

MOF (2022b). "JGBs Holdings by Foreign Investors." https://www.mof.go.jp/english/policy/jgbs/reference/Others/holdings02.pdf.

MOF (2023a). "Corporate Financial Statements." http://www.mof.go.jp/english/pri/reference/ssc/results_index.htm.

MOF (2023b). "Central Government Debt." https://www.mof.go.jp/english/jgbs/reference/gbb/index.htm.

Morelix, Arnobio (2013). "3 Facts You Probably Didn't Know about Venture Capital and Entrepreneurship." Currents Kauffman Foundation, May 13, 2016. https://www.kauffman.org/currents/three-facts-you-probably-didnt-know-about-and-venture-capital-and-entrepreneurship/.

Moriguchi, Chiaki (2015). "Table 2-b: Top Income Shares in Japan, 1947–2012." Top Income Shares and Income Mobility in Japan. https://www.aeaweb.org/conference/2016/retrieve.php?pdfid=14187&tk=keZ8h2yE.

Moriguchi, Chiaki, and Hiroshi Ono (2006). "Japanese Lifetime Employment: A Century's Perspective." In Magnus Blomström and Sumner La Croix (eds.), *Institutional Change in Japan*. pp. 152–176. New York: Routledge.

Morishita, Kae (2022). "Japan Celebrates Having the Most Companies That Are a Century Old." *Asahi Shimbun*, June 13, 2022. https://www.asahi.com/ajw/articles/14635072.

Motohashi, Kazuyuki (2011). "Innovation and Entrepreneurship: A First Look at Linkage Data of Japanese Patent and Enterprise Census." RIETI Discussion Paper Series 11-E-007, February 2011. https://www.rieti.go.jp/jp/publications/dp/11e007.pdf.

Mulgan, Aurelia George (2018). *The Abe Administration and the Rise of the Prime Ministerial Executive*. London and New York: Routledge

Murai, Shusuke (2015). "Almost 30% of Young People Don't Want to Work for a Company, Survey Finds." Japan Times, August 14, 2015. https://www.japantimes.co.jp/news/2015/08/14/national/social-issues/almost-30-young-people-dont-want-work-company-survey-finds/.

Nakamura, Gen, and Tatsuya Okada, Shinichiro Ibusuki (2014). "Japan's Materials Industry Facilities Literally Falling Apart." *Nikkei*, July 2, 2014. https://asia.nikkei.com/Business/Japan-s-materials-industry-facilities-literally-falling-apart.

Nakashima Propeller (2019). "Company Profile." https://www.nakashima.co.jp/eng/company/history.html.

Nakazono, Hiroyuki, Takashi Hikino, and Asli Colpan (2014). "Corporate Groups and Open Innovation: The Case of Panasonic in Japan." In Refik Culpan (ed.), *Open Innovation through Strategic Alliances*, pp. 253–276. New York: Palgrave Macmillan, Kindle edition.

Naoshi, Ikeda, Kotaro Inoue, and Sho Watanabe (2017) ."Enjoying the Quiet Life: Corporate Decision-Making by Entrenched Managers." NBER Working Paper 23804. http://www.nber.org/papers/w23804.

NEDO, New Energy and Industrial Technology Organization (2018). "Data Collection Regarding the Global Competitive Position of Japanese Manufacturing and Software Firms." https://www.nedo.go.jp/koubo/NA2_100050.html(in Japanese).

Nemoto, Kumiko (2016). *Too Few Women at the Top*. Ithaca, NY: Cornell University Press.

Nihon M&A Center (2020). "IR Report for Q2 Fiscal 2020." https://www.nihon-ma.co.jp/ir/pdf/210430_presentation1_en.pdf.

Nikkei (2010). "Job-Seeking Ice Age—Hiding One's Personality," September 16, 2010. https://www.nikkei.com/article/DGKDZO14757260W0A910C1MM0000/.

Nikkei (2014). "Japan Eyes Bigger Tax Break for Angel Investors," May 3, 2014. https://asia.nikkei.com/Economy/Japan-eyes-bigger-tax-break-for-angel-investors.

Nikkei (2018). "Major Japanese Companies Set for R&D Spending Binge," July 25, 2018. https://asia.nikkei.com/Business/Business-trends/Major-Japanese-companies-set-for-R-D-spending-binge.

Nikkei (2021). "Bain Creates $1bn Business Succession Fund Focused on Japan," April 26, 2021. https://asia.nikkei.com/Business/Business-trends/Bain-creates-1bn-business-succession-fund-focused-on-Japan

Nippon.com (2016). "Regular Full-Time Positions Increasingly Elusive for Japanese Workers." Citing data from MHLW's Survey of Employment Conditions 2014. https://www.nippon.com/en/features/h00133/

Nishiguchi, Toshihiro, and Jonathan Brookfield (1997). "The Evolution of Japanese Subcontracting." *MIT Sloan Management Review*, Vol. 39, No. 1 (Fall 1997), pp. 89–101. https://search.proquest.com/docview/224965800?pq-origsite=gscholar&fromopenview=true.

Nishimura, Itaru (2020). "Wages in Japan Part I: Why Does Japanese Wage Curve Have a Strong Seniority Element?" *Japan Labor Issues*, Vol. 4, No. 23 (May–June 2020), pp. 17–21. https://www.jil.go.jp/english/jli/documents/2020/023-04.pdf.

Noguchi, Yukio (1994). "Dismantle the 1940 Setup to Restructure the Economy." *Economic Eye* 15 (Autumn), pp. 25–28.

Noguchi, Yukio (1998). "The 1940 System: Japan under the Wartime Economy." *The American Economic Review*, Vol. 88, No. 2 (May 1998), pp. 404–407.

OECD (2001). Economic Outlook, Vol. 2001/1, No. 69 (June). library.org/economics/data/oecd-economic-outlook-statistics-and-projections/oecd-economic-outlook-no-69_data-00097-en

OECD (2009). "Employment Outlook 2009." https://www.oecd-ilibrary.org/oecd-employment-outlook-2009_5ksj0t54txbn.pdf?itemId=%2Fcontent%2Fpublication%2Fempl_outlook-2009-en&mimeType=pdf.

OECD (2010). "R&D Tax Incentives: Rationale, Design, Evaluation." https://www.oecd.org/sti/ind/46352862.pdf

OECD (2012). "Lessons from PISA for Japan, Strong Performers and Successful Reformers in Education," p. 47. http://dx.doi.org/10.1787/9789264118539-en.

OECD (2013a). "Science, Technology and Industry Scoreboard." https://www.oecd-ilibrary.org/oecd-science-technology-and-industry-scoreboard-2013_5k44x0hx8vxr.pdf?itemId=%2Fcontent%2Fpublication%2Fsti_scoreboard-2013-en&mimeType=pdf.

OECD (2013b). "Entrepreneurship at a Glance." https://www.oecd-ilibrary.org/industry-and-services/entrepreneurship-at-a-glance-2013_entrepreneur_aag-2013-en.

OECD (2013c). "Figure 21: Assistance to Low-Income Households Is Small in Japan." Economic Survey of Japan, 2013. https://www.oecd-ilibrary.org/oecd-economic-surveys-japan-2013_5k9475btsqjf.pdf?itemId=%2Fcontent%2Fpublication%2Feco_surveys-jpn-2013-en&mimeType=pdf.

OECD (2014). "Entrepreneurship at a Glance." https://www.oecd-ilibrary.org/industry-and-services/entrepreneurship-at-a-glance-2014_entrepreneur_aag-2014-en.

OECD (2015a). "Economic Survey of Japan 2015." http://dx.doi.org/10.1787/eco_surveys-jpn-2015-en.

OECD (2015b). *In It Together: Why Less Inequality Benefits All.* Paris: OECD Publishing. http://dx.doi.org/10.1787/9789264235120-en.

OECD (2015c). "The Innovation Imperative." https://read.oecd.org/10.1787/9789264239814-en?format=pdf.

OECD (2015d). "Employment Outlook 2015: Figure 4.7: Transition Probabilities from Unemployment and Temporary Work to Permanent Work." http://dx.doi.org/10.1787/888933239873.

OECD (2015e). "Science, Technology and Industry Scoreboard." https://www.oecd-ilibrary.org/oecd-science-technology-and-industry-scoreboard-2015_5jrxmkwcht8r.pdf?itemId=%2Fcontent%2Fpublication%2Fsti_scoreboard-2015-en&mimeType=pdf.

OECD (2016). "Financing SMEs and Entrepreneurs." https://www.oecd-ilibrary.org/financing-smes-and-entrepreneurs-2016_5jrqdkqh527d.pdf?itemId=%2Fcontent%2Fpublication%2Ffin_sme_ent-2016-en&mimeType=pdf.

OECD (2017a). "Public Expenditure and Participant Stocks on Labor Market Programs." https://stats.oecd.org/Index.aspx#.

OECD (2018a). "Unemployment-Benefit Coverage: Recent Trends and Their Drivers." Employment Outlook 2018. https://www.oecd-ilibrary.org/oecd-employment-outlook-2018_5j8s9ztvbcjd.pdf?itemId=%2Fcontent%2Fpublication%2Fempl_outlook-2018-en&mimeType=pdf.

OECD (2018b). "SMEs in Public Procurement." https://doi.org/10.1787/9789264307476-en.

OECD (2018c). "Financing for SMEs and Entrepreneurs, 2018." https://www.oecd-ilibrary.org/financing-smes-and-entrepreneurs-2018_5j90hl4ksj44.pdf?itemId=%2Fcontent%2Fpublication%2Ffin_sme_ent-2018-en&mimeType=pdf.

OECD (2018d). *Financing SMEs Scoreboard.* http://dx.doi.org/10.1787/888933665523.

OECD (2019a). "Financing SMEs and Entrepreneurs 2019: An OECD Scoreboard." https://www.oecd-ilibrary.org/deliver/fin_sme_ent-2019-en.pdf?itemId=%2Fcontent%2Fpublication%2Ffin_sme_ent-2019-en&mimeType=pdf.

OECD (2019a). "SDBS Business Demography Indicators (ISIC Rev. 4)." https://stats.oecd.org/Index.aspx?QueryId=45529.

OECD (2019b). *Measuring the Digital Transformation: A Roadmap for the Future.* Paris: OECD Publishing. https://doi.org/10.1787/9789264311992-en.

OECD (2019d). OECD Economic Surveys, Japan, April 2019." https://www.oecd-ilibrary.org/deliver/fd63f374-en..pdf?itemId=%2Fcontent%2Fpublication%2Ffd63f374-en&mimeType=pdf

OECD (2019e). "Compendium of Productivity Indicators 2019." https://www.oecd-ilibrary.org/industry-and-services/labour-productivity-in-smes-and-large-firms-manufacturing-and-business-services_6c6023d8-en.

OECD (2019f). "Pensions at a Glance 2019." https://stats.oecd.org/Index.aspx?QueryId=69414.

OECD (2019g). "Growth in GDP per Capita, Productivity and ULC." http://stats.oecd.org/Index.aspx?DataSetCode=PDB_GR#.

OECD (2019h). "R&D Tax Incentives: Japan, 2019." http://www.oecd.org/sti/rd-tax-stats-japan.pdf.

OECD (2019i). "Fig 5.13: Share of Households with Catastrophic Health Spending." Health at a Glance 2019. https://www.oecd-ilibrary.org/deliver/4dd50c09-en.pdf?itemId=%2Fcontent%2Fpublication%2F4dd50c09-en&mimeType=pdf.

OECD (2019j). "PISA 2018 Results, Japan," p. 5. https://www.oecd.org/pisa/publications/pisa-2018-results.htm.

OECD (2020a). "Median Disposable Income (Current Prices)." https://stats.oecd.org/Index.aspx?QueryId=66599#.

OECD (2020b). "Trade Union Density" and "Collective Bargaining Coverage." https://stats.oecd.org/Index.aspx?QueryId=90648#.

OECD (2020c). "Share of Self-Employed Who Are Employers, by Sex." https://stats.oecd.org/index.aspx?queryid=70935.

OECD (2020d). "National Accounts 5: Final Consumption Expenditure of Households." https://stats.oecd.org/Index.aspx?DataSetCode=SNA_TABLE5.

OECD (2020e). "Employment by Job Tenure Intervals." https://stats.oecd.org/Index.aspx?DataSetCode=TENURE_FREQ.

OECD (2020f). "Attitude towards Entrepreneurial Risk, by Sex" and "Feasibility of Self-Employment, by Sex." Social Protection and Well-Being. https://stats.oecd.org/index.aspx?queryid=54676#.

OECD (2020g). "Female vs Male Entrepreneurs in Japan." https://www.oecd.org/sdd/business-stats/FBS-Japan.pdf.

OECD (2020h). "Business Enterprise R&D Expenditure by Source of Funds and Number of Persons Employed." https://stats.oecd.org/Index.aspx?DataSetCode=BERD_S OF_SIZE.

OECD (2020i). *Education at a Glance 2020.* Paris: OECD. https://www.oecd-ilibrary.org/deliver/69096873-en.pdf?itemId=%2Fcontent%2Fpublication%2F69096873-en&mimeType=pdf.

OECD (2020j). "PISA 2018 Results (Volume V): Effective Policies, Successful Schools." https://doi.org/10.1787/ca768d40-en.

OECD (2021a). "High Growth Enterprises." SDBS Business Demography Indicators (ISIC Rev. 4). https://stats.oecd.org/Index.aspx?QueryId=45529.

OECD (2021b). "Economic Outlook Statistical Annex." https://www.oecd.org/economy/outlook/statistical-annex/.

OECD (2021c). "Incidence of Unemployment by Duration." https://stats.oecd.org/Index. aspx?DataSetCode=AVD_DUR.

OECD (2021d). *Education at a Glance 2021*. Paris: OECD. https://stat.link/n2rbd1.

OECD (2022a). "Level of GDP per Capita and Productivity." https://stats.oecd.org/Index. aspx?QueryId=54369.

OECD (2022b). "Dataset: Average Annual Wages." https://stats.oecd.org/Index. aspx?QueryId=25148.

OECD (2022c). "Patents." https://data.oecd.org/rd/triadic-patent-families.htm.

OECD (2022d). "Population with Tertiary Education." https://data.oecd.org/eduatt/pop ulation-with-tertiary-education.htm#indicator-chart.

OECD (2022e). "Contributions to Labour Productivity Growth." https://stats.oecd.org/ Index.aspx?QueryId=66347.

OECD (2022f). "Share of Employed Who Are Employers, by Sex." https://stats.oecd.org/ index.aspx?queryid=70935.

OECD (2022g). "Public Expenditure on Labor Market Programs." 2017 data. https://stats. oecd.org/Index.aspx?DataSetCode=LMPEXP.

OECD (2022h). "Gini (Disposable Income Post-Government Measures, 18–65 Age Group." Income Distribution Database: by measure. https://stats.oecd.org/index. aspx?queryid=66670#.

OECD (2022i). "Healthcare Expenditure and Finance." https://stats.oecd.org/Index. aspx#.

OECD (2022j). "Inequality by Country." Income Distribution Database. https://stats. oecd.org/Index.aspx?QueryId=66599#.

OECD (2023a). "Economic Outlook Statistical Annex." https://www.oecd.org/economy/ outlook/statistical-annex/.

OECD (2023b). "Dataset: Venture Capital Investments." https://stats.oecd.org/Index. aspx#.

Oh, Hak-Soo (2015). "The Unionization of Part-time Workers in Japan." *The Journal of Industrial Relations*, Vol. 54 No. 4, pp. 510–524.

Ohara, Takashi, and Bain & Company (2022). "Japan M&A: The Emergence of Transformative M&A." Bain & Company, February 8, 2022. https://www.bain.com/ insights/japan-m-and-a-report-2022/.

Oikawa, Akira (2019). "Japan's R&D Spending Hits Record for Nearly Half of Companies." *Nikkei Asian Review*, September 14, 2019. https://asia.nikkei.com/Business/Business-trends/Japan-s-R-D-spending-hits-record-for-nearly-half-of-companies.

Okamuro, Hiroyuki (2006). "Determinants of R&D Activities by Small Manufacturers in the Deflation Economy" (in Japanese). *Commerce and Finance*, Vol. 54, No. 6, pp. 5–19. https://hermes-ir.lib.hit-u.ac.jp/rs/bitstream/10086/17625/1/0100902301.pdf.

Okamuro, Hiroyuki (2008). *Survival of New Firms in an Industry Agglomeration: An Empirical Analysis Using Telephone Directory of Tokyo*. Graduate School of Economics and Institute of Economic Research, Hitotsubashi University. http://www.thebhc.org/ publications/BEHonline/2008/okamuro.pdf.

Okaseri, Hiroyuki (2017). "Analysis of Voting Results on Shareholder Proposals." Short Review, November 30, 2017, Nikko Research Center. https://www.nikko-research. co.jp/en/nfi-review/791/.

Okubo, Toshihiro, Alexander Wagner, and Kazuo Yamada (2017). "Does Foreign Ownership Explain Company Export and Innovation Decisions? Evidence from Japan." Research Institute of Economy, Trade and Industry (RIETI), Discussion Paper Series 17-E-099. https://www.rieti.go.jp/jp/publications/dp/17e099.pdf.

Okuno, Hiroki (2022). "FOCUS: From Apple to local Platforms, Japan Tackles Unfair Digital Trade." *Kyodo News*, January 31, 2022. https://english.kyodonews.net/news/2022/01/7ff76f760acd-focus-from-apple-to-local-platforms-japan-tackles-unfair-digital-trade.html.

Okunuki, Hifumi (2018). "Two Japan Supreme Court Cases Clarify When Discrimination against Fixed-Term Workers Is OK." *Japan Times*, June 24, 2018. https://www.japantimes.co.jp/community/2018/06/24/issues/two-japan-supreme-court-cases-clarify-discrimination-fixed-term-workers-ok/.

Olcott, George, and Nick Oliver (2014). "The Impact of Foreign Ownership on Gender and Employment Relations in Large Japanese Companies." *Work, Employment & Society*, Vol. 28, No. 2 (April 2014), pp. 206–224.

Ono, Arito, Koji Sakai, and Iichiro Uesugi (2008). "The Effects of Collateral on SME Performance in Japan." RIETI Discussion Paper Series 08-E-037. https://www.rieti.go.jp/jp/publications/dp/08e037.pdf.

Ono, Arito, and Iichiro Uesugi (2014). "SME Financing in Japan during the Global Financial Crisis: Evidence from Firm Surveys." Hitotsubashi University Repository Working Paper Series No. 6. http://hermes-ir.lib.hit-u.ac.jp/rs/bitstream/10086/26435/1/wp006.pdf.

Osawa, Machiko, and Jeff Kingston (2022). "Precaritization of Work in Japan." In Noriko Murai, Jeff Kingston, and Tina Burrett (eds.), *Japan in the Heisei Era (1989–2019)*, pp. 127–139. New York: Taylor and Francis.

Oyama, Tsuyoshi (1999). *Stagnation and Structural Adjustments of Nonmanufacturing Industries during the 1990s.* Tokyo: BOJ. http://www.boj.or.jp/en/ronbun/ronbun_f.htm.

Ozawa-de Silva, Chikako (2020). "In the Eyes of Others: Loneliness and Relational Meaning in Life among Japanese College Students." *Transcultural Psychiatry*, Vol. 57, No. 5, pp. 623–634. doi:10.1177/1363461519899757.

Pandey, S., and S. Rhee (2015). "An Inductive Study of Foreign CEOs of Japanese Firms." *Journal of Leadership & Organizational Studies*, Vol. 22, No. 2, pp. 202–216.

Paprzycki, Ralph, and Kyoji Fukao (2008). *Foreign Direct Investment in Japan: Multinationals' Role in Growth and Globalization.* Cambridge: Cambridge University Press, Kindle edition.

Patrick, Hugh (1994). "The Relevance of Japanese Finance and Its Main Bank System." In Masahiko Aoki and Hugh Patrick (eds.), *The Japanese Main Bank System: Its Relevance for Developing and Transforming Economies*, pp. 353–408. Oxford: Oxford University Press.

Paul, Justin, Philippe Hermel, and Archana Srivatava (2017). "Entrepreneurial Intentions: Theory and Evidence from Asia, America, and Europe." *Journal of International Entrepreneurship*, Vol. 15, No. 3, pp. 324–351. http://dx.doi.org/10.1007/s10843-017-0208-1.

Pearce, James, and James Carland, III (1996). "Intrapreneurship and Innovation in Manufacturing Firms: An Empirical Study of Performance Implications." *Academy of Entrepreneurship Journal*, Vol. 1, No. 2 (Fall 1996), pp. 153–171.

Pempel, T. J. (1998). *Regime Shift: Comparative Dynamics of the Japanese Political Economy.* Ithaca, NY, and London: Cornell University Press.

Penn World (2021). "Tables 9.1." https://www.rug.nl/ggdc/docs/pwt91.xlsx.

Penn World (2022). "Tables 10.0." https://www.rug.nl/ggdc/docs/pwt100.xlsx.

Prime Minister's Office of Japan (2022). "Speech by Prime Minister Kishida Fumio at the Guildhall in London." May 5, 2022. https://japan.kantei.go.jp/101_kishida/statement/202205/_00002.html

Rainforest Action Network (2019). "Banking on Coal Power—League Table." Banking on Climate Change: Fossil Fuel Finance Report Card 2019. https://www.ran.org/publications/banking-on-climate-change-2019/.

Rakoff, Jed (2014). "The Financial Crisis: Why Have No High-Level Executives Been Prosecuted?" *New York Review of Books*, January 9, 2014. https://www.nybooks.com/articles/2014/01/09/financial-crisis-why-no-executive-prosecutions/

Rapp, William. (1976). "Firm Size and Japan's Export Structure: A Microview of Japan's Changing Export Competitiveness since Meiji." In Hugh Patrick (ed.), *Japanese Industrialization and Its Social Consequences*, pp. 201–248. Berkeley: University of California Press.

RECOF M&A database (2021). https://madb.recofdata.co.jp/.

Reischauer, Edwin (1957). *The United States and Japan*. New York: Viking Press.

Rengo (2019). JUTC-Rengo 2018–19. http://www.jtuc-rengo.org/about/data/rengo2018-2019.pdf.

Research Institute for Higher Education, Hiroshima University (2020). "Figure 136, 137: Annual Earnings by Educational Background." Statistics of Japanese Higher Education. https://rihe.hiroshima-u.ac.jp/en/statistics/synthesis/.

Retherford, Robert, Naohiro Ogawa, and Satomi Sakamoto (1996). "Values and Fertility Change in Japan." *Population Studies*, Vol. 50, No. 1 (March 1996), pp. 5–25. http://www.jstor.org/stable/2175027?origin=JSTOR-pdf.

Reuters (2008). "Japanese Workers More Unhappy, Government Report Says." July 22, 2008. https://www.reuters.com/article/us-japan-labour/japanese-workers-more-unhappy-government-report-says-idUST30904520080722.

Reuters (2013). "Toyota Labour Federation to Push gor Higher Wages-Media." https://www.reuters.com/article/instant-article/idUSL4N0JK0S920131205.

Reuters (2019). "Japan Anti-Trust Regulator Accepts Amazon Japan Improvement Plan." September 10, 2020. https://sports.yahoo.com/japan-anti-trust-regulator-accepts-061939128.html.

Roberts, Edward, and Charles Eesley (2011). "Entrepreneurial Impact: The Role of MIT—An Updated Report." *Foundations and Trends in Entrepreneurship*, Vol. 7, Nos. 1–2 (August 2011), pp. 1–149. DOI: 10.1561/0300000030.

Rostan, Mike (2014). "The International Mobility of Faculty," January 2014. https://www.researchgate.net/profile/Ester-Hoehle/publication/278658754_The_International_Mobility_of_Faculty/links/573dbf2308aea45ee842d3d1/The-International-Mobility-of-Faculty.pdf.

Rothaermel, Frank (2001). "Incumbent's Advantage through Exploiting Complementary Assets via Interfirm Cooperation." *Strategic Management Journal*, Vol. 22, pp. 687–699.

Rtischev Dimitry (2016). "How the Sunk Costs of Incumbents Make Entrants Important for Innovation: A Model and Implications for Policy" *Gakushuin Economic Papers*, Vol. 52, No. 4, pp. 175–188. https://core.ac.uk/download/pdf/292915808.pdf.

Sachs, Jeffrey, and Andrew Warner (1995). "Economic Reform and the Process of Global Integration." *Brookings Papers on Economic Activity*, Vol. 26. https://www.gsid.nagoya-u.ac.jp/sotsubo/Papers/Sachs_Warner_1995.pdf.

Sakai, Koji, Iichiro Uesugi, and Tsutomu Watanabe (2010). "Firm Age and the Evolution of Borrowing Costs: Evidence from Japanese Small Firms." *Journal of Banking & Finance*, Vol. 34, No. 8 (August 2010), pp. 1970–1981.

Sakakibara, Mariko, and Michael E. Porter (2001). "Competing at Home to Win Abroad: Evidence from Japanese Industry." *The Review of Economics and Statistics*, Vol. 83, No. 2 (May 2001), pp. 310–322.

Sato, Fumika (2018). "Startups Not Status: Japan's Top Grads Rethink Success." *Nikkei*, February 25, 2018. https://asia.nikkei.com/Business/Business-trends/Startups-not-status-Japan-s-top-grads-rethink-success.

Schaede, Ulrike (2005). "The 'Middle-Risk Gap' and Financial System Reform: Small-Firm Financing in Japan." *Monetary and Economic Studies*, Vol. 23, No. 1 (February 2005), pp. 149–176. http://citeseerx.ist.psu.edu/viewdoc/download?doi= 10.1.1.598.341&rep=rep1&type=pdf.

Schaede, Ulrike (2020). *The Business Reinvention of Japan: How to Make Sense of the New Japan and Why It Matters*. Stanford, CA: Stanford University Press.

Sharp (2020). "Corporate Profile" Company Information. http://global.sharp/corporate/img/info/his/h_company/pdf_en/materials.pdf.

Shimizu, Hiroshi (2019). *General Purpose Technology, Spin-Out, and Innovation: Technological Development of Laser Diodes in the United States and Japan*. Singapore: Springer.

Simon, Ruth, and Caelainn Barr (2015). "Endangered Species: Young U.S. Entrepreneurs." *Wall Street Journal*, January 2, 2015. https://www.wsj.com/articles/endangered-species-young-u-s-entrepreneurs-1420246116.

Simons, Daniel (2010). "Counter-Intuition." Video of presentation at TEDxUIUC at https://youtu.be/eb4TM19DYDY.

Solomon, Richard (2014). "How Not to Lose Your Home When Going Bankrupt in Japan." *Beacon Reports*, April 21, 2014. https://beaconreports.net/en/going-broke-japan/.

SPEEDA (2021). March 3, 2001. https://jp.ub-speeda.com/.

Stam, Erik, and Mikael Stenkula (2017). "Intrapreneurship in Sweden: An International Perspective." *Financial and Institutional Reforms for an Entrepreneurial Society (FIRES)*. http://www.projectfires.eu/wp-content/uploads/2017/01/D5.4-Complete-paper.pdf

Stangler, Dane (2010). "High-Growth Firms and the Future of the American Economy." Kauffman Foundation, March 2010. https://www.kauffman.org/entrepreneurship/reports/firm-formation-and-growth-series/highgrowth-firms-and-the-future-of-the-american-economy/.

Statistical Yearbook (2012). "Table 16-12: Monthly Contractual Earnings of Regular Employees by Size of Enterprise, Industry and Age Group." https://www.stat.go.jp/data/nenkan/back61/zuhyou/y1612000.xls.

Statistical Yearbook (2015). "Table 13-2: Establishments, Employees, Annual Sales of Goods, Value of Goods in Stock and Sales Floor Space of Wholesale and Retail Trade by Legal Organization and Size of Employees." https://www.stat.go.jp/data/nenkan/back64/zuhyou/y1302000.xls.

Statistics Bureau (2016). "Farm Households by Degree of Engagement and Size of Operating Cultivated Land (2005 to 2015)." Statistics Yearbook 2016. https://www.stat.go.jp/data/nenkan/65nenkan/zuhyou/y650802000.xls.

Statistics Bureau (2017). "Table 16: Population (Persons Engaged in Work) by Sex, Marital Status, Education, Age, Number of Persons Engaged in Enterprise, Status in Employment, Type of Employment, Whether Starting a Business for Oneself—Japan." 2017 Employment Status Survey. https://www.e-stat.go.jp/en/stat-search/file-download?statInfId=000031738323&fileKind=0.

Statistics Bureau (2018). "Table 4:4 Distribution of Establishments by Major Group of Industries, When Establishments Opened, When Current Businesses Commenced and Age Group of Business Proprietors." Unincorporated Enterprise Survey. https://www.e-stat.go.jp/en/stat-search/file-download?statInfId=000031833319&fileKind=0.

Statistics Bureau (2019). "Yearly Average of Monthly Disbursements per Household— Two-or-more-person Households (2000～2017)." https://www.stat.go.jp/data/kakei/longtime/zuhyou/18-01-an.xls.

Statistics Bureau (2020). "Table 3: Monthly Receipts and Disbursements per Decile." https://www.e-stat.go.jp/en/stat-search/file-download?statInfId=000031353440&fileKind=0 https://newrepublic.com/article/153870/inequality-death-america-life-expectancy-gap.

Statistics Bureau (2020a). "Labour Disputes (2010 to 2016)." https://www.stat.go.jp/data/nenkan/68nenkan/zuhyou/y681929000.xls.

Statistics Bureau (2020b). "Amounts of Savings and Liabilities Held per Household." https://www.e-stat.go.jp/en/stat-search/file-download?statInfId=000031821255&fileKind=0.

Statistics Bureau (2020c.) "Table 3: Monthly Receipts and Disbursements per Decile." https://www.e-stat.go.jp/en/stat-search/file-download?statInfId=000031353440&fileKind=0 https://newrepublic.com/article/153870/inequality-death-america-life-expectancy-gap.

Statistics Bureau (2022a). "Consumer Price Index, Percentage Change from Year Before." https://www.e-stat.go.jp/en/stat-search/file-download?statInfId=000031431706&fileKind=1.

Statistics Bureau (2022b). "Employed Person by Age Group (Ten-Year Group) and Employee by Age Group (Ten-Year Group) and Type of Employment." https://www.e-stat.go.jp/en/stat-search/file-download?statInfId=000021915916&fileKind=0.

Statistics Bureau (2022c). "18-2-bn Yearly Average of Monthly Receipts and Disbursements per Household by Yearly Income Quintile Group, and by Number of Household Members (Workers' Households)." https://www.stat.go.jp/data/kakei/longtime/zuhyou/n1602000.xls.

Stevenson, Reed, and Tsuyoshi Inajima (2022). "Hitachi's $18 Billion Divestment Drive Kept Activists at Bay." *Bloomberg*, January 19, 2022. https://www.bloomberg.com/news/articles/2022-01-19/hitachi-s-18-billion-divestment-drive-kept-activists-at-bay.

Sucher, Sandra J., and Shalene Gupta (2018). "Globalizing Japan's Dream Machine: Recruit Holdings Co., Ltd." Harvard Business School Case 318-130, April 2018.

Sugihara, Junichi (2022) ."Japan's Top Business Lobby Wants to See 100 Unicorns by 2027." *Nikkei*, March 12, 2022. https://asia.nikkei.com/Business/Startups/Japan-s-top-business-lobby-wants-to-see-100-unicorns-by-2027.

Sugioka, Toshio (2002). "Angel Investment in Japan." *Capital Research Journal*, Vol. 5, No. 4, pp. 9–14. http://www.nicmr.com/nicmr/english/report/backno/2002win.html.

Suzuki, Daisuke (2020). "Entrepreneurship Beckons Japan's Bright Young Bureaucrats." *Nikkei*, November 14, 2020. https://asia.nikkei.com/Business/Startups/Entrepreneurship-beckons-Japan-s-bright-young-bureaucrats.

Suzuki, Kan (2022). "Japan's Education System: What's Good about It and What Needs to Change?" *Japan Zoominar*, May 3, 2022. https://youtu.be/TQ1AciEfEOs.

Suzuki, Kenjiro, and Narushi Nakai (2022). "Japan's Midcareer Job Seekers Flock to Startups." *Nikkei*, March 13, 2022. https://asia.nikkei.com/Spotlight/Datawatch/Japan-s-midcareer-job-seekers-flock-to-startups.

Suzuki, Wataru (2021). "Private Equity Bets Big on Japan." *Nikkei*, April 19, 2021. https://asia.nikkei.com/Business/Business-trends/Private-equity-bets-big-on-Japan-5-things-to-know.

Suzuki, Yosuke (2022). "Middle-Aged Job-Hopping Booms in Japan." *Nikkei*, April 24, 2022. https://asia.nikkei.com/Spotlight/Datawatch/Middle-aged-job-hopping-booms-in-Japan

Tachiki, Dennis (2013). "High Growth Innovative Enterprises: A Research Note on Japan." *Tamagawa University, Faculty of Business Administration Bulletin*, Vol. 21, pp. 61–75.

Taira, Koji (1962). "The Characteristics of Japanese Labor Markets." *Economic Development and Cultural Change*, Vol. 10, No. 2, Part 1 (January 1962), pp. 150–168.

Takahashi, Koji (2019). "Long-Term Employment as a Social Norm: An Analysis of the JILPT Survey on Working Life (1999–2015)." *Japan Labor Issues*, Vol. 3, No. 19 (November 2019), pp. 12–17. https://www.jil.go.jp/english/jli/documents/2019/019-03.pdf.

Takenoshita, Hirohisa (2008). "Voluntary and Involuntary Job Mobility in Japan: Resource, Reward and Labor Market Structure." *Sociological Theory and Methods*, Vol. 23, No. 2, pp. 85–104.

Takeuchi, Kosuke, and Junichi Sugihara (2019). "Japan Antitrust Probe to Target Amazon, Rakuten and Beyond." *Nikkei*, February 27, 2019. https://asia.nikkei.com/Economy/Japan-antitrust-probe-to-target-Amazon-Rakuten-and-beyond.

Tanaka, Aiji (2012). "Japan's Independent Voters, Yesterday and Today." *Nippon.com: Your Doorway to Japan*. August 16, 2012. https://www.nippon.com/en/in-depth/a01104/.

Terazawa, Tatsuya (2001). "Monetary Policy: A Drug or Anesthesia?" Research Institute for Economy, Trade, and Industry, February 20, 2001. https://www.rieti.go.jp/en/miyakodayori/010.html.

Thierry, Isckia, and Denis Lescop (2009). "Open Innovation within Business Ecosystems: A Tale from Amazon.com." *Communications & Strategies*, No. 74 (2nd quarter 2009), pp. 37–54.

Tiessen, James (1997). "Individualism, Collectivism, and Entrepreneurship: A Framework for International Comparative Research." *Journal of Business Venturing*, Vol. 12, pp. 367–384.

Tingwall, Eric (2020). "Electronics Account for 40 Percent of the Cost of a New Car." *Car and Driver*, May 2, 2020. https://www.caranddriver.com/features/a32034437/computer-chips-in-cars/

Todo, Yasuyuki (2006). "Knowledge Spillovers from Foreign Direct Investment in R&D: Evidence from Japanese Firm-level Data." *Journal of Asian Economics*, Vol. 17, No. 6, pp. 996–1013. https://www.sciencedirect.com/science/article/abs/pii/S1049007806001369.

Tsuji, Takashi (2017). "Japan's 1.2 Million Heirless Businesses at Risk of Closure." *Nikkei*, October 9, 2017. https://asia.nikkei.com/Economy/Japan-s-1.2-million-heirless-businesses-at-risk-of-closure2.

Uchida, Hirofumi (2011). "What Do Banks Evaluate When They Screen Borrowers? Soft Information, Hard Information and Collateral." *Journal of Financial Services Research*, Vol. 40, No. 1–2, pp. 29–48. http://dx.doi.org/10.1007/s10693-010-0100-9.

Uesugi, Ichiro, Koji Sakai, and Guy Yamashiro (2010). "The Effectiveness of Public Credit Guarantees in the Japanese Loan Market." *Journal of the Japanese and International Economies*, Vol. 24, No. 4, pp. 457–480. http://hermes-ir.lib.hit-u.ac.jp/rs/bitstream/10086/16255/1/pie_dp400.pdf.

UNCTAD (2022). "Foreign Direct Investment: Inward and Outward Flows and Stock, Annual." https://unctadstat.unctad.org/wds/TableViewer/tableView.aspx?ReportId=96740.

UNESCO (2022). "Students from a Given Country Studying Abroad (Outbound Mobile Students)." http://data.un.org/Data.aspx?d=UNESCO&f=series%3AED_FSOABS.

Usami, Jun, Arthur Mitchell, Nels Hansen, Shino Asayama, and Marina Tatsumi (2019). "Japan's 2019 Proxy Season Results Announced (Shareholder Activism Update)." *White & Case*, September 12, 2019. https://www.whitecase.com/publications/alert/japans-2019-proxy-season-results-announced-shareholder-activism-update.

van Kooij, Eric (1991). "Japanese Subcontracting at a Crossroads." *Small Business Economics*, Vol. 3, No. 2 (June 1991), pp. 145–154.

Van 't Veld, Erika (2020). "8 Side Jobs for Foreigners to Make Extra Money in Japan." *Gaijin Pot*, April 29, 2020. https://blog.gaijinpot.com/8-side-jobs-for-foreigners-to-make-extra-money-in-japan/

Vlastos, Stephen, ed. (1998). *Mirror of Modernity: Invented Traditions of Modern Japan*. Berkeley: University of California Press.

Wada, Taizo (2020). "Global Money Pours into Japan-Focused Funds at Near Record Levels." *Nikkei*, March 14, 2020. https://asia.nikkei.com/Business/Finance/Global-money-pours-into-Japan-focused-funds-at-near-record-levels.

Watanabe, Susumu (1970). "Entrepreneurship in Small Enterprises in Japanese Manufacturing." *International Labour Review*, Vol. 102, No. 6, pp. 531–576.

Whittaker, Hugh (1997). *Small Firms in the Japanese Economy*. Cambridge: Cambridge University Press.

Whittaker, Hugh, and Robert Cole, eds. (2006). *Recovering from Success: Innovation and Technology Management in Japan*. Oxford: Oxford University Press.

Whyte, Martin King. (1994). "Review of Gilbert Rozman's The East Asian Region: Confucian Heritage and Its Modern Adaptation." *Contemporary Sociology*, Vol. 23, No. 1 (January 1994), pp. 39–40.

Wolfe, Benjamin (2016). "Businesses Spent $341 Billion on R&D Performed in the United States in 2014." National Science Foundation: Info Brief, August 2016, NSF 16-315, Table 1. https://nsf.gov/statistics/2016/nsf16315/nsf16315.pdf.

World Bank (2000 and assorted years). "World Integrated Trade Solution." https://wits.worldbank.org/CountryProfile/en/Country/JPN/Year/2000/TradeFlow/Export/Partner/all/Product/Transp#.

World Bank (2022). "World Development Indicators." https://databank.worldbank.org/source/world-development-indicators#.

World Economic Forum (2020). "Global Gender Gap Report 2020." http://www3.weforum.org/docs/WEF_GGGR_2020.pdf.

Yamagishi, Toshio, Hirofumi Hashimoto, and Joanna Schug (2008). "Preferences Versus Strategies as Explanations for Culture-Specific Behavior." *Psychological Science*, Vol. 19, No. 6, pp. 579–584. https://journals.sagepub.com/doi/10.1111/j.1467-9280.2008.02126.x.

Yamaguchi, Kazuo (2011). "Labor Productivity and Gender Equality: Why Do Japanese Firms Keep Failing, What They Should Do, and What The Government Should Do?" RIETI Discussion Paper 11-J-069. https://www.rieti.go.jp/en/publications/summary/11100003.html (only in Japanese).

Yamaguchi, Kazuo (2012). "Promote Women's Participation to Improve Productivity." *Nikkei*, July 16, 2012. https://www.rieti.go.jp/en/papers/contribution/yamaguchi/06.html.

Yamaguchi, Kazuo (2016). "Determinants of the Gender Gap in the Proportion of Managers among White-Collar Regular Workers in Japan." *Japan Labor Review*, Vol. 13, No. 3 (Summer 2016), pp. 7–31. https://www.jil.go.jp/english/JLR/documents/2016/JLR51_yamaguchi.pdf.

Yamaguchi, Yuzo (2020). "Japanese Megabanks Face Growing Investor Pressure To Fight Climate Change." S&P Market Intelligence Platform, June 9, 2020. https://www.spglobal.com/marketintelligence/en/news-insights/latest-news-headlines/japanese-megabanks-face-growing-investor-pressure-to-fight-climate-change-58972698.

Yamamoto, Mari, and Jake Adelstein (2016). "Meet Yusaku Maezawa, The Billionaire Entrepreneur Rocking the Art World." *The Daily Beast*, May 13, 2016. https://www.thedailybeast.com/meet-yusaku-maezawa-the-billionaire-entrepreneur-rocking-the-art-world

Yamamoto, Isamu, and Sachiko Kuroda (2016). "The Effect of Labor Turnover on Firm Performance among Japanese Firms" (only in Japanese). REITI Discussion Paper Series 16-J-062, December 2016. https://www.rieti.go.jp/jp/publications/dp/16j062.pdf.

Yamori, Nobuyoshi (2019). "The Effects of the Financing Facilitation Act after the Global Financial Crisis: Has the Easing of Repayment Conditions Revived Underperforming Firms?" *Journal of Risk and Financial Management*, Vol. 12, No. 2, pp. 63–79. https://www.mdpi.com/1911-8074/12/2/63/pdf

Yamori, Nobuyoshi, Yoshihiro Asai, Masao Ojima, Kei Tomimura, and Koji Yoneda, eds. (2019). *Roles of Financial Institutions and Credit Guarantees in Regional Revitalization in Japan*. Singapore: Springer.

Yamori, Nobuyoshi, and Kei Tomimura (2019). "How Regional Financial Institutions Can Promote Regional Revitalization in Japan: Results from a 2017 Survey on Regional Finance." In Nobuyoshi Yamori, Yoshihiro Asai, Masao Ojima, Kei Tomimura, and Koji Yoneda (eds.), *Roles of Financial Institutions and Credit Guarantees in Regional Revitalization in Japan*, pp. 1–23. Singapore: Springer.

Yashiro, Naohiro (2011). "Myths about Japanese Employment Practices: An Increasing Insider–Outsider Conflict of Interests." *Contemporary Japan*, Vol. 23, No. 2, pp. 133–155. https://www.degruyter.com/downloadpdf/journals/cj/23/2/article-p133.xml.

Yashiro, Naohiro (2019). "Serious Flaws in Japan's New 'Equal Pay for Equal Work' Law." *East Asia Forum*, November 8, 2019. https://www.eastasiaforum.org/2019/11/08/serious-flaws-in-japans-new-equal-pay-for-equal-work-law/

Yasuda, Takehiko (2005). "Firm Growth, Size, Age and Behavior in Japanese Manufacturing." *Small Business Economics* 24 (January): 1–15.

Yasuda, Takehiko (2006). "Programs to Stimulate Startups and Entrepreneurship in Japan: Experiences and Lessons." PowerPoint, January 10, 2006.

Yasuda, Takehiko (2010). "Business Startups: An Analysis of Selection and Post-Startup Performance." RIETI Discussion Paper Series 10-J-020, February 2010. https://www.rieti.go.jp/jp/publications/dp/10j020.pdf.

Yomiuri (2014). "Number of People Unable to Go to Grocery Stores to Reach 5.98 Million in 2025," October 24, 2014.

Index

For the benefit of digital users, indexed terms that span two pages (e.g., 52–53) may, on occasion, appear on only one of those pages.

Tables and figures are indicated by *t* and *f* following the page number